THE FOURTH CROSS

Spike Adams

Published in the United States by CJ Sparrow Publication.

Grateful acknowledgment is made to Hal Leonard LLC for permission to reprint previously published material: an excerpt from the lyrics of Strange Fruit. Words and music by Lewis Allan. Copyright©1939

Edited by Jamie Shimeall, Rosolyn Daniels, and Tavleen Kaur

Cover design by Jim Dunn
Interior Design by Booknook.biz

Disclaimer
This book includes references to real people, events, and figures. These references are factual and are not intended as fictional portrayals. Any additional names, characters, events, or places not based on real individuals or events are products of the author's imagination or used fictitiously. Any resemblance to persons, living or dead, beyond those explicitly referenced, is purely coincidental. For permissions or inquiries, please contact: spike.adams@gmail.com

ISBN: 979-8-218-73371-1 (Paperback)
ISBN: 979-8-218-51294-1 (ebooks)

Trigger Warnings:
This book contains content that may be distressing to some readers, including references to racial epithets, suicide, lynching, child sexual assault, adult sexual behavior, and racial violence. Reader discretion advised.

Dedication

The world would lose much of its beauty, but for my soulmate and wife, Jamie; my amazing sons, Clayton, Dylan, and Evan; and my dear friend, Samer. I dedicate this novel to them.

1

Fight

Seventeen year old Tyrene Horn lay face down on the grainy concrete, wondering whether he should get up or stay put. Gradually, he became aware of a wet, sticky, coppery taste seeping from his upper lip. Probably split, he thought. Running his tongue over the wound caused him to wince. Definitely split, he decided. His head throbbed, and his body ached. Yet, he felt indifferent to it all. The pounding hadn't hurt that much. He'd expected worse. He was almost disappointed.

He knew he'd be jumped today. He'd even prepared for it. The day before, in the cafeteria, Wally had boldly announced to his fan club and wannabes that he was going to beat him up. After lunch, he had grabbed Tyrene's wrist in the hallway, twisting it just shy of a snap. He thumped Tyrene's temple twice with his other hand, as though he were testing a melon for ripeness.

"Tap-tap! Gonna crack this open after school tomorrow," he jeered, with a twisted grin. "Sleep well," he teased. The crowd's laughter followed Tyrene to his next class as Wally swaggered away feeling accomplished after seeing the fear in Tyrene's eyes.

After school, he'd donned extra clothes, wrapped a pillow around his body inside his shirt, and filled his cargo pants pockets with hand towels. However, his head remained exposed and unprotected.

Tyrene's face throbbed with intense pain. He smiled to himself. *Guess I should have worn a helmet or something*, he thought. But that might have been *way* too obvious. He already looked as though he'd padded up for a football scrimmage.

With a determined effort, he rolled awkwardly onto his side. Immediately, his body alerted him to multiple sites of pain. Slowly gathering his bearings, he sensed Wally circling him. They were the same age, but Tyrene was small for his age and Wally was big for his. At times, Wally's hulking figure would change direction, alternating between moving closer, taunting him, and backing away. He was playing him—entertaining the expanding crowd—while provoking a reaction to fuel his final attack. Tyrene tried to look at him but realized he could only open one eye. *Damn*! Wally had put a whipping on him, just like he'd said he would.

A sizable crowd had gathered to observe Tyrene's humiliation—not just Wally's "crew," but the "cool" kids, the jocks, and the wide-eyed girls who always seemed thrilled by the most inane goings-on.

Wally liked the attention. He needed the attention. But poor, dumb Wally confused curiosity and fear with respect and admiration.

Tyrene wondered why no one ever stood up to him. He knew kids in the school who were bigger, more challenging, and stronger than Wally, but maybe the idea of a mindless brute intimidated everyone and mocked the so-called good intentions of others.

Despite the random, sporadic attacks on his classmates, Wally seldom suffered any retribution or punishment—probably because his dad was a cop or because Wally's athletic prowess was the pride of Thomas Jefferson High School. One thing Tyrene knew for sure: when some kid's ass is getting beat, heroes and champions are hard to find. He could have defended himself, but worried about seriously hurting the boy if he gave way to his pent-up rage.

Tyrene heard Wally's voice. "C'mon! Stand up so I can knock your ass down. I want to hear that thud when you hit the ground." Wally sounded almost gleeful.

Tyrene struggled to climb to his hands and knees. He strained to raise his head but couldn't see much higher than the drawstrings of Wally's sweats. Wally stood not too far away and had finally worked himself up for another attack. Tyrene braced himself.

It was not that this beating was hard for Tyrene. His old man had done a lot worse. His father would grab anything within reach to wail on him—a broom, a book, a belt. He'd beat Tyrene hard because he said he was disrespectful and defiant.

"Honor thy father!" He would yell. "That's what the Good Book says."

One evening, when the old man was in a particularly nasty mood and had given Tyrene a vicious beating, his son looked him in the eye and said, "Fuck you and the Good Book!"

His mother told the physician that Tyrene had been in a car accident, but the doctor was more than skeptical. Patricia Horn could tell by the doctor's reaction that he'd encountered this kind of lie before.

Yet, he didn't call Child Protective Services. Maybe, after years of trying to help mistreated and abused kids, the doctor had become tired and frustrated or had just decided that he wouldn't make things worse for a family already in turmoil.

A day later, Tyrene's brother Duke and their mother picked him up from the hospital. The old man was not there when they returned home. He was probably out drinking somewhere.

The shuffle of footsteps warned him that Wally was coming very close now. Wally looked like he was preparing to kick him in the face.

"Leave him alone, Wally. He's had enough. You know… you da man, Big Wally." One kid cautiously tried to appease him. The words sounded weak.

Wally walked toward Tyrene as if he had nothing to fear. Tyrene told himself that after Wally gave him one good head kick, he would probably stop beating him. If the kick didn't snap his neck, it would just knock him out cold. Remembering his encounters with his father, Tyrene decided he was okay with that.

He let his mind drift away down a tunnel of nothingness, readying himself for the final assault. But then he heard Wally spout something just before reaching that welcomed place of acceptance. The words took a moment to register. Tyrene's mind started to return to him, delivering thoughts that caused his body to shake involuntarily. His face must have betrayed some emotion because the crowd sensed it. Some became quiet, exchanging uneasy glances.

Wally, pleased at Tyrene's reaction, repeated what he'd said, slowly drawing out the words. "You Li'l pussy."

Tyrene's mind began to reel. He felt an electrical impulse—not slight and tingling like the one he felt on his fingers when he attached the wrong wires in physics lab, but strong and surging—slowly starting to course throughout his entire body.

"Li'l Pussy!" That was the name the old man called him when he was getting a beating. He called his son a "Li'l Pussy" because Tyrene wouldn't defend himself.

The words hit hard. A metallic click triggered something inside him, causing his body to tremble, jerk, and tense.

Tyrene heard a slight gasp from someone in the crowd. Wally must have sensed something, too, because he paused to eye his prey.

Wally's past beatings of the timid and helpless must have blunted his sensibilities because he sauntered forward anyway. Feeling the muscles in his legs, back, and arms roll and coil, Tyrene waited for an opening.

From nowhere and everywhere, a voice whispered—startling him. He couldn't tell if it was real or just his imagination. Then he heard it again—someone calling his name.

It was his brother's voice. In his mind's eye, Tyrene saw Duke smiling that wonderfully grand smile—the kind that said, "Everything's just fine."

He felt the familiar, strong, reassuring weight of his brother's big hand upon his shoulder and heard him say, with crystal clarity, "It's time to put an end to this bad boy's stupid act."

Tyrene felt a surge of energy growing. Strength was returning to his limbs. Determination started to grip him. He heard Duke whisper, "Do it!" He was more than ready now. He took a deep breath and felt his body expand.

Tyrene hurled himself at Wally, springing toward him like a steel trap snapping shut. Wally drew back his leg to kick him. As it came forward,

Tyrene blocked his kick with his left arm and deftly slid it under his leg to seize his hip. His right arm shot forward to grab his other hip, and Tyrene pulled Wally toward him with murderous instinct like a lion in absolute control of his prey.

Tyrene heard the crowd cry out as he buried his head in Wally's crotch. His teeth closed on something soft and rubbery. Wally's shriek was astounding. As they both plummeted to the ground, Tyrene continued to bite as hard as he could. In his whole life, he'd never heard a sound like Wally made. It was almost inhuman. But he was an animal now and didn't care. Tyrene felt Wally's arms flailing, slapping, and pushing at his shoulders, his fists sometimes striking the top and back of his head.

Wally screamed, "Get him off me! Get him off me! God! He's killing me!"

Wally thrashed about wildly, trying to throw Tyrene off. He sounded like he was crying—blubbering, "I'm sorry! I'm sorry!" His wailing was almost deafening.

Frozen by the unexpected attack, the crowd began to yell frantically at each other.

"Help him! Help him!" someone yelled.

"Somebody pull him off Wally!" Tyrene heard a near-hysterical girl scream. "Do something, you guys!"

One boy shot back, "You do something, bitch! You ever try to stop a dog fight?"

After Tyrene heard Wally scream for his friend, he suddenly felt determined hands pulling at his hair, shoulders, and neck. Panicked blows and kicks began to come from all directions. Suddenly, the blows and kicks stopped.

Then he felt something hard hitting him in a slow, studied, calculated fashion. He heard the batteries reverberate inside the flashlight as it struck his back, arms, and shoulders.

Damn, a security guard! Where was she when I was getting my ass kicked?

He knew he had seconds.

He bit harder. Twisting his head like a dog with a chew toy.

Wally's struggles slowed. Became jerks. Then nothing. A pitiful whimper.

Then—

CRACK.

The flashlight hit Tyrene's head.

Everything went black.

2

To Serve and Protect

The monitor measuring Tyrene's vital signs displayed multi-colored numbers and lines rising and falling rhythmically. There were oxygen tubes inserted into his nose, but the antiseptic smell of the room reached his nostrils despite them. Unexpectedly, he felt the gentle pressure of a kiss on his forehead, then something wet dropped onto his cheek. Tyrene gradually realized that his mother was gently cradling his hand. The floral scent of her favorite perfume was a welcome greeting as he slowly became conscious on the hospital bed. He managed to see her through the haze of one eye.

There were tears in Patricia Horn's eyes, but there was also love—intense, powerful, and protective. It was the same look she'd given him when she came home to find him on the floor, bruised and beaten by his father.

On that evening, nearly three years ago, Tyrene had woken up to her touch and the scent of her perfume. He lay limp on the floor as she supported his head on her lap with her left arm under him. Her right hand had been trembling. In it was a serrated kitchen knife. He could see something wet and red on the blade.

"Where is he?" he'd asked vaguely, his voice sounding as if it were coming through a thick fog. Dimly, he had heard, "The bastard's gone."

That was the last beating he had received. The last time he had heard from or seen his father. That night, just before the police arrived, he had overheard his mother speaking to Grandma Emma.

"I told that sorry excuse for a man that if he ever made the mistake of showing up at our house or got anywhere near my Little Man Dude,

I would send his rotten Black ass straight to hell with a 'Do not pass Go' sign!"

Little Man Dude—that was his nickname. His brother Duke had given it to him as an expression of respect and affection. It was his special name, only used by his family. Duke had told him that he had earned it.

One evening, after a terrible day at school, he'd told Duke that two kids had jumped him just before his math test. He'd lost the fight but managed to knock a tooth out of a classmate's mouth. Even though he was disoriented, bruised, and upset when he took the test, he got an A.

Laughing, Duke had exclaimed, "Dude! As small as you are, you should always run for cover, especially when there are two knuckleheads."

Then his big brother had embraced him, kissed him on the top of his head, and said, "You are my Little Man Dude. The world better watch out." Duke gave him that grand familiar smile—the one that made Tyrene feel safe and secure.

He let the memory of Duke fade as his attention returned to his mother. Raising his right hand to touch her face, he felt a tug on his wrist. He jerked his arm several times, somehow expecting that his indignation at being handcuffed to the bed would cause the restraint to fall away. He suddenly realized that there were restraints bounding his ankles as well. He tested his limits by moving his legs under the sheets. It was clear that he could not climb down off the bed. Well, at least his left arm was free. Alarmed, he grabbed his mom's hand hard.

"Relax, honey," Patricia said. "It won't be for long. The nurse told me that they may be moving you soon."

Caressing her son's shoulder gently, she said. "Don't forget that the bully whose private parts you gnawed on is the son of a cop. Kensington is the one who had you restrained, even though no case has been filed and no arrest warrant has been issued. The nurse told me that he blew up when she refused to tell security to strap you to the bed. When his threats to have her fired didn't work, he went over her head. He lied to the on-call doc, saying that you were dangerous—a gangbanger and a high-run risk. Your nurse fought the doctor hard for you, so a compromise was reached, given your medical condition.

"But whoopee!" she continued sarcastically. "You get to have one hand free. It's Kensington's way of letting you know that he'll punish you any chance he gets. They'll remove the restraints after they get you to the juvenile detention center, but you'll wear them every time they transport you to and from court." She paused. "Remember when I got locked up?"

Meeting his confused gaze, she said, "You're going to be charged with some bullshit crime. Probably assault, but I don't want you to worry. Even Black people have the right to self-defense."

There was a hint of admiration in her voice. "You remember Henry, the skinny little boy that even the girls pick on? He told me that the security guard got winded while wailing on your back and shoulders with that big-ass flashlight that she attaches to her belt. She couldn't get you to stop so she hit you on the head. Henry said that you were like a pit bull on steroids."

She chuckled. "Henry told me that Wally's tea-bagging days are over." She moved her face close to his. "You did what you had to do, son. All those kids standing by...nobody doing nothing, just watching, seeing you get beat."

She stroked his hair gently. His face was bruised and swollen. Purple blotches dotted his forehead. There were painful-looking bruising on the sides of his neck where Wally had apparently choked him. Hot anger burned through her, but she restrained herself. Her son needed her to be calm to help him feel safe.

With one slender finger, she gently traced the long, narrow bandage that ran across his cheek. A smaller bandage covered part of his forehead. A chill went through her as she touched the side of his face.

Butterfly stitching? she wondered. *Not what the doc gave me after I got stabbed in county jail, she thought, but at least it won't leave a scar.*

"Well, son!" she said. "You have no broken bones, no fractures, but more importantly, no apparent swelling in the brain. Tests are still being done though. That's what the on-call nurse told me." She sighed. "But I wish I could get you to our doctor. Sometimes, Black folks don't get the same attention that white folks get. Your Grandma Emma can tell you that."

When Patricia's mother had severe stomach pain, the examining Medicaid doctor had only recommended an enema and Maalox. If she had waited one hour longer to get her mom to the hospital, her appendix would have ruptured, and she would've died.

Why is it that Black people tend to receive such poor medical care from white doctors? she wondered. *Don't they take an oath to do no harm?*

Cops, like doctors, take an oath too, she thought. *The boys in blue take a solemn oath to serve and protect. Aren't they both in the business of saving lives? Why do their efforts seem to crumble when it comes to helping Black people?*

"Maybe those doctors think that it takes a hell of a lot more to kill us than white people," she said, absentmindedly. "And maybe that's why cops shoot first and ask questions later."

When Tyrene looked puzzled. She smiled. "Not important, baby. How you feeling? Anything hurt real bad? If you feel okay, give me my 'Li'l Man Dude' smile. If you*'re* hurting, just nod your head."

Tyrene was sore and aching, but nothing screamed out—a slight dizziness, but that was all. He smiled at her and saw relief spread across her face. He held on to her hand and gave her a thumbs up.

Suddenly, an unexpected explosion of noise caused them both to jump. The pounding on the wall outside the room was loud and felt insulting. Tyrene tried to sit up quickly on the bed, but the movement almost made him nauseous. He pulled the oxygen tubes from his nose and waited. His mom, startled by the sound, tensed and turned to the doorway, freeing her hand from his.

Patricia carefully placed her tote bag, open and readily accessible, on the bed. Before the cop could step across the threshold and into the room, she pulled it toward her.

Tyrene looked at the burly, rotund officer, but the man wasn't looking at him. He was looking warily at his mother.

The cop stopped abruptly, just past the entrance. He placed his hand on the butt of his gun. His eyes were menacing.

She spoke first. "Whoa, Rambo! You kind of nervous, ain't you? With that gut on you, I can't imagine you just graduated from the police academy. Is this the best that you can do to assess whether you need to use deadly force or not?"

"Ya got a real smart mouth on you, lady!" He looked like he wanted to spit. "What would you know about deadly force?"

She looked at him demurely. "I got a TV." She paused. "I like that show *Cops*. Sometimes I watch *Law and Order.* I like seeing you guys in blue with your guns drawn and badges flashing, running around wild, kicking down doors, and screaming at all the drug dealers and gangbangers. Every now and then, one of you hotshot, holier-than-thou officers gets to pistol-whip a 13-year-old." She sneered and gave him a slow once-over.

"You protect my rights, right? I imagine you're here to protect my son's rights too." Tyrene threw a frightened look at her, yanking his arm as hard as he could against his restraint to get her attention. She needed to stop testing this cop's patience.

Patricia had developed a sharp edge when it came to cops. The edge had started after she'd stood up to her husband. She would have killed him that night if he hadn't escaped her attack. After being released from jail, she had been altogether different, although the soft parts of her love came through when she was with her sons.

Patricia was arrested the night his father had beaten him for the last time. She had swung the knife in a wild frenzy, cutting her husband in the neck, chest, and back. There was blood everywhere. He had raced to the emergency room as fast as he could. The ER attendant notified the police. His father lied, of course. He convinced the police that when he had tried to stop his wife from beating his son, she turned on him in a rage grabbed a knife and began slashing him.

The police didn't believe her. They believed him. She had the knife. He had the wounds. The investigating officer concluded that the crazy, knife-wielding Black woman had scared her son into lying. The detective decided that the husband was an innocent victim who got stabbed while trying to protect his son from his out-of-control wife. She was handcuffed and jailed for attempted murder."

Once, during a jail visit, Patricia explained to Duke that it's not just about what facts the police think they have, but the facts they choose to believe. "Someone decides how they want to interpret the facts and the spin they want to put on them," she told him.

Patricia always wondered how the same facts can mean one thing to one person, and an entirely different thing to another.

She told Duke, "I guess it all comes down to what you want to believe." She added, "When it comes to the police, sometimes it's not about finding the truth—it's just about getting a conviction."

She spent nine months in jail awaiting her day in court; but then, unexpectedly, the charges were dropped. Dismissal was a possibility that her attorney had not considered, but it was one that TicToc, her roommate in the county jail, had repeatedly emphasized.

TicToc had predicted, "He definitely won't show, Horn. Trust me on this! The Lord has got your back on this one."

Patricia's homecoming celebration didn't last very long. One week after the family was reunited, Duke took his life. He was only fifteen. One moment, he was there, and the next he was gone. Duke left a note that only baffled his family. Something had broken him, but no one knew what. The family figured he had waited for his mom to come home to say goodbye.

Tyrene thought his mom would be undone after Duke died, but she simply said, "All I can know — what I have to believe — is that he must have been in a lot of pain. Deep pain. Hidden pain we couldn't see. Dark pain we couldn't understand." What I *do* know is that he waited for me to come home so we could be together again—at least for a short while."

She paused, unable to hold back her tears. "He waited for me. Do you understand? He waited for *us*. So, honey, I choose to cherish not only our memories from that last week with him, but also those from his entire life."

Looking up from her tears, she held Tyrene's face in both hands and said, "I know this is a bit selfish of me and maybe even a little crazy, but I would've pled guilty to every charge and spent my life in prison if it meant that Duke would still be alive." Holding her son's gaze, she said, "I know he wouldn't have left you without me coming back home."

After Duke's death, they had to deal with the police and a social worker all over again. Had his mother not been at work at the time of Duke's death, she might have been arrested. A lengthy police investigation ultimately concluded that Duke's death was a suicide.

After his death, the light in her eyes went out. Her face became hard, and the only time you could hear genuine softness in her voice was when she spoke to Tyrene or Emma, her mother.

The officer's unexpected appearance in the hospital room triggered deep hostility within Patricia. Her arrest by the police after stabbing her husband had deprived her of precious time with Duke.

Keenly aware of the woman's defiant stance, the officer finally summoned the courage to come further into the room. His hand still on his gun.

"I know about you," he said. "Patricia Horn! You were in jail for trying to kill your husband. I looked it up. The DA had an airtight case against you. You only got off because we couldn't find your husband to testify."

"What's your name?" she asked indifferently.

He snapped at her, "It's on my badge, lady!"

"I don't want to get close enough to read your name on that badge any more than you want me to. Let's try this again." She repeated, curtly, "What is your name?"

"Quisling. Officer Quisling," he snorted. His hand squeezed the butt of his gun. His eye was starting to twitch.

"Well, officer, since you know who I am and I imagine you know who my son is, I won't waste your time with an introduction. Now, I'm going to walk away from my bag so that you can search for whatever you think might cause a problem for you. I saw your eyes bug out of your head when I pulled it to me. Guess you were taught in the academy that all Black people are dangerous."

Quisling waited until she had backed up against the wall. Then, he spoke.

"Okay, boy, toss me the bag," he ordered. "Toss it toward the foot of the bed. Toss it slowly, and make sure that's the only thing you toss."

Patricia protested, "You see he's hurt. He only has one free arm. Just waddle over to the bed and get it yourself."

Quisling felt his body jerk, smarting at the insult. Narrowing his eyes, he released the retention strap on his holster. Patricia lifted her chin high and put both hands on her hips.

A tiny bit of sweat appeared on Quisling's upper lip. He felt edgy. He resented being challenged—especially by someone Black.

Quisling commanded, "Do it!"

Groaning slightly, Tyrene picked up his mother's bag. It hit the metal bed board with a thud. Quisling moved quickly to rifle through it, still keeping his hand on his gun. He glanced at her while searching for any object that could be used as a weapon.

She looked at him in disdain. "You needn't be polite, Opie. Just dump it on the bed!"

Quisling stopped, stared hard at her, snatched the bag off the bed, and dumped its contents on the floor. Even though her personal items lay scattered everywhere, she looked at him as if he were pouring her a cool drink of water.

"Are you satisfied that you're safe now?" she mocked, observing her cell phone, wallet, and notepad on the floor. The face of her cell phone appeared cracked.

"Back up, Opie, so I can get my things," she said sharply.

The cop wiped his mouth with his hand and stepped back slowly. "Don't call me Opie again, lady," he snapped, "or I will—"

"Or you'll do *what*, Opie? Are you stupid as well as fat?" She paused, staring hard at him. "Remember, I ain't alone in a dark alley!"

An unexpected chill shot through Quisling. The memory of the lifeless expression on the Black man's face he had killed in a dark alley stole his voice. Quisling snatched his hand away from his gun butt like he had just touched a hot stove. For a moment, he looked vulnerable and uncertain.

"Don't worry," she said. "I'm not wasting time filing a complaint. It wouldn't do any good anyway. I'll bide my time and wait until you do something real stupid."

Quisling slowly returned his hand to his gun and began to squeeze and release the handle.

"You know I can take you in for interfering with an investigation," he growled.

"What investigation?" she demanded. "You bang on the wall like you own this room. You interrupt a private conversation between my son and me. You don't even have the courtesy to introduce yourself, and you don't explain why you're here! So, what investigation am I impeding?"

Quisling took a slow, deep breath, regretting that he had initially taken such an aggressive approach with the family, but still trying to show he was in charge.

"I came here to take your boy's statement!" he shouted, pointing at Tyrene.

"Oh, is *that* why you're here, Officer Quisling?" she said sarcastically. "Forget it! I'm speaking on behalf of my son. We want an attorney before any statement is made, before any statement is taken, before any statement is given. And he is *not* talking to you, not even to say 'hello', until an attorney is present. Is that clear?"

She didn't call him Opie this time, but her words punched the air like a smack across his mouth.

Quisling flushed crimson. He wanted to punish her for such brazen, disrespectful defiance. If his eyes had been laser beams, he would have cut this tall, skinny Black bitch in half. He had already wasted a good part of his evening driving here when he could've been finishing other reports, but he wanted to help Kensington—secure a confession, or at least an admission of guilt that could be used in court.

"You people!" he muttered under his breath.

"What?" Patricia snapped. "I didn't quite catch that."

"Well, let me be clear! We let your kind into our schools to get an education. You disrupt our classrooms, bring down the neighborhood, and attack our students." Quisling ground out, "Your boy tried to castrate a kid with his teeth! With his teeth!" he shouted in disbelief. "You niggers ain't nothing but animals. Your boy won't have a prayer in court. I'll make sure of that."

Surprisingly, Patricia started to laugh. "You idiot," she said. "You've been castrating our Black men for years? Now you target our sons. You use the media, the schools, the law, and the police. And when you use the courts, you say it's all in the name of justice.

She paused to pull herself together. "But not this time," she snarled. "By everything unholy within me, I will stop you. You will not have my son." The lioness had spoken, and the hyena was about to retreat.

Quisling now glared at her with wild-eyed fury. She invited his stare. The quiet in the room felt ominous. The officer started to back away to the doorway but then stopped abruptly. His mouth contorted, as if he wanted to say something but knew he shouldn't. He looked to the hall and saw movement. The presence of others convinced him that it was time to leave.

He remembered the anxiety he'd faced while dealing with Internal Affairs a few months back, when a deadly force investigation could have cost him his career.

During an evening patrol, he had come across a Black drug dealer in an alley with two white guys who looked like college students, judging by the way they were dressed.

When he hit them with the beam of his flashlight, Joe College and his friend took off running, but not the nigger. Shielding his eyes from the light, the tall, wiry Black man acted like he knew the drill that was about to unfold.

The Black man said mockingly, "Now, why you do dat, Officer? I'm just tryin' to earn me and mines a livin'. You know how hard dees times be." He began to laugh.

"Don't mock me, boy. I'll shove this flashlight up your Black ass," Quisling had shouted, trying hard not to be unnerved by the man's cool manner. In his most authoritative voice, Quisling ordered, "Don't move! Kneel down and put both hands straight into the air so I can see them."

"Well, officer," the Black man crooned, "if you don't want me to move, I can't kneel down. And if you want me to kneel, I gotta move." He chuckled as Quisling's nostrils flared violently.

"Why you white folks make it so hard on us dumb niggers?" Still chuckling, the dealer assumed a feigned, apologetic air.

A few feet away from the dealer, a dimly lit lamp hung over the top of a rusting metal door. The dealer started to walk casually toward the door, to stand beneath the light, raising his hands as he walked.

The unexpected movement caused Quisling to draw his gun. The gun discharged. The explosion was deafening. The man fell with a surprised, pained look on his face.

Quisling stood speechless. Frozen with panic and fear, his eyes darted about looking for witnesses. No one. Then he looked for signs of life. No movement. No sound came from the man. Quisling only heard the distant sound of street traffic and the wind whipping litter about in the alley.

Leveling his gun and flashlight at the man's head, Quisling walked cautiously toward the lifeless figure sprawled in the alley. When he was closer, he scanned the body again for movement and then swept the area with his flashlight. He exhaled in relief.

No eyewitnesses. No cameras. No passersby.

Quisling slowly knelt, placing his index and middle finger against the man's throat. Quisling's heart was pounding. The man felt warm, but he had no pulse. He cursed the dead man for the trouble his death would cause him.

A small stream of sweat trickled down his damp face. Looking around again furtively for bystanders, Quisling pulled a knife from his boot, wiped his prints off, and put it in the dead man's hand. He remembered something Kensington had told him about carrying a knife. "You never know when you might need it."

The administrative decision following the man's death was relatively swift. Officially relieved of duty with pay during the deadly force investigation, Quisling started hanging out with Kensington and his son Wally on the weekends. He needed emotional support to keep himself together.

Quisling didn't feel any guilt about killing the man. In fact, he felt an adrenaline rush—because he *had killed* a *Black* man. He just didn't want to lose his job or be prosecuted for manslaughter.

Kensington told him not to sweat any criminal charges coming from the District Attorney's office. Squeezing Quisling's shoulder to reassure him, he said. "It's got to be a solid case for the prosecutor to come after you.

"The DA doesn't forget that he has to rely on us—on our investigation, our reports, and our testimony—when it comes time to prove a case before a jury. So, most prosecutors won't be willing to risk their relationship with us for some random, small-time, Black, no-account drug dealer." Kensington chuckled. "Not in this county, anyway."

In the evenings, over a few beers, Kensington advised him on how to field the questions and monitor his body language with the Internal Affairs Division. He also gave him the name of a defense attorney who specialized in Internal Affairs hearings.

"You wouldn't have to deal with all this red tape in the first place if the nigger had gotten on the ground like you told him. It wasn't your fault, Quisling. Just an accident—pure and simple. I know you didn't mean to kill him. Mistakes happen."

Although the dead man's wife, relatives, and neighbors said that he never carried a knife, it was clear that he possessed a weapon on the night that he died. The Black community held its usual demonstrations and protests by outraged civic and church leaders who charged police corruption, claiming that the knife was a plant.

However, Quisling didn't worry. Supported by a stalwart police union, he knew that the system, sooner or later, would bend over backwards to protect its own.

Quisling might not have gotten through the investigation so smoothly if Kensington hadn't coached him. Word was out that the Internal Affairs Division (IAD) was starting to feel pressure from the American Civil Liberties Union (ACLU), the National Association for the Advancement of Colored People (NAACP), and watchdog committees, like Mothers Against Police Brutality (MAPB), over administrative findings that let cops off the hook.

The rise in deaths of unarmed Black men had drawn more scrutiny to the administrative review process. The IAD had to demonstrate that it was taking its investigations more seriously due to the public outcry over the deaths of Black men.

Quisling damn sure didn't want to be the police department's scapegoat. And he sure as hell didn't want to become the poster boy for some left-wing Jew group or the organization for the descendants of cotton pickers, either.

Now, in this hospital room with this Black bitch, Quisling definitely didn't want to deal with IAD on a biased-based conduct complaint. He didn't have time to do some bullshit diversity training. Deciding to leave well enough alone, he abruptly turned and stomped out of the room.

Holding her pen near her chest, Patricia followed him.

Quisling shouted a threat over his shoulder as he lumbered down the hall, "I'm gonna do everything in my power to have your son charged as an adult. We *will* get your son! You can count on that, even if I have to bend the law to do it."

Quisling's words seem to hang in the air. For the first time during this encounter with Quisling, Patricia seemed uneasy.

Returning to Tyrene's bedside, she said, "Everything will work out fine, baby. We just got to stay strong." She turned to stare at the doorway.

“This is a serious game we have to play with these cops now. We need to be careful and smart.” She caressed Tyrene's hand and gently leaned over to touch her lips to his forehead.

After examining her pen again, she lowered herself to the floor to collect the contents of her bag.

Brimming with anger, she repeated the words of defiance: “Not my child.”

3

An Unlikely Friendship

Officer Kensington pulled halfway up his driveway, turned off his headlights, and shut off the engine. He surveyed his house. It was shrouded in darkness. The streetlight that usually illuminated the entrance to his driveway flickered on and off, casting an eerie glow.

Years ago, when he'd arrive home, the porch light would be on, and his house would be alive with movement, music, the aroma of dinner cooking, and the delightful laughter of his wife as she spoke on the phone, effortlessly multitasking in the kitchen.

Most of Elsa's dinners were culinary delights. When he praised how good it tasted, Elsa would smile and say, "That's because I made it with love."

Usually, Wally's bedroom light would be on upstairs, but he wouldn't be there. Instead, he'd be in the living room, staring at his computer screen, with his earbuds connected to his iPad, listening to rap while laughing and typing away on Instagram with his friends—especially Allison, his "babe."

All that had been good, alive, and vibrant in his life had suddenly been swept away like dry stalks in a violent windstorm. The memory of that moment still haunted him:

The aroma of fresh green peppers, garlic, and onions wafted through the air as he walked into the kitchen. An assortment of spices lined the marble countertop. A thick slab of flank steak, prepared for seasoning, sat invitingly on a wooden platter. He stopped at the kitchen table to peruse the mail, smiling at Elsa's cookbooks, magazines, and clothing catalogs.

"Wally! Where's Mom?" Kensington shouted.

Sighing, he stepped into the living room. He had to touch Wally's shoulder to get his attention—he couldn't hear over the music from his earbuds.

He repeated, louder this time, "Where's Mom?"

Startled, Wally pulled one earbud from his ear. "I thought she was in the kitchen, but she might be upstairs. She said she was feeling a bit tired and might go lie down for a while."

Nodding his thanks, Kensington trudged down the hall and slowly climbed the stairs. His frame, once muscular, had been described by Elsa as "pleasingly plump." He'd jokingly told her he preferred "beefy"—it sounded more manly.

Entering the dimly lit room, he saw her slim figure lying across the bed, still dressed in her work clothes. She had kicked off her shoes. Her right arm was folded across her eyes; her left hand was clenched in a tight fist on her chest. He thought he saw a tear glinting in the corner of her eye.

"Elsa," he called softly. "Elsa," he repeated, even more gently. He sat down on the bed—and held his breath.

The physician explained that she had suffered a massive heart attack, likely experiencing faintness, dizziness, and difficulty breathing. "Her death," the doctor concluded, "was probably quick and relatively painless."

Kensington remembered the phrase "relatively painless."

Painless? he thought. Relative to what? What did this MD know about pain and death?

He knew both—intimately.

But in all his years as a cop, nothing compared to the raw, searing pain he had felt that evening as he fervently clutched his wife's hand and begged, "Elsa, please wake up. C'mon, honey, open your eyes. Just wake up."

Even though she'd been gone for over a year, Kensington still felt as though his soul had been sucked into a void he could never escape. At times, the pain nearly consumed him. He had even considered suicide but managed to move beyond that dark possibility—largely because Elsa believed his soul would be condemned to hell and eternal damnation.

And there was Wally to think of. To care for. He had to go on. Elsa would expect nothing less.

Coming home now felt like entering a house of darkness and shifting shadows. It was the same house, but no longer a home—just an empty shell without Elsa's loving presence.

His beloved wife was gone. And without her, he and Wally drifted apart.

After her death, when Kensington trudged home from work in the evening, he no longer found his son laughing at the computer or listening to his music. Wally mostly kept to himself, retreating to the solitude of his room.

As much as he tried, Kensington could not muster the will to knock on Wally's bedroom door unless it was absolutely necessary. Kensington seemed to need a reason to contact him—truancy reports, failing grades, fights at school, or household chores. Like his own, Wally's efforts and performance seemed to spiral downward.

Kensington had become more aloof at work, more cross, and more irritable. His performance as a police officer suffered. He received more civilian excessive force complaints in twelve months than in his entire 20-year career as a street cop.

Keenly aware of an increasing chasm between his life and Wally, he watched listlessly, knowing he was at a total loss about what he should do. He had no support from family. Only a few living relatives were around, and Kensington didn't like any of them. Besides, they were hundreds of miles away.

He was relieved when Quisling called him for assistance with his pending Internal Affairs Investigation, despite the serious nature of a deadly force allegation. An adverse determination by the department, although rare, could result in termination from the force, decertification as a police officer, loss of his pension, and potentially both a criminal prosecution and a civil rights lawsuit.

Quisling needed his help. Elsa always said that the best way to take your mind off your own troubles was to help somebody with theirs.

Quisling was direct when he spoke to Kensington on the phone. "I hear you have some experience with these official-type inquiries. Well, the department is up in arms because I killed this nigger drug dealer. I need to know how to game the process and what I need to do to prepare. Can we get together sometime soon? I can bring over a pizza or something."

After settling on a meeting date, Quisling said coyly, "Just wanted to let you know that your idea about carrying a knife—just in case—definitely helped me."

Kensington had once rescued an elderly man from his submerged car in a lake by cutting him free of his seatbelt with his pocket knife.

Covering up a crime was not what Kensington had in mind when he told Quisling about carrying a knife, but Quisling had other ideas. Planting a weapon by police was not new. It definitely works, particularly if you're not caught on video.

Every cop knows a "throw-down" can strengthen your case with the DA and Internal Affairs—especially if the person you killed has a weapon, even if it's only a two-and-a-half-inch pocketknife.

Quisling's comment about carrying a knife was testing Kensington to ensure he would still support him, knowing he'd committed a crime.

Kensington hesitated for an instant before replying to Quisling's comment. "Yep! Pocketknives come in handy for all sorts of things."

Over the ensuing weeks, Quisling became a frequent visitor to Kensington's home, usually around dinnertime. It was a nice change to have hot meals, even if they were fast food. The frozen meals had been getting old, and Wally was starting to complain.

Sometimes, Quisling would bring Italian, Chinese, or Mexican, and he always entertained them with a bizarre tale about growing up in the Deep South and "how it used to be."

"My great-granddaddy would tell me how Black people would step off the sidewalk if a white person was passing by—out of 'respect,' you know, to give their 'betters' more room to walk. And then there were the public signs that told a Black person where they could eat, drink water, use the bathroom, or sit on a bus."

Nodding his approval, he said, "It was a clear message to the darkies about the natural order of things. Besides," he added, "keeping them at a distance was a good thing. Like Thomas Jefferson discovered, Blacks have a strong and disagreeable odor because they sweat more than whites."

Kensington had wondered if Quisling was making up nonsense because he despised Black people.

He doubted that the author of the Declaration of Independence would make such an outrageous claim, even if he had owned over 600 enslaved people during his lifetime, according to Quisling.

Surprised by Quisling's comment, Wally raised his chin and blinked in confusion.

Heartfelt, dusty nostalgia caused Quisling to ramble on. "My favorite story was when great granddaddy was just 16, and he walked into a colored restaurant across the railroad tracks into nigger town with his Pa. He walked straight up to a table of Black men, all strangers to him, bold as he could be, and carried on a conversation with them, calling men 50 years his senior 'uncle' and 'boy.'" Quisling grinned from ear to ear.

"What my great-granddaddy enjoyed most," Quisling explained with relish, "is that the colored men were so intimidated by his presence that each man stared down at the floor. They were too fearful even to look him in the eyes." Quisling chuckled. "Those niggers knew that the wrong look or the wrong word to a white person could cost them a beating or maybe their lives. Now, that's power!" Quisling finished, beaming.

One memorable evening, Quisling invited Kensington and Wally to one of his favorite restaurants, located in a predominately Black section of town, reputedly known for its mouthwatering, spicy, Southern fried chicken, prepared from a family recipe generations old.

While stuffing himself with chicken and greens, Quisling, predictably, began reminiscing about the "good ol' days" again.

"You know, listening to my great-granddaddy reminded me of Senator Trent Lott from Mississippi when he talked about how different the country would have been if Senator Strom Thurmond had been elected

President of the United States in 1948. My great-granddaddy sent me a quote by that great man."

Quisling closed his eyes in an attempt to retrieve the words verbatim from memory. He began haltingly, gradually speeding up as Thurmond's words began to surface: "All the laws of Washington and all the bayonets of the army cannot force the Negro into our homes, our schools, our churches, and our places of recreation and amusement."

Quisling let out a self-satisfied sigh. "That's right. That's what he believed," he said, proud that he could conjure up the deceased US senator's words. He leaned back in his chair, folded his arms against his large stomach, and smiled.

Wally chimed in. "My government teacher discussed Strom Thurmond and his hard-line views on segregation. He said Thurmond filibustered the Civil Rights Act of 1957 for 24 hours and 18 minutes because he was against expanding federal protection to voting rights for Blacks. It was the longest single-person filibuster in the United States Senate."

"Yeah," Quisling agreed. "Thurmond had the right idea. You don't give power to ignorant people who are too damn lazy to register to vote. Like an old-time New York governor once said, "This is a white man's country. Let white men rule."

Wally lowered his eyes, looking down at the table. Eyes twinkling, he glanced at his dad, who wondered what mischief he was up to. Wally suddenly threw out a question that caught Quisling off guard. "Just curious, Officer Quisling, but didn't Strom Thurmond have a Black daughter?"

Quisling's face became blank. His eyes darted to the ceiling as if he could find the answer there.

Kensington chuckled. "Guess they didn't smell so bad after all."

"Well, I … Well, I …" Quisling stammered. "I think I may have heard something like that on TV."

Kensington couldn't resist. "Quisling, you might've heard it on TV because Dan Rather interviewed Thurmond's daughter on *60 Minutes*."

"You can't trust what you hear on the news," Quisling declared quickly. "The news media fabricates stories all the time. Rather might have hired some Black woman to say she was Thurmond's daughter and got false documents to prove her identity. You know, like Obama had that fake birth certificate made to say that he was born in Hawaii."

Wally furrowed his brow, uncertain. He didn't know what to believe. He waited to hear his dad's response.

Kensington stifled his laughter, enjoying Quisling's apparent defensiveness. "Well, no one came forward to discredit Essie Mae's story like they did Dan Rather's news report on President George W. Bush's military service."

Quisling's eyes lit up. "See! See! Goddamit! That's what I mean about trusting the news!" he exclaimed.

He nearly crowed. "So the newsman who interviewed this Black female imposter got in trouble for fake reporting about a US president!" He smiled, feeling redeemed.

Kensington arched one eyebrow while grinning at Quisling. Leaning forward, he shook his head. "But Dan Rather didn't get in trouble for the story on Strom Thurmond's daughter. Just Google it!"

Looking abashed, Quisling raised his shoulders in surrender. He frowned. "What was her name?" he asked, looking at Kensington. "Essie Mae? Was that it?" He shrugged. "I guess that's a good name for a colored gal." After shifting uneasily in his chair, he said, "You know, even if that rumor is true, it was generally accepted back then that a white man had to go through certain rites of passage before he could be considered a 'real' white man. One of those manhood rites involved having sex with a..."

Kensington sharply interrupted. "Damn, Quisling! That's enough. Wally doesn't need to hear that crap!"

Quisling looked sheepishly at Wally and apologized. Predictably, testosterone-driven Wally shouted excitedly, "Naw, Dad! I want to hear!"

Quisling and Kensington looked at each other with surprised, but amused expressions and erupted into raucous laughter. An elated Wally joined in. Quisling patted Wally's arm and said, winking, "I think I'll just leave it to your old pa to talk to you about the birds and the bees, son."

For the first time in months, father and son had started to reconnect emotionally, experiencing that same comfortable, familiar feeling they used to share when Elsa was alive.

Kensington jumped as a car backfired as it accelerated down the street, jolting him out of his reverie. He sat up stiffly. It was late, and he was bone tired. Seeing Wally in the hospital had worn him out. Hearing the pain and embarrassment in his son's voice was almost too much to bear. For the first time in his life, he'd heard Wally use the word "nigger." He'd spat it out with a vehemence and ugliness that echoed "the good ole days" that Quisling had talked about.

"I want to kill that nigger, Dad. I want to kill him for what he did to me. There's no way that he's not gonna pay for this."

The fierceness of Wally's words and the pained look in his eyes left his still grieving father with only one possible response—a silent nod of agreement. They embraced, and Wally's tears felt like they would burn through his father's skin. They held each other tightly, their pain and loss fusing into a perverse bond.

Kensington had used the racial slur before. He'd thought nothing of it. A lot of cops on the force used the word "nigger." They'd become more careful, in this woke world of political correctness, when and where they said it. Besides, if a cop didn't want to spend his time in some mind-numbing Racial Intelligence Training and Engagement program, he had to be careful about what he said—at least in public.

Hell, even niggers call themselves "niggers." They don't own the word. If nigga is a good enough lyric for Snoop Dogg, Kensington thought, it's *good enough for me.*

As Kensington sat in the car, his mind was troubled. Why was he so bothered that Wally had used that particular word? Prejudice, discrimination, bigotry, and racism were as American as apple pie. It's woven into *America's DNA,* he thought. Then, his conscience revealed what he should have known all along.

Elsa! If Wally had used that word in front of her, she would've been rendered speechless. She would have challenged him. "Do you think you're superior because your skin is white? God doesn't have a favorite color!"

Had his son started to cross over that bridge into the world that Quisling spoke of? Kensington wondered if he'd always stood on the other side of that bridge alongside Quisling but had never acknowledged it.

Kensington scoffed at the thought, shaking his head. He hadn't burned a cross on anybody's lawn. He hadn't fired a round into anybody's back. He hadn't bombed a church or placed a noose around a Black man's neck. He was nothing like the men who Quisling admired.

Quisling had recounted, quite graphically, the lynching of a Black man in front of thousands of white men and women with a twisted sense of pride, as if relishing the gruesome details passed down by his great-granddaddy. Even little white children were allowed to witness the brutal killing of a human being—to hear the terrified cries of pain, ignored pleas for mercy, and smell the acrid odor of burning flesh. Sometimes, body parts were cut away as souvenirs, depending on the crowd's mood. His great-granddaddy once told him that a charred body could smell like burnt roast pork.

Quisling observed proudly, "They were all good, God-fearing Christian folks back then—standing up for the white race."

Kensington felt conflicted. *How could anyone claim to be Christian and still stand by while some poor soul was savagely murdered, with people cheering on as if it were some kind of carnival attraction? Who was truly guilty—the ones who carried it out, or the ones who watched and did nothing?*

Elsa would have described such behavior as sinful, not just a travesty of the Christian faith, but pagan, barbaric, grotesque, despicably cruel, and soulless. Elsa would not have been confused about the issue of culpability.

He could imagine her wounded outrage. "To be human means acting like one—with compassion and conscience, not like some rabid animal or bloodless ghoul. How can anyone witness such horror and live with themselves, without staining their soul?"

Kensington groaned with the truth of Elsa's convictions. She would never have allowed Quisling into their house or tolerated his relationship with the family. If Elsa had been alive to ask him, "What side of the bridge are you on, Kevin Kensington?" He might have waffled, trying to convince her that white pride was different from white supremacy.

"The 'N' word is a word of hate, Kevin, with a legacy of dehumanization and death older than this country," he imagined her retort. "Whether you believe in white pride or white supremacy, the message is the same when you say that word."

Isn't it enough that I try to be a good person, earn a decent living, take care of my family, obey the law, and pay my taxes? Kensington thought.

He sighed deeply and slapped the steering wheel, as if trying to silence the nagging thoughts in his head. He got out of the car and bounded toward the front door, fumbling for the key in the pitch-black darkness. After finally unlocking it, he stumbled inside and let out another heavy sigh.

Silence. Darkness. Emptiness. The musty smell of a house that felt like it had been abandoned for years. He walked down the hall to the kitchen tables where mail was piled in stacks and dishes cluttered the sink. He dropped himself heavily into a chair, which groaned beneath his weight. He avoided turning on the light.

Thinking back to when he was at the hospital with Wally, Kensington remembered the doctor's prognosis—the words that likely triggered Wally's racial slur. The memory of the doctor's words echoed in both father's and son's ears:

"The damage to Wally's reproductive organs is so extensive," the doctor said, "that he may not be able to father a child naturally."

Looking out the sliding glass door, Kensington searched the sky in vain for even the faintest glimmer of light. Then, unexpectedly, he noticed a light turned on in a neighbor's house across the yard.

Before he died, his father told him that when he first moved into the house, there were no other homes for miles—no nearby neighbors, and hardly any traffic noise.

Kensington began to reflect on how the neighborhood had gradually changed. The grocery store had cosmetic products for Blacks and magazines for Spanish speakers. Indian clerks, with their awful accents, mutilated the English language while bagging his groceries. Early in the morning, in a few white suburban neighborhoods, he had to endure the racket of roofers pounding and ripping off tile, jabbering away in Spanish. Driving down the street, he bristled at the sound of booming hip-hop music or Spanish lyrics he didn't understand. What happened to good old country western music? He no longer recognized his world.

As he drummed his fingers hard on the kitchen table in muted darkness, he remembered a book that Quisling had given him. Reaching back to flip the light on, he saw the book on the table half-buried under unopened mail. He pulled out the bookmark to read a passage out loud that Quisling had underlined:

We desire to live in our own neighborhoods, go to our own schools, work in our own cities and towns, and ultimately live as one extended family, in our nation. We shall end the racial genocide of integration.

Kensington saw a few short sentences that Quisling had scrawled alongside the quote: *Segregation now. Segregation tomorrow. Segregation forever.*

Kensington began to speak out loud, as if Elsa were sitting in a chair across the table from him.

"Life was so much clearer when you were here, sweetheart. I'm used to following rules. I'm comfortable following rules. When I needed to deal with something that didn't fit the rules, you always tried to help me understand what was right. All I've ever wanted was to have a family, be a good dad and husband, and be a good cop."

Kensington felt that his moral compass was gone. He sighed, longing for a response that he knew wouldn't come. He searched his memory for Elsa's words. They used to feed his soul, but now they faded in and out like a weak signal on a transistor radio.

What Kensington heard, more clearly and powerfully than any message he'd ever heard before, emerged from deep within.

There is right and there is wrong. And then there is blood. And blood is more important than any rule devised by man or God. At least, this you know to be true.

Kensington pulled up Quisling's name on his phone. It rang several times before the familiar voice answered.

"Hey, Quisling. It's Kensington."

There was momentary silence on the other side, and then Quisling spoke, "How's Wally doing?" The emotion in Quisling's voice was unmistakable.

"That's why I called," Kensington said, clearing his throat. "Well, I need your help, but I'd rather not talk on the phone."

"I'll get there as soon as I can," Quisling said.

"Not tonight," Kensington replied. "I feel like I've been through the wringer. Maybe we can meet up at your place sometime soon."

"Sure, no problem," Quisling answered. "Just let me know. Anytime. We'll get together whenever you want."

Quisling initially thought about telling Kensington that he'd contacted the Black bastard who had maimed Wally, but quickly dismissed the thought. It was not a good time.

"Thanks, Quisling. You're a butthead but a real friend."

There was silence on the other end. Then Quisling said, "I'll do whatever I can for you and Wally. You know that." Emotion crept into his voice again.

"Soon," Kensington said.

"Yeah," Quisling responded.

Kensington ended the call and tossed his phone on the table. He reopened the book and stared vacantly at the pages. Slowly, the image of Elsa crept into his mind, her presence almost tangible, as if silently reproaching him for the dark path he was choosing to embark on.

If she could speak to him, she would tell him that what he was planning to do wasn't just wrong—it was evil.

4

Money Talks

Looking down the long row of kids dressed in bright orange uniforms triggered a deep sadness within Tyrene. *Everyone here is somebody's child,* he thought. *Everyone here has made a mistake and has been caught up in the system.*

A parent or grandparent waited anxiously for answers to questions they didn't know to ask. They didn't understand the charges, the process, the jargon, or the formalities. Meanwhile, armed strangers assumed responsibility for their children's safety and well-being.

Sighing softly, Tyrene looked around the courtroom, searching for his mother. She hadn't arrived yet, but he had no doubt she'd appear. In the hospital, she warned him it was a serious game they needed to play. He knew that his mom would be a fierce competitor.

Suddenly, the locked door, which required a magnetized badge to open, made an audible click, signaling the arrival of more young individuals in orange jumpsuits.

Deputies escorted three chained juveniles from the corridor through the access door into the courtroom. Security precautions for high-risk offenders, no doubt. His group of ten had been herded through the same door about 45 minutes prior.

This group of three in bright orange uniforms slowly shuffled into the courtroom. The metallic clinking of the chain-link shackles around their young ankles evoked images of prison gangs and convict leasing that his teacher had discussed in his US History class.

Their expressions were varied—anxious, fearful, angry, bewildered, tearful, confused. Just kids. Kids who had screwed up. Kids who had broken the law and would soon be labeled as juvenile delinquents, regardless of how minor the offense.

Some tottered along, hands secured close to their bodies, held snugly by a belly chain, hinged cuffs, and leather straps. Others were more fortunate. No restraints. More boys than girls—more Black kids than white. A few appeared to be high. Some were crashing, coming down from drugs.

Despite his honor-roll status, a clean record, and the absence of gang affiliation or drug use, Tyrene was now one of these kids. One angry, desperate act of self-preservation had landed him here.

A moment later, a well-dressed man and woman, each carting several boxes of files, glanced anxiously at the wall clock as they rushed into the courtroom. The tall, awkward, and angular man, nearly tripped over a long black cord that emerged from the centermost part of the floor, connected to a microphone on the podium. The slight, athletic-looking woman, her face pinched, was meticulously groomed, except for a long strand of brunette hair that dangled over her forehead. As the harried duo entered, a slim, mousy-looking woman bolted from a chair just in front of the waist-high wooden barrier that separated the court area from the audience.

She stammered through an apology about the reports being prepared late due to the high number of kids arrested. The man and woman frowned as they took the reports from her hands.

"Jesus," the lanky man said as he surveyed the sea of orange suits and the thick stack of papers he had to digest before the judge took the bench. "It's gonna be a long fucking morning!"

As he flipped through pages detailing charges, delinquent history, mental health issues, substance abuse, and other miscellaneous facts, one case caught his attention—attempted murder and assault charges, accompanied by aggravating factors for a violent juvenile offender.

A kid had nearly castrated another kid with his teeth! He glanced at their faces, trying to identify which kid was the culprit. The man nodded knowingly as he located a small figure at the far end of the back row. The bandages and facial bruising were an immediate giveaway.

Observing the extent of the kid's injuries, he wondered if he could beat a self-defense theory at trial. He hoped no one had photographed the boy's injuries. *By the time he goes to trial,* he thought, *he should be all healed up. Any self-defense claim will suffer without photos.*

Quickly thumbing through the report, he realized that the victim was the son of veteran police officer, Kevin Kensington. Kensington had testified in several cases that he'd tried in juvenile court. He remembered him as a decent cop, although he had heard troubling rumors about citizen complaints involving excessive force stacking up against him.

As the assigned assistant deputy district attorney for the morning docket, he knew he'd request a no-bond hold. *This kid would not return home anytime soon,* he thought. Self-defense or not, it wasn't his job as a prosecutor to argue for the kid's release—that was the defense attorney's job. The kid was going to need a good one, too: white victim, son of a decorated cop, a repugnant act, a Black youth offender, and probably an all-white, male jury.

"This is going to be a hot one," he said absentmindedly.

Overhearing him, his female associate asked quizzically, "What?"

He shoved the report over to her as if it were a burning piece of coal, pointed to the charges, and stabbed at the last name of the victim. Her nose wrinkled as if she'd sniffed something offensive.

"Oh my God," she gasped. "Kensington." She let out a long, slow, deep breath. "You can keep that one," she declared.

"Not a problem," he responded. "Although I bet you dinner this case won't stay in juvenile court past the filing of charges deadline."

She nodded and remarked, "That kid better put his big pants on. He's about to be charged as an adult."

The hour was nearing 8:30 a.m., and people were starting to wander in. The mousy-looking female handed reports to professionally attired individuals. Some moved about the courtroom with ease. A few young attorneys appeared confused, as if they didn't know what they were supposed to do or where they should sit.

Maybe young attorneys, she thought, *most likely sworn in as licensed lawyers as early as this morning.*

The metal door clicked again, and the sea of young heads turned to see an older female with silver gray-blue hair emerge from the back hallway, demanding, in an inordinately loud voice, "Who is the guardian ad litem on duty today? Anybody from social services?" She then demanded, "Have we got an on-call defense attorney?"

A few hands went up dismissively. "Well, let's get moving, people! We've got a heavy docket this morning, and the judge has a meeting he has to get to by noon." The woman looked around. "Where is Amy?" she snarled, her beady eyes scanning the seating area for the small figure, who instinctively shrunk in her seat. "What happened to the reports?" she snapped after spotting her. "Did you drop the reports off at the division?"

Amy Walker popped up from her seat, trembling. The shy, sylph-like woman from pretrial services looked thunderstruck.

"I'm … I'm sorry. I forgot. I was in such a rush to get everything done. I was still working on some of the reports when the DAs walked in." She appeared to be on the verge of tears.

The judge's clerk stood with one fisted hand on her hip, staring hard at Amy, her ample bosom heaving. "The judge is always the priority here," she bellowed. "He gets those reports before anyone else—before the district attorneys, the on-call attorneys, social service, or any Tom, Dick, or Harry."

A few spectators seem surprised that a staff member would speak so abrasively to a fellow employee in open court. Others looked away, embarrassed for the young woman.

"Give us our copies, please!" the judge's clerk barked, emphasizing "*our*" with a sarcastic sneer. The young woman approached her hesitantly with a large stack of reports.

The matron hissed, "Be prepared to be eaten." She snatched the reports from Amy's hands, turned abruptly, and huffed toward the door. The resounding click of the door reminded Amy of her dad racking the slide of his Glock when he chambered a bullet.

Clusters of people arrived and began wandering about. Parents, relatives, and friends were coming in droves to support their child as the noise level steadily increased. Agitation, confusion, and sadness also rose as the families in the gallery spotted their loved ones supervised by deputies. For security purposes, families were not allowed to speak to or touch their children, but some family members waved excitedly anyway.

One distraught youth fought back tears. Another child, about ten years old, began to weep uncontrollably. "I want to go home!" he cried upon seeing his grandmother.

A heavyset Black woman with graying hair rushed toward the jury box where the kids were seated. People parted quickly as this mountain of energy began to roll toward them. Seeing a possible security breach, a deputy sheriff, who looked like he could move mountains himself, stepped directly in her path before she could enter the well of the court—the area where court business is conducted. His sudden appearance didn't seem to faze her.

He said in a firm but calm voice, "I'm sorry, ma'am, but we can't allow any contact with the kids. Safety procedures, you understand."

"My name is Darlene Moore," she pointed to one of the shackled young men in the jury box. "And that's my grandson."

The deputy nodded sympathetically, his voice softening, "I understand. I do. I have kids of my own." His concern seemed genuine, and Darlene hesitated as she eyed him suspiciously.

Calling out to Amy, he asked, "Can you provide Ms. Moore with some information about visitation over at the detention facility?" Amy smiled, pleased to be of service to someone after the public scolding she'd received from the court clerk.

"Please come with me, ma'am. My name is Amy." She said gently, as she carefully guided her away from the well.

Frustrated and upset, Darlene turned to face the audience, ignoring the busybody stares and whispers. Lifting her head high, she let Amy lead her away. Her round, fleshy shoulders sagged slightly, but she maintained a spirited spring in her step. The strain on her face was evident; her spirit was bowed, but not broken.

The desperate face of her grandson gripped her with a furious intensity. Her thoughts raced, skipped, and jumped as she frantically searched her mind for some way—any way—to get him out of this dismal place.

The gentle pressure of Amy's hand, cupped beneath her elbow, guided her toward the doors leading to the hallway. Amy leaned into the heavy door, bracing herself, but nearly stumbled when Patricia Horn suddenly pulled it open.

"Oh, excuse me. Are you okay?" Patricia asked.

"Fine. I'm fine." Amy responded. "Just surprised me. Caught me off balance." Amy's attention, however, was drawn to the long scar on the attractive African-American woman's face. She was slender in her mid thirties, with light brown skin and sharp intelligent eyes.

The elderly Black woman chimed in, "Well! I'm not fine. Dey got my baby boy in there. I don't know how I'm gonna get him out."

Patricia looked at her sympathetically. The woman's vibrant energy reminded her of her mother, Emma. She felt an immediate kinship.

"You must stay strong," Patricia said. "Keep hope and faith in God. He'll see you through this."

Patricia's eyes were kind, but the strain behind them was apparent to the older woman.

Amy, small and white, was suddenly aware that she stood between two different generations of Black women who had come to an alien and hostile forum to do whatever they could to rescue a loved one. They forced brave smiles, but their eyes reflected their anxiety.

"Well, c'mon, young lady!" Darlene said spiritedly. "Tell me what you can do to help mah boy!"

Amy excused herself with a deferential smile toward Patricia, took hold of Darlene's elbow again and proceeded down the hallway.

She explained, "My office is on this floor. Just a bit down the hall. We have a few minutes before the judge starts the docket, and we can talk while we walk."

As they started to walk away, Amy heard a voice behind her. "Just a moment, please. Your voice sounds familiar. My name is Patricia Horn. I think we talked on the phone the other night about my son, Tyrene."

Looking over her shoulder, Amy acknowledged her, without breaking stride, "We probably did. I always try to confirm information in my reports by contacting as many parents as possible, but we can talk later. Okay?"

Turning away from the two women, Patricia wondering what escape was possible for young men of color from a system that seemed determined to stigmatize them. Taking a deep breath, she grasped the brass handle, pulled open the door, and stepped into the courtroom.

Her attention was drawn to the two rows of kids in orange jumpsuits seated to the left of the judge's bench. Her heart skipped when she saw him. And when Tyrene saw her, the smile on his face was magnificent. She nearly ran to the front of the courtroom to be closer to her son.

Finding a suitable vantage point, she sat down. When she looked back to her son, she saw a man in a suit holding a file speaking to him.

Probably the public defender, she thought, remembering her first appearance in felony court for the attempted murder of her husband.

Patricia scanned the courtroom. Seeing only a few white children in custody, she glanced around to gauge how many white parents were present. There were more white kids than Blacks in the audience with their parents. Most of these white families were dressed formally for court—men in suits and ties and women in dresses, pants suits, or skirts—while many Black adults were casually attired or dressed for work in company uniforms.

Her gaze shifted to white men in dark suits with expensive-looking briefcases resting on their laps, as they conferred with their white clients and adolescent children. She noted that none of the Black families appeared to have legal representation.

It was the same dynamic she'd experienced when she was brought to court in waist cuffs and ankle bracelets to face her own criminal charges.

Race and class are clear lines of demarcation in America's criminal justice system, she mused.

"History is repeating itself," she muttered.

Several years ago, her two sons had sat in the audience with their grandmother, teary-eyed and frightened, as they watched their mother shackled in a jury box. Now, here she sat, witnessing the re-enactment of a process that could lead to an outcome as arbitrary as a spin on the Wheel of Fortune.

Suddenly, several metallic clicks echoed, overlapping each other, as two doors were opened: one from the outside hallway near the corner of the jury box where the kids were seated, and the other higher up behind the raised bench, allowing the judge to enter and be visible to all.

"All rise!" a male bailiff announced as a mild-mannered judge, with kind eyes, robed in black, entered the room. There was a delayed response from the audience as they slowly became aware that the judge was about to take the bench. The two lawyers at the prosecution's table, directly before the judge's bench, snapped to attention.

A solitary lawyer at the defense table rose halfway to his feet. The attorneys seated behind the tables, just in front of the wooden railing, stood quickly. The entire audience followed, rising slowly from their seats.

However, some juveniles in the jury box were not as responsive to the order to rise. Most of them finally complied as a massive officer walked over to the jury box and made several quick, impatient gestures with his hand for them to stand.

The judge's voice was low, measured, and oddly soothing as he intoned, "Please be seated." He frowned at the paperwork that had been placed on the corner of his bench. He quickly leafed through the documents, shuffled through a few files, and inserted the documents within the appropriate folders. Looking up from his stack of papers, he asked, "Which cases are ready to be called?"

The male prosecutor announced, "Morning, Judge Jones! I have a private case that's ready."

The judge looked uneasy. He didn't like giving the impression that affluent individuals received priority in his courtroom. Some courtrooms called private attorneys first, earning those judges unmerited favor in the eyes of those attorneys who benefited from preferential treatment. A judge was ever mindful of judicial evaluations and upcoming elections. Well-connected lawyers could sometimes upend a judge's career.

"Ladies and gentlemen," Judge Jones began slowly, "some families are here with private attorneys. These attorneys charge by the hour, so I hope to help those families save a little money. I hope you understand. I will try to get to everyone's case as quickly as I can because I know that you all have important matters to attend to today. Please be patient."

Someone in the audience shouted mockingly, "We understand, Your Honor. Money talks!"

The judge blanched. Visibly offended. He looked down at his desk. He felt a headache coming on. He placed his fingertips to his temples as if the pressure would be sufficient to prevent the pounding in his head. The courtroom became deathly still. A few attorneys shook their heads in disapproval.

Clearing his throat, the judge spoke slowly. "Regardless of anyone's feeling or perception about the process, if anyone is unwise enough to yell out another inappropriate and disrespectful comment on the record in open court, he or she will have an opportunity to reflect on their indiscretion in a jail cell. I hope I've made myself clear."

He looked over at the deputies, who nodded their understanding that an adult might go to jail today. The judge's eyes were cold now, as he scanned the audience, seemingly daring someone else to speak.

"Call your first case, counsel," he said flatly.

"Yes, sir," the DA responded quickly. "People in the Interest of Thomas Alexander Montgomery, III."

From the rear of the courtroom, a distinguished gentleman with thinning, sun-bleached hair and age spots emerged, a file in one hand and a briefcase in the other. A well-dressed couple strode behind, their lanky teenager trailing after them. The boy wore a dark gray pinstripe suit with a stylish tie, his shoes were polished to a mirror shine. The family stood out conspicuously, even among other well-dressed white families in the courtroom.

"Good morning, Judge. Marcus Robert Pettigrew from the law firm of Tower, Bankshank, and Millandorf," he announced as he placed his briefcase on the table. "Tommy, my client, and his parents Mr. and Mrs. Montgomery are in attendance."

"Pete Miller for the People, your Honor," said the DA enthusiastically, who'd called the case.

"Thank you, gentlemen," responded the judge.

Before the judge could speak, Attorney Pettigrew asked if he could be heard briefly. The judge gave a perfunctory nod.

"Your Honor," he began, "I've spoken to the Chief Deputy of the District Attorney's Office concerning this case, and we've reached an agreement to vacate the warrant and set a personal recognizance bond."

The judge interrupted. "Counsel, I read the affidavit for the arrest warrant, and it appears that your client is currently being investigated for a series of burglaries throughout the metropolitan area. Moreover, he was identified in a lineup, in this particular case, as one of the individuals who possessed a loaded handgun that was used to threaten a homeowner. An outstanding warrant for his arrest has been issued in this jurisdiction, and the bond is currently set at $100,000."

The public recitation of the criminal allegations sounded far more stark to the parents, causing them to fidget uncomfortably. The anemic-looking boy stared at the floor. Sensing where the court might be heading, Pettigrew looked at Miller, the assistant deputy attorney, for help.

Picking up the cue, Miller said, "Ah, yes. That's correct, Your Honor. I was informed by my supervisor this morning, who'd spoken to the Chief Deputy, about how we were to proceed in this matter.

"Your Honor, we've agreed to quash the warrant and convert the $100,000 bond to a personal recognizance bond based upon several important mitigating factors. This is, of course, subject to the court's approval." The corners of the judge' mouth turned down as he sensed a political favor in the making.

Welcoming the opening created by Miller, Pettigrew interjected hastily, "That's correct, Judge. This agreement was reached based on several important considerations. Specifically, Mr. and Mrs. Montgomery have arranged for their son to participate in individual therapy twice a week with a renown psychotherapist. He's also attending a support group through a highly reputable licensed agency. He has submitted UAs on a random basis, and his THC level is steadily decreasing. Moreover, he is being evaluated independently by Dr. William Clausen, who specializes in bipolar disorders."

"What about public safety, counsel?" the judge asked incredulously. "Your client is alleged to have burglarized three homes, at times with a weapon, and you are asking this court to quash a warrant and release him to his parents on a signature bond?"

Before Pettigrew could answer, the judge snapped at Miller, his voice resonating with disbelief. "Your office agreed to this?"

Miller looked slightly embarrassed. He knew the judge remembered that just days before, he'd aggressively argued for a $100,000 bond for a Black teenager who was charged with two counts of aggravated robbery and menacing at a convenience store, even though the gun involved wasn't real. The boy had been homeless, was hungry, and had no prior juvenile history.

Miller cleared his throat. "All I can say, Judge, is that the case was carefully reviewed and approved by our Chief. Given the proactive steps that counsel and the family have taken in good faith, I feel confident that the community would not be at risk." The judge continued to look perturbed.

Miller continued. "This is a real wake-up call for this young man, Your Honor." Miller was choosing his words carefully. "I know he's been made aware that his case could potentially be transferred to adult district court if he is non-compliant with the treatment program established by his parents. If he's tried as an adult, he understands he is facing up to 75 years in prison."

Mrs. Montgomery looked like she was going to faint. And Mr. Montgomery appeared increasingly agitated. He was obviously a man accustomed to getting his way.

Pettigrew raised his hands, almost in supplication. "Your Honor, I'm well aware of your genuine concern for the welfare and safety of the community. Had I not truly believed that the plan we've put in place will provide the necessary protective safeguards, I wouldn't be making this request on my client's behalf."

To shore up his plea, Pettigrew added, "It also appears, if I may respectfully point out, that the community and safety concerns of the Chief Prosecutor of this district were clearly satisfied by the treatment and safety plan established by the parents after lengthy consultation with numerous specialists in the field."

"I need a moment," the judge said curtly, clearly displeased with the agreement. He sat back in his chair. Everyone in the courtroom was watching him. The mocking words… "Money talks!" echoed in his head.

His eyes caught sight of a group of African-American students seated in the very rear of his courtroom. Unusual. All boys. All wearing ties. No uniforms. Dressed for court? A field trip?

Leaning forward, he began. "Alright. As it appears that the Chief Deputy has been consulted and has given her approval, I feel obligated to accept this agreement, particularly since I know little about the facts of this case or the mitigating circumstances surrounding it."

The judge could see relief seeping into the parents' faces. The private attorney's smug *expression* prompted the judge to throw a curve ball into the deal.

"However," the judge continued, "Given the seriousness of the allegations, I'm ordering Mr. Montgomery to be placed on pretrial release and supervision while he's on bond." He added, "The Court also orders an ankle bracelet at pretrial's discretion."

Noting the confusion in the parents' faces, the judge explained, "Pretrial is an agency of the court that monitors juveniles in the community to assure compliance with certain conditions. With the program's participation and involvement, the court can ensure that the treatment regimen implemented is being followed and that contact is made by pretrial with Mr. Montgomery regularly. More importantly, the agency is additional protection to ensure that the community remains safe."

The judge paused. "You must understand that if Mr. Montgomery fails to comply with the program requirements, he will ultimately be wearing an orange jumpsuit like the kids sitting over there in the jury box."

"Your Honor," Pettigrew protested, "that wasn't our agreement. My client is presumed innocent of all charges."

The judge responded calmly. "You needn't shout, Mr. Pettigrew. I'm not deaf." The throbbing in his head was beginning to subside. "If you want the personal recognizance bond, it will be with pretrial release. If you are refusing pretrial release, tell the parents to give their son a hug because the deputy sheriff will take him into custody right now."

Pettigrew appeared stunned. He glanced at his client's parents and shrugged his shoulders. Montgomery shook his head, openly disappointed with the attorney.

Gathering his scattered wits, Pettigrew stuttered, "Thank you, Judge. I understand." Any semblance of smugness on Pettigrew's face had vanished. Pettigrew acquiesced. "Pretrial conference as a condition of the PR bond...of course."

The judge looked over the heads of the parents and attorney then out into the audience. "Where is pretrial? Where is Amy Walker?"

At that moment, the courtroom door swung open, and Amy dashed forward, a panicked look on her face as she heard her name called. She began speaking rapidly as she hurried down the aisle. Darlene Moore followed closely behind her and promptly took a seat.

"I'm so sorry, Your Honor," Amy said, her face flushed as she struggled to catch her breath. I needed to speak with a mother regarding her child's case. It took a lot longer than I anticipated."

The judge responded with measured formality, "Ladies and gentlemen, I apologize for the interruption."

He turned to Amy. "Ms Walker," he said, gesturing to the young man, "Mr. Montgomery is being placed on the pretrial release program. These are his parents and their attorney, Mr. Pettigrew. Please assign a case manger to supervise the young man. My clerk will provide them with the necessary paperwork and a new court date. Now, folks, please return to your seats."

"Next case, Mr. Miller. Let's call someone in custody this time."

"Right, Judge," Miller responded, trying to mask his frustration about the Montgomery case.

"People in the Interest of Tyrene Horn," Miller announced. When Judge Jones looked over the courtroom, he saw a bruised, bandaged boy stand up. His small stature made it difficult to determine his age, though he had to be at least ten—the minimum age for juvenile court. The judge observed the boy scanning the audience, his eyes anxiously searching for someone before he stepped out of the jury box.

Tyrene's mother raised her hand high signaling her presence. Almost immediately, another arm waved enthusiastically from the far back corner of the courtroom, where the judge had noticed a group of African-American boys seated together.

Li'l Bits! My best friend from middle school is here, Tyrene thought excitedly. He hadn't seen him since he and his mom had left the old neighborhood. Tyrene had told Li'l Bits that his mom wanted to move so he could attend a better school, but they both knew the truth: she couldn't bear to live in the house where Duke had died.

Tyrene smiled broadly toward the back of the courtroom. He straightened his posture as much as his injuries allowed and nodded enthusiastically at his friend.

His mother moved swiftly toward the table designated for juvenile defendants. Taking her cue, Tyrene began making his way forward, the metallic jingle of the chain marking each step.

Undaunted, he shuffled forward and tottered to the table where his mother was now standing. The man who introduced himself as his attorney was whispering to her. All the while, the audience's eyes remained fixed on Tyrene's bandages. Some of them, particularly the African Americans, assumed his condition was the result of a vicious beating he'd received after running from the police.

Judge Jones, concerned, leaned forward on his elbows and propped his chin on his folded hands studying the young man carefully.

He waited for the mother and child to be seated, quietly observing the well-dressed, poised African-American woman before him.

Her dark brunette hair was cropped close and neat. A thin, long scar ran down the left side of her face over a prominent cheekbone to the corner of her mouth. The scar lent her a formidable appearance, but her attire softened the impression: a white silk shirt with a floral bow paired with a well-tailored blue suit, signaling to the world she was safe—as long as you didn't cross her.

Patricia Horn revealed no emotion as she sat down. It wasn't until she looked at her son that the judge saw a fierce expression of love. They did not touch, but in that instant, they conveyed the profound intensity of their mother-child bond.

The judge instinctively understood that she would not tolerate any insult, trespass, or offense against her son. He glanced at the prosecutor, who remained oblivious to the formidable opponent seated just ten feet away.

Before the prosecutor began, the judge spoke aloud, addressing no one in particular, "Has this young man received adequate medical care?"

Amy Walker stood up and asked for permission to speak. As a non-attorney, she needed the judge's approval before addressing the court.

"By all means," the judge replied politely.

"Tyrene was released from the hospital only yesterday evening," she said. "The doctors recommended keeping him under observation for an additional 24 hours to ensure there's no bleeding in the brain or complications from his concussion. I spoke to a nurse yesterday, who assured me he was stable enough to be released. Nevertheless, the juvenile detention staff is monitoring him closely. As you can see, he has several injuries still in the process of healing."

The judge lifted his chin. "Young man," he began, "how are you feeling now?"

Tyrene glanced at the judge, then at his mom, and back to the judge. He responded with a smile and a nod.

"Well, are you in any pain? You look like you took quite a beating," the judge said, his concern evident. Tyrene remained silent.

Amy shifted uneasily. "Your Honor, may we approach the bench briefly?"

Judge Jones appeared puzzled but motioned the prosecutor, the public defender, the on-call guardian ad litem, and Amy to come forward.

Once assembled at the bench, the parties leaned in to hear Ms. Walker's report. She began in a whisper. "Your Honor, I omitted some information about Tyrene in his report this morning. I felt some of the details were just too personal."

The judge acknowledged her caution with a nod, "Go on, Ms. Walker."

Amy sighed. "Your Honor, he won't talk to you. He won't talk to anyone. He doesn't even speak to his mother."

"That's right, Judge," the Public Defender added. " He didn't say a word to me this morning."

"Are you telling me he's mute, Ms. Walker?" Judge Jones asked.

"No, Judge. Well, yes, in a way. I'm sorry. It's complicated. Something traumatic happened to Tyrene several years ago." Unexpectedly, Amy felt her eyes tear up.

"Tyrene came home after school. He usually was the first one home. When he arrived, he heard music. He realized that the music was coming from his brother's room. He called out to him, but didn't get any response. After calling out several times, he decided to go to his room."

A tear welled in the corner of her eye, which she quickly wiped away. "I'm so sorry," she mumbled, aware that certain emotional displays violated professional norms.

She continued. "When Tyrene walked into his brother's room, he saw him on the bed. He was not moving. His brother had tied a plastic bag around his head with a twist tie. An empty bottle of sleeping pills sat on the bedside table. A note in his brother's hand read, *'I couldn't pretend anymore that I was okay. It's been so hard for me for such a long time. I have to stop this awful pain. I know you won't understand, but it's not about you. It's not your fault. You're not to blame. I love you both with all my heart.'*"

Amy paused to collect herself before continuing. "Since that day, he hasn't spoken a word."

"If Tyrene was the only one home and he stopped speaking after he discovered his brother's body, how do you know what happened after he arrived home?"

"From a reliable source, Your Honor. His mother told me he disclosed much of that information in his journal entries to his trauma therapist."

Pursing his lips, the judge leaned forward. "What else did you learn?"

"The Department of Human Services conducted a child abuse and neglect investigation. I reviewed the file, and a child protective team determined a petition was not warranted. The file also indicated that the police investigation found no evidence of foul play. The coroner's report ruled his brother's death a suicide."

She paused. "I want you to know, Judge, that Tyrene is a bright kid in honors classes and not a problem student."

Before she could complete her presentation, the DA interjected dryly, "Not a problem student until now."

The on-call defense attorney felt compelled to respond. "Have you forgotten the presumption of innocence? This is the kid's first appearance."

The DA paused and then countered, "Your client nearly castrated another boy while attacking him at school. What's your presumption of innocence? It wasn't an assault? The kid was hungry and just needed a snack?"

The judge raised his hand. "Folks," he said, "this is not the time to start squabbling about the merits of the case. This morning, we are only dealing with probable cause for his arrest and setting of bond. Please return to your seats."

As the attorneys walked back to their assigned tables, glaring at each other, the judge said," A moment, Ms. Walker." She returned to the bench.

"A good report, Ms. Walker. Thank you."

Amy's eyes brightened at the compliment. "I try to be thorough, sir."

The judge asked, " Are you meeting with Tyrene's mother later."

She nodded, "Of course, sir."

As gently as he could, the judge advised, "I know you care deeply for all the families you work with, but I need you to be careful about maintaining appropriate boundaries." He worried that she might feel overly sympathetic toward this family.

Amy looked at him quizzically.

He explained, "Keep the professional and personal aspects of the job separated. I know it can be difficult when personal details are shared."

Uncertain, Amy nodded again.

"Of course, Judge!" She said, smiling at him as she returned to her seat.

Clearing his throat, the judge addressed Patricia and Tyrene. "I apologize for excluding you from the bench conference. Occasionally, it's necessary to address delicate matters at the bench to respect a family's privacy."

The judge announced, "I'm ready to make my findings. He began, "Tyrene Horn appears in court today because it's alleged that he has committed a delinquent act. Having reviewed the statement supporting a warrantless arrest, I have determined that probable cause does exist to arrest him. The question remains whether he should be detained. Now I need to hear from the attorneys about the issue of bond. Mr. DA, your position?"

"Thank you, Your Honor," DA Miller said. "Based upon the savage nature of the delinquent act, the possible filing of attempted second-degree murder, assault with a deadly weapon, assault resulting in serious bodily injury, and the realistic possibility that the People will ask that this case be directly filed into adult district court, the People are requesting a 'no bond hold'. The People ask that this young man remain in detention until charges are formally filed in—"

The defense attorney interrupted, "As usual, your Honor," the DA contemplates not only overcharging but also stacking the charges," he exclaimed. "It was a school fight! Do you see his injuries? Do you see how small he is? It's clear that he was acting in self-defense. Mr. Horn has absolutely no record, no delinquent history. Besides that, he's an honor student."

The defense attorney glared at the prosecutor as he spoke, his voice quaking with anger. "As the court acknowledged earlier this morning, pretrial release is available to ensure public safety."

The judge turned to the guardian ad litem. "Do you have any statements to make in the child's best interest?"

The GAL declined. "I haven't been appointed yet, Judge."

"Well, Madam GAL, you are appointed now. Please obtain the family's contact information from Amy, as well as a copy of the pre-trial report."

"Now, the question of bond," he turned to Patricia. "Ms. Horn," the judge asked softly, "Would you care to make a statement regarding the issue of bond?"

This concession was highly unusual, as her son was represented by an attorney, and she wasn't licensed to practice law.

Patricia rose slowly from her seat, proud and dignified. Her voice was clear, and unlike most parents, she was not bewildered or intimidated.

"Your Honor," she began, "my son is a good boy. He doesn't look for trouble, but he doesn't run from it, either. He did what he absolutely had to do to defend himself from a vicious attack. Do you see what that boy did to my son? Does justice favor the one who is injured the most, even though that same person initiated the attack?"

Her words were even and measured, devoid of emotion, but compelling. "The defense claims that this was just a fight at school. He gravely mischaracterizes what happened here. My son defended himself against a bully who was physically bigger and stronger. He fought back against an unprovoked assault while his classmates stood by, cheering the bully on. No one intervened to help him, although a large crowd had gathered to watch. My son did what he needed to do to survive a vicious and brutal attack. No reasonable jury, if fair, will see it otherwise."

For a brief moment, her voice nearly broke. "Judge! There's no way I can afford a high bond." She paused, as if she wanted to say more, but thought better of it and sat down.

Surprised by her quiet eloquence, the judge took a moment to respond. "A 'no bond' hold is inappropriate, given the circumstances of this case. Moreover, the court declines to find that Mr. Horn's teeth constitute a deadly weapon, regardless of the manner in which they were used in this alleged assault. The recommended minimum bond amount for first-degree assault is $50,000 cash or surety. The court is setting the bond at the recommended amount."

"Judge!" the DA protested, "Are you forgetting about the attempted murder charge?"

"Thank you for reminding me, Counsel. So that the record is clear, I'm finding probable cause as to the second-degree assault with serious bodily injury only, not the attempted second-degree murder charge," Judge Jones said, arching an eyebrow.

The DA looked as if he had been kicked in the chest, unable to believe the court's ruling.

Mindful of the overly generous bond set in the first case, the defense counsel suggested an alternative. "Would the court consider a PR bond to the mother, along with pretrial supervision release?"

The judge pondered the request briefly before shaking his head. "No. That would mean he would be released for a few days, only to be taken back into custody again, if charges are direct filed in adult court and a new bond is set. Make that request again, Counsel, if this case remains in juvenile court, and I maintain jurisdiction."

5

Our Brother's Keeper

After Judge Jones' decision, Patricia sighed deeply and turned to Tyrene.

"Okay, my Little Man Dude," she said. "Stay strong. I need to meet with pre-trial this morning. I think it's with Ms. Walker. She sounds like the woman I talked to last night."

Then she leaned in close, whispering, trying to contain her excitement. "Remember my friend, TicToc, the one I met years ago in county?" When Tyrene nodded, she continued. "I've got a meeting with her today. She said she's going to help us!" Patricia's voice trembled with nervous anticipation.

TicToc had been released from jail about 60 days before her. In the jail cell, just before her release, TicToc had gently touched the bandage covering the wound on the side of Patricia's face.

"I owe you, lady," TicToc said fiercely. "You ever need anything, I mean *anything*, and I'll be there. You may not be able to find me, but I'll definitely find you."

Although Patricia had been unable to find or contact TicToc for nearly two years, TicToc always came to mind whenever life felt overwhelming. To her, no woman was more formidable—or more resourceful—than TicToc.

Patricia leaned over and gently pressed her head against her son's.

Tyrene kissed her on the cheek and stood up. She watched as he shuffled back to his place in the jury box. She then walked out of the well to the public seating area. She turned to wave goodbye to him, her heart heavy, but her expression unwavering.

Just then, she felt a tap on her shoulder and turned to see Amy Walker. As Patricia and Amy headed toward the doors, she noticed someone, waving excitedly from the back of the courtroom. The figure moved swiftly down the long wooden benches, carefully stepping over shoes, past crossed knees, and outstretched legs.

At first glance, he could have been her son—at least, in size. It was Li'l Bits, Tyrene's friend. They were the same age and had been born on the same day. Best friends, they had been inseparable in middle school.

Before he could speak, Patricia raised her finger to her lips, signaling him to be quiet and motioned toward the doors leading out of the courtroom. Amy led the way out into the hall.

After seeing her son, Patricia could finally breathe. It felt as if a heavy weight had been lifted from her shoulders, easing the tightness in her chest.

Tyrene was safe, and her friend TicToc—the same friend who had mysteriously disappeared after being released from county jail—had returned to help them.

Frenetic, youthful energy exploded before the door closed behind them. Li'l Bits was bursting with excitement. "Ms. Horn! So good to see you! Is Tyrene okay? Somebody beat him bad! Where are you living now? Will you be able to get Tyrene out? Can I visit him?" His words gushed like water from a broken pipe.

Li'l Bits was a whirlwind of bubbling elation. Thick, dark curls hung low over his high forehead, and his bright brown eyes—alive with intelligence—framed his oval face. His warm, winsome expression felt like a welcoming embrace to Patricia. He measured no more than five foot four, earning him his nickname, yet his presence filled the hallway with a radiant power.

"Whoa! Slow down, Li'l Bits," Patricia said, laughing. She reached over to give him a tender hug. "I'm as excited to see you as you are to see me, but what are you doing here?"

Nodding her head toward Walker, she said, "Matthew Michael Carver, this is Ms. Walker, someone from court who might be able to help Tyrene."

"Aren't you supposed to be in school, young man?" Walker observed in jest.

Cocking her head, Patricia snapped, "He came to see my son. Can't you suspend your judgment for a minute?" The strain of court had drained her patience.

Surprised by her sharp tone, Li'l Bits looked at Walker and warily eyed Patricia before speaking again.

Politely, he explained, "I'm on a court tour with students to see the justice system at work, but I really came to see Tyrene. Someone posted on Facebook about his arrest, so my mom called the county clerk to find out when Tyrene's case was set. I got last-minute approval with the help of my mom and a friend for the trip. My teacher is really cool. She knew the real reason why I wanted to come."

"I assume your teacher is in the courtroom with the rest of your friends?" Walker asked tentatively, still confused by Horn's sharp tone.

"Oh, she's not with us, but the Professor is." Li'l Bits explained. "I mean, Doug Joiner. We call him 'the Professor'! He's inside with the rest of my group, but he's not a teacher at my school. He's a retired cop. He runs an independent class for African-American kids in his home. He was the one who contacted my Government Studies teacher to get the trip approved."

"Well, it's a smart thing to know how the system works. Learn a lot, Mr. Carver, but we don't have much time. Ms. Horn and I have to excuse ourselves. We have some important matters to discuss."

"About Tyrene?" he asked, his eyes wide.

"Among other things," she replied.

Shaking his head, he said, "Tyrene looks beat bad. This wouldn't have happened, if I'd been there, Ms. Horn. Excuse my language, ma'am, but I would've kicked that bully's ass."

Patricia knew Li'l Bits was not making an idle claim. Tyrene had once told her about an incident in middle school where three Black kids had been harassing a white boy after the last school bell. The boys took turns knocking the books out of his hands every time he picked them up. Tears steaming down his face, he'd begged them to leave him alone, but they just laughed and continued their taunts. Li'l Bits stepped in to intervene and dropped the big kid before he could blink. The movement was so fast that it seemed like a blur. The sound of his foot striking the kid's head echoed with a sharp thwack. Stunned, the other two pulled him to his feet and carried him away.

After the drubbing, Tyrene asked Li'l Bits why he'd bothered to help that white boy. Li'l Bits asked Tyrene what he would've done if the boy had been a friend or a family member. Tyrene told him that he would have tried to protect him.

"That's the point, Tyrene. If you saw that boy as someone you knew—family, a friend, even a neighbor—his color wouldn't matter. And if you could imagine him as somehow connected to you, you wouldn't have seen him as a stranger either."

Li'l Bits paused. "Remember the story of the Good Samaritan. He helped a Jew who despised his people. We are all our brother's keeper."

Tyrene protested, "But he didn't even take the time to thank you for saving his sorry ass."

"If you do something you think is right, that should be thanks enough."Then, with a smile, he added, "it *is* nice, though, when someone shows their gratitude."

Li'l Bits and the two women stood in the courthouse hallway as Amy cleared her throat to get Patricia's attention.

Li'l Bits reached out to touch her arm. With his soft eyes and warm smile, he gently asked, "Ms. Horn, where'd you go?"

Startled, Patricia apologized for becoming so distracted. She looked at him, so physically like her son, and returned his smile.

"No, Li'l Bits. Kicking his ass wouldn't have been a good idea. Then you'd be in there chained up, and we'd be out here trying to figure out how to get you out, too."

Li'l Bits nodded, acknowledging her point. "*Can* you get him out? $50,000! My dad barely makes that in a year. That's a lot of money."

Patricia sighed and shrugged. "Don't know yet. Got to talk to a friend of mine about the bond. Funny… it's been about two years since I've seen her, about the same amount of time since you last saw Tyrene." She fell silent for a moment and placed her hand on Li'l Bits' shoulder. "I'm sorry we didn't stay in touch more with you, son. It's just that ... you know ... after Duke died..." Her voice trailed off.

He placed his hand on top of hers, which rested gently on his shoulder. "No need to explain, Ms. Horn," Li'l Bits said. "I understand."

Patricia looked at him, remembering the sleepovers and birthday parties. She could hear Duke's infectious laughter as he teased and joked with them. Those were truly wonderful moments. She regretted letting her emotional pain interfere with the boys' friendship.

"Ms. Horn, is there any chance I can visit Tyrene? I mean… visit him when you go?"

Walker interjected. "Only family members are authorized to visit. However, since you're so close to Tyrene, Ms. Horn can contact me, and I'll see what I can do. Okay? But I can't make any promises." Amy admired the young man's loyalty.

"That's great! That's great!" he repeated excitedly. "Ms. Horn, please call me if I can visit Tyrene."

"I will, son. Now, you'd better get back in there with your friends. We'll talk again soon." She kissed him on the top of his head. "Goodbye for now, Li'l Bits. Thanks for coming. You've always been a good friend. Tell your mom I said, 'Hi'. Now, I need to find out if Ms. Walker can help Tyrene get released from this awful place."

Li'l Bits nodded and said, "Nice meeting you, Ms. Walker. Please do what you can to help my friend!"

Patricia heard his voice break when he said, "my friend," waving at her as he walked away.

The two women exchanged a glance, signaling that it was time to go. Walker said, "My office is straight down the hall. It will afford us some privacy."

Turning to face Amy, Patricia said, "The man in court who said, 'Money talks,' spoke an ugly truth about the criminal justice system that many government employees prefer to deny or ignore."

Amy softly exhaled, bracing herself for what was to come.

"Do you know who Bryan Stevenson is?" Patricia asked.

"Of course I've heard of him," Amy responded, almost defensively. "He's a well-known lawyer who represents indigent defendants on death row."

"Well," Patricia continued, "Attorney Stevenson was defending a poor Black 14-year-old boy in a criminal case. He wanted to find a way to convince a judge to give his young client fair and equal treatment in court. So, as lawyers do, he wrote a motion to the court."

Amy shrugged, "Nothing unusual about that."

Patricia chuckled. "Yes! But the motion was unusual and brazenly creative. You might even say it was extraordinary! Attorney Stevenson titled his motion in language that was impossible to ignore: 'Motion to try my Poor, 14-Year-Old Black Male Client Like a Privileged White 75-Year-Old Corporate Executive.' He caused an uproar in court. The judge was furious." Patricia started laughing.

Amy cocked her head, wondering if Horn's tale was a Black urban myth.

Patricia said, "So I want you to imagine my son as a white teenager from an affluent, well-connected family—the kind with deep political ties and generational wealth. Picture him dressed in designer clothes, sitting beside a high-powered Ivy League attorney who charges more per hour than most people make in a week."

Clicking her tongue, she continued ruefully, "Let's see if those optics can help shift your perspective about what you can do to help my son."

Amy pressed her lips into a thin line and sighed. *This is going to be a long meeting,* she thought.

6

White Privilege

Walker unlocked a door that opened into a tiny room. There was barely enough space for two people. Her desk was cluttered with files and professional journals. A wedding photograph of a Black and white couple teetered on the edge of her desk. Several diplomas and certificates hung from the otherwise bare walls.

"I ordinarily don't like to display my credentials," Amy confessed, "but I thought I needed to show that I do have degrees. Otherwise, folks might think that I was just a female janitor in this tiny room," she said with a wry smile.

"You're a state employee working in the juvenile system and a woman at that. I'm surprised you have an office at all," Patricia commented absentmindedly. "However," she added, "I'm not impressed with credentials, Ms. Walker. I'm impressed with results. Can your program help Tyrene and me? Can it help him like that white boy was helped this morning? If, as the judge says, your program helps ensure community safety, it should help my son get released. You know he has no priors whatsoever—no violent past, no weapons offenses, nothing to suggest he's a threat. Besides, as the lawyers say, this assault charge is an accusation only. It's not evidence of any wrongdoing."

"Please have a seat, Ms. Horn."

Amy eyed Patricia as she navigated the tight space to get to her chair. She believed her to be different from the typical African-American moms she'd previously encountered. Well-spoken and educated, she didn't use the stereotypical "ghetto" language often heard in interviews. She also appeared confident and unafraid of the court system. Observing her in a slightly dated, yet smartly tailored suit—perfect for court—Walker had to admit that Patricia Horn was impressive.

As she lowered herself into her chair, Walker's attention was drawn again to the long, thin scar on her face. Despite her delicate features, the scar looked menacing at a certain angle. Patricia caught her staring. She'd gotten accustomed to the stares. People, particularly white women, were always curious about the incongruity of an attractive Black woman bearing what appeared to be a nasty battle scar.

Patricia launched into her main concern. "The prosecutor said something that suggests Tyrene won't even be considered for your program."

Amy smiled politely. "I do my best to ensure every child has a fair chance of being released on bond."

Patricia said bluntly, "Pardon me, but you didn't answer my question. Will the DA block my son's chances of getting released?" Walker's expression changed.

Amy said softly, "Unfortunately, our legislature is not as generous to youth when it comes to violent crimes."

"The DA said something about a direct file to adult district court," Patricia noted. "Isn't he the one who decides whether a child is charged as an adult?" The question sounded more like an accusation.

"That decision is entirely within the discretion of the prosecutor. The law defines the basis for exercising that discretion." Amy's tone was almost apologetic. "I know your son is only seventeen, but the law allows a case to be transferred to adult court if the charges are serious enough."

Patricia pressed her. "If the case is transferred to adult court, he is no longer considered a juvenile, is he?"

Taking a deep breath, Amy said, "Yes, if that happens, Tyrene will have to defend against these charges as if he were an adult. Based on the charges, if he is convicted, he will face a lengthy prison sentence."

Patricia sighed and raised a hand to her face, now etched with strain. "You remember the white boy who appeared with his parents and his fancy attorney this morning? The judge said he's under investigation for several burglaries and has been identified as being in possession of a gun while committing a home invasion. He looked about the same age as my son. I understood that he only faces adult court if he violates his pretrial release conditions."

Amy nodded her head in agreement. "Yes, that's what the judge said."

Patricia leaned forward, "But a transfer to adult court is already being considered for my child. He doesn't get a chance to avoid being treated like an adult."

Avoiding her eyes, Amy meekly responded, "That's correct."

Her voice rising, Patricia said, "So that white kid, who commits home invasions with a weapon, is released today on a PR bond with pretrial services, while my child has to post a $50,000 bond for fighting a bully at school." Her voice echoed her disbelief.

Amy swallowed hard. "That's also correct," she replied, shifting nervously in her chair.

"I get the picture now, loud and clear." Patricia muttered, "Just us—not justice."

Her instincts had told her not to expect much from a justice system that tends to favor the rich and discriminate against the poor. She'd hoped, however, that the process would be different and fairer in juvenile court.

But why would it be different? she asked herself. *Children grow up to be men. They still represent a threat!*

She berated herself for being so naively optimistic. *Being Black in this system means that laws are applied differently. The courtroom setting doesn't matter; laws are conveniently ignored when they serve particular interests.* She'd seen as much this morning when the judge set a PR bond for the well-connected family.

"I don't know your personal feelings or beliefs about how the law treats Black people, Ms. Walker, but this process reminds me of Swiss cheese. Black and brown people and the poor are the ones who routinely fall through the holes. Only well-connected lawyers know the random patterns that keep their clients safe."

Amy understood her frustration and indignation. After learning about the family's trauma and loss, she hoped to make a difference for them.

The previous evening, Amy had met with Tyrene at the juvenile detention center to interview him and prepare her report. Although she sometimes encountered kids who refused to speak to her because they saw her as part of the system, Tyrene was different.

He was not at all guarded. Tyrene was polite. He merely smiled at her and said nothing. Observing his badly beaten state, she initially assumed that he couldn't speak because he'd sustained an injury to his vocal cords or, perhaps, English was not his native tongue. She made a referral to the duty nurse, but the nurse already knew about his situation.

The nurse explained, "His hospital discharge summary did not indicate damage or trauma to his throat, so I gave him a piece of paper and a pencil and asked him to respond to my questions in writing."

She continued, "The bottom line is that he can speak, but chooses not to. I confirmed this with his mother. Tyrene's therapist called it 'traumatic mutism'. The therapist explained it this way to his mother: Tyrene and his brother had a very close relationship that sustained and nurtured Tyrene on many levels. Duke's death was traumatic for him—not only because he died, but the way he died. Tyrene can no longer call his brother's name and expect a response. By choosing not to speak, his silence denies his brother's death. More importantly, it's Tyrene's way of keeping Duke alive.

"According to the therapist, Tyrene will speak again when he can accept and embrace death, even inexplicable death, as part of life." The nurse paused, then added, "Something so powerful might occur—so deeply stirring—that Tyrene will feel compelled to speak. He'll be unable to remain silent. In that moment, when he does speak, his healing will begin."

Walker glanced at Horn, who had fallen silent and was staring into space. With a slight quiver in her voice, she said, "Ms. Horn, I hope you believe me. I do my best to catch the children before they disappear into those holes."

Patricia sat back in her chair, and exhaled deeply. Finally, she turned to look at Amy.

"Ms. Walker, can you please explain to me the meaning of the image of the woman wearing a blindfold, while holding a scale in one hand and a sword in the other."

"You mean the idea that justice is blind?" Amy asked.

"Yep! That's the one. It's a powerful image. The blindfold is supposed to symbolize impartiality, fairness, and the principle that justice should be administered without bias, favoritism, or preferential treatment, regardless of race, class, gender, or sexual orientation. Maybe one of these days, that blindfold might mean something," Patricia said dryly.

Nodding slowly, Amy replied, "Believe me, I understand. I'm with you. Even with the advantage of a jury, God help you if you don't look, sound, or act like the people who decide your fate. But for what it's worth, I hope that some day soon, justice *will* be blind."

Patricia was surprised by the sincerity in her voice, but she still felt profoundly disappointed. *This program can't help me. Patricia thought. Can't help my son. Walker's good intentions won't change a damn thing.*

She sighed, reminding herself there was nowhere to go until the much-anticipated call came.

Looking over at the wedding portrait on the corner of Walker's desk, Patricia said, "Well, at least it looks like love is blind."

Amy followed Patricia's eyes to the wedding picture of her and her Black husband. She welcomed the conversational shift, grateful to talk about something more pleasant.

She smiled broadly. "If I had listened to my parents and my friends, we definitely wouldn't be married. But after we got to know each other, I no longer saw or thought about his color. I just saw a decent human being."

Appreciative of her response, Patricia said, "I bet you two met in college."

Laughing, Amy said, "You are so right. I knew Oscar from an English Lit class, but we never spoke."

"Well, how did you guys get together?" She asked.

"You really want to know? It's not the typical boy-meets-girl story."

"If you're comfortable, I'm comfortable."

Taking a deep breath, Amy began, "Oscar and I were at a frat party. Everybody was drinking and having a good time. A lot of my school friends were there, so I was a bit wild, chugging shots and playing drinking games. I was feeling a little woozy, so this guy said he would take me to the bathroom because I told him I was going to be sick. I didn't know who he was, but I did feel like I was going to be sick."

Patricia nodded. She knew where this story was headed.

"He carried me upstairs, but instead of taking me to the bathroom, he took me into a bedroom.

"I vaguely remember him laying me down on the bed. I was starting to feel like I was going to throw up." She paused for a minute to collect her thoughts.

"I was in an alcoholic fog, but I could feel him touching me, unbuttoning my blouse. I think he kept telling me how pretty I was. He started to unfasten my jeans, and I felt him tugging at my pants. I felt so weak and drunk that I could barely lift my arms, but I do remember I started yelling 'Stop!' At least, I think I did."

Patricia cautioned," Are you telling me more than you want to?"

"No! No! Of course not," Amy said. "Besides, it has a happy ending. The next thing I knew, I heard the door open, and this guy yelled, 'What the hell are you doing to my girlfriend?' The guy on top of me freaked and started apologizing in a panic."

He pleaded, "I'm sorry, man! I'm sorry! I didn't do anything. I guess we both had too much to drink. She asked me to bring her up here."

"In any case, the guy took off. Oscar called one of his female friends to get me dressed and back to my dorm. Someone told me he stood on guard outside the room until they dressed me.

"The next morning, my sorority friends told me how he'd rescued me. I saw him in class sometime that week and thanked him for helping me. We went out for coffee after class. We've been together ever since."

"No regrets?" Patricia asked.

"Absolutely no regrets. When I'm with Oscar, it just feels so right, so natural. I can't imagine my life without him."

Amy thought about the risk her husband could have potentially faced if he'd been found alone with a partially undressed white woman. She said, "Even though Oscar spoke about his fear of being accused of rape, I never realized how real that fear was for him."

Patricia asked, "What do you mean?"

Amy shook her head slowly as if trying to deny a painful memory. "I read about a man who died in prison. He was Black. He was accused of raping a white woman. Somehow, the police focused on him because he'd tried to pick up an undercover cop during a surveillance operation to catch a serial rapist. He was the only Black man to approach the undercover cop. There was no solicitation. No crime was committed. I guess he liked what he saw and wanted to meet her." Amy paused.

"Go on, please," Patricia said, leaning forward.

"A serial rapist had been raping a lot of young white women from campus and town for about a year. He was known as the Texas Tech Rapist. The victims had identified the rapist as a Black man. The police set up surveillance in a part of town where they thought he would strike again."

She continued. "Well, the Black guy who approached the female cop was arrested. This one victim said she was certain about who raped her. She picked his picture out of a photo array and later picked him out in a lineup. I believe she wrote, in an affidavit after the lineup, 'I'm positive of my identification, and there is no doubt in my mind.'"

Amy sighed. "Did you know that about seventy percent of wrongful convictions are based on eyewitness misidentification?"

"Heard it was high. Didn't realize that it was that high," Patricia said.

Amy continued, "There was no forensic evidence to speak of. No one else identified him as the rapist. The jury was not allowed to hear about the evidence of other rapes in the area or the year-long police investigation to catch the serial rapist. The truth later emerged that another Black man was the rapist who had assaulted her and all the other women. He was not the man the victim had positively identified."

Amy shook her head and said, "I guess the rapist had a conscience because he contacted the courts to confess that they'd convicted an innocent man. But he waited until he couldn't be prosecuted for the crime. It took him ten years to reveal that the wrong man had been charged, prosecuted, convicted, and sentenced.

"According to the news, the rapist reached out to the district attorneys and the courts and confessed. His first attempt was in 1995. After several months without a response, he contacted the courts again to confirm they'd received his letter. He was informed that they had. Yet another five years went by with no response, so he reached out once more."

Shaking her head again Walker said, "It was too late. The rapist didn't know it then, but an innocent man had already died in prison in December 1999 for a crime he didn't commit. He died from a childhood illness—asthma," she paused. "My Oscar suffers from asthma."

Both women were momentarily silent: one remembering the tragedy, the other trying to make sense of it.

"What was the man's name—the one who died?" Patricia asked.

"Timothy Brian Cole," she recalled. "He had a family, served in the military, was working toward a college degree, and spent thirteen years in prison for a crime he didn't commit."

"That bit of news about Mr. Cole's innocence didn't renew my faith in the system, but I think it may have helped the family," Amy said.

"How was that?" Patricia asked.

"The family was able to clear his name. DNA tests confirmed that he didn't commit the rape," she said. "The state of Texas actually issued a formal apology."

"How white of Texas!" Patricia said sarcastically.

"A detective on the case was asked if he thought that he owed the Cole family an apology. Let me read to you what he said." Amy appeared visibly agitated.

She swung her chair around to retrieve a news clipping from her bulletin board. She began to read. "There's one perfect system and one perfect individual. I don't think that, here on earth, we have it right yet." She tossed the clipping on the desk.

They both fell silent again, reflecting on the travesty of justice that had occurred. They wondered how those in power, having participated in such an obscenity, could so easily deny responsibility.

"You remembered his name," Patricia said quietly.

Amy, surprised by the question, responded, "How could I *not* remember his name? It's the least I can do. I need to remember him. I *want* to remember him. Remembering him is a way of honoring him, and it's my very small way of acknowledging the family's loss. I feel like I owe the family an apology."

"You… apologize?" Patricia said curiously. "For what?"

"Oscar and I have been talking about this. I mean… about what responsibility we owe to others. Our church pastor has introduced us to many new ideas that I hadn't previously considered. We're taught about our responsibility to the homeless, the orphans, the poor, and those imprisoned."

Pointing to a certificate on the wall above Patricia's shoulder, Amy said, "In our community, we have a neighborhood watch program where we look out for the well-being of others, including strangers, simply because they live in our neighborhood."

Patricia raised her chin and nodded. "Keep talking. You remind me of a little fellow I know who has similar beliefs."

Amy paused, biting her lip. "It's not that we cause or are personally responsible for those tragedies. It's about what we need to do to help those who have suffered because of those tragedies."

"Come again?" Patricia said, trying to understand her meaning.

"Someone can argue that Timothy Cole died unnecessarily, for all sorts of reasons: the police did a sloppy investigation, the prosecutor wasn't interested in justice—he was just out to get another win; the judge and prosecutor didn't take the time to investigate the confession of the self-proclaimed rapist—you can go on and on.

"But, even though that injustice occurred at a different time, in a different state, it was still my government—our justice system—that prosecuted and convicted that poor man. It was in my country that an entirely innocent man died for nothing," she said.

Patricia added somberly. "Yes. Injustice anywhere is a threat to justice everywhere." She thought back to Li'l Bits' words: *If you believe that we are all connected, it doesn't matter who the person is, even if he is a total stranger.*

Walker smiled at the photo of herself and Oscar during a day at the amusement park. She said, "We're planning on having children someday. I want them to grow up in a country that is just and fair."

A concerned look crossed Patricia's face. It didn't go unnoticed by Amy.

"What are you thinking, Ms. Horn? You don't seem like the type who would condemn interracial marriage or advise against having mixed children for the child's sake. I have the right to marry whoever I want and have children with the man I love, regardless of his skin color," she said her tone, unexpectedly defensive.

Patricia said, "You have a good heart, Ms. Walker. You'll be a wonderful mother. You have the right to marry anyone you love."

"I'm no fool, Ms. Horn," Amy said with an edge in her voice. "The small Midwestern town where I was raised had its share of bigots. Oscar and I have discussed the prejudice and discrimination that our biracial children will face from both whites and Blacks."

"Well, it's important that you and Oscar have discussed those issues," Patricia said carefully. "But I'm talking about something more personal to you."

Walker frowned. "What do you mean?"

"Have you ever noticed that when you're with Oscar—like in a restaurant—you end up waiting longer to be seated, or the waitress is rude for no reason? Or you apply for a loan with Oscar, but a problem pops up just before your loan is approved?"

"Yes," Walker said. "Some of those things have happened. They happen to everybody, though. I don't think much of it, but Oscar gets upset. I just tell him he is being overly sensitive. But he gets even more upset when I say that. He just says that I don't understand. When he tells me that, it always makes me mad. I feel like I'm stupid or something."

Amy frowned, tapping her finger on the desk. "Oscar told me that it's hard for me to understand something I've never experienced. Then he said something odd."

"Which was?" Patricia asked.

"It's an African proverb. Oscar said, 'The fish is the last to acknowledge the existence of water.'"

Patricia laughed, falling back against her chair. "Makes sense to me. Did he explain it to you?"

"No! He said that when I can figure it out, then I'll understand what it feels like to be Black in America. What do you think it means?"

Patricia laughed again. "I'm not going to piss Oscar off. That's your job!"

Amy liked this woman. There was something very steadfast about her. She was confident and self-assured.

"So… " Amy said, folding her hands on the table. "You still haven't explained to me the price I've apparently paid for marrying Oscar."

Patricia arched her eyebrows. "Oscar has been trying to explain it to you, but you don't get what he's saying. You listen, but you don't understand. You dismiss his feelings when he speaks to you about perceived racial slights. He's more attuned to those slights because he's had to learn how to cope with them. It's all new to you. It's not something you fully understand."

Amy was confused, wondering what she still failed to understand.

Noticing her frown Patricia added, "It's the soul-crushing insults, insensitive comments, ignorant racial jokes, and the bigoted put-downs that Oscar has to endure in a world that dehumanizes Black people. When you're out in public *without* Oscar, you're afforded your 'white privilege.' You may lose it when you're with him, in his physical presence."

"White privilege?" Amy muttered, her voice tinged with confusion.

Patricia searched her mind, trying to find a way to help her understand.

"Have you ever heard of a Black person 'passing' for white—completely severing ties from family, friends, and community to build a new life, unburdened by the weight of racial prejudice and white resentment. Did you ever wonder why someone would do that?"

Seeing a hint of comprehension dawn in her expression, Patricia continued, "You've probably been experiencing minor losses of white privilege, ever since your relationship started with Oscar. The experiences just have not registered in your consciousness. The insults or slights are probably fleeting, and perhaps they're subtle, barely noticeable to you, falling beneath the frequency of your cultural experience. You lack the tools to understand the social cues and interpret those experiences and micro-aggressions because there was no need to teach them to you. If you had grown up as a white person in a Black family, you would understand what those survival tools are."

Amy said, with a hint of sarcasm and a flash of anger, "It sounds like whatever you are talking about needs to drop on me like a grand piano falling from a ten-story building."

Trying her best to be patient, Patricia replied, "That piano you are talking about could kill you." She folded her hands in her lap then continued. "The most extreme loss of white privilege occurs when someone from a hate group decides to kill you because your interracial relationship is perceived as a threat to the preservation of the white race or a violation of the established social order. That person feels entitled—even obligated—to end your life."

"But society is far more accepting of interracial marriage than it was 50 years ago," Amy protested. "This is the twenty-first century. We had a Black president, and we now have a Black woman vice president."

"Yes," Patricia agreed. "But begrudging tolerance is not acceptance. What society is willing to tolerate could change significantly in the future.

"And as for President Obama's election creating a post-racial society..." She rolled her eyes. "America yearned for social transformation without doing any of the work. After Reverend King gave his '*I Have a Dream*' speech, white America hoped King's vision had finally come true with President Obama's election." She shook her head, "But look how far the pendulum swung when Trump was elected."

Patricia scoffed, "How could anyone believe that placing a Black man in the White House would somehow undo centuries of oppression and exploitation? Yet, many white Americans naively clung to the elusive hope that the nation had turned the proverbial racial corner." She laughed. "Black folks aren't that naive. We can't afford to indulge in self-delusion. Not even with a Black woman VP in the White House."

"I was not raised that way, Ms. Horn," Amy protested. "My parents raised all their children to believe that it is the heart and soul that matters, not the color of one's skin."

"That may be what they taught you," Patricia replied, "but didn't you tell me that your parents didn't want you to marry Oscar?"

Amy explained, "Yes! But they didn't want me to deal with the prejudice that they knew I would face in an interracial marriage."

"Okay," Patricia conceded. "I don't know your parents, so I'll just accept what they said." She added, "God bless them if they truly embrace Oscar. I wish our society had more people like them." She paused. "If you and Oscar decide to have children, I believe it's important you help them understand what they will have to deal with as they grow up. Oscar will help you."

Amy was quiet, still struggling with the notion of white privilege. She finally said, "I don't know, Ms. Horn. I'm not sure if I want to put so much emphasis on race. I just want them to be proud of who they are."

Patricia sighed deeply and shook her head. "You can try to ignore the realities of '*race*' if you want. But this country reflexively judges the world and its people through the lens of race—a practice that began even before this nation was born." Patricia leaned forward. "Have you heard of a book called *White Fragility?* Do you watch documentaries like "*13th*" or "*Who We Are?*" to educate yourself?"

Amy visibly stiffened at the suggestion that she was uneducated. *How very rude,* she thought. *I have a college degree.*

Patricia continued to press her argument. "Our national identity has evolved by defining itself based upon a caste system and a racial hierarchy. And the fact that we had a Black president in the White House only tends to heighten racial anxiety for some white people. Did you know that a far right extremist segment of this society hoped the election of President Obama would spark a race war? And after Trump was elected they seemed to be gaining traction."

Amy stared at her as if she was suddenly speaking a foreign language.

Patricia leaned back in her chair, folding her arms. "Race is and has always been America's original sin," she said. At the exasperated expression on Amy's face Patricia thought, *Never try to discuss race with a white person. White privilege always gets in the way.*

Amy responded hotly. "Even if what you say is true, which I think is absurd, I know there are not enough of those kinds of people out there to start a race war. It would be suicidal."

Patricia shrugged. "It's the trying that causes the devastation, destruction, and death—not the success."

Amy was quiet. The emotional bond she had felt for this woman was being pulled away, like a helpless swimmer caught in a rip current.

Patricia continued, "Life is precious. If one person dies, white or Black, because of those kinds of racist beliefs, that's one life too many." She paused, wondering what else she could say to help her understand.

She chose the nuclear option. "Maybe if your beloved Oscar becomes one of the victims who dies because of the color of his skin, you might start to understand what I mean."

Amy felt as though all the air had been suddenly sucked out of the room. Before she could protest, Patricia's cell phone went off, causing both women to start.

Patricia said, "Excuse me while I take this." She quickly retrieved the cell phone from her suit jacket. "You're where? What are you wearing? I'll be down in ten minutes." Glancing over at Walker, still visibly seething, Patricia whispered, "No! Better still, make that five." She returned the phone to her pocket.

"My friend is having me picked up. She wants to talk to me about Tyrene's situation."

Amy made a half-hearted attempt to smile. Visibly irked, she said dismissively, "Have a good day, Ms. Horn."

Patricia ignored Walker's feeble attempt to be polite and walked out, closing the door softly behind her.

Walker listened to the muffled footsteps fading away and groaned. She snatched a pencil from her desk, snapped it in two, and flung the pieces across the room.

How dare she lecture her about white privilege! How dare she presume to tell her how to raise her child! What gall!

Agitated and offended, she sank back into her chair and kicked her feet onto the desk, sending a stack of folders tumbling to the floor.

Staring at the photo of Oscar, she began to ponder the nature of fish and water.

7

Boss Lady

Patricia walked briskly down the hallway to return to the division, hoping to catch one last glimpse of Tyrene before she left. Outside the double doors of the courtroom, she saw a small congregation of African-American adults—men and women. The family resemblance between some individuals was obvious. A few lounged on chairs and benches in the waiting area along the hallway, while others milled about outside the doors. A few paced back and forth, sighing with each troubled step. Patricia instinctively knew that a loved one had lost their freedom and, perhaps, faced a lengthy prison sentence.

She nodded and smiled at those who looked at her. Peering through the narrow, wire-meshed glass panels, she scanned the courtroom for Tyrene. But the court was in recess. The deputies had removed Tyrene, and a new batch of kids had been delivered.

She let out a weary sigh, then made her way toward the elevators. After the doors closed, a tinge of excitement began to build as she pressed the button for the first floor. She hurried through the doors as soon as they opened and rushed to the nearest exit.

Out of the courthouse she looked for the mountain of a man she was supposed to meet. When she had asked what he was wearing, he'd simply replied, "You can't miss me. I tend to stand out," his voice rang with amusement.

About thirty feet to the east of the courthouse stood a towering Black man, resplendently dressed in an Italian-styled dark blue suit. His continental appearance and build reminded Patricia of a larger than like Idris Elba, but scale up to nearly seven feet tall. He had a similarly muscular physique, though with much broader shoulders and a much heavier frame, likely weighing close to 400 pounds. A gasp escaped her lips as her head tilted back in awe.

Though he seemed aloof and inattentive as he stood casually near the Lincoln limousine, his cool surveillance of pedestrians coming and going on the courthouse grounds suggested otherwise.

She approached him with awe, excitement, and uncertainty in equal measure. Up close, he was extraordinary — gargantuan, built like a defensive lineman or a powerlifter. In another era, a warrior — a man forged of Carthaginian salt and iron.

He wore his history on his face: a jutting jaw, broad forehead, hard eyes, facial scars, and a nose that had been broken too many times. Despite his daunting size, she still noticed a prominent bulge on the left side of his chest. He was armed. As she inched closer, she noted tiny scars on high cheekbones and around his eyes. She held her breath, waiting for him to speak.

His voice was magnificently deep, seeming to resonate and rumble from the depths of his soul. "Ms. Horn!" Controlled excitement filled his voice. "I'm so pleased to meet you. I've heard many good things about you."

The measured pleasure in his voice eased some of her fear, but despite that, his smile conveyed a sense of quiet, understated lethality. He extended an arm the size of a tree trunk to shake her hand.

As a child, she visited the beautiful forests of a California National Park with her parents. She had stood in awe beneath a towering sequoia. She'd felt so incredibly insignificant in the presence of such magnificence. That same feeling returned to her as she stood in the shadow of this man.

He smiled in a way that showed he understood what she was feeling. Unfazed, he deftly slid his hand from hers and opened the car door. "Do you need the restroom before we start, Ms. Horn? It's a bit of a drive, and I've been instructed not to make any stops unless absolutely necessary."

She paused, wondering about the need for this instruction. "No. I'm fine. I'd like to get going."

"Yes, ma'am. Have a seat. Someone is very much looking forward to seeing you. Please make yourself comfortable." Again, that reassuring, understanding smile—the tension in her body was starting to fade.

This time, when he spoke, she detected a slight accent. She thought of the African and Caribbean students she'd met in college: intelligent, highly motivated, gracious, warm, and kind. She wondered if he'd immigrated to the States.

Closing her door gently, he opened the driver's side door to enter the car. It felt as if the limousine sagged when he sat down.

Breathing in the rich scent of leather, she scanned the expansive interior of the car. To her right, she saw a small steel-framed refrigerator next to a fully stocked bar. An old-fashioned glass filled with an amber-hued liquid rested in an ice bucket beside her seat. The scent of that familiar concoction stirred pleasant memories.

Suddenly, guilt stabbed her. *Such luxury,* she thought, a*nd my baby is languishing in a detention center.* She desperately hoped that TicToc could get him released. The image of Tyrene's hopeful face and Li'l Bits' exuberance warmed her heart.

The boys were born on the same day, about an hour apart, in the same hospital, but on different floors. The circumstances leading up to Tyrene's birth were not exceptional, but Li'l Bits' mother shared a story about her son that left Patricia enthralled.

"When I was about nine months pregnant," Ms. Carver began, "and more than ready to deliver, my husband told me about something very odd that happened."

"As I was sleeping," she continued, "he was getting ready for work. While tying his tie and looking into the mirror, he became aware of the room becoming brighter behind him. It wasn't the sun coming through the window because the room was getting bright too quickly. He turned around and saw an area by the window glowing with this incredible light. He didn't know what to make of it. He was fearful at first, but as he watched the light, he felt more awe than fear."

"Then, to his amazement, a light, brilliant and white, rested on my belly. It stayed there a moment, and then it was gone as suddenly as it had appeared. He woke me to tell me what he'd seen. He was nearly incoherent, trying to explain the light. I scoffed. I told him he was daydreaming.

"He swore he hadn't been dreaming. He kept saying it was some kind of message. He believed that it was a message from God about our child. He said our child would be special."

There was no brilliant light illuminating my bedroom before Tyrene was born, Patricia thought, *but both boys are extraordinary in their own way.*

Patricia picked up the classic old-fashioned glass from the ice bucket and brought it to her nose. TicToc hadn't forgotten—A Rusty Nail, and chilled! Her favorite. Her friends often teased that a Rusty Nail was a "man's drink" and that she should try something more "feminine" like a Mint Strawberry Moscow Mule or a Blue Hawaiian with a tiny umbrella. Polite laughter was her response to her friends' attempts to mold her into a so-called lady.

Patricia quietly nursed her drink and looked around the warm interior with its soothing light. She noticed that the glass privacy panel separating her from the mesmerizing Black Titan was impenetrable.

With such a fancy ride, these darkly tinted windows might be TicToc's way of avoiding unnecessary attention from the police. A Black driver in a fancy car was one thing. A Black passenger in an expensive car was another. A Black passenger with a Black driver in a sleek, high-end car was like waving a red flag in front of a police cruiser. Whatever the need for privacy, Patricia could not deny that it was incredible to lounge in this vehicle.

She tapped on the window to get the driver's attention. She slid the thick partition back. Excuse me, sir. I'm sorry, but I don't know your name."

"It's Carl, ma'am, and you don't have to tap on the window. There's a intercom system in the car. Just press the button. You need only speak above a whisper, and I can hear you."

"Carl, I can barely see out of the windows. I can't even see you. Is there a reason for that?"

"Yes, ma'am, there is, but I will let Boss Lady explain that to you."

"You call TicToc, Boss Lady?" she asked.

"Yes, ma'am. She's my boss, and she's a lady. So that's what I call her," he replied matter-of-factly. "Boss Lady."

"Have you known TicToc long, Carl?" Patricia asked, a smile in her voice.

"Pretty much all my life, ma'am. I'm sorry, but I need to focus on my driving. Traffic at this hour can sometimes feel like the Indianapolis 500. If you have a specific request, like adjusting the compartment temperature or sound system, just let me know."

"What if I get a bit loopy after drinking all this scotch and need a bathroom? This car is fancy and all, but I don't see any bathroom in here," she joked.

Carl laughed. "Don't worry. If you need to stop, we can. But I'll ask you to put on some very dark glasses, and I'll escort you to the lavatory door because you won't be able to see with the glasses on." He quickly added, "But you can take them off once inside. You just need to put them on when you come out." Patricia wondered why there was a need for the cloak-and-dagger routine.

Carl seemed to read her mind. "Boss Lady will explain everything to you, ma'am. Let me say it's a precaution taken for your protection."

She mulled over Carl's explanation about his employer's need for secrecy. TicToc was very private about her life while they were in jail.

"Did TicToc tell you how we got to know each other in jail?" She asked, taking another sip of the sweet, dark liquid, appreciating its calming effect.

"Yes, Ms. Horn. She told me how you risked your life. I saw the scar on your cheek. I don't think you know how special you are to her. If you didn't know, you'll learn very soon. She feels indebted to you, ma'am. That means that I am also indebted to you."

TicToc was released from jail about two months before Patricia's charges were dismissed. Patricia waited for a visit, a phone call, or even a letter—anything—but received nothing. She rationalized that TicToc's criminal activities on the outside kept her busy; but Patricia could not—would not—accept that TicToc had simply forgotten about her.

After the DA dismissed her case and she was released from jail, she did everything she could to find her, especially after Duke's death. She desperately needed to connect with her dear friend to share the unimaginable pain of losing her firstborn. Ironically, searching for TicToc was a welcome distraction, acting as a buffer against her raw, aching grief.

Patricia Googled Tanya Mason, TicToc's real name. She paid for an online locator service, contacted the county jail for a forwarding address, checked with the motor vehicle department, and tried to obtain her identity and criminal history information through the FBI as well as records from the court. But she couldn't find anything.

There wasn't even a case under her name in a statewide index search of civil and criminal cases. During the entire time they'd spent together, TicToc had no visitors and never mentioned a family member. In her frustrated attempt to find her, Patricia realized that she knew practically nothing about her friend, except that she habitually prayed and read the Bible. Oh, and TicToc loved a good game of dominoes. But now, after all this time, she was grateful that she hadn't forgotten her.

Sighing softly, she closed her eyes and sank into the soothing comfort of the seat. As she relaxed she thought back to the moment she first laid eyes on her enigmatic cellmate.

It was at the evening meal in the jail cafeteria. Inmates would approach TicToc's table in the far corner of the room where she seemed to be holding court. The progression of bodies to and from her table appeared regulated by an invisible traffic light. Patricia learned from other inmates that drugs were being sold. It seemed that TicToc conducted her business only on certain days when two particular guards were working—a buff, short fire hydrant of a man called Bull and a tall, overweight woman called Wanda.

One evening, when Patricia had finished her meal of unsavory mashed potatoes, soupy gravy, and mystery meat, she picked up her tray and headed toward the tray rack that sat a few feet from TicToc's table. Without warning, a big, brawny, tattooed inmate who called herself the Behemoth, appeared before her, tapping hard on Patricia's dinner tray and pointing to another tray rack across the room. Patricia hesitated momentarily, staring up at her more out of fear than defiance.

Unaccustomed to slow responses, the Behemoth narrowed her eyes and leaned forward. Patricia wondered if she was in the process of a sex change. Her large pectoral muscles had swallowed her tiny breasts, and no feminine sign of softness was present in her features.

When the Behemoth clenched her hand into a fist that looked like it had pounded sandbags, Patricia backed up slowly, and moved toward the other tray rack.

After dinner, she returned to her jail cell, a 6-by-8 room with concrete block walls, a cement floor, a double-deck steel frame bed, a metal sink in one corner, a toilet in the other, and a couple of shelves.

The room smelled of despair. This would be her home for God knows how long, until she pled guilty or was found guilty of the charge of attempted murder and assault. All the while her husband, the batterer, the abuser, the control freak, was free. *He should be in jail,* she thought, *not me.* But the law didn't always work to protect the innocent.

He'd reported the "crime" first. He told the emergency physician, the EMT, and the nurse treating his knife wounds that his wife had attacked him when he tried to stop her from beating their son. Her husband's despicable lie to save his own skin had put her in this hellhole.

If Tyrene had been less evasive when answering the cops' questions, the outcome might have been different. However, it wasn't fair to blame him. He'd lied so many times to cover up his dad's physical abuse that it was no wonder he was uncertain and confused.

She heard someone walking toward her cell. Even though she'd only been in jail for less than a month, she knew the difference between the sound of a guard walking and an inmate. The footsteps stopped abruptly at the entrance to her cell.

Patricia looked up to see a lean, toned African-American woman, her thick, slightly graying hair pulled back in a bun. She was maybe in her late forties, early fifties. Her skin was olive and her eyes hazel. Her nose was long and straight, and her lips were thick and sensual. Most whites would not have recognized her as a Black woman, but Patricia knew. She wore what Patricia had come to learn was trustee garb, a special uniform given to inmates who had earned the guard's respect. She cradled a Bible in her arm.

She smiled. "I've been reassigned to your cell. Had a conflict with my celly. My name is Tanya Mason, but I go by TicToc. What's your name?"

Disarmed by TicToc's open, straightforward manner, she returned the smile. "Patricia Horn," she replied.

"How do you like to be called?" TicToc asked.

Patricia shrugged. "No preference."

"Okay. I'll call you Horn." She stepped into the cell and asked, "Horn, would you pray with me?"

Since that first meeting every morning before breakfast and just before lights out, they would read their favorite passages from the Bible. Often, Patricia would talk about her family and her life on the outside. TicToc never appeared guarded, but disclosed no details about her family, personal, or social life. And she never discussed her business in the far corner of the chow hall.

One evening, TicToc entered the shower while Patricia was there. She was startled to see ugly brown spots marring TicToc's wiry, well-defined body. She couldn't help but stare.

Discolored patches stood out starkly against her skin on her upper back and shoulders. Some appeared as though they'd been seared into her skin with a hot poker. Other areas were puckered—their rough, uneven texture impossible to miss. *Were those from bullet wounds?* Patricia wondered.

TicToc smiled, seeing her startled expression. "I know. Not very pretty."

Recovering as best she could, Patricia joked, "Dissatisfied customers?"

TicToc laughed. "You could say that. Customer relations hit the skids a couple of times. It wasn't a contract hit. Just some disgruntled customer who didn't like my product. Comes with the territory. If you survive, you keep learning from your mistakes."

Business dealings in the jail started to change several months before TicToc was nearing her release date. Word had been circulating that a new, rough-looking inmate called Sideways had gang and drug ties on the outside and wanted to take over the business on the inside.

Sideways didn't want to compete with TicToc. She didn't want a percentage of TicToc's business. She wasn't looking for a partner either. She wanted to be top dog and had no intentions of waiting for TicToc to be released from jail.

TicToc ignored Sideways' messages delivered by her runners, rejected every proposal to meet with her, and laughed at her death threats.

TicToc assured Patricia of her safety, her tone calm but firm. "You have nothing to worry about. They're after me. I just need to be careful. It would be best to keep your distance from me outside of our cell."

Changes began to unfold quickly. The number of TicToc's regulars started to dwindle. The brute who had stopped Patricia from approaching TicToc on that first day was seen keeping company with a new inmate—a young, intimidating woman in her thirties. She was marked by a snake tattoo on her neck and a teardrop tattoo beneath her eye. TicToc told Patricia that the teardrop meant she'd killed someone, possibly for revenge.

TicToc grew increasingly cautious. She altered her schedule and daily routine—showers, meals in the hall, walks in the yard, even time in the community room. She no longer allowed Patricia to accompany her. The only moments they shared now were the Bible readings in their cell.

TicToc had a no nonsense approach to the situation. "Remember, this bullshit doesn't concern you, Horn. Besides, you got two boys to take care of when you get out of here. I got no one."

Several days after that conversation, Patricia heard a loud commotion as she was walking past the community room. A few inmates rushed out, their faces pale with panic. A short, round woman with tattoos up and down both arms, grabbed Patricia's arm. "Don't go in there. You can't help her!"

"Get the guards!" Patricia shouted. "Someone call the guards!" But the women ignored her pleas and scattered in different directions.

Heart pounding, eyes wide with panic, Patricia dashed into the room. The scene was chaotic. The TV screen was shattered. A couch was overturned, and chairs were strewn across the floor. An inmate, named Bender, was sprawled on the ground, moaning as blood streamed from her nose and mouth. Nearby, the woman with the muscular build who called herself the Behemoth crouched low, circling cautiously, searching for an opening to attack TicToc.

TicToc kept her distance, her steps deliberate and measured as she carefully moved around the room. About six feet away, a petite, wiry woman known as Squirt, glared at TicToc, her lip curled in a snarl. She yelped and barked like a rabid animal, her shiv glinting in her hand.

Both women were armed, but TicToc held them off with a broken wooden table leg. When she spotted Patricia, TicToc jerked her head sharply, signaling her to leave.

"If you relax, TicToc, I'll make it quick for you," the Behemoth hissed. "You keep on fighting, and you are gonna piss me off. If I get pissed, I'm gonna open you up slow like a stuffed pig."

"Bitch," TicToc said coolly, "you're about to take your last breath in this world. I'm sending you and your half-pint whore straight to hell."

The menace in TicToc's voice was bone-chilling. The smaller woman, Squirt, stopped barking and glanced at the Behemoth, seeking reassurance. Squirt took a few steps back.

Finally finding her voice, Patricia yelled, "Leave her the fuck alone, you stupid cunts!"

"Horn! Get out of here!" TicToc yelled, her voice now laced with panic.

Startled, the two women turned toward Patricia. Seeing nothing in her hands, Squirt lunged, slashing the dagger wildly at her face. Patricia instinctively jerked her head back but underestimated the swiftness of her attacker's speed. She felt a sharp, searing pain as the shiv slashed her cheek.

Squirt swung again—even more wildly this time—lurching off balance. Patricia shoved Squirt's arm away then she landed a hard punch to her face. The woman howled and dropped the blade.

Patricia leaped behind Squirt and snatched her hair with both hands, yanking her back. Squirt screamed in pain.

Patricia spun her around and slammed her headfirst into the wall. Squirt dropped with a dull thud, leaving a trail of blood down to the floor.

Without warning, something struck Patricia hard, high between her shoulder blades, knocking her forward. Before she could fall down, she was yanked back against her attacker's body. Her mind froze when she saw the knife raised high above her head. Duke and Tyrene's faces flashed before her eyes.

A moment later, the would-be assassin suddenly stiffened and gasped, before she was pulled away. The shiv clattered to the floor. Patricia collapsed, catching herself on her hands, as her would-be murderer let out a chorus of startled grunts—reeling under a flurry of bone-jarring blows.

Patricia heard the assailant's heavy knees suddenly hit the floor. She turned just in time to see TicToc swing behind the Behemoth—mounting her back and locking her arms around the woman's massive throat in a brutal chokehold.

With a murderous cry, TicToc yanked her backwards so violently that Patricia thought she heard a popping sound.

The Behemoth desperately tugged and flailed at TicToc's arms, her eyes bulging wildly, her face twisted in panic as she fought to escape. TicToc's forearms swelled and her biceps bulged. Like an anaconda coiling around its prey, TicToc steadily squeezed the life from her. Panicked gurgles and convulsive gasps signaled her impending death as TicToc hissed, "Whose bitch are you now!"

For an instant, a dark, maniacal expression flashed across TicToc's face, making her almost unrecognizable. Patricia almost felt sorry for the Behemoth...almost.

Darkness pressed in from all sides, Patricia's vision clouding—its light dimming like a dying candle. Her body shook. With every fiber of her being, she fought to maintain consciousness but couldn't. Her back felt hot and wet. She fought to keep her eyes open but blacked out to an ugly, unforgettable sound—the crisp, sharp snap of bone breaking.

8

The Cover-Up

During Patricia Horn's incarceration, Captain Buford Perry served as the Bureau Chief of the County Jail. He was a gaunt man with an oddly distended appearance, as if he had swallowed something far too large for his frame. Patricia learned from a cop who'd interrogated her that Buford would lead the investigation into the inmates' deaths. However, she was later surprised to learn that it was not the murders in his jail that would cost him his job.

Alone in his office, Perry meticulously examined the photos of the women's bodies. One image, in particular, stood out as the most chilling.

Throughout the jail, the woman in the photo was known as the Behemoth, a figure feared by nearly every inmate. Even the male guards couldn't suppress their instinctive fear when she turned her gaze on them.

Yet, there she was—nearly six feet tall and easily 195 pounds of solid muscle—thick arms splayed wide. Her head hung like a broken doll at an unnatural angle.

A few feet away, Squirt's body lay slumped against the wall, her throat nearly flattened into the floor from the force of the blow that had killed her. Perry winced as he looked at what used to be her neck, hollowed out like a smashed yellow squash. The coroner concluded that someone had deliberately rolled the body over and delivered a devastating blow to her throat—likely from a heavy object or a powerful kick. Then there was the third victim, Bender, who succumbed to brain hemorrhaging after repeated blunt-force trauma to the skull.

Perry tapped the photos rhythmically, shuffling them into different patterns, as if rearranging them might unlock the truth about what had happened. The scene was a forensic nightmare: blood trails in the hallway, an overturned couch, two splintered tables, a smashed TV, shattered glass, broken chairs, blood smears on the walls, a pool of blood on the floor, and three dead bodies.

Perry was determined to avoid a thorough investigation into the deaths of the three inmates. By keeping the inquiry narrow, he felt more confident about controlling the outcome, especially with the help of a police detective who had been on his payroll for years.

The news media could pose a challenge, but fortunately only criminals—not guards—had been killed. This meant the situation would attract far less interest. There were no sympathetic victims to rally around, no public outrage to fuel the headlines.

Past tabloid coverage of the jail had taught Perry that even the smallest criminal investigation could spiral out of control, potentially leading to grand jury indictments—especially if corruption was involved. His predecessor's downfall, a sordid sex scandal that had left multiple inmates pregnant, was a stark reminder how quickly things could unravel.

Using his position as bureau chief, Perry had orchestrated a scheme that granted a drug cartel access to an incarcerated dark web drug manufacturer. The manufacturer had coincidentally ended up in Perry's jail after receiving consecutive sentences for multiple DUIs.

A clandestine lab was set up for "the cook" in a restricted area of the jail, and the cartel supplied all the chemicals she needed. Once a month, a food delivery vendor dropped off chemical supplies, while cartel-affiliated inmates at the sally port loaded the truck with the finished product— packages of fentanyl and meth. Handpicked guards at the gate conducted superficial searches of the truck's interior and undercarriage. Perry insisted that routine inspection procedures be followed meticulously to avoid suspicion.

The cartel had established a network to distribute drugs outside the jail, and TicToc was chosen to handle sales on the inside. It was exactly the kind of scandal that could put him in federal prison for decades. He had to tread carefully.

A flicker of regret crept in as Perry thought about the criminal enterprise he'd set in motion, but the opportunity had been too lucrative to ignore. Besides, he'd built enough layers around himself to stay untouched—to keep his hands clean.

A few discreet phone calls to his DEA informant was all it took to set the wheels in motion with the cartel, and he'd delegated the day-to-day operations to his jail captain to ensure everything ran smoothly.

Business was lucrative enough for him to afford keeping both his wife and his mistress happy. He'd spent part of his take on a brand new Volvo XC40 for his wife and used the rest to keep his mistress happy—with lavish gifts, five-star dinners, and nights away from her abusive husband.

He'd been thrilled when his young paramour suggested stealing away to Vegas, but he needed a larger bankroll. When outside sources informed him that another inmate could nearly double his profits, he authorized TicToc's elimination if she refused to step aside.

Studying the photos again, Perry shook his head. The death of one inmate wasn't considered a major issue. But an inmate confessing to killing one woman in self-defense—while claiming ignorance about how two others had died in the same room during the fatal brawl—was another matter entirely.

He was confident the district attorney wouldn't want to play the role of Hercule Poirot to solve a multiple, murder mystery. However, he worried the prosecutor would be pressured to charge someone—likely TicToc—given the brutal nature of the deaths.

Perry had to ensure TicToc wasn't prosecuted. The only other possible suspect was TicToc's cellmate, but Horn had been unconscious when she was found. TicToc was the obvious culprit, especially since she confessed to killing one person. If charged with murder, she might be inclined to provide state evidence about the drug operation, which could ultimately put *him* in an orange jumpsuit.

Perry needed to offer the prosecutor a plausible theory to explain the inmates' deaths as well as a convincing argument not to prosecute TicToc.

Perry set aside the only two statements of interest—Horn's and TicToc's—on the left corner of his desk. In Horn's statement, she wrote that one woman was already on the floor when she entered the room. The injured woman was moaning and bleeding but still alive. Horn was certain Squirt had been breathing after she threw her into the wall. She recalled seeing TicToc defending herself against the Behemoth just before she passed out. She also mentioned that the Behemoth and Squirt had been armed with shivs.

TicToc's statement was as unhelpful as those from the panicked women who'd fled the room. Despite their apparent injuries, those inmates gave the typical con response: "Didn't see nuthin'. Didn't hear nuthin.' Don't know nuthin'."

TicToc claimed she vaguely remembered someone entering the room as she lay dazed on the floor from a blow to the head. The intruders had allegedly announced they weren't there for her. She insisted she hadn't seen who they were or what they'd done.

Of course, Perry didn't believe her bogus story about being confused and disoriented from a head injury—she didn't have a scratch on her. Her claim that she'd killed the Behemoth was even more absurd.

Perry speculated that some inmates had seized the opportunity to settle grudges—killing Bender, Squirt, and the Behemoth. Alternatively, if TicToc had arranged for protection, perhaps her hired enforcers were the killers. Puzzled, he ran anxious fingers through his thinning hair.

He had to act quickly to contain the damage. A well-conceived plan was essential to close the case as expeditiously as possible. He needed a story that would explain the three deaths, tie all the pieces together, and exonerate TicToc.

He mentally sifted through past incidents where he'd imposed discipline for inmate squabbles that turned violent. *Of course,* he thought. *It's so obvious! Why didn't I think of it sooner? A lover's triangle! Makes total sense! Anger! Jealousy! Resentment! Betrayal! That's enough to get any inmate killed.*

He murmured, "And loyal friends—especially cons—always take sides in a fight." His lips curled into a sly smile.

He had a decent chance of persuading the DA that lesbian jealousy had sparked the melee, arguing that simmering resentment and anger between rival lovers had boiled over into violence. Other inmates had naturally taken sides in the killing spree. *Yes!* he thought excitedly.

Of course, TicToc would want to claim responsibility for killing the Behemoth. Her reputation as a badass would skyrocket in jail, but snitching on the real killers would put her own life in danger. Perry's smile widened. It was as clear as the nose on his face—TicToc had lied about killing the Behemoth.

Perry mentally rehearsed the scenario he would present to the district attorney. His pitch to dissuade the DA from prosecuting TicToc was taking shape, as he practiced his spiel in his head:

TicToc has no violent criminal history—just drug dealing, prostitution, fraudulent schemes, and petty theft. No jury could imagine that a woman her size was capable of murdering the Behemoth, let alone two other inmates.

Besides, TicToc had a solid self defense argument. It was three against one, and two of the women had knives. Her attorney could contend that the other women were killed by unknown assailants.

Pleased with his clever narrative, Perry imagined his concluding argument exploiting a prosecutor's greatest fear—losing at trial.

In the most dramatic fashion possible, he'd say: *Just imagine if TicToc gets acquitted! Her acquittal could only produce negative political capital for us. Can you imagine the embarrassment? Besides, it could take two painful weeks to try her case and would be a needless waste of taxpayer money.*

Perry grinned broadly, already tasting victory. To tie up any loose ends, he'd arrange a few perfunctory visits by his detective, a lunch or two with the DA, and a carefully crafted media statement. Then his grand lie would wrap everything up like a birthday gift, topped with a decorative bow. He smirked.

As for the unsolved murders, he would deliver the standard bromide:

The three unfortunate victims will be the subject of a thorough ongoing investigation until the culprits are apprehended and vigorously prosecuted to the full extent of the law. He chuckled. *Sounds good,* he thought.

Perry decided against disclosing the cause of death to the press. He would fall back on the usual explanation about the potential prejudicial impact that public disclosure could have on pending criminal proceedings. Truthfully, he wondered if the deaths were too unsettling for the public to handle. He, also, feared the violent nature of their deaths might invite undue scrutiny.

His detective and the DA would convince the coroner to withhold that information arguing it could compromise their investigation. From experience, he knew that news reporters would be satisfied with crime scene photos, criminal records of the deceased, and an interview with him. After all, those people who died were nothing more than sorry dregs of society. Nothing newsworthy there.

A month later, the news headline read: *Deadly Lesbian Feud Claims Three Inmate Lives. Two Inmates Survive.*

After undergoing surgery—requiring twelve stitches in her back and seven in her face—Patricia spent a week in the hospital before being transported back to jail.

TicToc embraced her warmly as she entered the cell but let go quickly when Patricia groaned. "Go easy. I'm still sore."

"Well, little sister," TicToc joked, eyeing her bandaged face, "your mama told you that you'd never win a beauty contest. Now you got proof."

"Not funny! Next time yo' ass is in trouble, I'm gonna pull up a chair and cheer for the other side."

"All good, Horn, as long as you don't help them. You put a hurt on that yelping bitch." TicToc laughed. "Guess she really annoyed you."

Patricia squeezed TicToc's hand affectionately and walked gingerly past her friend to sit on the edge of her bunk bed. TicToc sat beside her. She touched Patricia's arm and said quietly, "Thank you, Horn."

Inhaling deeply, Patricia whispered, "When I got stabbed, three women were alive. When I woke up in the hospital, three women were dead. I found that out from the detective. I get it that you had to put the Behemoth down, but the other two? That one woman on the floor was moaning when I rushed in. That other one who kissed the wall with her head got knocked out, but she was still alive—"

TicToc pressed her index finger to her lips and glanced slowly around the cell, her eyes darting back and forth to suggest that the room might be bugged.

"Several people rushed in while I was holding you. I didn't recognize them. One said, 'We're not here for you.' I was too dazed to focus. That's what I told the detectives."

Patricia understood and released a soul-heavy sigh. Her very dear friend murdered two helpless women. *Maybe it was necessary,* she thought. If the would-be assassins had survived, they might try again. *Maybe their deaths were needed to send a message to other potential killers.*

TicToc picked up her Bible, flipped through the pages, and pointed to a verse. She said, "Please read it to yourself, Horn."

The verse read, *For all have sinned and fallen short of the glory of God, and all are justified by his grace through the redemption that came by Jesus Christ.*

When she looked up TicToc whispered, "When you come for the head of the king, be prepared to die."

The luxurious comfort of the limousine ride did little to dispel the terror of Patricia's near-death experience at the hands of the Behemoth. But, oddly, what haunted her most was the heart-chilling rage in TicToc's expression just before she broke the Behemoth's neck.

Her attention snapped back to her surroundings when the limousine phone rang. "It's for you, ma'am," Carl said politely.

"Horn!" TicToc exclaimed. "It's been a minute." She laughed, the lilt in her tone disarmingly light. "I'm back." Skipping over the details of her sudden disappearance, TicToc said simply, "I had to leave the country for an assignment, Horn. But I'm back now—and I'm here for you."

"I'm prepared to kick your ass, TicToc!" Patricia yelled. "Do you have any idea how I've searched to find you? For years, I didn't know whether you were dead or alive. And then, poof, out of the blue, you reappear with a text message!"

Patricia's voice nearly broke. "I didn't want any help back then, TicToc. I just needed to talk to you. I'm damn sure, with today's technology, you could have gotten in touch with me. I bet a carrier pigeon would have even worked."

TicToc laughed. "You're right, Horn. But, whether you realize it or not, I've been with you one way or the other over the past few years. You'll understand after we talk," she promised.

"You're into something big time by the looks of this ride," Patricia observed as she glanced around the limo's interior.

TicToc replied, "You have no idea, Horn. It worries me sometimes when my services are requested by certain organizations—not from the standpoint of danger, but from the standpoint of power. That kind of power can go to your head. You sometimes forget how power can be used irresponsibly. As George Washington, our first U.S. president observed, 'Government is not reason; it is not eloquence. It is like fire, a dangerous servant and a fearful master. It should never be left to irresponsible action for even a moment.'"

"What organizations are you talking about, TicToc? Are you talking about one of those unknown alphabet black op secret agencies? I bet I won't be able to find it on a Secretary of State 501(c)(3) list or in the records of the Better Business Bureau," she teased.

"Just think of me as a hard-working woman trying to make a buck," she chuckled. "It's best to be careful about what I share with you, Horn. Just know I have returned to help you and your son, Tyrene. I hope you'll let me do that for you."

Patricia sighed, "What you do professionally, TicToc, is none of my business. You want to help my son. That's all that matters."

"Horn," TicToc said gently, "you do need to understand one thing. When I'm out to win," she paused briefly, "I don't play nice. As long as you can accept that, I can help you."

A momentary silence crept between them. "Does that include killing, TicToc?"

“Well!” TicToc said pensively. “I hope it doesn’t have to come to that. “But,” she paused, as she took a sip of her drink. “You already know that I don’t have a problem with shedding a little blood,” she said casually. “Does that upset you?” There was a challenge in her voice. “You didn’t have a problem with shedding blood when you opened up your old man with that knife.”

“I was protecting my child!” Patricia protested.

She heard TicToc sigh through the phone. “Same situation here, Horn. A mother does what needs to be done to protect her child—even kills, if necessary. Only this time, it’s not one person attacking Tyrene. It’s the entire criminal justice system coming after him.

“They claim legitimacy by labeling their actions ‘law and order.’ They convince themselves they’re keeping the streets safe—even when they imprison the innocent or kill unarmed Black people they deem ‘suspicious.’ As long as they wrap it up in the guise of due process and call it justice, we’re all fair game. No one is safe once the system marks you.”

Patricia wavered, thinking about her son, but reluctant to condone death. She remembered his eyes—so much like Duke’s. She pictured the bruises on his face and the innocence in his eyes at the hospital and court. Then there was that unnerving visit from Quisling. His threat to get her son had triggered a primal fear and anger.

Not my child, she thought, echoing a primordial instinct as old as time—a mother’s fierce, unyielding drive to protect her young at all costs.

TicToc’s lips curled slowly into a smile. “I take your silence as a yes. Just so you know, Horn, I will only resort to violence if all else fails. Besides, I think I’ve got a plan that should leave everybody breathing. Okay?”

“Okay,” Horn responded slowly, still uncertain but relieved.

“Look! Enjoy your drink! Relax! Take a nap! I will see you in an hour or so. We’ll talk more later.”

After a pause she said. “Horn, I’m deeply sorry about Duke.” Then she ended the call.

Patricia allowed herself to sink further into the warm embrace of the expensive leather. Taking a drink, the sweet, burning sensation of scotch and Drambuie slid down her throat. A stream of troubling thoughts threatened to disturb her tranquility—Tyrene's hospitalization, his incarceration, and the court appearance with the overbearing prosecutor. She'd felt a hollow, gnawing fear of helplessness… until TicToc's message arrived. Odd, she thought—it came the same day Tyrene was hospitalized."

After one last sip, Patricia secured her glass in a holder. She was starting to feel the sudden seductive lure of sleep. She allowed the peace and restful darkness to envelop her, with the comforting thought that *Tyrene would be safe.*

An hour later, Patricia woke with a start. The drink had relaxed her more than she'd realized. She pressed the intercom and said to Carl, "I'm almost in need of a bathroom break, sir. How much further?"

The car jolted as it rumbled over unpaved road while pebbles and rocks clattered against the undercarriage. "Carl," she said, "Where the hell are we?"

"We're here, ma'am." The car slowed to a halt, and Carl turned off the engine. Moments later, the ground beneath them began to shift. Mechanical gears groaned and the vehicle shook several times as the car started to descend.

"What the hell, Carl?" Patricia exclaimed, gripping the door handle.

"Nothing to worry about, Ms. Horn. Just a few more feet."

The car jolted and bounced for nearly two minutes before shuddering to a stop. "Sorry about the ride down, ma'am. The drive mechanism needs a little work."

Before Patricia could respond, she heard movement outside. Carl waited in his seat. The doors unlocked, and the rear passenger door swung open. A flood of light illuminated the interior. Two feet away, Patricia saw a pair of dark red pumps in a stance she knew all too well.

"Horn!" TicToc said cheerfully. "You're just in time for a lovely meal."

9

Dead Man Hanging

Kensington sat on Quisling's porch and scanned the litter scattered across the unkempt premises. *Not quite a dump*, Kensington thought, *but close to it.* He checked his watch again. No Quisling. He was tired of waiting.

He looked toward the dirt road that led up to Quisling's trailer. Bushes, trees, tall grass, and weeds had claimed the site. It was wild and unpicturesque. If Quisling had wanted rural country, he'd certainly found it.

Kensington eased himself out of the chair to stretch and turned to survey the home. The corrugated aluminum structure was in dire need of repair, its exterior marred by rust, discoloration, and chipping. The small wooden porch was weathered and worn. The door handle had been improvised with a wire hanger. The windows looked like they hadn't been washed in years.

Two objects stood out conspicuously on both sides of the uninviting entrance—the flag of the United States and the flag of the Confederacy. Each flag was mounted securely on a gold-plated bracket. The poles appeared to be made of white fiberglass. Atop the U.S. flag was a brass-plated eagle while the Confederate flag was crowned with a plastic gold acorn finial. The incongruity was striking: a dilapidated structure adorned with two brilliant flags.

Before the controversy about pledging allegiance to the flag peaked in his elementary school, Kensington had placed his hand over his heart and recited words he didn't fully understand. He knew the ritual was important because the class couldn't begin until those solemn words were spoken.

Kensington looked at both flags and spoke aloud. "One Nation under God, indivisible, with liberty and justice for all." The incongruity deepened. *Whose nation? Whose God? Whose justice? Did "all" include all of humanity?* Kensington knew that Quisling had no uncertainty about the answers to those questions, but Kensington was no longer sure.

Kensington noticed a swirl of dust rising from the road before he caught sight of Quisling's truck. He rechecked his watch and swore under his breath. Quisling's Dodge truck bounced and rattled along on the uneven dirt road and parked a few feet from his car. Quisling exited the truck quickly, looking exasperated.

"Sorry, Kensington. Damn truck overheated. Needed to cool down."Quisling called out, "I brought food. Stopped off at the burger place after I got the truck running." He held up two white bags with grease stains at the bottom. "Let's go on in and eat," he said enthusiastically. "If I'm hungry, I know you're starving." His laughter shook his belly.

Kensington jerked his head toward the trailer. "You sure it's safe in there? Your place should be condemned if the inside needs as much work as the outside."

Quisling shrugged. "It's not comfortable like your place, Kensington, but it'll do. It ain't fancy, but it's clean inside," he said, unapologetically. "Besides, I got a couple of cold beers in the fridge."

"Okay, Quisling. Let me know when I need to watch my step when we get inside so I don't trip over something dead or fall into a hole."

"Real funny! You ought to be glad I could arrange time off so we could meet. You know how my jerk supervisor is. By the way, did you tell Wally I said 'Hi'?"

"Yeah." Kensington suddenly fell silent.

Quisling studied him for a moment. "Not doing well, is he?"

Kensington shook his head. "Not well mentally or physically."

"That fucking Black animal bastard," Quisling swore. "C'mon. Let's go inside. Food is getting cold."

Quisling jiggled the makeshift door handle until it opened. He then stepped inside, announcing, "Welcome to my humble abode."

Kensington followed him into a room dimly illuminated by speckled sunlight that struggled to break through window blinds. Surprisingly, the air in the room smelled fresh and clean. Kensington noted a portable air purifier on the kitchen floor.

Quisling's home was even more sparse than he'd imagined. The living room consisted of a futon that apparently doubled as a bed. A rustic pine wooden coffee table sat in front of the futon. Quisling's only apparent luxury was a well-worn leather chair.

Quisling took the food and napkins out of the bag, then tore it open to use it as a tablecloth. He spread the napkins on the table to act as makeshift plates.

Kensington moved several books and magazines from the table to the floor to make space. Among them were *The Turner Diaries*, *Mein Kampf*, and *Notes on the State of Virginia* by Thomas Jefferson.

Quisling gestured for Kensington to take a seat on the futon. After arranging the wrapped food on the napkins and distributing the packets of condiments, Quisling shuffled over to the leather chair and pulled it closer to the table. With a soft grunt, he sat down and hunched over the food.

"Okay! What's on your mind, Kensington? How can I help you and Wally? You know that boy is special to me."

Kensington didn't respond. He was looking at the wall in front of them. Quisling smiled. He was proud of that wall.

Kensington put his food down and walked over to study the three striking prints. Quisling had framed only one—obviously his favorite.

Kensington examined the picture of a tall, slender Black man dressed in overalls and a white long-sleeve work shirt, with a wire noose high and tight around his throat. His arms, bound at the wrist, dangled limply in front of him. His feet hung about a foot above the ground at the base of a pine tree. A crowd of white individuals—mostly men, but also some women and four children—encircled the tree, their gazes fixed on the lifeless body.

Kensington glanced to the print of Hitler, his arm outstretched in the standard Nazi salute as he stood majestically before a crowd of tens of thousands. His eyes moved quickly to another image, which looked like a baby Hitler held standing on his mother's lap. It was this two-by-three-foot fine art quality print that intrigued him.

Quisling couldn't contain his pleasure at Kensington's puzzled reaction to his giclée print. He hurried over to explain.

"I'm really proud of this one," Quisling gushed. "It's a work of art. I saw the original in an exhibit in Denver some years back. I saved for months to buy a print. With shipping and insurance, it cost me over $2,000." Quisling paused and proudly announced, "It's called Epiphany I: Adoration of the Magi."

Kensington carefully studied the artwork, which seemed more like a documentary-style photograph than a painting. Although drawn to the picture, he felt something strangely disturbing about it.

The focal point of the picture was an attractive blonde Aryan woman holding a naked, dark-haired toddler on her lap. Surrounding her and the child were five Schutzstaffel officers. Only the child's gaze is directed out of the painting, while the mother casts her eyes downward. The picture's title seemed to suggest that she was the Madonna, and the infant on her lap was the Christ child. It suddenly dawned on Kensington that an infant Hitler was being depicted as the Messiah!

Collectively, the prints unsettled him. Kensington had always indulged Quisling's nostalgic ramblings about the "good ole days" and his monologues on white supremacy with polite detachment. At times, he'd even taken a strange pleasure in hearing Quisling speak of white pride and his past affiliation with the National Association for the Advancement of White People. But until now, he'd never fully grasped the depth of Quisling's dark obsession.

Obsession or not, Kensington needed him. His plan to avenge his son couldn't succeed without Quisling's help. And in this moment, that obsession—twisted as it was—had become an asset.

Quisling pointed to the symbol just above the Death's Head in the print and announced proudly, "That's their national emblem—a German eagle with outstretched wings. I couldn't quite make it out in the print, but the eagle appears to be clutching a swastika in a wreath. Now, look at their collars. All of them have the lightning bolt SS patch." Quisling grinned broadly, not at Kensington, but at himself, proud of his knowledge of German symbols and insignia.

"Man!" Quisling exclaimed. "I would look some kind of sharp in one of those uniforms."

Kensington asked, "Who did you say the artist was?"

"An Austrian. A guy by the name of Gottfried Helnwein. He's my hero. Someone finally got it right. He's shown the world that Hitler was the Messiah, our Savior—not only for the German people but for all of us—the white race.

"Hitler almost did it! He had the right idea—the final solution. That's what we need in America. A final solution for the Jews and the mud people." Quisling's round face beamed, his blue eyes sparkling with exuberant delight at the thought of national genocide.

It didn't escape Kensington's attention that Quisling's deep-seated hatred of Blacks would fit his plan nicely.

Quisling was a true believer in white supremacy. To him, Black lives had no value. They were nothing more than vermin that needed to be exterminated. In fact, he took pride in having killed that drug dealer—seeing it as a righteous act. He needed no persuasion that a debt to Wally had to be paid, particularly if it meant the ultimate destruction of a Black teen's future.

A Black boy had nearly castrated his son! To Quisling, this was the ultimate offense against the white race. Given the opportunity, Quisling would probably kill the boy himself.

Besides, Quisling deeply cared for Wally. Kensington was now confident that he could keep his promise to his son. The nigger would pay, just as Wally had asked.

With raised eyebrows, Quisling asked Kensington, "You ever hear of *The Turner Diaries?* That's a book that every white man has gotta read."

"Can't say that I have," Kensington replied, curious. "What's it about?"

"It's our final solution to the Jews and the coloreds." Quisling replied excitedly. "An ordinary white man stands up to the government. He organizes a violent overthrow of the federal government by white guerrilla militants. The hero, along with other white nationalists, wage a deadly race war. Any white person who does not support the revolution is considered a traitor and is killed. A bloody uprising spreads beyond the United States to the rest of the world. It's a white uprising, and we win. We win! We ultimately kill all the Blacks and Jews. The white race is saved!"

Quisling could barely contain himself. "You have *got* to read the book, Kensington! It will help you understand the danger that the white race faces—a white genocide."

Kensington was astonished. He had no idea that such a radical book existed.

Quisling returned to his chair and sat down to eat. Kensington watched him bite into his burger. "This race war thing is crazy, don't you think, Quisling? I mean… given the government's firepower and all the state and federal resources, what chance would anyone have of overthrowing it?"

"Well, Kensington," Quisling said, wiping his mouth with the back of his hand, "it really wouldn't take much. People just need to be scared and fed up. Threaten their sense of security, combine that with some real hard times and take away their hope. You'd be surprised what people are capable of. All it takes is one small spark. You never know when the spark will happen or where it will come from. Hell! We thought that making that nigger president would be the spark to start a race war. And now we've got a nigger woman VP of all things." He shook his head.

Kensington sat down on the futon. "You mean, like the economic conditions that put Hitler in power?"

Quisling started laughing. "Kensington, I thought you understood human nature better than that. We don't need a great depression or a crippling economy. Just create enough fear, anxiety, distrust, insecurity, resentments, anger, and you got the powder keg you need."

Kensington sat down and bit into his burger. "I just don't think that any state in this day and age—or the nation, for that matter—would tolerate any political leader who openly subscribes to racist views. I think that most Americans would consider that un-American."

Quisling laughed again. "The American Civil War didn't end our commitment to white supremacy, Kensington. It just plowed soil over so we could start sowing again."

Quisling paused as he chewed. "The past is never far from us, Kensington. If you read *The Turner Diaries*, you will begin to understand something vital—that a small group of committed people can change the world. The hero in the book, Earl Turner, realized that if you want real change, you can't rely on the government or political institutions."

Kensington looked at him blankly, waiting for an explanation.

"What did the abolitionists do?" Quisling asked. "They forced Lincoln into a civil war. What did the Blacks do? They marched, protested, and sang to bring about the civil rights revolution. Just think about it! Whether it's women's rights or gay pride or La Raza, they all pulled the system along, kicking and screaming, until they got what they wanted."

Kensington nodded in agreement. "Grassroots movements! You're right, Quisling. I never thought about it that way. Every major social or political change happens as a result of sustained, organized protest."

"Yep! The government ain't gonna do shit for you," Quisling maintained. "We, as white patriots, have to organize and do for ourselves ... or we are gonna get wiped out as a race, as a people, as a culture."

Kensington leaned back against the futon and studied Quisling. "Well, Quisling, which one are you pulling for, the extreme right-wing Republican Party or the overthrow of the government?"

Quisling explained, "The Republican Party might keep a lid on the Jews and the mud people temporarily, but most of them are too chickenshit to push for a final solution the way Hitler did."

Quisling rubbed his chin thoughtfully. "You know, America has no qualms about getting rid of its undesirables, Kensington. Think what we did to them red-skinned heathens. Made treaties and broke them. Moved them from one sorry place to another. Starved them! Shot them! Just slowly killed them off with broken promises and lies."

Quisling's eyes lit up. "You know ... we could have started our own extermination program with the Japanese when the government rounded them up during World War II and put them in internment camps." He snickered. "Just needed a few gas chambers in three or four states to start getting rid of those slant-eyes."

Kensington was mildly intrigued by the idea of white power, but the notion of killing innocent white people to promote it, along with exterminating non-whites and so-called white traitors to ensure racial purity, was beyond what he could accept.

What kind of people would populate such a world? Who else would be on their death list? At what point would the killing stop? he wondered.

Kensington recalled an award-winning documentary called *'Genocide'* narrated by Orson Welles he'd watched with Elsa. *He'd thought, The LGBTQ community, the physically challenged, the mentally ill, progressive intellectuals, journalists, political activists—all would be targeted in a pogrom of 'undesirables'.*

Kensington chewed on his lower lip, imagining U.S. military troops and state and local police—armed with high-powered weapons and flash bombs—marching through the streets in helmets and riot gear. They'd descend on integrated neighborhoods and diverse communities, rolling in with tanks and army trucks to seize people from the streets and drag them from their businesses and homes. University campuses would be overrun. Libraries destroyed. Professors and administrators would vanish.

Whoever said it can't happen here? It already did—with the internment of 120,000 Japanese Americans!

Disbelieving and incredulous, Kensington stared down at the floor, trying to fathom the real possibility of a Holocaust in America or even a second civil war. It was too surreal to contemplate—like imagining a mob storming the U.S. Capitol in broad daylight.

Troubled by the idea of war and images of death, Kensington's attention returned to the SS officers surrounding the mother and infant. He got up and walked back to study the print again.

"I heard what you said about the kid being Hitler as the infant Jesus—I mean, the Messiah and all—but I'm getting a different read, looking at the expressions on these German officers' faces."

Quisling furrowed his eyebrows. "What'd you mean?"

"Look carefully at their eyes and body language," Kensington said. "They don't appear to be particularly humbled in the infant's presence. They appear to be inspecting the kid and studying his mother. This one guy to the right looks like he's trying to see if the kid has been circumcised, which is a dead giveaway for a Jew boy. If he is circumcised, it's off to the oven for the both of them."

Quisling got up and stood by Kensington. He appeared more than slightly agitated.

Kensington continued, "See the guy nearest the woman? He's got a piece of paper in his hand. I think that it's something incriminating. She's looking at the paper as if it's an accusation."

"What the hell are you saying, Kensington?" Quisling exclaimed, insulted.

"Well, the whole scene reminds me of an official investigation that is being conducted. It's like she is high up in society, and the SS has uncovered some information that indicates that she is not who she says she is. The SS is there to confront her with a document—that incriminating piece of paper."

"What kind of investigation?" Quisling asked sarcastically. "It's obvious that the artist is representing the Hitler child as the incarnation of God in human form."

Kensington thought for a moment, sensing Quisling's increasing agitation. Then he exclaimed, "I got it! The only reason any SS officer would confront this woman was if she had managed to conceal her Jewish identity. But someone, perhaps an informant, stumbled across damning evidence, like an employment or school record from her village, that proved she was a Jew passing as an Aryan."

Kensington turned to Quisling and exclaimed. "Hah! She's busted. Fraulein Jew has been discovered!"

"Kensington," Quisling started slowly, "I invite you into my home, treat you decent, serve you food, give you a beer, and you try to turn the hero of my $2,000 print into a goddamn Jew. That's blasphemy!"

Kensington's sudden burst of laughter was so spontaneous and unrestrained that Quisling managed a sheepish grin. Within moments, he began to laugh as well.

Quisling said, "Okay. I'll give you the bullshit saying that 'art is in the eye of the beholder,' but as long as you live, never open your mouth to repeat your twisted ideas about my artwork again!" He added quickly, "Don't repeat that crap to Wally. I want to show this print to him, too, and I don't want you poisoning him with your warped ideas."

Puffing his chest out, Quisling put his hands on his hips and declared, "That's baby Hitler, incarnated as the true Messiah."

Kensington barely managed to mask his amusement and said, "I promise to let Wally come to his own conclusions."

Kensington returned to his seat, waving Quisling to join him. But Quisling, still fuming about Kensington's comments, remained staring at the print. With a grunt, he finally turned and stomped back to his chair.

"Quisling," Kensington said, "Remember a few nights ago when I said I needed your help?"

Quisling nodded, rubbing his hands together. "Been waiting to hear."

"Well," Kensington started, "I need you to help me do something that is risky as well as illegal. If caught, we could be criminally prosecuted and lose our pensions." Quisling's eyebrow arched sharply.

"I want you to take your time to think about this before you decide." Kensington paused and added, "You are not indebted to me for helping you with IAD."

"You've never handed me a bill for the IAD investigation, and I don't see one in your hand now," Quisling said.

Kensington acknowledged his remark with an appreciative nod and continued. "The last time I visited Wally in the hospital ... he was feeling bad ... real bad. Besides being hurt and embarrassed, he was angry."

Quisling interjected, "He wants blood?"

"No ... not exactly! He didn't put it that way, but it's clear that he wants payback. Wally said, 'I want that nigger to pay.' He was crying, Quisling. I've never heard him cry like that—not that way—not even when his mom died. Maybe that's because he felt what happened to his mom was natural. What happened to him..." Kensington paused, searching for the right word. "What happened to Wally was unnatural—something no man should endure, let alone a boy growing into manhood."

Quisling snorted, "Particularly a white boy."

Kensington leaned forward, his voice low. "We are good to get the kid tried as an adult. I spoke to a DA friend who will take care of that. No sweat in that department.

"Every conceivable serious count is being considered, including attempted second-degree murder and first-degree assault. The problem is getting a guilty verdict on the attempted murder charge. I mean... even if we get an all-white jury, I just can't see a jury wrapping its head around an attempted murder charge, given the nature of the injury and the use of teeth as a dangerous weapon, particularly if the public defender can present evidence of self-defense." Kensington took a swig from his beer.

Quisling gave a silent whistle of appreciation for Kensington's analysis. It was the reason Quisling sought Kensington for his help with his internal affairs investigation case.

"I see what you mean. He walks on the most serious charge if the jury doesn't agree that a bite to the groin area is attempted murder. And the nigger walks on everything if the jury buys a self-defense argument."

Kensington leaned back on the futon. "Even if we're lucky enough to get the assault conviction, we'd have to deal with some serious mitigating factors at sentencing," Kensington said. "I heard that the kid is a model citizen, gets good grades, and is college bound." Kensington rubbed his forehead in frustration. "And, on top of all of that good shit, he's also got a great sympathy factor."

"Sympathy factor?" Quisling asked, furrowing his brow.

Kensington explained. "Several years back, the boy came home to find his brother lying dead on his bed. He'd committed suicide by wrapping a plastic bag around his neck with a twist tie. An empty narcotics bottle was by his bedside. Since then, the boy ain't said a word, not even to his mother."

"Sounds mighty suspicious to me," Quisling observed. "You know that woman tried to kill her husband. Sounds like she went after her son and staged his suicide after the murder attempt on her husband failed." Quisling said, nodding, "she didn't get to kill her husband, so she killed the son who reminded her of him."

Kensington frowned at Quisling's pseudo-speculation, then continued. "I saw several investigative requests from the DA's office about the case. Looks like the DA was contemplating murder charges. Forensics showed the mother's fingerprints were on the pill bottle. A noisy neighbor said the woman argued with her son the day before. A handwriting expert made a preliminary determination that the mother had written the suicide note."

Kensington narrowed his eyes. Sighing, he said, "Then the paperwork stops. Completely stops! No more investigative reports! No supplementary reports! No expert forensics report! No nothing!" Nagging suspicion etched his face.

Quisling hunched forward, wondering if someone had made a backroom deal.

"Then, an internal memo is filed a few weeks later, recommending that the case be closed." Kensington said. "No explanation was given. Somebody, somewhere, pulled some strings. Somebody powerful 'cause everything just came to a standstill."

Equally perplexed, Quisling rubbed his jaw. "So, where does that leave us? If your hunch is right, that somebody might still be around, pulling strings."

"Yeah! Maybe, but that was years ago," Kensington said. "Things change. Time moves on. People die off. In any case, we can still frame him for a crime that would make it impossible for him to get acquitted. We can mark him with a stigma so humiliating, his dreams will shrivel up like spoiled fruit."

"Okay, Kensington. Let's hear the damn plan. Let's get this nigger bastard."

"You remember Wally's girl, Allison? You met her once, over at the house."

"Yeah. Sweet kid," Quisling said.

"We persuade her to lay a rape charge on that boy. You know how Black-on-white rape offenses tear at a white jury's guts. "Negative stereotypes and prejudices about Black men raping white women cause white people to act irrationally, like a pack of lemmings rushing off a cliff."

Quisling smiled in agreement, nodding at his print of the lynched Black man. "That's the way we used to handle attacks on our women."

"More importantly," Kensington continued, "it's not even a 'he said/she said' situation. Get a sweet, white girl crying about how a Black boy violated her, and no jury is gonna believe anything else—not in this country. Besides, how's the boy gonna deny it?" Kensington paused, relishing their good fortune. "He don't talk."

Quisling slapped Kensington's knee enthusiastically. "That's right. It's great! It's *not* a he said/she said situation. It's all just a 'she said' situation! We got him!"

Without asking directly, Quisling had let him know he was more than willing to break the law and violate his sworn oath. As an investigating officer, Quisling could coach Allison about writing her statement, run interference with her mother, gather evidence, and act as a conduit to the DA's office. Both could practice with her and prepare her for testifying in court.

"With a violent felony rape conviction on his record, he'll be required to register as a sex offender for life and will be subject to lifetime supervision," Kensington crowed. "He can forget about getting a decent job. His employment options will be limited. Even finding housing will be tough. He'll be a social pariah. That rape conviction will be an albatross around his neck until he dies. Just like Wally will live every day with the emotional pain of his injury, this boy will carry the stain of 'sex offender' for the rest of his miserable life."

Quisling smiled broadly at Kensington. "You're the kind of man we need for our movement."

Simultaneously, they raised their beers in a silent toast to their plan.

Kensington asked, "Can I count on you?"

Quisling put his beer can down, reached over, and placed his hand on Kensington's shoulder. "It will be an honor, Kensington. It will be a goddamn honor."

"Allison will be at the hospital visiting Wally tonight. She'll be alone. We can get things rolling this evening." Kensington smiled, "This also gives Wally a legitimate reason for fighting that boy—he was simply defending her honor."

"It's music to my ears, Kensington," Quisling crooned loudly. "That's what we white men do. We uphold the sanctity of our women."

Quisling glanced at the lifeless body of the Black man hanging from the tree—and smiled.

10

An Eye for an Eye

Laughter echoed within the cavernous walls mingling with the soothing sound of a cascading waterfall. Imbued with a chapel-like tranquility, slivers of artificial light streamed through crevices in the ceiling. The dark earth surrounding the pond was adorned with water shrubs, plants, flowers, and small trees.

Patricia gazed admiringly at the translucent pond where koi fish glided beneath the surface in swirls of red, gold, and orange, their movements sending ripples of light throughout the pond. Standing barefoot at the water's edge, she stretched her arms upward, took a deep breath, and slowly exhaled, releasing the weight of her troubled spirit.

TicToc gazed appreciatively at the calm on Horn's face, so unlike the strained, drawn expression she'd worn when they'd bunked together in the county jail. She quietly observed the woman who had risked certain death to protect her. Horn had no conscious thought of her two beloved sons, who were waiting anxiously for her return home. She'd rushed forward instinctively to protect her.

Horn could've died that day, but self-preservation never crossed her mind. Her courage reminded TicToc of a botched assignment in Syria when a firefight unexpectedly erupted. She was hit several times, but another agent had thrown himself in harm's way to save her life. He absorbed a spray of bullets meant for her. Like him, Horn was a warrior.

After a moment of quiet meditation, Patricia turned to her friend. "I'm sorry, TicToc. Your subterranean hideaway is so beautiful. I just felt..." She hesitated, her voice trailing off.

"Transcended?" TicToc offered.

"Transcended. Exactly. I felt transcended," Patricia said.

TicToc intuitively understood. "I've always cherished my sanctuary. It's the only place where I can truly experience a deep sense of inner peace. While I occasionally reach moments of total tranquility, they often slip away from me. More often than not, they elude me." She paused. "Dark memories intrude… She sighed. "But I'm so pleased that you feel..."

"Blessed." Patricia finished the thought for her. "Even though Tyrene is in jail, you've given me reason to hope for his release and exoneration. The plan you shared with me during our meal will likely compel the prosecutor to either reduce the charges or possibly dismiss the case entirely." Standing before the waterfall, Patricia saw the faint arc of a rainbow and smiled. "I've never had a friend like you," Patricia confessed. "I was worried that I'd never see you again."

"I would never let that happen, Horn." TicToc's eyes glazed with tears, revealing her deep fondness for this woman. "Let's head back to the living room. I've got a secret to share."

Patricia furrowed her eyebrows. TicToc wasn't one for sharing—especially personal matters. Throughout their time in jail, she'd been a closed book. She studied her friend, noting that she had acquired several more gray hairs at her temples in just a few years. Yet she still looked remarkably fit—lean, toned, and athletic.

Patricia padded across the marble tiled floor and settled onto the silver-gray couch next to TicToc. She angled herself to keep the waterfall in view, her gaze following the cascading water upward to the cavernous ceiling high above.

The ceiling, a natural rock canopy, stretched over 100 feet high, blanketing the circular room in its vastness. Five breathtaking, life-size African sculptures stood towering and vigilant, animating the space with an air of quiet grandeur.

"Wow," Patricia exclaimed. "Can't believe you have so many of Woodrow Nash's pieces." She shook her head, marveling at her friend's incredibly lavish lifestyle.

TicToc chuckled, waving her hand toward the figures. "I draw strength and serenity from their beauty. Quite majestic, yes?"

Patricia smiled at TicToc. "Way different from that cage at the county jail."

"Yeah!" TicToc said thoughtfully, her eyes circling the room. "I wanted a place that felt sacred, a refuge. I dreamed of my sanctuary at an early age and, thankfully," she shrugged, "things worked out for me."

Patricia knew better than to question TicToc's ability to amass such wealth and create a secret hideaway that could only be described as idyllic.

"I'm truly happy for you, TicToc. Thanks for inviting me." Her voice trailed off as an unspoken question lingered in her mind.

TicToc voiced it. "Why all the secrecy?"

"Yes. Was it really necessary to blindfold me for a bathroom break, or all the precautions taken to prevent me from knowing our destination?"

"I'll explain as much as you need to know, but I can summarize everything in one word," she said reassuringly. "Safety."

Patricia crossed her arms tightly across her chest. "I'm listening."

TicToc had vowed that if their paths ever crossed again, she would let Horn see the person who had shared a cell with her for seven months.

"I consider you a friend." She paused to meet Patricia's eyes, "which is a liability in my line of work."

"Which is...?"

TicToc stood up and walked over to a white silk curtain that shimmering like a canvas. She pulled the cord, raising the curtain to reveal the figure of a crucified Jesus, suspended without a cross. It was constructed of wood, stood approximately six feet tall, and was suspended mid-air by nearly invisible cables attached to the ceiling. Jesus' expression and form inspired a profound sense of divinity and sacrificial glory.

Patricia gasped, "I've seen this sculpture before. It was in a religious art magazine. It's beautiful. It's a reproduction of Michelangelo's bronze depiction of Christ. His portrayal of Christ's left leg crossing over his right, is somewhat unusual in Italian Renaissance crucifixes, which traditionally had the right leg crossing the left. But Michelangelo's sculpture was less than two feet tall."

Impressed with her knowledge of the piece, TicToc cocked her head and smiled. "Remember when we prayed every night in the county jail?"

"It wasn't *every* night. Remember, I spent nearly a week in the hospital from that knife wound."

TicToc chuckled. "I told you to leave, but you were..." correcting herself, "...*are* just too damn stubborn. But I did pray for you, darlin', while you were away."

Patricia said, tongue in cheek, "I didn't doubt that you would."

"I had this sculpture made because of our faith—to remind me of what His sacrifice means to me," she paused and said, "and how I ought to live my life."

"*Ought* to live your life?" Patricia echoed, uncertain of her meaning.

"So many times, I've stood beneath this cross asking His forgiveness for what I've done. I know I'm a sinner, but I try to do right when I can for others, particularly those people I care about."

Patricia saw guilt flash across TicToc's face. "TicToc! What have you done?"

TicToc walked back to the couch and sat down. "Sometimes, I've had to be... an avenging angel for others." She flashed a rueful smile. "The thing is, Horn, it's not just what I've done...and I've done plenty. The problem is, for the most part... I enjoyed it."

Patricia recalled the terrified, panicked sounds of the Behemoth struggling to live and the maniacal expression on her friend's face.

"I suspected as much," Patricia said softly.

She wanted to comfort her friend and reassure her. Her mind raced for something compassionate to say—but what do you say to your dearest friend who enjoys killing?

"It's okay, Horn. You don't have to say anything. I just needed to tell someone who might understand the contradictions between my faith and my life. Someone I trust. Someone I care for."

Patricia fell silent, reflecting on the enormity of TicToc's spiritual dilemma. Then, unsure where the words came from, she said, "Soldiers kill in war—out of duty. Cops kill, they say, to protect themselves. Extremists kill to espouse a cause. Psychopaths kill for sport. You kill…" her voice trailed off.

TicToc said, "I don't kill for sport, Horn. I usually kill for money, but only when bad folks need killin'."

A shiver raced through Patricia's body. Though she appreciated TicToc's honesty, her friend's unsettling confession still left her uneasy. She touched TicToc's arm, surprised to find gratitude in her eyes.

Deciding it was best to shift to a more innocuous topic, Patricia glanced around the luxurious room once more.

"You didn't have to remain in jail," she said. "With your resources, you could've gotten out anytime."

"I was incarcerated for a reason," she explained. "I was paid to gather intel on a long-running drug cartel operation."

"Why you?" Patricia exclaimed. "The government has the FBI, the DEA, and local law enforcement."

"Who said anything about the government? My client was an irate, cuckolded husband who wanted to destroy the career of the bureau chief of the county jail who was screwing his wife. Around election time, Buford Perry got his 15 minutes of fame." TicToc laughed. "Actually, about two weeks of prime time plus 12 years in prison.

"Seems a bit excessive merely to embarrass and trap a philandering fool," Patricia said. "But destroying his rival's life so publicly must have been sweet revenge for a vindictive, jealous husband."

"Buford was involved in the drug cartel operation. He was making and selling drugs in the jail." TicToc shrugged. "He was dirty. I'd say, he had it coming." She noticed their empty glasses.

"Looks like it's time for another round." She yelled, "Carl, the desert's dry."

Patricia was thoughtful for a moment, then she said. "Explain to me again why you're hesitant to bond my son out."

"Safety, Horn. He's a Black teenage kid who wears his hair like Jean Michel Basquiat. He caused a horrendous injury to a white kid whose father is a decorated cop. If he isn't on the streets or at home, there's less risk of being harassed by the kid's father or one of his cop buddies. In detention, Tyrene becomes less of a target."

Seeing doubt in Horn's eyes, TicToc continued. "Consider a traffic stop where an officer claims that Tyrene made 'furtive movements' before they shot him—or where he is killed on the sidewalk because he supposedly looks 'suspicious.'"

TicToc leaned forward. "Do you remember Elijah McClain, a young Black man who played his violin for stray cats in pet stores because he believed it soothed them. He was just walking home one evening, listening to music—before the police put him in a chokehold. Then, paramedics injected him with a fatal dose of ketamine. What was Elijah's crime?" she scoffed. "Like Trayvon Martin, someone thought he looked 'suspicious.'"

TicToc shook her head. "Are you hearing me? Tyrene's life could be in danger on the street or in a car. Right now, he's safer in juvenile detention than at home. I told you that if he's transferred to the adult jail, I already have a bondsman standing by to bail him out. Besides, I have eyes on him in juvenile detention as we speak."

Patricia frowned. "Why would anyone want to harm my child?"

"Wrong question, Horn. Perversity is fueled by an ugly emotion, not reason, decency, or morals. Mix in racial hatred and combine it with a deep-seated grievance, and you'll witness unimaginable barbarism."

TicToc sighed. "You might think that I'm being paranoid. I'm not. I know what dirty cops are capable of and what they do." Her eyes narrowed. "There's nothing worse than a corrupt cop."

"I can keep him safe at home," Patricia protested. "Especially with your protection."

"You ever hear about cops executing a no-knock drug warrant on the wrong address and shooting up the house? You do know about the illegal raid on Breonna Taylor's home, don't you?" Not waiting for an answer TicToc continued. "Think about this, Horn. Instead of cops being reckless, stupid, and incompetent, executing a warrant on the wrong house, imagine a death squad coming to your home in a pre-dawn raid , using a no-knock warrant as a ruse to kill Tyrene, like the Chicago police killed Fred Hampton!"

Patricia inhaled sharply and cupped her face with her hands.

"I can't risk that much exposure by getting into a shootout with cops at your home," TicToc said tersely. "Leave Tyrene safe in detention, where I can minimize risk and maximize protection. I'd rather be paranoid and wrong than naive and wrong."

Seeing Patricia's frown she said, "You need to trust me, Horn. Remember when I left you in the county jail, and told you I'd be here if you ever needed help?"

"Yeah, but you disappeared ... for years," Patricia said.

The confusion and hurt in her eyes made TicToc look away. Fortunately, Carl arrived with their drinks, easing the tension. He then exited as quietly as he'd come. TicToc took a slow, deliberate sip from her drink before speaking.

"I believe you had a lot of questions about who paid Duke's funeral expenses. The funeral director told you that the benefactor wanted to remain anonymous. Remember?"

Patricia's face was blank, but her eyes burned intensely.

"My son committed suicide," she said, her voice breaking. "One week after I was released from the county jail." Her eyes began to brim with tears.

TicToc placed her glass on the table, and rested her hand on Patricia's arm. "I was on assignment in Prague when I heard."

"Why didn't you contact me?"

"I'm sorry. My assignment was... sensitive. The nature of my work is dangerous. It puts anyone connected to me at risk."

"But you've contacted me now," Patricia protested, confused, wiping away her tears.

"It's a calculated risk, but I took every precaution I could think of. Besides... I had to. You need my help, but I'll have to leave soon. Not sure when I'll get another chance to see your ugly face again," TicToc teased.

"Well, I don't look particularly attractive when I cry," she said. A sudden stillness descended between them. Staring intently at TicToc, she asked, "When you say, 'not sure', you mean that you might not return?"

TicToc shrugged. "I knew the challenges involved when I chose this line of work."

"Some line of work, TicToc! Don't you think that it's just a bit hypocritical to do what you do and still profess to be a person of faith?"

"No. Not at all," TicToc said matter-of-factly. "Who would need forgiveness and redemption more than me?" She looked over at the sculpture of Christ. "I'm absolutely perfect in my imperfections. I'm a human being first, before I am a Christian, if you can appreciate the distinction."

Patricia sighed deeply. It was clear that TicToc had made peace with the bewildering contradiction in her life. Nothing she could say would change her mind. What mattered most was that TicToc was here with her now.

"When I told the funeral director that I couldn't afford any of my son's funeral service packages, he just smiled and said, 'Expense is not a problem. Everything has been taken care of. He wouldn't give me any information about who paid for what."

Patricia looked at TicToc, realization dawning on her face. "TicToc! It was you!" She threw herself at her friend, hugging her tightly.

"Well, Horn. That ain't all," TicToc said, mischief in her voice. "I have copies of the school's security tapes of the attack on your son! Carl hacked into the school's security system to access surveillance tapes. I was worried that the DA might announce that they had been accidentally erased or lost, so I arranged to have Carl collect that footage the evening of the assault. Copies were made and delivered to Clayton Marshall, Tyrene's lawyer." TicToc beamed.

"You got the tapes?" Patricia exclaimed in disbelief.

"It's great evidence for the defense," TicToc explained. "It's clear that your son endured a vicious beat-down for a considerable amount of time. A crowd of kids was around. No one was helping him. A few seemed to be cheering the bully on, aggravating the situation. Although your son did cause some serious damage to that kid, a jury, after seeing those tapes, might agree that the bully got what he deserved."

"TicToc! That's wonderful news!" Patricia was nearly beside herself with excitement. "When can I see the footage?"

"You can watch right after we finish here. The clarity of the footage is good, except for one particular spot. I've looked at the film about five times, and an area on the tape appears blurry just before your son retaliates."

"A blurry image?" asked Patricia. "Is it the camera angle?"

"No. When you watch the footage, someone appears to be kneeling or crouching by your son. The image is unclear and hazy. It seems like a faint, shadowy outline of a person, but I can't quite make it out. My tech people couldn't enhance it to make it clearer."

She paused. "The one thing that I am certain of is, just before your son lunges at that kid, Tyrene's facial expression changes completely. You can even detect a perceptible physical change throughout his body. It's quite remarkable! It's almost as if he's transformed and then attacks in a fury." TicToc said, reflecting on how the shadowy image turned him into someone utterly fearless.

"We have a saying in our business," TicToc said.

"What's that?" Patricia asked.

"Beware of the dead. It's when you think your target is dead or incapacitated, and you get careless and sloppy. You drop your guard. You think that you're safe, but you're not. The bully made that mistake with your son." TicToc looked at Patricia. "Your boy has the heart of a lion."

"He does," she agreed proudly. "But don't you try recruiting him," she added teasingly. "He's going to college."

TicToc laughed.

Patricia suddenly became quiet. She stared at this remarkable woman, wondering what TicToc ever saw in her.

TicToc smiled knowingly. Seeming to read her mind, she said, "It's your heart, Horn. It's a good heart. You remind me of my sister, Marla. Such a sweet, beautiful person."

"I didn't know you had a sister," Patricia said, surprised. "Where is she?"

"She's dead," Tic Toc said. Her voice flat. "Some very dangerous men murdered her. They tortured her for days, but she didn't break."

Stunned, Patricia stuttered, "I'm... I'm so sorry, TicToc. That's awful. Why? What did they want from her?"

"Me. They wanted me," TicToc said quietly. "One of our foreign competitors had fed false information to a group of terrorists that identified me as the assassin of one of their military leaders.

"Apparently, the terrorists were closing in on one of their double agents, and they needed time to divert attention from the double agent to someone else. Because only a few snipers in the world can make a kill shot from over 3,000 meters, it was easy to pin the murder on me. Our competitor made sure that I was in the area at the time of the assassination. We met at a village coffee shop about two miles from the target. I was set up. They wanted me. To find me, they needed my sister."

TicToc smiled grimly. "It's alright," she said. "I got them all—the ones who tortured and killed her and the one who gave the order. It took a while, but I got them all."

Patricia blanched at her confession.

"I considered eliminating all of their family members, but thought that might be a bit excessive, so I decided to kill only one. I chose the family member of the man who targeted my sister." TicToc took a sip from her drink. "He had an older sister whom he adored. We kidnapped her from her apartment in Amsterdam while her husband and two children were sleeping. We smuggled her into Rome."

Patricia barely managed to stifle a gasp. She felt her heart pounding.

TicToc's expression had been subtly changing as she described her revenge. Her eyes narrowed, and the hazel color of her eyes transformed into a cold glint.

"I made him watch his sister's death before I killed him. An eye for an eye," she said her voice cold. "Good Old Testament justice."

Patricia struggled to understand how TicToc could kill an innocent person for revenge, even if Old Testament law allowed it. The thought of a mother being murdered made her numb. A chill settled over her. Strangely, killing the men didn't disturb her—Patricia believed they deserved to die. But she knew, instinctively, their deaths hadn't been quick or easy. TicToc's expression told her as much.

"I saw pictures of my sister's body," TicToc continued. "I showed them to the man moments before I shot his sister. He knew it was useless to beg for her life after he saw those pictures of Marla." A tear appeared in the corner of TicToc's eye. She quickly wiped it away.

"It was a clean shot, close range, through her heart. She died instantly, but he didn't. I made sure of that."

Patricia couldn't suppress an involuntary shudder.

"Just so you know, Horn, I also located the genius who devised this dumb plan to protect his double agent."

Patricia raised her hand quickly in silent protest. When she was able to speak, she said weakly, "I don't think that I want to know anything else, TicToc. It's too much."

Patricia reached for her glass, her hand trembling. She took a long, drink. Swallowing hard, she welcomed the burning sensation in her throat.

"I understand, Horn. I'm so very sorry. I forget that my world is alien to anyone who isn't used to..." her voice trailed off.

"Let's talk more about how I can help you and Tyrene," she said quickly. "Those tapes are powerful visual evidence to support a self-defense argument. The only problem is that the law provides that the right to self-defense may be abandoned if excessive force is used. It just depends on who's on the jury. If it's an all-white, all-male jury, we may have a problem, but I can work on that."

"I can't believe you got those tapes!" Patricia repeated, in disbelief. "So you think you can manipulate the jury pool, if necessary? And it also appears that you can kill with impunity." She looked at TicToc in bewilderment. "Who are you really, TicToc?"

"Let's just say that I'm one of those people in the world you don't fuck with. But, because of the nature of my job, we'll never be able to have a normal friendship. I'd put you and your family, even those close to you, at risk. You'd become more vulnerable, and I'd become more vulnerable."

"Took a minute, but I am getting it now—safety," Patricia said.

She looked at TicToc, impressed by her, in awe of her, frightened for her, and unsure of what to say.

Patricia allowed herself to accept—*no, not accept, tolerate* TicToc's "work." She couldn't deny their profound bond and shared faith. For all her extraordinary contradictions, she'd grown to love her like a sister. She understood, too, that TicToc felt the same about her. She raised her glass ceremoniously and announced, "A toast to my dear friend!"

Patricia closed her eyes, attempting to recall the exact words. Initially, they came slowly, but soon they flowed easily.

"*Time is too slow for those who wait, too swift for those who fear, too long for those who grieve, and too short for those who rejoice; but for those who love, time is eternity.* To my dear friend TicToc, the daughter of time."

TicToc smiled, obviously flattered. "That's very nice, Horn. Thank you. Who's the author?"

"Henry Van Dyke. He was a clergyman in the early 20th century. He was also a lecturer and author who had a fond regard for our Lord."

TicToc raised her glass. "Let's toast the plan to release your son. What shall we call our operation? I know! What about Cake Walk? That's the name of a dance that slaves created to mock white aristocratic society."

Patricia thought for a moment and then shook her head. "No! I really don't have a problem with white people as a whole. It's the ones who claim to be colorblind but aren't; those who call themselves Christian, yet ignore the teaching to love thy neighbor; those who have no understanding of white privilege and couldn't care less; and those who refuse to acknowledge that they have benefited from slavery, whether or not they or their ancestors ever owned a slave."

"The last one about refusing to see that they benefited from slavery covers about 90% of them!" TicToc laughed.

Patricia laughed. "No, really—I refuse to stereotype them as a group the way most do us."

"Okay. My arm is getting tired. Let's come up with a name and make this toast!"

"I got it. Let's call it Operation Freedom."

"Not exactly a code name that we ordinarily use for a mission of this nature," TicToc chuckled, "but okay."

TicToc looked across the room. "There's someone over there who we need to bless our mission." Patricia followed TicToc's gaze to the statue of Jesus. They clinked their glasses, took a celebratory sip, and placed them on the table.

TicTok took Patricia's hand to guide her to the statue. They stood under the suspended figure. Neither spoke; words would have been superfluous. After several moments, they knelt together, eyes closed, each clasping the other's hand. With their free hands, they lifted high in praise and adoration. It was not unlike praying in the county jail—there too, they had found peace.

There was a subtle movement high above them. TicToc glanced up just in time to catch the glint of light reflecting off a small, round object spinning rapidly as it descended toward the floor. Patricia felt TicToc move and opened her eyes.

In one fluid motion, TicToc snatched the object from the air. It was a buffalo nickel, shiny and clean as if newly minted. Patricia's heart began to pound. She took the nickel out of TicToc's hand. "I don't believe this!" she said. Intrigued, TicToc waited patiently as Patricia studied the nickel. She finally said, "It doesn't happen often—just every now and then. I haven't quite figured a pattern, but this is the first time that one has appeared in the presence of another person."

"What's going on, Horn? I don't usually have money dropping out of nowhere in my home."

Patricia struggled to explain the remarkable appearance of the coin.

"It all started after the Kensington boy attacked Tyrene at school. I'd find a buffalo nickel somewhere near me—maybe on the floor or on the bed or in my bureau drawer. One day, a nickel just fell out of the blue into the tub when I was showering."

TicToc inhaled deeply and said, "That's too weird, Horn."

"I know. I've been thinking more and more about Duke and wondering why he took his life. The thought of him dying like that has always tormented me. I wish I understood. I blame myself—but then, I don't know what I should blame myself for. I loved that boy so very dearly. My heart broke when he died."

Patricia began to sob openly now. The deep anguish of her loss erupted with a violence that shook her with spasms of raw emotion.

TicToc glanced up at the serene face of Jesus above them and hugged her friend tightly.

"If I didn't tell you before, Horn, I'm sorry I couldn't attend Duke's service," TicToc murmured, her voice tight with regret. "This may be difficult for you to consider, but I want you to talk to someone for me. Something is going on that's beyond our understanding with these coins. I can't explain their appearance, but I know someone who might be able to help—if you're willing."

Patricia nodded slowly, emotionally drained, she whispered, "I need to know."

"Look at me, Horn," TicToc said sternly.

Surprised by the tone of her voice, Patricia pulled away and wiped the remaining tears off her face.

"Remember when we read about the seven gifts of the Holy Spirit in the Bible?"

Horn nodded. "Yes. We read about the gifts of wisdom, understanding, knowledge, fear of God, and other gifts."

"Yes, that's correct. The person I want you to see has a special gift, but it's not one of the seven gifts, and it is definitely not of the Holy Spirit, according to the Bible."

Patricia looked confused as she struggled to understand what TicToc was trying to tell her.

TicToc cautioned her friend, "This is important. You must make this decision yourself. I can only tell you that what I'm about to propose is frowned upon in the Bible."

Baffled by what TicToc might suggest, Patricia asked, "Do you think this person can help me?"

"I'm more than confident that she can."

"Why are you so confident, TicToc?"

TicToc took the coin from Patricia's hand and studied it.

"This coin is a sign or a message of some sort, and the woman I mentioned has a gift for reaching beyond this world."

"What on earth are you talking about, TicToc?"

TicToc placed the coin in Patricia's trembling palm. "I know she can help you, Horn, because…she helped me speak to Marla."

11

Payback

Allison hurried down the hospital corridor. Reaching Wally's room, she stood in the doorway and gazed wistfully at her childhood sweetheart. He looked pale and sickly, a mere shadow of the guy she knew and loved, which caused her to fear for his recovery.

Heavily sedated and breathing deeply, he looked exhausted—eyes closed tightly, as if he never wanted to wake again. She was confused, frightened for him, and concerned about their relationship. She'd been told that his injury wasn't life-threatening, but the healing process would be multifaceted and complex. The doctor cautiously advised that it was a delicate medical condition requiring months of observation. However, the somber tone in the doctor's voice hinted at something more troubling, leading her to fear that he was alluding to the psychological impact of Wally's injury.

Maybe he'll suffer from depression or grapple with body image and identity, she thought. Allison worried whether she had the emotional strength to support him through his trauma.

It was a "manhood" thing, she told herself. She shook her head and frowned. How could such a relatively small part of his anatomy define so much about what it means—physically and sexually—to be a man? A damaged penis could achieve an erection and still function, but only if Wally didn't think that he was irreparably damaged goods.

Callous comments had already started at school. Allison knew that most teenage boys lacked the capacity to be sensitive about a classmate's misfortune, especially when it involved something as personal as one's sexuality.

Some of Wally's buddies had even joked about "pitch-hitting" for him if he couldn't "get it up." They'd gone from worshipping him to kicking him while he was down.

Whether she and Wally would ever have passionate and wildly exhausting sex again no longer mattered to her. What she craved most was the physical closeness—the quiet, seductive intimacy of his embrace during those stolen moments in his bedroom, when they simply lay still, holding each other.

She sighed and walked over to Wally's bedside. Leaning down, she inhaled his familiar scent. The soft stubble of his unshaven face brushed against her cheek, sending a faint tickle across her skin. She smiled tenderly, her lips hovering just above his, when a loud, voice shattered the moment.

"Hold on, young lady! You 'bout to molest a helpless male?" Quisling teased, his broad grin stretching across his face.

Allison jerked back, her face flushing with heat. She looked up to see Wally's dad, Kensington, and his friend, Quisling, standing in the doorway. Kensington looked apologetic, but Quisling was clearly clueless. She struggled to regain her composure. The intrusion had shattered a deeply private moment.

Kensington immediately recognized her discomfort and apologized for the interruption. Quisling, however, remained dumbly unaware. He bustled noisily into the room, accidentally bumping into the bed. The jolt roused Wally.

"Dad! Officer Quisling! Hey! How are you?" Wally's voice was soft and sluggish. The scent of Allison's perfume gave her away before he saw her. As soon as he realized she was there, his expression softened, and a quiet warmth spread across his face.

"Allison," he said softly. He reached for her hand. "Hi, babe."

Allison grasped his hand. She turned it over and pressed soft kisses to his palm. Tears welled in her eyes, and the sound brought a smile to Kensington's face—it reminded him of the way his wife used to wake him up for work, smothering his face with gentle kisses.

God, how I miss her, he thought.

"It's good to see you, son," Kensington, said, moving to the opposite side of the bed. He ruffled Wally's hair affectionately. "You're looking much better," he lied. "I can't tell you how good that makes me feel."

Wally met his father's gaze; his own eyes clouded with frustration and pain. "I don't feel okay, Dad. I feel broken. I'm angry. It feels like my life has been trashed."

Quisling, standing at the foot of the bed, nodded sympathetically. "You're gonna be alright, Wally Boy. Count on it. Takes some time, but you *will* be alright."

Wally managed a weak smile, and Allison glanced at Quisling with gratitude.

"Allison, this is Officer Quisling," Wally said. "You know, the guy I've mentioned a hundred times to you."

"Wally," Allison replied gently, "you may be a little groggy from the meds. Your dad introduced me to Officer Quisling once at your house before the… uh ... incident at school."

She turned to Quisling. "Thanks for visiting. Good to see Wally's Southern Confederate rebel again. He's spoken so highly of you. You don't know how much Wally has enjoyed your company and stories."

It was Quisling's turn to feel embarrassed. He wasn't used to people holding him in such high regard.

Kensington was grateful for Quisling's part in helping him and Wally reconnect after his wife's death. Despite Quisling's morbid fascination with stories of the old South—particularly the violent ones—and his obsession with perpetuating white supremacy, he'd managed to ingratiate himself into their lives through humor and good-natured kindness.

"Yep," Kensington interjected, a teasing glint in his eye. "I must say that Officer Quisling has become an undeniable presence in our lives. The jury is still out whether knowing him will be a blessing or a curse," he joked.

The room erupted in soft laughter, creating a sense of comfort and ease.

"Well, Wally has told me a lot about you, too, Ms. Allison," Quisling said. "You get prettier every time I see you."

Allison blushed at the compliment, offering a demure smile in return.

Turning to Wally, Quisling blurted out, "Your dad's got a foolproof plan to handle this court thing, Wally. It's gonna set things right."

Pleased that his father remembered his desire for revenge, Wally asked excitedly, "What plan, Dad?"

Kensington attempted to mask his frustration with Quisling. He wasn't prepared to broach the topic so soon. It had been a while since he'd seen Allison, and he assumed she might be grappling with abandonment issues after her father's abrupt departure. He wanted to make sure she was emotionally grounded before delving into something that could frighten her.

Earlier, when Kensington asked about Allison, Wally confided, "She's been feeling down, exhausted. Her dad packed up and left without a word, and her mom made her get an after-school job to help with the bills.

"The only time he makes contact is when he sends a few dollars through the mail—no return address, no note, nothing. She really misses him."

"We'll get to the plan, but we need to make sure that our conversation is private."

Puzzled, Allison stole a glance at Wally. He smiled reassuringly at her and made a weak attempt to sit up in his bed, but he collapsed back onto the pillows. The drugs in his system left him sluggish and uncoordinated. His body wouldn't cooperate, but his mind was clearing somewhat. Allison carefully arranged the pillows behind his head.

Kensington looked at Quisling and nodded toward the doorway. Quisling caught the cue and got up to station himself outside the room. "Yell if we get company," Kensington said firmly.

Quisling stepped into the hallway, leaving the door slightly open, and assumed his position with an air of extreme importance.

"Allison," Kensington nodded to the remote on the bedside table. "Turn on the TV and raise the volume, but not too loud." Uncertain, Allison complied.

Kensington began haltingly. "Allison, did you tell your mom that you were meeting with me at the hospital?"

"I did," Allison replied, "but I don't understand why. I mean... you'd be here anyway to see Wally, right?"

Ignoring her question, Kensington continued, "Was your mom curious about you asking me to be here?" Kensington watched her closely.

"No. Not really," Allison said. "She just asked if everything was alright."

"What did you tell her?"

"I did like you told me to," Allison replied. "I just said that I needed your advice about something."

"Did she ask anything else?" Kensington pressed.

"She asked if I had gotten in trouble with the law."

"Anything else?" Kensington asked, his tone probing.

"Yeah!" Allison responded, laughing. "She wondered if I was pregnant." I said, "Not yet, Mom." She looked tenderly at Wally and squeezed his hand.

With a bitterness in his voice that surprised Allison, Wally said, "Pregnant? Maybe never! Anyway, not by me."

Allison was silent for a moment and then turned on him fiercely. "If not by you, Wally Kensington, then it damn sure won't be by anybody else." She leaned toward him, her voice quaking with emotion. "If you care about me—really care—you will never say something stupid like that to me again."

Wally flinched at her words. He saw the injured look on her face, as well as her hot anger.

"Sorry, babe. I'm not feeling real good about myself right now."

She kissed him gently on the lips. "I can feel good for us both, Wally, until you're better. Don't you ever forget that."

For the first time, Kensington fully appreciated the depth of Allison's feelings for his son. He now felt more confident that she might be open to his plan, even if it meant telling a lie.

Kensington began to explain his idea slowly. "Well, what I've been thinking about," he paused, shifting his weight, "This plan won't work without your help, Allison. It's the only way I can get real justice for my son."

"I don't understand, Mr. Kensington. How can I help? I wasn't even there when Wally was hurt."

"I know, Allison. You weren't there when it happened, but you could provide a reason to the jury to understand *why* it happened. The reason for the fight, I mean."

When Kensington said the word "jury," Allison's mouth fell open. Confused and now fearful, she shook her head in protest. "I still don't know what you mean, Mr. Kensington. You want me to be in front of a jury?" She looked at Wally for help, then back to his dad. "What… what kind of reason could I give?"

Kensington reminded himself to take it slow. He couldn't risk Allison rejecting the idea before he could explain it.

"Allison, what if you told Wally that this boy had done something inappropriate to you, and Wally became angry? No! Better still, Wally was outraged! He decides to confront the boy. In the process of confronting him, the boy gets pissed off and hits Wally. You know how Black boys get when they think they've been dissed."

Unsure, she nodded slowly in agreement and mumbled. "I guess."

"That's why the fight started—inappropriate sexual contact! Wally learned that this kid hurt you. So you, Allison, can provide the reason why the fight happens. That was Wally's motivation."

Confusion swirled across Allison's face, which appeared to lose more color as Kensington spoke. Shaking her head, Allison asked plaintively, "How could I possibly be harmed, Mr. Kensington? I've never even spoken to that boy. I've seen him, but I don't know him."

Taking a deep breath, Kensington took slow, deliberate steps around the bed and placed his hands gently on her shoulders. "Before I answer that question, Allison, I need to give you the big picture about the probable outcome of this trial, based upon my 25 years in law enforcement. This kid will be charged as an adult." Kensington explained. "I made sure of that. Even if he's found guilty of assault and goes to prison, he'll get out eventually. He'll be able to move on with his life. The bottom line, Allison, is that, after doing his time, Wally's attacker won't have any real stigma attached to his life. He won't be reminded about what he did to our Wally."

Wally managed to nod his head vigorously in agreement.

"But Wally..." Kensington continued cautiously. "Wally won't have that luxury. He won't have that advantage. He'll be forever reminded of that humiliating moment every day of his life. The physical trauma may leave him someday, but the memory will never die. The scar will remain. It'll be even worse if he is not able to father a child with you."

Kensington fell silent. The room had become uncomfortably still. He shot a quick glance toward Quisling, who was engaged in conversation with a technician in the hallway. Quisling caught his eye and responded with a reassuring thumbs up.

Kensington could see her hesitation, uncertainty flickering behind her eyes. She pulled away from him; his hands dropped from her shoulders.

Wally and Allison were silent, the weight of recent events heavy between them. They grappled with the fear of Wally's injury, uncertain how it would shape their future—or how this plan might alter their lives forever..

Kensington waited for Allison to speak, aware that her next words would be pivotal to the success of his plan.

"Wally?" she said, her voice trembling. "What do you think?"

Wally's face tightened, his expression pinched with anxiety. His voice carried a sharp, angry edge.

"I've got to be honest with you, babe. I want to get this guy for what he did to me. What he did to *us*. Let's listen to what my dad has in mind, Okay?"

Allison nodded slowly. "Okay. Please continue, Mr. Kensington."

Kensington adopted a look of feigned concern—his most solicitous expression.

"There is one sure way to put a stigma on that kid for the rest of his life," Kensington said. "Even after he's served his time, no matter where he goes, no matter what he does, this will follow him — just as it will follow Wally for the rest of his life." Kensington paused, leaned in, and whispered, "We get him labeled as a sex offender."

Allison inhaled sharply, her eyes widening as if they might envelop her face. "You want me to accuse him of raping me?" she gasped. Her voice faltered, tight with panic.

"We've got an expression in law enforcement, Allison, that recognizes the limitations of the justice system. Police officers understand that for certain offenses, the punishment will never fully match the severity of the crime. So, we do what we can to make it right for the victims. If necessary, we even create evidence to make sure that some rotten bastard gets everything he deserves. We call it 'just desserts.' We give a criminal scumbag what is due: a metaphorical eye for an eye.

Kensington paused, allowing the moral justification of his plan to sink in. "The justice system can never restore a victim's sense of safety, dignity, or self-respect. It's not designed to do that. The victim of a violent crime, like Wally, is left to pull his life back together again unless…" he paused, his gaze steady, "we can get retribution another way."

"Retribution?" Allison mumbled. Her voice broke with uncertainty as she nervously chewed on her lower lip.

Kensington, drawing on his experience as a police officer, took a deep breath and steadied his tone. He was trained to manage difficult conversations.

"I've gotten close to victims of crimes. You've got to if you want to do your job right. When a wound is inflicted, it can affect you on many different levels. Deep, painful levels. Words can never convey the loss. Some wounds never fully heal, no matter how much time passes. Wally has suffered one of those wounds."

"Wally will heal. He's young and strong. Don't tell him that he won't heal, Mr. Kensington," she pleaded, fighting back tears.

"Of course, he'll heal *physically*, Allison," Kensington said placatingly. "But will he recover *emotionally*? This is something that you can do to help him. You can help him with his emotional pain. This is a gift that only you can give—a gift that he'll never forget."

Allison was visibly trembling, her hands shaking as she fought to steady herself. Sensing her distress, Wally gently urged her to come closer so he could hold her hand.

Kensington pressed on, his voice steady but insistent. "We can make this work, Allison. We can coach you, support you, and guide you every step of the way. You don't even have to say that he raped you if you don't want to. You only need to say that he tried to assault you. Just that he touched you..." Kensington's voice trailed off. "You know. He touched you in a bad way."

Allison shrunk inward, her shoulders slumping as her head dropped to her chest.

Kensington gently turned her from Wally to face him. He could feel her slender frame shaking beneath his touch. He lifted her chin carefully, his eyes locking with hers—steady, resolute, and quietly reassuring.

"We'll help you prepare a statement," Kensington said soothingly. "We'll keep the facts simple. We'll work with you until the story becomes second nature. We'll be with you every step of the way."

Allison exhaled sharply, taking several deep breaths to steady herself—clearly in distress. Yet, Kensington remained relentless—determined to make his plan work.

"Lying in court..." Her voice cracking as the words escaped her lips. "Lying under oath." Tears welled in her eyes again.

"Allison," Kensington said softly, "lying under oath is practically expected. People lie in court all the time. I overheard this lawyer joking with another lawyer about people lying in court. The lawyer said, 'The very first lie that a witness tells is when he raises his hand and swears to tell the truth, the whole truth, and nothing but the truth.'"

Allison's gaze grew distant, her eyes seemingly looking past Kensington. He hesitated, wondering what she was thinking, but he persisted.

"Wally has told me about your interest in acting. He told me that you're really good. All you have to do is play a role—the role of a victim who has been…" Kensington paused, carefully choosing a less charged word. He said, "Sexually assaulted."

Kensington kept his voice soft and his tone warm, aiming to reassure her. "This is a scenario that will work," he said confidently. "Think how natural it would be to confide in Wally about the assault—someone you love. Wally has noticed that your mood has changed, and that you tend to be more emotional and preoccupied. He asks you if you're okay. Initially, you tell him it's nothing—that you just miss your dad.

"But the thought of that boy touching you—and how he touched you—really starts to bother you, to eat at you. You can't keep it to yourself anymore, and you finally tell Wally at school after you see the boy walking down the hall."

Allison shook her head. "No! That won't work, Mr. Kensington. My friends told me that they heard Wally promised to beat him up after school."

Kensington shrugged. "That's okay. Doesn't change the reason for the fight. Even if Wally started the fight, the jury would know why."

Allison was tormented. She looked at Wally, searching for guidance. Wally appeared to be weighing the situation himself. He wanted reassurance that Allison would be safe—that she wouldn't be at risk because of the lie.

Kensington added, "Oh, I forgot to tell you one very important fact."

Allison and Wally looked at Kensington, wondering what he'd omitted. He said, "This kid doesn't talk." They stared at him, bewildered.

"What… what do you mean, he doesn't talk?" Allison asked, her voice rising, brittle with panic. "What are you saying?"

Kensington explained, "He suffered some kind of trauma a while back, and he hasn't said a word in years."

Wally's eyes widened in realization. "Oh! That's why he didn't say anything when I was hitting him!"

"Trauma! He suffered some kind of trauma, and you want me to add to it?" Allison dropped her head into her hands, her shoulders shaking. Both Kensington and his son tried to quiet her at the same time.

Quisling, eavesdropping on the conversation, abruptly left his post and entered the room. In the most soothing voice he could muster, he said, "Allison! There is probably something that you don't understand."

Allison slowly lifted her head, eyeing him warily as she waited for him to explain what he clearly thought she hadn't understood.

"My great-granddaddy told me a long time ago that Black people don't feel the way we feel—pain, grief, heartache. They don't hold on to those emotions the way we do. That's why it was so easy for slaves to go on with their lives after their families were separated in slave auctions and on plantations. Hell, even President Thomas Jefferson understood that Black people are not like us. In his book, *Notes on Virginia*, he said that their emotions are fleeting."

Shaking her head, she said incredulously, "What! You really believe that crap?"

Quisling looked like he'd been hit with a cattle prod. Before he could respond, Kensington swiftly ushered him out of the room. Kensington didn't want Quisling to launch into a rant about the 'bestial nature' of Black people and risk alienating Allison entirely.

Quisling yelled over his shoulder, "History books always try to be politically correct. They leave out a lot. They don't teach what's true in school nowadays."

As Kensington returned to Wally's bedside, Allison asked anxiously, "What if he does start talking again right after I testify in court? Doesn't he have the right to tell his side of the story?" She wiped a tear from her cheek.

"It won't matter even if he does, which is highly unlikely. But if he does, Allison, it's still your word against his. Besides, you're white, and he's not. And he won't be tried by a jury of his peers. He'll be tried by a jury of *my* peers."

Kensington studied her face, noting the way her thoughts appeared to race behind her troubled expression.

"What about my mom, Mr. Kensington? What do I tell her?"

Kensington smiled reassuringly. "You won't have to explain anything. She doesn't need to know any details or specifics. In fact, I'll have a member of the victim advocate's office impress upon her that she shouldn't attempt to talk to you about what happened. Talking about it again might re-traumatize you."

Allison released a deep, shuddering sigh, relieved at knowing that she wouldn't be quizzed by her mother, but tears continued to well in her eyes.

"Allison," Kensington said gently, "that's why I told you to tell your mom you needed to speak to me. You wanted me to be here with Wally when he explained the reason for the fight."

"Please don't cry, babe," Wally interjected. "This is a good plan. I've seen you act at school. You just need to play the role of a traumatized victim, like in one of those Law-and-Order Special Crime shows. I know you can do it. My dad will watch out for you. Hell, he's the law!"

Her eyes darted back and forth between father and son, as a heavy sense of dread settled over her. She looked down at the floor and muttered, "This is so wrong."

Fear was etched across her face, and a sickening knot twisted in her stomach: she felt trapped, torn between two impossible choices. *Would she lose Wally if she said no? If she said yes, would their relationship survive a lie that could destroy an innocent person's life?*

She tried to reconcile his father's dark plan with her beliefs. "I need a minute," Allison murmured, her voice small and broken.

Several moments passed. It felt like an eternity to Kensington. His heart was in his throat. Finally, she inhaled sharply and released a shuddering sigh. "If you want this Wally, I'll do it. But if I make this commitment to you, you have to make a commitment to me."

"Sure, babe! Anything you want! What do you need?" Wally asked, relieved.

She whispered in a small, childlike voice, "You can't ever leave me, Wally. We have to stay together! I mean—always! I want us to get married."

Wally and Kensington looked stunned. The room became eerily quiet, and then they exploded in laughter. Confused and mortified, Allison blanched with embarrassment and would have escaped from the room, but Wally had gripped her wrist. Kensington quickly held up his hands to block her exit. She tried several times to jerk away but couldn't.

"Let me go, Wally." She felt weak and ashamed.

Wally made quiet, soothing sounds to her. Then he brought her hand to his lips, and pressed a gentle kiss on it. Grinning mischievously, he asked, "Can we wait until after graduation?"

Her body relaxed, and her face lit up with relief. She threw herself into his arms, kissing him deeply. "Oh, Wally," she sighed. "I love you."

"Love you, too, babe, "he said.

Kensington apologized, his voice gentle and sincere. "I'm so sorry, Allison. I had no idea what you were going to ask, and when you said you wanted to marry my son…" He shook his head, a smile tugging at the corners of his mouth. "Well, it was just…" Kensington paused, searching for the right words before exclaiming, "It was just pure joy!"

Kensington and Wally burst into laughter again, their voices filling their room. This time, Allison joined in.

Quisling watched them out of the doorway, his expression puzzled as he tried to figure out what was going on. Allison's earlier rebuke of his remark about Blacks lacking emotional depth still irked him.

"Graduation and not one minute later," Allison said, her face beaming with excitement. She leaned over and kissed Wally long and passionately.

Kensington teased, "Hey! Easy on my son. He's still recovering!"

Turning to Quisling, Kensington called, "It's a go! We've got our team." He added, "And I've also acquired a beautiful future daughter-in-law." He turned back to Allison.

"We'll work on a preliminary statement for the DA. I've checked out the boy's attendance records and yours, so I know when both of you were in school. I've canvassed the school and have identified a couple of possible isolated locations—blind spots—for the assault to occur. We just need to develop a narrative... a convincing scenario that makes sense. We will probably want you to provide us with a blouse and a pair of slacks or jeans that we can submit as evidence."

He paused, his gaze steady. "Pick a blouse that you usually wear to school. A friend in the lab, who owes me a favor, will get the kid's saliva off Wally's pants. Once we've got the blouse and pants, we'll smear the kid's DNA on your clothing. A forensic expert will be able to testify where the boy's DNA was found."

He leaned forward, his voice lowering slightly. "An old bracelet or necklace with a broken clasp will also be damaging evidence that you were attacked." Kensington was visibly excited. "This will be way easier than you can imagine, Allison." Though not entirely persuaded, her commitment to Wally remained unshakable.

Kensington looked at Wally and Allison. "Everyone okay with this?" he asked.

Wally nodded, a faint but unmistakable smile of approval on his face. Allison, her heart lifting at the sight of Wally's smile and his high spirits, nodded in agreement.

Kensington said, "You kids have a moment to yourselves. I'm going to let Quisling know what's going on. Then, I'll make a call to your mom. I'll follow you home tonight to speak with her. I think I can get a friend from the victim's advocate program to meet us at your house tonight. We'll make sure that your mom doesn't ask you any questions. She'll be advised how to best help and support you."

Allison looked puzzled. "Will this woman from the victim's advocate program know what we're doing?"

Kensington smiled. "She'll have a general idea, but she doesn't need to know specifics. I just have to tell her 'just desserts' and inform her about the nature of the crime. She'll understand what she needs to tell your mom. She'll take it from there. She'll emphasize that your mom should not pry or ask you any questions but wait for you to come to her when you are ready to open up."

Kensington gave Allison's shoulder a gentle squeeze before stepping away from the bed, a noticeable bounce in his step. He was satisfied. He would finally get the payback that his son requested. It would be full, extensive, lifelong, and complete.

As Kensington's mind raced ahead, he envisioned the next steps. Once Allison's statement was prepared and signed, Quisling could deliver it to the filing deputy along with his investigative narrative and report form.

He thought, *It might be just in time for the DA to prepare a felony complaint with the attempted sexual assault count. Too bad it won't be a violent rape charge but that might have been too much for Allison to handle. It doesn't matter, though. With a sex offense conviction, that punk bastard will still be required to register as a sex offender for decades.*

Kensington called over his shoulder as he walked away, "Kids, sit tight. Quisling and I need to talk."

Wally responded enthusiastically, "Okay, Pa!"

Kensington called out to Quisling, "Hey, Quisling! We got some work to do. Let's go down to the cafeteria to map this thing out."

Quisling smiled, his tone eager. "Right with you, boss. I'm right with you."

12

Be Strong

"He's not here." The voice was flat, laced with an undercurrent of hostility.

Patricia Horn turned around to see Amy Walker standing behind her, a stack of files cradled in her arms, and a frown crept across her face. Amy didn't seem particularly pleased to see her again.

"What do you mean he's not here?" Patricia asked, her voice sharp with suspicion. "Where is he?" she demanded.

Amy gestured for Patricia to step aside, guiding her away from the entrance to the juvenile court division. "Tyrene's case was called earlier—about an hour ago," she explained.

"Why didn't you contact me to let me know?"

"Ms. Horn," Amy said evenly, shifting the weight of the files to her hip, "cases get called when the court is ready to call the case. The DA wanted your son's case called earlier because he wanted to inform Judge Jones that it's been transferred to adult court. The deputies didn't even bother to bring your son into the courtroom."

She paused, then added without emotion, "I'm sorry, but you still have time to get to the courtroom upstairs. It's right above this one on the next floor."

Without thanking her, Patricia dashed down the hall toward the elevator. The ride up seemed to take an eternity. When the doors finally opened, Patricia ran out, her eyes wild and her heart pounding—her 17-year-old son was being charged as an adult!

Patricia's greatest fears were unfolding: Tyrene didn't have a guardian like TicToc to watch over him. She feared he would inevitably face a grim choice—either seek protection from a jailhouse enforcer for sexual favors or risk unspeakable violence. The stories she had heard were horrifying— sexual predators would knock out a man's teeth so they couldn't bite down when forced to perform oral sex.

*TicToc's plan to sabotage the prosecution's case has got to work—and soon! But we need that bond posted **now!*** her mind screamed. To hell with safety—dismissing TicToc's concern about police retaliation. Every moment counted, and failure wasn't an option.

Even if this new judge reinstated the attempted murder charges and increased Tyrene's bond, TicToc had assured her that she could post a $750,000 cash bond if necessary, though she'd need 24 hours to arrange payment.

Years ago, she'd been shackled in this very courthouse, facing potential ruin and the loss of her family if convicted. Now, her only child was about to stand in the same courtroom, confronting a similar fate. The weight of the past pressed upon her as she watched history threaten to repeat itself.

Patricia entered the courtroom through the double doors, stopping abruptly in the aisle, stunned. A wave of fear washed over her as her eyes fell on her diminutive teenage son sitting among a group of men in the overcrowded jury box. Their expressions were a chaotic mix—some vacant, some menacing, others angry, and some utterly indifferent. Court staff and attorneys moved briskly, seemingly oblivious to the gravity of the inmates' situation—shuffling paperwork and preparing their submissions for the court.

Tyrene was struggling to maintain his composure–his posture stiff, his face tense–but she knew he was terrified. He was just a boy—small, vulnerable, and surrounded by obvious repeat offenders: hardened criminals with menacing faces and cold, indifferent eyes. The thought that she'd failed him tormented her. She'd known what awaited him at his first appearance in adult district court, but she allowed herself to believe that the prosecution would never charge a boy as an adult—not for a school fight.

When Tyrene saw her, he bolted out of his seat. He caught her eye, and he silently mouthed *"Mom."* The deputies immediately intervened, sternly commanding him to remain seated until his case was called.

Patricia scanned the room. It felt hollow and lifeless—devoid of the familiar hum of family, relatives, and friends who usually filled juvenile court. The sparse attendance left many rows of benches empty.

Just as she had observed years ago, most of the inmates were brown or Black—a stark reminder of the systemic inequalities that continue to plague the justice system.

She started down the aisle toward the wooden railing near the counsel table to sit closer to her son but changed her mind and chose a seat near the door instead—to keep watch for Tyrene's new attorney. TicToc said she had spoken to him the day before Tyrene's first appearance in juvenile court.

As usual, Patricia asked for a physical description of the man. As usual, TicToc didn't give one.

"Like Carl, you'll definitely know him when you see him," TicToc said. Besides, you won't find many Black attorneys gracing the halls of justice. And he already knows what you look like. I sent your picture and your son's to his cell phone the same night I spoke to him."

The clerk's voice suddenly filled the room, commanding, "All rise! The Honorable Judge Thadeus R. Davidson presiding."

The orange mass of bodies rose unevenly–one here, another there—until they were all finally standing. The judge entered the courtroom with a stern expression, barely acknowledging their presence as he impatiently waved his hand for them to sit. He ignored the few people who stood in the gallery.

"Madam Clerk, who's up to bat?" he asked gruffly.

Your Honor," she said, holding up a file with a bright red "Priority" sticker. "I had a request to call a case out of order because the senior assistant deputy DA appearing this morning is pressed for time and needs to get to a meeting."

"Joe Morton! Is he here?" the judge asked, surprise in his voice.

“Right here, Judge,” a deep, resonant voice replied. “I was just talking to the new DAs assigned to your courtroom. I’m advising them on how you like your courtroom run and offering them some useful tips that might save their legal lives.”

The judge‘s gaze drifted to the back of his courtroom, where Morton stood surrounded by a cluster of young wide-eyed female attorneys.

The judge appreciated Morton’s efficiency—he rarely went to trial, preferring to resolve cases through plea bargains. On the rare occasion he did, it was only high-profile cases that captured the media’s attention. The judge expected as much; he knew Morton had political ambitions.

Judge Davidson chuckled. “You make sure you get them in line. I don’t like upstarts who think they know what they're doing, but don’t.”

Morton emerged from the group, exuding the confidence of a man in complete control. He’d developed a slight paunch over the years, though traces of his former quarterback’s build were still evident. Despite his weight gain, the judge noticed that a few young female lawyers blushed in his presence.

Morton had mastered the art of using his charisma and commanding presence to his advantage. He wielded his charm like a weapon, effortlessly swaying jurors and even earning the occasional envious glance from male colleagues as he worked his magic in the courtroom.

“Mr. Morton, what case do you want called?” Judge Davidson asked affably. “As you can see, I’ve got a heavy docket this morning. If you want to be heard, you’d better do it damn quick.”

With a crowd of impressionable new hires behind him and obviously in the court’s good graces, Morton thought, *Showtime.*

“If you don’t mind, Madam Clerk,” Morton said smiling, “I’ll do the honors.” He retrieved the file from the court and announced, like a circus ringmaster, “People versus Tyrene Horn, case number BC10880.”

Hearing her son’s name, Patricia jolted upright. Her eyes darted toward the door, frantically searching for the attorney TicToc had assured her would arrive within five minutes.

She restrained herself from calling out, "*Wait! Not yet! My son's lawyer isn't here!*" Instinctively, she calmed herself, fearful of how she might be perceived if she disrupted the proceedings. More importantly, she had to remain calm for Tyrene's sake.

Tyrene and his mother rose and approached the podium from different areas of the room, their movements nearly in sync—an unspoken testament to their deep bond.

Morton noted their familial resemblance and watched them closely, his eyes scanning for any evidence of weakness he could exploit at trial. He assumed she would serve as a character witness—testifying to her son's peaceful nature, portraying him as a gentle soul who would never resort to violence without provocation.

Morton suppressed a smile. He could shred her testimony like tissue paper, twisting her maternal love and their mother-son relationship to discredit her. He would conclude his cross-examination with a crippling question, "Would you lie to protect your son?" The question always seemed to unravel a parent on the witness stand—no matter how firmly they denied it, especially if their child was facing prison.

Judge Davidson appeared visibly irritated as he studied the Black woman briskly walking toward the young defendant. He shouted sternly to her before she could reach the podium, "Miss, you need to take your seat in the back! You're not permitted to be up here with the attorneys!"

Patricia stopped abruptly.

She said, "Your Honor! Forgive me, but that's my son. He's just a boy. I believe the law requires a parent to be present when the child is a minor."

"Miss! You're not presuming to educate me about the law, are you?" the judge spat. "You're not even an attorney. Did you do some kind of legal search on Google?"

Joe Morton's gaze lingered on Patricia, his eyes sharp, weighing her every gesture. Would she react in anger? Would she cave? Would she become defiant? This was a prime opportunity to gauge the kind of witness she'd be before a jury.

Tyrene's anxious eyes darted to his mother, who met his gaze with unwavering calm. Her expression was unreadable, save for the faintest wink—so subtle it could have been dismissed as a nervous tic. Tyrene pressed his lips together to suppress a smile, but Morton, ever observant, smiled as he caught the silent exchange between mother and son.

The seasoned trial attorney filed away several mental notes: *Very close relationship, a 'me and you against the world' attitude,* and *'this ain't my first rodeo'.*

Patricia spoke in a conciliatory tone, her voice even and subdued. "I apologize, Your Honor. I meant no disrespect. An attorney explained to me that a parent must personally appear with her minor child or be held in contempt of court. I want to be clear that I did not learn this information from the internet."

She quickly added, "Please know, Your Honor, that my son has never been in trouble. And he's an honor student."

Morton's eyes remained fixed on her. He observed how she'd folded one hand into the other; her posture was relaxed, and her hands rested calmly at her waist. Her body language was non-threatening; her tone, dutifully solicitous; and her expression, quietly submissive.

Morton sensed the judge starting to relax. He walked over to her and extended his hand. "Ms. Horn, I presume. My name is Joe Morton. I'm a senior district attorney assigned to the case."

She ignored him, leaving his hand dangling awkwardly in space. He quickly withdrew it with a tight smile and made another mental note—*rude Black bitch.* She nearly—but not completely—masked the burning contempt she held for him—if not him personally, then for his office in general and his position in particular.

"Young lady," the judge roared, his voice echoing through the courtroom, "We do not consider your son a minor on this floor. I don't care if he's going to be a valedictorian. He's an adult in my courtroom."

"Yes, Your Honor," she replied, her voice soft. "I'm doing my best to adjust to that reality, but it's very hard." Her facial expression shifted to that of a vulnerable, frightened woman and deeply concerned mother. Even the judge began to soften.

"Goddamn," Morton muttered under his breath. He thought, *She's a fucking actress, too!*

"Well, Miss," the judge said, his tone measured but still with an edge of authority, "your son is here for his first advisement. That means the authorities file charges, inform him of his rights, and argue bond."

Turning toward Morton, the judge chided, "Did you folks run out of serious cases to try? What's this kid doing in my division?"

"Judge, Tyrene Horn appears before you on serious, multiple felony charges," Morton explained. "He's being charged with attempted second-degree murder, assault with a deadly weapon, menacing, and..."

Before Morton could finish his recitation of charges, a voice boomed from the back of the courtroom.

"Excuse me your honor!"

All heads turned, as the judge reared up to see who had interrupted his court proceedings.

A Black man, impeccably dressed in a bespoke suit, strode confidently down the aisle. In one hand, he carried a luxurious leather monogrammed briefcase, in the other, a neatly organized file. His age was difficult to determine. His movement radiated authority, each practiced gesture reflecting years spent in courtrooms and the halls of justice.

The judge leaned forward with unabashed curiosity, scrutinizing the stranger. He noted the man's athletic build, recognizing him as someone of stature and prestige, despite his being Black. The deputies exchanged glances, silently questioning if anyone recognized him. Several young female DAs in the gallery whispered and stared.

He strode toward the podium with notable confidence, unfazed by the curious glances that followed him. He smiled, then nodded at Patricia. Looking at Tyrene's legal savior Patricia was struck by his impressive demeanor and physicality–his barrel chest and broad shoulders. His tight, natural curls were styled like a regal crown, framing piercing eyes that emanated intelligence and strength.

"Ms. Horn. Tyrene. Please take a seat at the table," he said, his voice melodious and rich. As they moved forward, he turned to the judge.

"Judge Davidson, my name is Clayton Marshall, attorney registration number 14578. I am orally entering my appearance on behalf of Tyrene Horn. Please excuse my tardy arrival. I came directly from the airport. My flight from Paris was delayed."

Marshall eyed Morton cautiously, uncertain of what to expect. Their falling out nearly twenty years earlier still left bitter feelings between them.

"Well, Clayton. It's been a while," Morton said, his smirk thick with disdain.

"I don't tolerate such informality in my courtroom, Mr. Morton. You, of all people, should know better," Judge Davidson said sternly.

"Sorry, Judge. I know Mr. Marshall—or rather, I should say I *knew* Mr. Marshall. It's been nearly twenty years since I've seen him. I've followed his impressive accomplishments in the National Law Journal. We played on the same college football team a lifetime ago."

Acknowledging the prosecutor with a curt nod, Marshall responded, "Joe." Catching his mistake, he immediately corrected himself. "Sorry, Your Honor. I mean, Mr. Morton."

With deliberate indifference, Morton turned his back to Marshall to face the judge, "May I continue, Your Honor?"

Judge Davidson nodded, only half-attentive, still intrigued by the Black attorney—*Was he really mentioned in the National Law Journal?*

"As I was saying, judge, after reviewing the aggravating facts of this case and screening it with my deputies, I decided to transfer the case to adult court." He paused briefly, his upper lip curling into a sneer as he glanced at Marshall, then quickly shifted his focus back to the judge.

"We're requesting an additional forty-eight hours to file more charges. Just so you know, judge, we do have a complaint prepared for the attempted murder and assault charges, which I can give to counsel now. However, it's come to my attention that there may be additional charges involving a separate female victim."

"What are these other charges, Counsel?" Judge Davidson asked, his voice sharp with curiosity.

"I just spoke to an Officer Quisling late last night. He's an investigator on the case who advised me Mr. Horn may have committed criminal offenses against the victim's girlfriend. Officer Quisling is in the process of completing his investigation, but we anticipate filing kidnapping, attempted rape, and perhaps other related sexual assault charges."

A sharp gasp escaped Patricia's lips. Tyrene stared slack-jawed at the scene unfolding before him, his head shaking frantically in silent denial. Marshall maintained a poker face and reached over to squeeze Tyrene's shoulder.

Morton barely held back a chuckle, his expression carefully neutral. *What was the quote?* he thought. *Revenge is a dish best served cold. Well, it has been 20 fucking years, and now is better than ever.*

Morton placed copies of the criminal complaint involving the victim, Wally Kensington, and the probable cause statement for the female victim on the podium in front of Marshall. He handed the original copies to the clerk, who gave them to Judge Davidson.

Davidson paused to read the probable cause statement and complaint. Clucking sounds could be heard as he read. After reviewing the allegations in the arrest warrant, his eyes swept over Tyrene, with unmistakable disgust.

"Forty-eight hours for the other charges?" he asked, his tone clipped.

"Yes, sir," Morton replied, dutifully.

"Excuse me, Your Honor," Marshall interjected, "but I categorically object to granting the DA more time to file additional charges. Under the rules of criminal procedure, the filing should occur no later than today. He can always file an amended complaint. More importantly, I'm requesting that these restraints be removed from my client."

Marshall paused, studying the judge's reaction. Judge Davidson, renowned for his old-school cantankerous demeanor, was often regarded as a loose cannon by litigants.

Marshall added, "Moreover, Your Honor, I'll be asking this court to determine whether this case should be returned to juvenile court under the newly enacted law—one I trust the court is well acquainted."

The judge scoffed. "Well, the necessity of restraints is determined by court security, not me. I *am* granting the DA more time, Counsel. The boy is in district court now, not juvenile court. Mr. Morton has already prepared the complaint involving the charges for the male victim. Waiting to receive the charges on the female won't make much difference. We can set a preliminary hearing today so your client won't be prejudiced. You just need to waive an advisement of the charges and his rights. Besides, you still need to file a written motion opposing the transfer to adult court."

Sensing he was in a no-win situation, Marshall said, "Well, I would like to address the issue of bond."

Without consulting the DA—a clear deviation from standard procedure—Judge Davidson snapped, "I'm not setting any bond at this time, Counsel. Your client is dangerous. Based upon what I have read, what has been filed, what is anticipated to be filed, and the possibility that your client may have sexually assaulted multiple victims, community safety demands that there be a no-bond hold in this case."

"What, Judge?" Marshall exclaimed, his voice filled with astonishment. "The prosecutor only mentioned one female. Where did you get multiple sexual assault victims?"

Patricia was shocked. TicToc assured her that she could cover a $750,000 cash bond. Now, it was clear that even $10 million dollars in cash meant nothing if the judge refused to set bond. She raised her head, lifted her chin high, and placed a firm hand on her son's arm.

If the Judge Davidson had glanced her way, he would have flinched at the rage burning in her eyes. She was keenly aware of the judge's arrogance and his troubling approach to the law: *I'll do anything I damn well please because I wear the black robe. B*ut she decided to challenge him anyway.

"My son will not get justice here. I can see that now." Patricia declared, her voice steady, but bristling with anger. "This is a kangaroo court!"

Judge Davidson recoiled violently, his head snapping back as if he had been slapped. "Hold your tongue, young lady! You don't have a right to speak unless I give you permission!" he barked.

Patricia stood up, her posture rigid and indomitable. Her voice clear and strong, "You're supposed to be fair, but you've unlawfully denied my son bond, driven by emotion and passion instead of logic and reason, swayed by knee-jerk reactions to the charges rather than a reasoned application of the law."

Audible gasps rippled through the audience.

Judge Davidson was stunned. No one had ever spoken to him with such disrespect, let alone a Black person. He began yelling, his face red with fury. "I told you to be silent! You need to be silent!" he fumed. "One more word out of you," he stammered, "and.. and… and I'll hold you in contempt." The deputy sheriffs stiffened, their muscles taut, poised to spring into action.

Patricia stood eerily still, unwilling to give the deputies justification for intervening—but she wouldn't comply with the order to be silent, not until she'd fully articulated her grievance.

She glanced at Marshall, whose eyes flashed a warning, but she raised her hand—signaling him not to interrupt. She felt Tyrene tug sharply on her arm, but she didn't falter—she wasn't finished.

"My son didn't kill anyone. Killers don't get bonds," she said, eyes smoldering with contempt.

"I'm warning you, young lady!" Judge Davidson bellowed, his voice rising to a shrill cry. "Do you want to go to jail?"

Tyrene pulled harder on his mother's arm, trying to drag her back into the chair, but she ignored him.

"Wearing that robe only means that people get to call you judge. You're not a judge. You're a laughable caricature of a third-world bully!"

Judge Davidson's face drained of color, turning ghostly white. He opened his mouth to speak, but no words came–only incoherent sputtering. He lurched to his feet, his voice rising to scream. "Arrest that Black bitch!"

Patricia sneered, her voice smoldering with rage. "Your robe is the wrong color, Davidson. It should be white...." She paused, her eyes narrowing as she added "...with a hood."

Before the deputies could seize her, she leaned toward Tyrene again, whispering. "Be strong, Little Man Dude."

A moment later the deputies seized her, nearly lifting her off the floor as they dragged her out of the courtroom. A wave of muffled laughter spread through the few spectators seated in the back of the gallery. The prisoners remained deadly quiet, fearing the judge's wrath.

Marshall turned to address the court. "Your Honor," he began, his tone measured, but firm, "given your unfortunate characterization of my client's mother and your clear expression of racial bias, with all due respect, sir, I can't see how you can ethically continue to preside over this case."

The judge slumped into his chair, looking emotionally spent. His eyes were fixed ahead, his thoughts swirling as he tried to make sense of what had just happened.

"What did you say, counsel?" His voice was faint, almost pleading. What are you suggesting?" He seemed confused.

"Your Honor, you called my client's mother a 'Black bitch'. As you can see, my client happens to be Black, as well. I doubt there's an appellant court in this country that wouldn't describe your comment as racially motivated, biased, and unprofessional."

Attempting to steady himself, the judge countered "I didn't call her a bitch." He began to fumble for words. "I called her ... I called her ... I called her a witch. Yes. That's what I called her—a witch. I called her a witch," he repeated the words as if trying to convince himself.

Morton chimed in, his tone smug, "That's what I heard, Mr. Marshall. The judge called her a witch." The judge shot Morton a look of gratitude, his relief palpable.

Marshall gritted his teeth and glared at Morton, his voice low but razor-sharp. "Even if we entertain the idea that he said 'witch,' he specifically called her a *Black* witch. That distinction carries undeniable racial connotations."

"No," the judge said sharply. "I strongly disagree. Using the word 'Black' is merely descriptive of her race. If I had called her a 'white witch,' that description would have been inaccurate. Using 'Black' in this context, sir, is not racist," Judge Davidson declared, his voice laced with indignation, "And I take umbrage–great offense–at the suggestion that I am a racist." He concluded with a self-righteous huff.

"I can get a transcript of the record, Your Honor," Marshall said firmly. "The record will clearly show that you referred to her as a 'Black bitch.' The record will speak for itself."

By the clerk's station, Gladys, his long-time employee and trusted assistant, stood to the side of the judge's bench. Clearing her voice, she spoke up, a feigned tone of alarm.

"Judge! I apologize. I just realized that I didn't turn the recorder on this morning. She shrugged. "We don't have a record of anything said."

The judge eagerly seized this unexpected gift from his clerk of 15 years.

"Was it off all morning?" he asked, simulating concern.

"Yes, sir. I'm so sorry," she replied sheepishly. She avoided Marshall's burning glare, focusing on the judge, who appeared to be regaining his composure.

"Don't worry about it, Gladys. These things happen, and nothing of import was said." Color was gradually returning to his face.

Marshall closed his eyes and took a long, deep breath. It felt as though he'd stepped into a Jim Crow time warp. It had been a long time since he'd had to deal with such blatant and unapologetic bigotry. He was used to political cover-ups, criminal frames, police corruption, and double-dealing. Still, he'd never witnessed such egregiously offensive behavior by a judicial officer in open court, especially in front of witnesses.

Lies and more lies, he lamented to himself silently. *From public officials who are supposed to demonstrate character, integrity, and honesty.*

Marshall finally said, "Excuse me, judge. I need a moment to collect my thoughts." Although visibly irked, Marshall maintained a calm composure.

As he considered the legal procedure necessary to have the judge removed from the case, Gladys approached the bench with a fresh cup of water. The judge nodded in thanks and took a gulp.

The words "Black bitch" continued to reverberate in Marshall's mind. As far as he was concerned, Judge Davidson might as well have called Ms. Horn a nigger.

From the judge's perspective he'd merely made an unfortunate comment in the heat of the moment, triggered by what he saw as an inexcusable provocation from a grossly disrespectful woman who happened to be Black.

Morton broke the awkward silence. "Judge, why don't you call another case so I don't hold up your docket. I need to confer with Mr. Marshall about this case."

The judge quickly agreed, grateful for the opportunity to be rescued from his embarrassing faux pas.

Had Judge Davidson noticed Tyrene's malevolent stare, he might've held him in contempt too—a clear reflection of his zero-tolerance policy for disrespect. The judge had no patience for defiance of any kind in his courtroom, and his biases toward Tyrene would only amplify any punishment imposed.

To him, Tyrene personified the ghetto trash that he had to deal with: a hip-hop-loving, pot-smoking gang member—probably the type who sagged his pants and wore his cap backward. Judge Davidson frowned at Tyrene's hair, which seemed to sprout in every direction like Buckwheat in *The Little Rascals* TV series. He wondered what kind of drugs he might be using.

The judge grimaced slightly as he instructed the sheriff to escort Tyrene back to his seat in the jury box.

Marshall gestured to Morton to meet him outside the courtroom. He exited first, while Morton lingered behind to speak with the three assistant district attorneys, who wore bemused smiles. As Marshall stepped into the hallway, he heard the judge calling another case.

Morton began speaking as soon as he walked through the doors. "I know what you are thinking, Clayton. If you can't get a transcript of the hearing, you can get affidavits from the people in the courtroom to prove that the judge allegedly said 'Black bitch.'"

"Go on," Marshall said sharply.

Morton glanced around to ensure their conversation remained private. Smirking, he moved closer to Marshall. "Who do you think you're going to get affidavits from? Those prisoners in there?" He chuckled derisively. "Do you think any of those sorry excuses for human beings in the jury box will risk signing an affidavit? They might have to appear in front of Judge Davidson for sentencing. And the same goes for those people in the audience. Either they're here because they've got a case, or they're here for someone who has a case."

Morton paused, studying Marshall's reaction as his words sank in. "No DA from my office will back you, and you can forget about that wimpy public defender. You think he'll risk his career for your client?"

"Why wouldn't he?" Marshall snapped.

"That kid, the public defender, is no different from anyone who wants to continue to practice law in this county. If he submits an affidavit suggesting that Judge Davidson is a racist, he'd be crazy to appear in front of him again. And the other judges in the building won't take too kindly toward a whistle blowing attorney, either." Morton cocked his head. "Denigrating the reputation of a highly respected jurist nearing retirement—what's the value in that?" he asked.

Marshall scowled. He thought, *Highly respected jurist, my ass.* Morton's arrogance was insufferable.

"And don't count on the deputies getting involved. They have a job to do, but it doesn't involve sticking their necks out for your client."

They stood locked in a glare, the air between them crackling with animosity. Marshall drew a slow breath, steadying himself. He needed Morton to meet with him tonight—especially after the no-bond hold. The meeting was imperative, but he had to retreat from their conflict without yielding an inch.

"My hope, Joe, is simple," Marshall said calmly. "I want my client to be treated fairly. Racial bias has no place in the administration of justice—"

Morton didn't allow him to finish, "Nobody promised your client a perfect trial—just a fair one," Morton retorted. "Twelve jurors will weigh the evidence, determine the credibility of the witnesses, and use their independent judgments to determine beyond a reasonable doubt whether your client is guilty of a crime."

He leaned forward, his voice low and deliberate. "If he's found guilty, he might be able to appeal to the United States Supreme Court," Morton declared. "That's as fair as it's gonna get."

It took all of his restraint not to smack the smug, self-righteous look off Morton's face.

"Tell me something I *don't* know, Joe. I've been practicing law longer than you," Marshall grumbled.

Morton's grin widened, triumphant. "Well! This is something you don't know, counselor," Morton crooned. He was nearly beaming. "Our renowned state-certified forensic lab will be checking your client's DNA on some of the rape victim's clothing."

Marshall frowned. "DNA evidence is a two-way street, slick. Nearly 575 wrongly convicted people have been exonerated based upon DNA evidence, and about 53 percent of those freed nationwide have been Black." Marshall paused. "You do remember the legal maxim that it's better to let ten guilty people go free than to convict one innocent person."

"Well, Clayton," Morton taunted, "I guess the system worked! All those so-called innocent people, even the *Black* ones, were freed. Given the time period for the appeal process, maybe the court will exonerate your young Black client after serving a little time." He laughed. "I think prisoners are released after serving an average of 14 years, according to the Innocence Project." Morton chuckled, "Your client won't even be middle aged."

Marshall studied Morton before speaking. "You've got this all figured out, haven't you, Joe?"

"Yeah. I do. You don't get this far in your career without learning a thing or two," Morton said with a broad grin." He enjoyed verbally lashing his old college teammate. However, he was still concerned about the repercussions that Judge Davidson might face if his outburst became local news.

"You can get two affidavits filed in support of your motion to recuse Judge Davidson—one from your client and one from his mother—but they won't be credible given their connection to the case. However, if the press picks up this bogus 'race' thing, it would be like dropping a piglet in a shoal of piranhas."

Morton shrugged, "Particularly if his comment is blown out of proportion. It would be highly embarrassing to Judge Davidson. Besides, I like the old guy. He's been like a mentor to me. I don't want to see him hurt or humiliated. And I damn sure don't want an errant slip of the tongue to taint his reputation."

"Some slip," smirked Marshall.

"Don't get cute with me, Clayton. I *do* have an idea that might work for you and the judge."

"I'm listening," Marshall said, his voice tinged with skepticism. "It better be good."

Morton said,"If you agree to forget about any recusal motion, I think I can persuade the judge to release Ms. Horn."

Marshall narrowed his eyes. "She needs to be released immediately, and I want Davidson off this case."

Morton smiled. "That's a lot to ask, Counselor. Judge Davidson is a proud man."

"I don't give a damn how proud he is." Marshall shot back. "Get him off the case or win or lose, I'm filing that recusal motion based upon racial bias. And Joe..." Marshall paused, choking back his anger. He leaned in, voice low and cold. "Word *will* get to the press. I've learned a thing or two myself along the way." His glare was piercing. "Count on it."

Morton's eyes sparkled with amusement at Marshall's attempt to intimidate him. After all these years, having Marshall under his thumb was deeply satisfying.

"I'll see what I can do," Morton said, his tone conciliatory, but sarcastic. "Understand that I won't ask him to recuse himself. I will ask that he reassign the case, but that still won't be easy," he added, clearly enjoying the upper hand.

"Just make it happen, Joe," Marshall said sharply. "And one more thing."

Morton folded his arms. "You got all you gonna git, son."

"Relax, Joe. This ask is easy. I want to get together to talk about the case. Maybe over dinner tonight. I've gathered some solid evidence that will sink your case like the Titanic."

Morton raised an eyebrow. "Do you actually think you have something to help your boy?" he asked, cynicism evident in his tone. "I'm not offering him any deal unless he pleads guilty to everything. I do mean *every* felony count. If he does, I'll agree to remain silent at sentencing," Morton remarked dryly, his amusement obvious.

"That's a real gracious offer, Joe," Marshall said, his voice heavy with sarcasm. "I'll probably have to fight my client to keep him from taking it."

"Don't matter a whit to me, Clayton. I prefer to whip your ass in trial. I plan to send your client away until he's eligible for Social Security."

Marshall ignored his boast. "Dinner tonight, about 7 p.m. That steakhouse on 14th and Broadmore? Jake's Steakhouse. Is it still there?"

Morton eyed Marshall, weighing the offer. The "solid" evidence that Marshall claimed to have magically acquired piqued his interest.

After mulling the offer over, Morton relented. "The steakhouse is still there, but management has changed over the years. It still has the reputation for the best steaks around. Dinner! Why not? We can catch up on old times. That was where we held our victory dinner before we left to celebrate at coach's house. Remember?"

Morton's expression darkened momentarily at the mention of coach's house. Marshall deliberately steered clear of discussing their victory celebration. He sensed that broaching that subject might jeopardize his dinner plan.

Marshall deftly switched subjects. "So, do we have an agreement about Ms. Horn's release and Davidson's recusal?"

Morton nodded. "Okay! Ms. Horn will be released when she apologizes profusely on the record in open court in front of the judge."

Marshall gave a barely perceptible head shake. He didn't like Morton when they'd played ball together, and time had failed to diminish that feeling.

"You know how this works, Clayton. No apology, no get-out-of-jail-free card."

Marshall hesitated. "If I can tell her he's off the case, she might be more inclined."

Morton crossed his arms again and leaned back. "Her call," he said. "Tell her that 'pride goeth before the fall.' She can put her son first or her ego. Makes no difference to me. If she agrees, she can deliver her apology at the close of the court's business today." He chuckled, adding, "That lady needs some jail time to remember her place."

"Her… *place*?" Marshall asked, a challenge in his voice. "You mean, some time to cool off."

"Whatever, Clayton," Morton snickered. "Just get it done if you want her out."

Marshall shrugged nonchalantly. "I'll see what I can do."

"As for Judge Davidson," Morton said, "I think I'll be able to help him see the light about turning the case over to another judge–but it's not going to be called a recusal. I repeat! It will be a reassignment. The case is going to be reassigned due to docket congestion. Understood?"

"I don't care what you call it, as long as he's off the case," Marshall said. "Now, let's go back in there and recall the Horn matter."

Marshall started toward the door but stopped. Eyeing Morton, he said," I'm particularly interested in the evidence your office has regarding this alleged sexual assault. Somehow, you managed to convert a garden-variety school fight to include charges of attempted rape and kidnapping."

Marshall added, his voice thick with distrust. "It's damn curious how the alleged victim's girlfriend suddenly remembers that her virtue was compromised. How convenient for your prosecution." Marshall huffed, his tone heavy with contempt. "Do you even have a name for this mystery girl?"

"Ain't nothing garden variety about this fight," snapped Morton. "Your client nearly chewed the boy's dick off. The damage might not have been so extensive, if he'd been wearing denim jeans or, at least, some shorts under those sweats. As for the girl, she's why the fight started in the first place. The victim didn't take it too kindly that your client took liberties with his girlfriend, so he did what any red-blooded American would do. He confronted your boy." Morton paused. "Her name is Allison Ruddick."

"Sounds like your vic started the fight." Marshall said, his tone confident.

"Nope. You're mistaken," Morton crowed. "The victim was upset about what your boy did to his girlfriend, but your client threw the first punch."

"You sure about that, Joe?"

"I'll have three witnesses testify to that point," Morton insisted. "The kid has a lot of friends—good, loyal friends. And, you know, most teenagers will go along to get along. Peer approval. Peer acceptance and all that good shit."

Morton was starting to gloat. "Besides, you are at a bit of a disadvantage, aren't you, Clayton? I was informed that your client suffers from traumatic mutism." Morton laughed, his tone both mocking and patronizing. "Even with your supposedly vaunted legal prowess, it's going to be a stretch to argue self-defense when your client can't speak."

"The fat lady hasn't even begun to sing yet, Morton," Marshall said flatly. "I've got a surprise for your arrogant ass. Wait until dinner tonight."

Morton deliberately sauntered ahead of Marshall, who took a deep breath and reminded himself to remain cool. As he entered, Marshall's gaze shifted to the jury box, where Tyrene sat rigid among the dull mass of imprisoned men. Marshall stopped in the middle of the aisle, made a fist with his right hand, and struck his chest twice. Tyrene acknowledged the gesture by giving a slow, deliberate nod.

When a lull occurred in the cattle call of cases, Morton interjected, "Judge, can we recall the Horn case now? Defense counsel has a demanding schedule," Morton remarked, his tone condescending.

Judge Davidson's expression hardened as his gaze shifted to the Black attorney standing before him. He thought, *Affirmative action was probably the only way you got admitted into law school.*

Davidson struggled to decipher Marshall's demeanor. It was either exaggerated confidence or hidden contempt for him. Uncertain, but suspicious, he tightened his grip on the file.

He skimmed it slowly, occasionally glancing up to study the attorney— searching for any hint of disrespect he could use to his advantage. He barely suppressed a smile at the thought of throwing the attorney in jail for contempt.

Folks in the courthouse would talk about it for years, he mused. Attorneys, clerks, and deputies would gossip about how he had jailed two Black people in a single day–a Black attorney and the defendant's Black mother.

Refusing to call the case himself, Davidson handed the file to his clerk. "You call it, Madam Clerk," he said dismissively.

Tyrene heard his name echo through the courtroom, the sound strange and foreign to his ears. Carefully stepping over the feet of other defendants, his cuffs and chains chattered as he shuffled his way down from the jury box toward Marshall who smiled softly at him.

After hearing charges of rape and kidnapping, the courtroom had dissolved into a dizzying blur to him—the voices of the judge and attorneys receding into a distant hum. For the first time since discovering Duke's body, he longed to hear his own voice–to scream, to protest, to break the suffocating silence.

His mind drifted to the horrors of the antebellum South. *Was he being treated like a modern-day slave?* He winced at the bitter sorrow that marked a slave's life. He thought:

Enslaved people were treated like livestock—chattel property to be bought, branded, bartered, bred, and sold—whipped until broken, even killed for refusing to bend to an owner's will. But their humanity meant nothing to the enslavers—only grueling, backbreaking, soul-crushing labor from "can't see to can't see."

And yet, Tyrene thought, Th*ey were human beings—flesh, blood, and bone who laughed, prayed, dreamed, created, sang, mourned, and loved—who had no rights, who had no voice—only an unshakable faith that one day, somehow, they would be free:*

Free from the chains.

Free from the whip.

Free from the noose.

Free from terror.

Free.

At least he was in a courtroom, where the law was supposed to protect him. At least he had a lawyer. At least, he had a chance to be free.

Still, Tyrene was gripped by a profound sense of dread. His mother had been jailed for daring to confront the judge who controlled his freedom—a man who was, at least, a bigot; at worst, an outright racist who refused to set a bond, imprisoning him. The district attorney had advised the court of his decision to transfer his case to adult court which meant he would be housed in county jail, where accused rapists, pedophiles, and murderers were held. And now this insane accusation about a sexual assault. What kind of nightmare had swallowed his world?

He remembered an expression used by his literature teacher to describe a dark, surreal, nightmare—*Kafkaesque*!

This is crazy, Tyrene thought, barely managing to hold back tears.

Little Man Dude! He heard his nickname. Startled, he looked around.

He felt a hand on his shoulder—large and comforting. He saw his brother's smile and the kindness in his eyes.

A voice whispered, *Never forget who you are!*

He straightened up, pulled his shoulders back, and lifted his chin. Setting his jaw, he heard the echo of his mother's words: *Be strong!*

13

The Phantoms of Our Past

Joe Morton descended the cantilevered staircase, admiring the decorative prints of artists from the French Romantic Period. He remembered a few names of famous French painters from college but couldn't connect any painter with the works tastefully displayed on the walls.

Pushing through the heavy mahogany doors that stretched toward a vaulted ceiling, Morton immediately felt its quiet sense of restrained elegance. The new owners had kept the name of the landmark restaurant, but its style and atmosphere were far different from the restaurant that had hosted his football team championship dinner nearly twenty years ago.

It was his senior year. He'd been the quarterback who sealed the victory by throwing a 60-yard Hail Mary in the final seconds of the fourth quarter with no timeouts left to spare. The pass, nearly intercepted by the MVP safety of the reigning championship team, was tipped high and wide, falling perfectly into the outstretched arms of his diving receiver, who tumbled over the goal line. The stadium erupted in deafening pandemonium. Despite being a 10-point underdog, his team had snatched victory, as the proverbial expression goes, from the jaws of defeat.

Young Morton stood ecstatic, incredulous, staring at the goal line where his teammate had fallen. There, lying on his back with the football held high in his hand was number 86—Clayton Marshall, his go-to wide receiver. Almost instantly, a mob of jubilant spectators stormed the field, screaming as they completely engulfed Marshall on the ground, while others rushed to the goalposts, tearing them down for souvenirs.

Morton surveyed the dining room. The physical interior of the room had changed—but the memory of that triumphant night, and what followed, remained brutally vivid. He shook his head sharply, as if trying to dislodge the nagging, uncomfortable memories of the after-party celebration.

Why hadn't he simply made a brief appearance at the party at his coach's house like Sally, his girlfriend, had suggested?

They could have spent a romantic evening at her place, if he'd just listened to her. He'd adored her, and she loved him. He'd never doubted they'd marry after graduation.

Returning to this restaurant, a place that dredged up a punishing memory that had haunted him for decades, was ill advised. Tonight, he was going to break bread with number 86, the man who was the source of all his pain, suffering, heartache, and resentment.

He chuckled ruefully. *If God lacks a sense of humor, He certainly has a keen sense of irony.*

Standing in front of the maître d's stand, Morton, absorbed in his thoughts and unaware of the attentive dining room attendant, struggled to pull himself out of his reverie.

"Excuse me, sir. Are you alright?" asked the well-dressed, silver-haired man behind the stand.

"I've been trying to get your attention for a while, but you seemed lost in thought. I assume you're looking for a table." The maitre d' paused. "Or, perhaps, a booth? Maybe you'd prefer a seat at the bar?" He flashed a smile, revealing even, white, polished teeth, obviously dentures.

Shaken from his reverie, Morton smiled. "Sorry. I was thinking about something that happened a long time ago."

"Ah, yes," the maître d' said knowingly. "The past. It can, unfortunately, be as much with you as the present. It's always wise to make peace with one's past, if possible. Too often, we find ourselves at war with the phantoms of our past in one form or another."

The maître d', who prided himself on being a keen observer of life, fell silent. He noticed the man's posture stiffen and his expression darkened. Intuitively, he realized he'd said too much—a fault that hadn't gone unnoticed by restaurant management. The maître d's apology was quick and profuse.

"Forgive me, sir. I meant no harm. You came here for an enjoyable evening, not to listen to the babbling of an old man."

Morton's inner turmoil, stirred by the maître d's words, was discernible but fleeting. It was like being caught off-guard by an opponent in court and having to adjust quickly to regain one's balance.

"Not to worry," Morton replied casually. "I'm here for dinner, though I doubt it will be a relaxing evening. It's a working dinner. I'm expecting someone. I'm surprised he's not here." Morton smiled at the maitre d', easing the man's discomfort. He added, with a soft chuckle, "But my guest has had a very challenging day."

"What's his name, sir? Once we have you comfortably seated, I'll keep an eye out for him."

"That's very kind of you. His name is Clayton Marshall."

The maître d' retrieved a pen from his breast pocket and jotted down the name. He smiled at Morton and gestured grandly with his arm as if to beckon someone.

Morton walked a short distance from the host stand to get a better view of the dining room. He saw nothing in the room that reminded him of that chaotic, unforgettable night. The energy of that evening had been electrifying—fans clamoring for autographs, teammates backslapping and embracing one another, snapshots and toasts abounding, and school football fight songs belted out with raucous abandonment. Morton had felt on top of the world, and Sally had been there to share it all with him.

With his parents' blessing, Morton had purchased an engagement ring a month before the game, planning to propose to Sally—but only if his team was victorious. He'd planned to ask her after the party, when they could be alone and savor the moment in complete privacy. But that precious opportunity had been stolen from him.

Morton closed his eyes and inhaled sharply. He felt vulnerable. *Would he lose control when Marshall arrived? Could he keep his phantoms at bay?*

Then, without warning, the memory at the coach's house assaulted him. His sense of vulnerability instantly dissolved into a ball of white-hot anger. He felt his body expanding, his suit jacket now uncomfortably tight. He was surprised to find his hands clenched into hard, angry fists. He murmured self-reassurances, trying to get his body to relax.

This is what happens when you don't make peace with the past, Morton said to himself. *One ugly memory leads to another, and then the memories grow wings.*

"Excuse me, sir. I didn't get your name," the maître d' said, interrupting Morton's thoughts.

Morton casually spoke his name over his shoulder, his attention drawn to the faces of several diners who appeared to be turning slowly in his direction.

Some stole quick glances, though not at him; others were bold and unabashed, openly staring at someone behind him.

Morton sensed her presence before he saw her. The scent of her perfume wafted toward him, soft and enveloping, like milky clouds drifting across a moonlit sky. As he turned, eyes around the room seemed to follow. But his froze when they met hers—two captivating pools of night shimmering with impish desire.

"Ah, Jetta. You're here!" sang the maître d'. The elderly man looked at her like a moonstruck adolescent. He reached out to gently touch her shoulder.

Morton, like most men, had only seen extraordinarily beautiful women in glamour magazines or movies. Occasionally, while shopping with his wife at the supermarket, he'd pick up a magazine and flip through the glossy pages, admiring the allure of petulant smiles and come-hither looks.

However, he'd never been physically in the presence of a face that could launch a thousand ships. She took his breath away. He felt uncomfortably self-conscious in the presence of this goddess and was completely at a loss for words.

She smiled at him, fully aware of the profound effect she had created.

"Good evening, sir. My name is Jetta. I'll show you to your table." Her voice was sweet and light as acacia honey.

"A booth, please, Jetta. Mr. Morton has a business meeting tonight and may require a bit of privacy," the maître d' said, his hand still resting lightly on her shoulder.

"Of course, sir," she acknowledged with a nod. "If you would follow me, Mr. Morton."

To his surprise, she took Morton gently by the arm to guide him toward the booth. Instead of holding his arm at the elbow, she entwined her arm under his, gently clasping his wrist with her hand. He felt the warmth of her body and the full, soft curve of the side of her breast against him.

Morton still hadn't spoken a word. He listened to her chat about the restaurant and her employment, mentioning how lucky she was to find work so quickly after moving to the state just a few days ago.

Finally, after clearing his voice, he managed to speak. "Well, all I can say is that I'm certainly glad to be at Jake's Steakhouse tonight."

Jetta turned toward him with a questioning look on her face. After satisfying herself that his tone was politely flirtatious, she smiled and pulled his arm tighter against her. Morton felt a hot sensation shoot straight up his arm and down his body.

"Well, I'm glad you came here this evening, too, sir," she purred. "Your wish will be my command."

It was now Morton's turn to try to fathom what she meant. Was she flirting with him or just buttering him up for a big tip? Though she didn't need to hold his arm in this fashion, snug against her body, he certainly wasn't going to complain. This could be the last time that he'd ever be graced with such beauty, and he was going to enjoy every moment.

Captivated by her, Morton imagined Abyssinian royalty—like the sculpted images he'd seen once in National Geographic. Her forehead was high, framing a nearly perfect oval face. Wide, dark, cat-like eyes sat hypnotically above prominent cheekbones. Her long, narrow nose flared like a delicately shaped arrowhead, arching just above achingly full lips. She moved gracefully, her step sure and silent, like a jaguar. The rich, deep blackness of her smooth, unblemished skin made Morton appear sickly, anemic, and frail in comparison.

She guided him toward a booth with a leather-covered back. After releasing his arm, he slid across the seat and gave her an appreciative smile.

"Will you be my waitress?" he asked softly.

She hesitated before responding. Straightening to her full six-foot height in stiletto heels, she stood tall and elegant, her long svelte frame commanding attention. He couldn't help but notice the way her round, full breasts rose and strained against her white, starched shirt. He swallowed hard and looked away, embarrassed by his desire for her—determined to keep it hidden from her arresting gaze.

Leaning forward, she lowered herself slightly over the table. In a soft voice that had become unexpectedly sultry, she whispered, "You're not seated in my area, but I'm sure I can arrange to wait on you if you'd like."

He felt consumed by her gaze. Looking at her directly, careful to modulate any overt tone of impropriety, he said teasingly, "Remember, Jetta. My wish. Your command."

Her laughter was quick, easy, and spontaneous, like wind chimes in a soft summer breeze. "Would you like an aperitif or something a little stronger before ordering?"

Feeling more confident, he challenged her, "Surprise me."

She smiled and responded seductively, "I already have."

He sat back against the soft leather as she turned to walk toward the bar. He followed her body as she walked, admiring her full hips. Without warning, she stopped and turned to look back at him. She knew he'd be watching.

He inhaled sharply and began to fidget with the silverware. He accidentally knocked over his water glass. Fortunately, it was empty. He felt giddy. He tried to remember when he had felt this excited about a woman before.

Looking down at his worn, tarnished wedding ring, he thought of Sally—the girlfriend who'd become his wife—and how much he used to love her. She hadn't changed. If anything, she had become even more lovely. He didn't doubt her devotion. She had campaigned tirelessly for him when he ran for county district attorney, rallying her many friends to make phone calls, distribute leaflets, and go door-to-door. She even managed to secure media exposure for him. But none of it could counter his opponent's accusation that he was soft on crime. Despite her unflagging efforts to get him elected, it couldn't erase the past—or how deeply it still haunted him.

Morton looked up to see Jetta walking toward the table with his drink on the tray. He loved the way she moved, so relaxed and fluid. Maybe it was just the nature of youth. He realized he wasn't the only one in the room enthralled by her graceful, flowing movements. Nearby males continued to steal glances at her as she walked by. Women smirked or pretended to ignore her.

"Hey!" she said, placing his drink on the napkin. "I left you smiling, and now you've got a frown on your face. What's up?"

Morton explained. "Just a wasted trip down memory lane. But now that you are back, I can't help but smile."

"That's more like it. I like to keep my customers happy. Would you like a menu, or do you want to wait? Mr. Beaumont, the maître d', said you're expecting someone." She brushed back a strand of long dark hair that had fallen across her forehead, waiting for his answer.

"I'll wait," Morton said. "He should be here soon. You'll like him. Tall, dark, and handsome. He dresses well, too."

"Sounds attractive, but is he married?" she asked, eyes flitting to Morton's ring. He resisted the urge to drop his hand into his lap.

"Dunno. Don't think so. I believe he's a very available bachelor."

Jetta clicked her tongue, shaking her head with a playful smirk. "Nope. Not my type. Single men tend to cling."

She nibbled her lower lip, her eyes lifting to meet his. She added with a pout. "I'm a bad girl. Married men tend to fit my lifestyle. Besides," she added with a mischievous grin, "a fling with the right guy can be a lotta fun."

Morton's heart skipped. He felt a shiver run down his leg. Before he could respond, she pressed a slender finger to her lips. "Hush. We'll talk later. I'll be back."

She glided away as he stared, unabashedly at her voluptuous figure. He made no effort to hide his desire, half-hoping she'd turn around to catch him admiring her. Morton's imagination was starting to get the better of him. He needed to slow down. If there was any chance of being with Jetta, he didn't want to blow it.

She preferred married men, and he didn't have any qualms about betraying his wife tonight. Although he still loved Sally, the knowledge of what she'd done twenty years ago gave him precisely the excuse he needed to taste forbidden fruit.

He'd buried this secret far too long. The maître d' was right. It was time to confront the phantoms of the past. He took a sip from his drink, wincing slightly at the burning sensation in his throat.

Whether Marshall showed or not, this was shaping up to be a worthwhile evening.

Jetta! Sweet, intoxicating Jetta. Her fragrance lingered in the air like morning dew glistening on jasmine petals. He felt another shiver run down his leg. He wondered what distant land had created this exotic creature.

He looked at his watch, muttering, "What the hell is keeping Marshall?"

14

An Old Wound

Marshall couldn't think of a worse time to have a dinner meeting with Morton, but TicToc's plan left him no choice. He was physically drained from dealing with that pompous-ass judge and emotionally spent after meeting with Tyrene and his mother.

Although he felt confident he had a defensible case, trying to convince an irate judge to set bond posed difficulties he hadn't anticipated. TicToc did not like surprises. The no-bond hold complicated everything.

Judge Davidson refused to reconsider his ruling and wouldn't entertain the idea of allowing his client to post a $750,000 cash bond. Even the request to post a million-dollar cash bond was categorically denied. Davidson still smarted from Patricia Horn's scathing insults. He had no intention of freeing her son.

Marshall explained the tit-for-tat arrangement to Ms. Horn when he met with her that afternoon. The look on her face was a mixture of anger and pain.

"Can't do much good for my boy if I'm locked up in jail," Patricia sighed. "God is going to have to give me the determination of Fannie Lou Hamer to go back into the courtroom and kiss that white man's ass."

In court later that day, Marshall thought she might be tempted to insult Davidson again as she stood in front of him. But she played it smart. She apologized in a way that reminded him of Marc Antony's famous funeral speech in *Julius Caesar*. On the surface, her comments sounded like praise, but an astute observer would have heard something different. Marshall had also checked to make sure that the recorder was working before she addressed the court.

Patricia concluded her apology with high praise, "Judge Davidson, you are a virtuous and honorable man. No one would ever believe that you uttered the words 'Black bitch' in anger. People are proud to know that you serve our state with such intelligence, character, and dignity. Your integrity is impeccable, your unsullied reputation is well deserved, your judicial temperament enviable. You were born to wear a robe."

Davidson looked slightly befuddled but nodded. Marshall looked down at the floor and smiled. Morton was about to say something but bit his tongue. Patricia was released.

Heading into the restaurant, Marshall rubbed his forehead slowly with his fingertips, trying to dispel the stress from his long day. His clothes felt sticky. He wanted a shower, but there was no time. He was late enough as it was.

He pushed through the mahogany doors and walked straight to the host station where the silver-gray-haired maître d' stood. Marshall expected the usual courtesy of a personal acknowledgment, but none came. Marshall waited. The maître d' continued to look down, seemingly engrossed in studying seating charts. After waiting a few minutes, Marshall said, "Excuse me!"

The maître d' looked annoyed, gave Marshall a quick, perfunctory once-over, and returned to reading his charts.

Marshall shook his head. "In this day and age, I didn't think I'd need to check whether this restaurant was listed in the Green Book."

The maître d' put down his pen nonchalantly and studied Marshall from head to toe as though he were a vagrant who had wandered into the restaurant by mistake. Noting the expensive looking but slightly wrinkled suit, he crinkled his nose before finally speaking.

"What did you just say to me? The Green Book? Are you referring to *The Travel Guide for Negro Motorists*?" He huffed, "This restaurant has never been segregated—not for over fifty years anyway."

"I'm glad you can see me now. I thought I was invisible for a moment." Before the maître d' could respond, Marshall added brusquely,

"Table for two, please." He scanned the room for Morton, worried that he might have changed his mind.

"Do you have a reservation?" the maître d' asked curtly.

Marshall looked over the maître d's head into the room. "No, no reservation. But it looks like you have several free tables."

"Those tables are free because they're reserved. A pity you didn't think to call ahead."

Marshall sighed. He knew this game all too well. "When do you release a table?" He asked, his eyebrows furrowing in frustration.

"It depends. We've held tables as long as an hour or more for our favorite customers," he replied, smirking.

Marshall leaned over the podium, a prominent vein pulsating in his thick brown neck. The maître d' stepped back quickly. Catching himself, Marshall straightened up and reconsidered the impulsive act he'd nearly taken. He said, "I'll wait for my friend. We have a business meeting. He should be along shortly, and then we'll decide whether to stay or leave."

His curiosity piqued, the maître d' asked, "Are you Clayton Marshall?"

"Yes, I am." Marshall replied blandly.

"Well, why didn't you say so sooner? You're late! Mr. Morton has been waiting for you! He's seated in a booth just past the bar."

"Well, damn! Looks like I finally got my pass," Marshall muttered, irked that he had to deal with a pretentious bigot just to get a table. When the maître d' looked puzzled, Marshall turned and made his way to the booth.

Morton looked up from his menu and smiled, savoring the sight of Marshall's disheveled appearance.

"Well, Clayton! You look worn out. What a difference a day makes—from suave, debonair attorney to a whipped, tired dog." Morton laughed.

"Laugh now, Joe, but remember… every dog has his day." Marshall slid into the booth beside Morton and opened his attaché case to pull out his laptop.

"What's this?" Morton asked.

"It's footage from the school fight," Marshall answered. "If you watch the video, you'll see why this attempted murder charge is bogus," he said. "Just hit the play button, please."

Morton slid the menu aside and took a large sip from an almost empty glass. He eyed Marshall as he pulled the computer to him. Just as he was about to start the video, Jetta appeared. She looked at the tired-looking Black man in the wrinkled suit and said, "Looks like you could use a drink, sir."

Morton leaned toward Marshall, whispering, "Don't get any ideas."

Marshall looked up at the dazzling Black waitress. Her energy, beauty, and good nature almost caused him to forget how drained he was. It felt reassuring to see another person of color, particularly one who wasn't shackled.

"I'm Jetta." She said, her eyes sparkling.

"Make it whiskey, please, Jetta. Straight up, and make it stiff and big," Marshall said.

"Now, Clayton," Morton said, smiling at Jetta, "I thought you were saving yourself for me."

Marshall glared at Morton, dumbfounded that he'd made such a grossly inappropriate joke.

Jetta chuckled at Morton's words. "You're nasty!" She teased, amusement in her voice.

"I know," Morton replied. "It's my most endearing quality."

"I'll be back in a moment with your drinks," Jetta said, smiling.

"Jetta, you already brought me a drink," Morton said.

Jetta winked, "I know. The next one is on me."

Both men admired Jetta's figure as she walked away. "Looks like you two have become quite chummy," Marshall observed, surprise in his voice.

"Jealous, Clayton? Not every woman is awed by your charms," he snapped. His pale skin flushing slightly.

"What the hell is going on, Morton?" He wondered how much he'd had to drink. "Is there something you need to tell me?"

Morton wavered. He felt ambivalent. Had he lost his resolve—or maybe it was his courage? Arguments raged in his head. One voice protested, *Hell! It's been twenty years. Twenty fucking years! Why bring that night up now?* He took a hurried sip from his near-empty glass.

Jetta returned with a highball and an old-fashioned glass on a tray. Seeing Morton's dour expression, her happy, carefree manner gave way to one of concern. She set Marshall's drink down without looking at him, her eyes fixed on Morton.

She placed Morton's drink in front of him, deliberately brushing his hand. He didn't look at her. He didn't want her to see the rage building inside him or his vulnerability. She placed her hand on top of his.

"You alright, Mr. Morton?"

Drawing on his seasoned experience as a trial attorney, he reined in his feelings, placing a metal shutter over his flayed and confused emotions. He managed a smile. "I'm okay, Jetta! Thank you."

He looked down at her hand on his, stirred by the warmth and softness of her skin. He wondered if her entire body was as soft as her touch.

He handed her his empty glass and looked sternly at Marshall. "He and I are going to take a little trip down memory lane."

"You two have history?" She asked, looking quizzically from one to the other.

The casual familiarity with which she communicated with Morton intrigued Marshall. "Yes, Jetta," Morton said quietly. "We go way back. About as long as you've been alive."

"Maybe you should give us some time, Jetta. I'll let you know when we're ready," Marshall said.

She nodded. "I'll be around. Just let me know."

The table became uncomfortably quiet after Jetta left. The tension between them was thick.

Their relationship had never been close, even though they'd played football together for three years. They had spoken in the locker room and gotten together to study plays, but they hadn't really socialized until the victory dinner.

That night, they were the shining heroes of the season. The team—and the entire town—celebrated their remarkable win. The victory facilitated a superficial social interaction, at least for that unforgettable evening.

Morton pushed the laptop away and began to twirl his butter knife around in a circle on the tablecloth.

Marshall finally said, "Okay, Joe! Just spit it out! I hear that confession is good for the soul."

Morton laughed derisively. "Ain't my confession. Damn sure ain't my soul."

Marshall looked at him, bewildered. "What the hell are you talking about? I've never done anything to you."

"I know what you did that night at the coach's house." Morton said, not trying to mask the contempt in his voice.

Marshall leaned back in the booth, his eyes narrowing as he studied Morton's face. "Are you talking about Sally?"

Morton slammed his fist on the table, causing the silverware to clatter. "Don't play fucking games with me, Clayton. You know damn well it's about Sally."

Marshall suspected as much. "Jesus, Joe!" he said plaintively. "Be reasonable. That was how long ago? Twenty years? People were drunk! You know how things can get."

"Did you get so drunk that you forgot that she was my girl?" Several patrons glanced toward their table.

"Joe, look. I'm sorry." Marshall said, attempting to placate him.

"Liar! You're a goddamn liar!" Morton hissed.

Marshall held up both hands. "Honest, Joe. I'm not lying. She followed me into the bathroom, and before I knew it, we were kissing." Rage contorted Morton's face. "Let me explain, Joe. Please!" Marshall's words were slow and deliberate. "I was drunk. I only kissed her once. When I realized what I was doing, I stopped. I had to push her away."

Without warning, Morton threw a punch at Marshall. Marshall pulled back as the punch glanced off his chin. In the background, someone yelled for the maître d'. Morton reared back again to strike, but Marshall seized his wrist mid-air. A few patrons fled their tables, while most stared at them in shock.

Marshall was no longer apologetic. "If you want to fight about a kiss that happened twenty years ago, let's go outside."

Morton snatched his arm away, glaring at Marshall. Looking around, he realized he was causing a scene.

"A *kiss*?" he sneered in a hushed voice, "You fucked her! You fucked her right in the goddamn bathroom." His voice grew hoarse with emotion.

Wary of the restaurant patrons' growing interest, Marshall lowered his voice. "You're out of your goddamn mind. We never did anything like that!"

Morton shook his head, his voice trembling. "Stop lying to me. I heard you and Sally. I was playing cards with some of the guys. You were watching the game, sitting across the table from Sally. I saw you get up and leave. Before I knew it, I looked around, and Sally was gone. After the game finished, I searched for her on the first floor. Then, I went upstairs to see if she was in the bathroom.

"I went into a back bedroom and saw light coming from a doorway. I walked into the room up to the door. I realized it was a bathroom because the door was partly open. It wasn't open wide enough for me to see faces, but it was open enough for me to hear.

"I heard bumping against the wall. It became louder and louder. At first, I thought it was funny. I thought one of the players had gotten lucky with one of the cheerleaders. Then I heard a girl's voice. I wasn't sure who it was at first because she was moaning. Then I recognized it was Sally! She was moaning, 'You're so big! You're so big!'" Morton avoided looking at Marshall directly. He felt humiliated. "I was shocked. I didn't know what to do. I just froze. I couldn't bring myself to go in and see her like that. I just couldn't, so I just ran out. I ran out of the house and down the street. I was bawling the whole time. I could hardly breathe."

Morton's breathing was heavy and ragged. He took a long, deep drink and stared at the bottom of his near-empty glass.

Marshall began speaking quietly and slowly. "Did you hear her call my name, Joe? Did you even hear my voice?"

Morton thought for a moment, trying to remember. He hadn't stayed long enough to recognize the man's voice. All he heard were low, guttural, sounds, hard, rhythmical bumping, and Sally's moans. Morton squeezed his eyes shut.

Marshall continued, "Did you ever speak to Sally about that night? Did you ask her who was in the bathroom with her?"

Morton looked at him incredulously. "Are you crazy? I was supposed to get a confession out of *her* for something *you* did?" He scoffed, "You're not getting out of this that easily."

"I don't need to get out of anything, Joe. I've got nothing to hide." Marshall leaned back and crossed his arms. "Let's go to your house right now and ask her."

Morton's face became ghostly pale, then beet red. "You're out of your goddamn mind if you think I'm going to ask her about this now... on your say-so."

But Morton was perplexed. *Why would he suggest confronting Sally? If she said he was lying, could he believe her*? But, Morton thought, *What if she fesses up?*

His mind began to race. He'd always believed it was Marshall because he'd left the table first, and Sally followed minutes later. But if it wasn't Marshall, who could it have been? The house was full of drunk football players. Some were known to try to fuck anybody's girl. Their motto was, "It takes two." But if it wasn't Marshall, who could it have been?

"Nice try, Clayton! It had to be you. I know she liked you. Sally would sometimes tell me she wanted to touch your hair, to see what Black hair felt like. Once, she told me that being around you made her feel nervous. I always thought she had some kind of weird attraction to you. Besides, I'll never forget her voice that night, saying how big you were and how good it felt."

Marshall leaned forward again, his tone incredulous. "So, the only proof you've got that it was me banging Sally in the bathroom is that you heard her tell the guy how big he was?" He shook his head. "You know I didn't have a rep for being a yard dog, Joe. Remember Smitty, our fullback? He fucked half the girls in that sorority house. You never heard anything like that about me!"

Doubt was starting to creep into Morton's mind.

"Joe," Marshall said quietly, "Do you buy into that myth that all Black men are well endowed, or are you just telling me that white men can't fuck?"

Morton flinched at the racial stereotype. "I don't appreciate your black humor."

"It wasn't me, Joe," Marshall insisted.

Both men fell silent. Marshall stared intently at Morton's face, but Morton's mind was elsewhere—back at that bathroom door listening to the rhythmic, relentless, thump! Thump! Thump! Morton threw back his drink, emptying his glass.

In a voice tinged with confusion and despair, Morton asked, "If it wasn't you, Clayton, who was it?"

Marshall shrugged, looked away, and frowned. "It's been twenty years, man—twenty years. Let it go."

"Do you know who it was?" Morton demanded.

"If it's so important to you after twenty damn years, you should ask Sally."

"If you know, Clayton, please… just tell me." Morton pleaded, his demeanor a stark contrast to the arrogant, condescending man he'd been in court earlier today.

Marshall hesitated before speaking—a long, thoughtful pause that felt like a lifetime to Morton.

"You want me to beg, Marshall? Is that what you want?"

Sighing deeply, he said, "It was Tater."

"Tater?" Morton muttered, stunned. "Tater?" he repeated incredulously. "That big bull moose from Idaho? No! No! It can't be Tater! That slow-witted idiot? Sally would never have anything to do with him. He's not her type."

Morton shook his head, eyes wide with disbelief. He reached for Marshall's drink, took a long gulp, and leaned back, his face drawn and pinched.

"How do you know it was Tater?"

Marshall shrugged. "He told me! Tater told *us!* He bragged about it the next day."

"What did Tater tell you?" Morton spat the words.

"You sure you want to hear all this?" Marshall asked. "You're just causing yourself unnecessary grief."

Insistent, Morton badgered him. "Tell me!"

Marshall glanced around the restaurant. Patrons stole nervous glances at their table. "Alright, Morton. If you feel the need to twist this knife."

Marshall closed his eyes and took a deep breath. "Tater told us that he might not be able to score any points in the game, but he'd scored a touchdown with your girl."

He heard Morton inhale sharply and watched him shift uncomfortably in his seat.

Marshall studied Morton, who now stared down at the tablecloth. "No one believed him, or wanted to believe him at first," Marshall said. "The guys knew how you felt about Sally, and how she felt about you."

"How many people did that bastard tell?"

"About five of us were packed into his car when he said it. Tater boasted, 'If you don't believe I tapped that, she has a birthmark in the shape of a clover leaf on her upper thigh. Ask Joe. I hope he knows that by now.' Then Tater started laughing."

Morton felt sick. "Damn! Tater did screw her! That bitch! That fuckin', whorin' bitch!" Morton was deathly quiet for a moment. Then he looked up at Marshall. "But, you kissed her! Even if you didn't screw her, I know you didn't stop with a damn kiss." He pointed an accusing finger at Marshall.

Marshall rolled his eyes in frustration. "Jesus! I've had a long day. I don't need this shit. I'm outta here." He started packing up his laptop. "I'll see you in court."

Morton was quiet now, his embarrassment and humiliation palpable, as if Sally's infidelity occurred just yesterday.

Marshall slid out of the booth, stood up, and said, "You've nursed this imaginary grievance against me for twenty years. You've let it eat at you, haunt you, and torment you. It's probably affected your relationship with Sally. Have you held back a part of yourself from her, wondering if she'd ever cheat on you again? Have you ever thought she might be struggling with guilt all this time? Maybe she was afraid to tell you, worried she'd lose you over one drunken mistake. It's time for you to bury it. It's time for you and Sally to resolve this so you two can move on."

"I didn't know someone designated you as my Magic Negro. I damn sure don't need advice from you," Morton scoffed. "I'm gonna beat your ass in trial. I'm gonna do everything in my power to get a conviction. I won't break the rules, but I know how to bend them just to the breaking point. The courts always give the prosecution the benefit of the doubt. Your client will go straight from jail to prison. That's some long-overdue payback for putting your mouth and hands on something that doesn't belong to you … *boy!*

Marshall scowled. *Boy! He called me a goddamn boy!* Something hot surged in his stomach but quickly faded. Morton's tactic was as obvious as a poorly made snare.

Marshall recalled a veteran community leader describing a hate-filled mob—spitting, cursing, and hurling rocks, bottles, and slurs—during Reverend King's 1966 Chicago Freedom Movement in Marquette Park. "Calling a Black man 'boy' or 'nigger'," the man said, "is the desperate gasp of someone clinging to a fading sense of power. It's the bark of a frightened dog."

Marshall loosened the top button on his dress shirt and pulled his tie down. He didn't attempt to disguise his anger and disdain, choosing to ignore Morton's attempt to insult him.

"I don't need you to forgive me," Marshall said coolly. "I didn't owe you anything back then, and I damn sure don't owe you a damn thing now. I'll apologize for the kiss, but that's all you get." He paused, allowing his words to register with Morton. "You won't get blood, and you will *not* get my client. I can play hardball, too."

Morton was about to stand up when Marshall said calmly, "If you get out of that booth, I will do my very best to break your face in three places."

Both men remained tense and poised. Marshall's face showed little emotion, while Morton's was a mix of confusion and rage. Morton eyed Marshall intently, waiting for him to relax his guard so he could strike. But, in his seated position, Marshall clearly had the advantage.

Jetta appeared suddenly, her voice cutting through the tension. "Gentlemen, please! The maître d' called the police. They should be here soon."

Looking at Marshall, she added, "I suggest that you leave and quickly, sir."

Marshall backed away cautiously. Once he reached a safe distance, he turned and left without another word. Morton opened his mouth to yell after him, but Jetta gently touched his lips. The scent of her perfume, warm and intoxicating, seemed to envelop him like a soothing balm.

"Hey, Mr. Morton," she said softly, leaning over and sliding her arm around his shoulders. "Take a deep breath. I'll bring you another drink. It's over."

The maître d' approached the table, his face a mask of exasperation. "The police are on the way. What a commotion that awful man caused! That's what happens when you allow people like that into a high-class restaurant."

Morton pulled out his cell phone and hit a number. "Hello? Dispatch? This is Joe Morton." After a pause, he said, "I'm fine, thank you. No! I don't have the duty phone this week. You just got a call from Jake's Steakhouse about a possible disturbance." After a brief pause, Morton said, "Well, the call concerned me and another gentleman, but he's left the premises." Morton nodded a few times, holding the phone to his ear. "I understand. The maître d' is here, but I don't think he's interested in filing a complaint. I just think he wants to make sure that the gentleman knows that he and his kind are no longer welcome in his restaurant."

Morton looked at the maître d'. "Is that correct, sir?" He nodded his agreement.

"Yep. That's what the maître d' wants. Cancel the call. Notify the responding officers not to come. The restaurant is open until 11 p.m., if they still want to take a report. Anyway, I'll be talking to that attorney in the next few days. I'll let him know that he will face a trespass charge if he returns."

Morton shifted his weight in the booth and paused again. "What? Oh yes, the attorney's name is Clayton Marshall. We're scheduled for an upcoming bond and preliminary hearing. "Morton was nodding again. "Right. Right. Thank you. Have a good night."

Morton looked at the maître d' and Jetta. "It's all been taken care of. The police, if they show, might arrive around closing time. This incident is no longer a rush." Morton put his phone away and decided to finish Marshall's drink.

"Are you some kind of government official?" the maître d' asked.

"Just a minor one. I prosecute criminals," Morton said, after draining the glass.

Impressed, the maître d' smiled. "By the way, the drinks are on the house."

"That's very kind of you, but it's not necessary," Morton said.

"It's my small way of apologizing for that man's behavior. Besides, I hope you make our restaurant a regular stop."

Morton glanced at Jetta, "As long as I get the kind of special service that I've received this evening, you can count on it."

The maître d' smiled at Jetta. "I need to apologize to our guests," he said. He then gave a low, obsequious bow and hurried away.

"So… you're a prosecutor?" Jetta asked.

"Yeah, but don't tell anyone else. I don't need the attention."

"Okay. I get that, but tell me why someone in law enforcement would take a swing at another attorney. If the police question me, I'd have to tell them the truth."

"Yeah. I guess it was a good thing I missed. I'd probably have to get off this case, for sure, if a police investigation was initiated. Conflict of interest. Appearance of impropriety, you know."

"So, what was it that set you off?" Jetta asked. She scanned the room. Not seeing the maître d', she slid into the booth.

"Jetta, it's ancient history," Morton said dismissively.

She laughed. "Like hell it is. It might've happened a while ago, but it still has a hold on you."

Her cell phone buzzed. "Excuse me," she said, glancing at the screen. "It's my roommate."

She started to leave the table. Morton grabbed her arm. "You don't have to leave," he said.

Jetta answered the call. "Hey, girl! You on your way? I get off in about an hour." Her expression flashed irritation. "*What*? You said you'd pick me up!" Frustration crept into her voice. "Never mind. That guy is no good for you. I'll get a Uber, but you'll pay for the fare." She ended the call and slid her phone back into her pocket.

"Problems, Jetta? I can give you a ride home if you need one."

"I can't ask you to do that, Mr. Morton," she replied.

"Joe. Please, just call me Joe." He shrugged. "Besides, it will be my pleasure. You intrigue me. I'd like to get to know you better."

Jetta eyed him, a playful gleam in her eyes and a smile on her lips. "Is it me or my body you want to get to know?"

Feeling emboldened by the alcohol and Jetta's brazen question, Morton leaned over and whispered, "It's really that amazing killer body of yours."

Jetta's laugh was spontaneous and throaty. "I was hoping you'd say that. I'll meet you out front at 9, but that means you won't have a chance to eat. Maybe I can fix something for you at my place, if that's okay. It'll be partial payment for the ride."

"There's food for the stomach and food for the soul. Being with you would satisfy both appetites," Morton replied.

"The one good bit of luck is that my roommate will probably be gone all night. Do you have to get home early?" She asked, placing a hand on this thigh.

Morton almost jumped at her light touch. He felt an excitement he hadn't experienced in years. "No, I have a little time," he said smiling.

Jetta leaned in toward him seductively, her breasts pressing against her shirt. Morton caught his breath.

"Do you see this body?" she challenged. "You're going to need a lot more than 'a little time' to take care of this," she said suggestively.

"I'll call in sick to work if I have to," Morton said breathlessly.

She chuckled. "Wonderful. I just got me a ride home, and you are going to get the ride of your life tonight. I'll get you another drink." Jetta reached across him to collect his empty glasses, rubbing her breasts against his shoulder. Morton gasped.

As she walked away, Morton pinched himself. *No, this isn't a dream.* A beautiful woman had just told him that she was going to fuck his brains out tonight and, perhaps, into the next day.

Morton looked down at his wedding ring. He'd never cheated on Sally before. Despite countless opportunities, he'd never yielded to the temptation, telling himself he would remain faithful to her, even though she hadn't been faithful to him. He'd taken a sacred vow before God to love, honor, and cherish her, forsaking all others. But then, he'd never met anyone like Jetta.

Jetta embodied every man's fantasy, reminiscent of a Sports Illustrated swimsuit model whose sensual appeal could make magazines disappear from shelves in hours.

This was a once-in-a-lifetime opportunity that he wasn't about to pass up. Besides, Sally had given herself away to someone else on the night of their big victory—the same night he was planning to propose to her. Tater had scored with his girl. It was time for him to even the score.

Jetta returned with his drink and placed it in his outstretched hand letting their fingers touch briefly. Pursing her lips, she blew him a kiss. "I'll be outside as soon as I can."

Trying his best to sound relaxed and casual, Morton replied, "Dark blue, four-door BMW. My emergency flashers will be on."

When she walked away Morton unlocked his phone to text Sally—*Don't wait up tonight.*

15

Everything He Wanted

Morton sat patiently in his car, listening to his playlist. He was starting to feel incredibly relaxed but, at the same time, slightly euphoric. Those strong drinks that Jetta served him definitely did the trick. He had to be careful that a cop didn't pull him over.

A soft drizzle began to fall. *In the Wee Small Hours of the Morning* was playing. *Frank Sinatra. Man, he could sing!* Morton thought. He hummed contentedly, enjoying the pleasant glow of his intoxication. With a serene smile, he closed his eyes and waited.

A few minutes later the door swung open and Jetta slid across the seat, the smell of rain and cool fresh air upon her. With her left hand, she pulled his head toward her and kissed him softly on the mouth. She placed her right hand gently upon his crotch and began to stroke him slowly. He was surprised at how quickly he became erect. She started to gently explore his mouth with her tongue while she continued to touch him. She was no novice. She stopped suddenly and pulled away.

With a playful look on her face, she said, "Miss me?"

Morton's head was spinning, but it was a delicious sensation. "Jetta, you make me dizzy!" He started to laugh. A feeling of anticipation was stirring within him.

"That's the effect I like to have on my man," she said, leaning in and nuzzling his neck. "Ready to go?" she asked. "My place isn't far. About 10 minutes away."

He reached over to cup her breast. Although she wore a coat, he could feel the full curve of it, firm and heavy in his hand. He was about to kiss her again when she said, "Plenty of time for that, Mr. Prosecutor. Let's get home so we can get comfortable."

"Good idea," he said. He reluctantly pulled his hand away and dropped it on her thigh. "I don't even know your last name," he said.

"It's Erzulie."

"Is that your last name, or is that its ethnic origin?" Morton's felt lightheaded. He felt remarkably relaxed in her presence.

Jetta laughed. "It's a Haitian name. Erzulie is known as a love goddess and a protector. Supposedly, she came into being in Haiti to protect families from being broken apart by their enslavers."

"Well, I don't think anyone could have given you a more fitting name. You are a goddess! I can't keep my hands off you." He reached for her again. This time, she didn't resist. His kiss was passionate and hungry. He pressed fiercely against her. He marveled how her body felt so good. She ignited a passion that had long been dormant.

"Whoa, big fella. I don't want you to pop before we get home. Just so you know, Joe, I enjoy a lot of foreplay."

He pulled back, allowing her to straighten her clothes. "You're right," he said breathlessly. "We have all night."

She stroked the inside of his thigh. "I'm going to fuck you, Joe, but I want it to be romantic. Okay?"

"That sounds absolutely wonderful to me," he said. "Now… where to, goddess?"

"Just head down the street, and I'll tell you when to turn."

They chatted as she gave him directions. She kept her hand on his thigh as he drove, occasionally stroking his penis. Morton felt it throbbing with her touch. As she stroked him, she studied his face to note what gave him the most pleasure.

He was also feeling a delicious headiness that he'd never felt before, but he attributed it all to his Black love goddess. She made him feel powerful. He felt like he was 21 again.

Morton parked in the underground garage of an apartment complex. Feeling slightly giddy and pleasantly high, he carefully maneuvered his car into the designated visitor space. He laughed when he knocked over a trash can.

"Wait! Don't get out," Morton said, as he rushed to open her door. He felt like he was walking on air.

Jetta stepped out and pressed her body against his, forcing him back against the car in the adjacent space. Morton felt every inch of her body against him. He could barely breathe. Every part of him tingled with excitement and desire.

"C'mon. I'll race you to the elevator." Jetta said as she took off like a gazelle.

He followed her—a mixture of laughter and clumsy steps—his movements more of a stagger than a run.

After the elevator door opened, Jetta stepped inside and wrapped him in an embrace that stole his breath. She kissed him lightly on both sides of his face and then passionately on his lips. While squeezing his butt with one hand, she reached behind him with the other and pressed the elevator button for her floor. Her mouth—hot, wet, insistent—stayed on his the entire ride, nibbling, sucking, kissing. Morton thought he might faint.

The elevator chime signaled their arrival, and they exited and drifted down the hall hand in hand.

She opened her apartment door and said coyly, "Make yourself at home. Throw your jacket on the chair over there. I want to slip into something more comfortable. There's scotch and glasses on the table."

She disappeared into the bedroom as Morton meandered across the room to toss his coat over a chair. The room was unpretentious, with only the minimum necessities: a love seat, couch, and side tables. Several posters adorned the walls—vivid depictions of Haitian voodoo imagery, a lively carnival, and a bustling market decorated the walls. From the tiny living room, he could see the kitchen nook behind the couch. The refrigerator stood off in the corner, but he decided to forgo ice in his drink. He felt warm and euphoric and didn't want to spoil that feeling with something cold.

"Hey, Joe!" Jetta called out. "Put some music on for us. In the entertainment center, you'll find some CDs. Put on something slow. Slow dancing turns me on. You're gonna be my Fred Astaire tonight."

Morton laughed. "I can't dance a whit, Jetta, but if you hold on to me, I'll follow your lead."

Jetta's voice was deep and throaty. "Joe! All you gotta to do is squeeze me tight and hold on to my hips. You won't know where you begin and where I end." Morton felt his heart skip.

Morton surveyed the sparse selection of CDs. He was not familiar with most of the Black artists' names. He wondered who still listens to CDs with today's streaming music platforms. He called out, "Which one is your favorite?"

There was a brief pause. Then Jetta replied, "Put on Gerald Albright's *Bermuda Nights*. Go to his cut—*In the Mood*. That's one of my favorites."

He inserted the CD and sat down to pour himself a drink. The sax melody began—slow, haunting, and seductive. A piano joined in teasing the alto sax along, ushering the melody forward with a rapid introduction of shimmering cymbals. The drum percussion made its dramatic entrance, adding a steady, solid beat. The sax moaned like a suitor's plea—softly coaxing, sweetly enticing, tenderly entreating while a chorus of voices whispered promises of pleasure yet to come.

He heard Jetta singing along in the bedroom. Her voice grew louder as she approached the living room. She twirled before him, wearing a flowing white satin robe and pajamas. The stark contrast of her beautiful black skin against the white garment made her appear almost surreal. Morton slid lower on the couch, his legs spread wide, inviting her in.

Jetta stepped between them and began to dance, slowly undulating her hips with the seductive lure of the music. She arched her back, running her fingers through her long dark hair, gyrating her hips slowly from side to side. Morton couldn't suppress a moan as he watched her. He was mesmerized by her beauty and seduced by the sway of her hips.

Without warning, there came a loud banging at the door. Jetta stopped suddenly and looked wide-eyed at Morton, who seemed slightly befuddled.

"Jetta! Jetta!" a plaintive voice cried. "I misplaced my keys. I'm locked out!"

"I don't believe it!" Jetta grumbled. "She's back. Already! Dammit!"

Morton eased himself up slowly. "Who's back? Who's at the door?"

Jetta sighed heavily. "My roommate, Tara. She wasn't supposed to be back until tomorrow. I tried to tell her that her boyfriend was a jerk. They probably had a fight."

Tara was starting to wail outside the door. "C'mon, Jetta. I know you're in there. I hear music."

Morton said, "She sounds drunk!"

"When Tara goes out to party, she always gets drunk. She's as wild as they come. I'm surprised she's still alive." Morton heard the irritation in Jetta's voice.

More banging at the door! Then they heard her kicking it. "*Jetta*!" Tara yelled.

"All right! Hold up. I'm coming. What the hell did you do with your key, anyway?" Jetta demanded as she stomped toward the door.

Morton lifted his head, trying to hear their conversation. Jetta was whispering.

Morton heard Tara yell, "I don't... I can't hear you. Hurry up and open the door. I gotta pee!"

Jetta emitted a long sigh. "Hold on, Tara. Don't get your panties in a bunch."

Tara started giggling. "I ain't wearing any," she yelled. "I left them at that jerk's apartment."

The light from the hallway entered the room as Jetta opened the door. Tara was spouting obscenities about her boyfriend. "Do you know what that bastard wanted me to do? He wanted me to screw two of his friends. Can you imagine that?" she giggled. "Though, I might have, if they weren't so fuckin' ugly!"

Jetta made several failed attempts to tell Tara that she had company, that she was entertaining, but Tara was lost in the golden glow of her inebriated world.

Within moments, Tara stumbled into the living room. When she could focus, she saw Morton and stopped short. She started laughing. "Oh, girl, you been holding out on me. Who's the stud?"

She plopped down on the couch next to Morton and leaned forward to inspect him. She murmured, "If my boyfriend had a buddy who looked like this, I would still be fucking." Jetta stood above them with her arms folded, her expression a blend of frustration and amusement.

Tara's long blonde hair cascaded in waves across her face. Morton watched as she clumsily brushed the thick mane from her eyes, revealing deep blue orbs that were slightly glassy. Her ample bosom contrasted with her classically elegant features.

Morton couldn't help but notice that she had a model's build straight out the fifties—voluptuous and curvy—but her breasts appeared to be disproportionately large for her frame. Her blouse was unbuttoned in several places, exposing generous mounds of pale white flesh that quivered with her every move. Morton caught a strong, minty odor of alcohol on her breath. Indulgently, he gently cupped her face. Despite her profane mouth, she exuded an innocent vulnerability that he found oddly compelling.

Tara said, "Oh! I like him. He seems like a gentleman." She looked at Jetta and said, "Can we share, Jetta? We can take turns or have a ménage a trois. Really! Any way you want, Jetta. Please?"

Her words were slurred but tumbled out quickly. A petulant, childlike quality in her voice made Jetta smile. Morton sat motionless, enthralled by the thought that he might experience his first threesome.

Jetta glanced off into the distance trying to decide what to do. She looked over at Morton who was ogling Tara.

She shrugged in apparent defeat. "Are you game, Joe?"

Morton looked admiringly at both women. He felt strangely and unusually amorous. He was aware that he was fully erect but was not at all self-conscious.

Both women admired the erection tenting his pants.

"Oh my!" Tara blurted, her eyes captured by the prominent bulge. "I think he just gave us his answer!"

Jetta dropped down on the couch beside Tara and kissed her deeply on the mouth. Morton heard an appreciative moan from Tara.

Catching her breath, Jetta said laughingly, "Okay. Let's party!"

"Let me use the bathroom first before I wet myself!" Tara slurred, as she dashed out of the room.

Jetta slid over to Morton and eased onto his lap. She began to kiss him slowly around his face, on his neck, and down his throat. Pulling back from him, she looked at him closely. "You sure you're okay with this, Joe?"

"I'm okay if you are, Jetta," he said, nibbling her earlobe. Eyes glazed and words slurring, Morton urged her, "You own me tonight, Jetta. I belong completely to you. Your wish. My command."

Jetta tossed her head back, laughing, her thick black hair fanning behind her. When she leaned forward and bit his lip. Morton moaned and kissed her with a hunger that surprised him.

Pulling back, she said, "Remember, Morton! Tonight, I am the Haitian Goddess of Love. You'll have to beg me to stop."

Eyes twinkling, she purred, "Be prepared to show your best side, Joe, because Tara loves taking pictures of herself naked.

"As long as I can get copies," Morton mumbled, feeling elated and strangely high. "I never want to forget this night."

At the sound of Tara's voice, Morton and Jetta turned to see her standing naked in the doorway. The light behind her made her skin seem luminescent. Like she was bathed in moonlight.

Morton heard Jetta chuckle when he gasped, astounded to be openly gaping at this voluptuous, hypnotic woman slowly floating toward him like a succubus in an erotic dream.

Jetta's laughter, light and carefree, echoed in his ears just before he felt the full weight of Tara's soft, enticing body envelop him.

16

Fight Fire with Fire

Outside the apartment complex, Marshall sat in his car listening to the radio. He'd nearly overslept, falling into his hotel bed after leaving Morton at Jake's Steakhouse. Exhaustion almost wiped him out. Dealing with Morton's pathetic narrative as a husband betrayed topped off a day from hell. A quick shower and a cup of instant coffee had revived him. Unsure how long he'd need to wait, he wore comfortable clothes, donning a hoodie, faded blue jeans, and sneakers.

The rain had died down, leaving the pavement glistening under street lights. He yawned, stretched, and glanced impatiently at his watch. He'd arrived at 4 a.m., exactly as the text message instructed.

He hadn't noticed the figure approaching his car and was startled to hear a knock on the passenger-side car window. He hit the automatic locks, the door opened, and a small duffle bag was thrown into the back. The leather made a soft rustling sound as she slid across the seat.

"Did you get it?" he asked casually.

A small, dark hand passed Marshall a tiny plastic encasement. "It's inside," she said. Her voice was tired.

"How many did you take?" Marshall asked.

"Well, we took over 40 pictures between the three of us. It took some maneuvering to get shots that wouldn't reveal our faces."

"But you did get Joe's face in the shots? I mean, you wouldn't have to guess it was Joe Morton's face, would you?"

"That's what TicToc told me to do. We got the shots. You name them, we got them—close up, medium shots, full body shots, high angle—but if you see any shots you want to use that might identify us, make sure you Photoshop our faces out."

"No! I don't want to do that. I don't want to give him any room to argue that the photos are fake. If your faces are in the photos, we won't use those."

Satisfied with her report, Marshall reached over and patted her hand. "Thanks, Jetta. TicToc will be pleased." Jetta acknowledged his approval with a nod. "Where's your friend?" Marshall asked.

"She's on her way out of town. She had her man pick her up. She was too tired and too drunk to drive." Jetta laughed. "Tara wore Morton out. He's sleeping like a baby now," she chuckled. "I need a ride to the airport. My plane leaves at 7:50."

"No problem. Happy to oblige." Marshall said, pulling onto the road. At that time of night there was hardly any traffic.

Jetta leaned back in the seat and sighed. "I thought this job would take a couple of weeks, at least. Man! Everything fell into place like clockwork. The timing couldn't have been better."

I'm glad," Marshall said. "TicToc only gave me a couple of weeks. And with that no-bond hold, I need to get these charges dropped for Tyrene like yesterday. And you're gonna make it happen, Jetta. You were the key."

"Do you think that the photos will do it?" she asked.

"Maybe! Maybe not!" Marshall shrugged. "Sex scandals don't seem to faze politicians the way they used to. However, Morton might not want to deal with the public embarrassment, jeopardize his professional career, or risk his marriage. Personally… knowing his over-inflated ego, these in *flagrante delicto* images will probably pull the rug out from under him."

Jetta sighed in relief. "Hope so, Mr. Marshall. I don't want to disappoint TicToc." She paused then asked, "Do you feel at all guilty blackmailing this guy? I mean… you did play ball together."

"Did you feel any guilt setting him up?" he snapped.

"No, Mr. Marshall, I didn't. But I'm not an attorney," she answered coolly. "I didn't take an oath to uphold the law. I'm just a working girl. I do what I'm paid to do, which usually means breaking the law. Sounds like you took offense. I didn't intend any."

"Sorry, Jetta. I'm edgy and tired. The best answer I can give is the old diatribe that you got to fight fire with fire. Playing by the rules won't get you anywhere, particularly if the system is corrupt. It's hard to fight injustice in a broken system."

"If the deck is stacked against you, your only chance is to cheat. Right?"

Marshall frowned. "I guess you could put it that way. Sounds pretty bad when you say it like that though."

It was Jetta's turn to be quiet, thinking about fighting fire with fire. "Ever try fighting fire with water, Mr. Marshall?" she asked.

"What do you mean?"

"I was thinking about what Reverend King was able to do. The deck was clearly stacked against our people, but he refused to fight fire with fire," she said, pushing a loose strand of hair from her face. "King used water to fight fire. You know what I mean. All the fires of hate could not withstand the healing power of His water. It was like pouring living water into the evils of Jim Crow and the hardened hearts of segregationists, offering forgiveness, not wrath—restoration, not revenge."

A puzzled look crossed Marshall's face. "Beautifully said, Jetta, but who are we talking about here? Are we talking about Reverend King, or…" Marshall paused. "…or God?"

Jetta's tone was reflective. "Reverend King was God's instrument to fight segregation. Only God's power could prevail against centuries of racial hatred to destroy nearly one hundred years of Jim Crow."

Marshall chuckled. "You sound like TicToc."

Jetta smiled. "I consider that a compliment." She turned to face Marshall. "So, what do you think about my idea—fighting fire with water?"

Marshall smiled, his eyes on the road. "Interesting idea, Jetta, but I don't think it would work in a court of law. It's a different kind of battle."

Jetta sighed. "If it can't work there, Mr. Marshall, then I'm worried for our country. I think there's something truly noble when we speak about seeking justice and doing the right thing."

Marshall nodded in agreement. "The problem is that far too few conduct themselves in a noble fashion, Jetta. What is pursued in court—hell, in life—is winning. Sometimes, at any cost. If the ultimate goal is just winning, words like integrity and justice become empty noise."

Jetta studied his face. He looked tired. "You sound a bit jaded, Mr. Marshall."

Marshall glanced at Jetta, marveling at her spunk. Maybe he'd experienced too much—seen too many innocent lives ruined by a system run by individuals who didn't give a damn.

"Remember King's 'I Have a Dream' speech, Jetta, when he talked about refusing to believe that the Bank of Justice is bankrupt?"

"Yeah! I loved his metaphor about America defaulting on a promissory note to people of color—that this country owes us the rights and freedoms promised in its founding documents."

"Well," Marshall said, "with all due respect to Dr. King, I *do* believe that the bank is bankrupt."

"You don't have hope anymore, Mr. Marshall? Things have changed. I mean… really changed. Did you ever think we would have a Black president? And now we have a Black female Vice President. Do you know how incredible that is... given the history of this country?"

Marshall considered her protests quietly but shook his head. He replied softly, "Jetta, if you study history—*really* study our struggle to survive in this country—you'll understand how many of our people have died at the hands of racists who were not prosecuted and who will never be prosecuted.

"I'm not talking about racists murdering a few hundred people. I'm talking about thousands. Black people—women, men, and children—randomly murdered by solitary individuals or a mob that decided to kill someone Black just for fun or because some white woman cried rape."

Glancing at her, he said, "Did you know that two thriving Black towns—Tulsa, Oklahoma, and Rosewood, Florida—were razed in the early 20th century, all because a Black man was falsely accused of assaulting a white woman? In the Tulsa Race Massacre, homes, businesses, schools, and churches were burned to the ground. Men, women, and children were slaughtered. White pilots dropped dynamite on the town from planes. Over three hundred people were murdered. An estimated 700 injured. Eight to ten thousand left homeless. Not *one* person was prosecuted."

He shook his head. "Think about the documented racial terror perpetrated by white Americans between 1865 and 1950: nearly 6,500 Black men and women lynched to uphold white supremacy."

Marshall inhaled sharply, raw emotion causing his voice to crack. "Words cannot describe the unimaginable horror and cruelty of white mobs—racial violence deliberately ignored at every level of government. Innocent blood stains this land for no other reason than the victims happened to be Black. The racial trauma has not ended. As far as I'm concerned, Jetta, it's a debt that America owes. It's a debt that America can never repay."

Jetta heard his anguish and understood his rage, but she had to cling to hope. If everyone felt as he did, it was just a matter of time before the world tore itself apart.

"Jetta, only a handful of these murderers have been prosecuted. Most of them have never been brought to justice. There was no trial. No one had to pay for these crimes. Some murderous hand took the life of a loved one, maliciously and violently, with impunity, under America's sacred banner of 'equal justice for all' while the law—our law—gave its blessing and Lady Justice looked on blindly."

"Mr. Marshall, what are we talking about here? Unsolved murders that are fifty or one hundred years old?" She shrugged. "I don't know much about the law, sir, but you need witnesses and evidence to prove a case. I'm pretty sure no one seriously investigated a case back then if it meant arresting someone white. Maybe it's better not to stir up a family's pain again—to give them false hope."

Confused by Jetta's response, Marshall said, "Some of these families don't even know how, why, or who killed their grandfather, uncle, husband, father, mother, aunt, or sister. Sometimes, a body was never found.

Don't you think those families deserve answers? Don't you think they want closure?" He sighed deeply. "The system just wants to let sleeping dogs lie. Don't cause a fuss. Don't rock the boat. Leave the hornet's nest alone. Don't unearth the past."

He asked, "What's the victim's family left with? Nothing but painful, ugly memories remain. Just heartache—and a lingering sense of suspicion and distrust toward a system that was supposed to protect their loved ones!" He gripped the steering wheel as he battled with his emotions.

"The Man holds us accountable when we commit murder, but a Black man is more likely to get the death penalty for murder than a white man, particularly if the victim is white! Who holds the white man accountable? The system? But who runs the system, Jetta?"

He sighed. "How can a family ever begin to heal—let alone find closure—when there's no legal acknowledgment of the wrong, no one held accountable, and justice is nowhere to be found."

Feeling the need to educate her about the symbolic importance of a trial, he began patiently. "A trial is, at its core, a ritualized community drama. The person who has violated a social norm is held accountable for their antisocial behavior. A sentence is imposed. Punishment is exacted. The harm is acknowledged, the victim vindicated, and the community's sense of justice restored. Someone pays a price for the wrong committed. The tear in the moral universe is mended. Only then can the universe be made right—and healing begin."

Marshall continued, "This is the awful truth about white America, Jetta. For generations, Black Americans have been brutalized by white racial terror—and there's been no real healing, only survival. This country was built on our suffering, and white society would rather bury that truth than face it."

"But if you can accept that trying a hundred-year-old crime is unrealistic, Mr. Marshall, and that justice will never be served, then what do you want? Revenge? From whom? Blood does not redeem blood. Blood will never satisfy hate."

"I want what every victim wants, Jetta. For every Black human being who was shot, stabbed, bludgeoned, tortured, burned, drowned, or lynched; for everyone who cried out to God for mercy and deliverance from a relentless, rabid mob or killer; for every person who pleaded in abject helplessness to spare their lives—I want justice!"

It had begun to drizzle again. Suddenly, the wind picked up, sounding like a mournful howl in the early morning darkness. Remembering Marshall's burning words, she imagined she saw the dark, anguished faces of people in the throes of death and heard the wail and cry of family members who'd learned of their loved ones' savage murder. She felt something wet on her cheek and was surprised to discover she was crying.

Marshall's voice dripped with bitterness. "Jetta, when the law is denied, and justice is mocked, and the anguished cries of thousands fall upon deaf ears, it feels as if God has turned his back on you."

"I think that we have a different view about God's grace and love, Mr. Marshall. I think that God was never closer to one of His children than when they sighed their last breath at the hands of a racist.

Jetta turned back to face him. "The dimension you speak of—your legal world—would suggest that justice is bankrupt and the universe is out of kilter. I guess the question for you is, 'What can you do about it—particularly for a victim of lynching that occurred a century ago? Hold a mock trial?" Jetta paused. "I think forgiveness is the only way. Remember, five people of deep faith forgave Dylan Roof for murdering their loved ones at Mother Emanuel."

"You need someone to be repentant before forgiveness is given, Jetta." He turned to watch raindrops steadily strike his windows, merging into winding, downward streams, only to be swept away.

"Have you ever heard of Preston John Porter Jr., Jetta?"

When she shook her head he said, He was a 15-year-old Black boy burned alive while chained to a railroad stake in Limon, Colorado, in 1900, while a mob of 300 white people stood by and watched. His only crime was being born Black." For a few minutes, the only sound was the rain hitting the windshield and the rhythmic swoosh of wipers. Then Marshall spoke. "I don't want the stolen lives of people like Porter to be lost, wiped away — like tears forgotten." He motioned to the rain on the windshield.

Uncomfortable with the turn their conversation had taken, Marshall thought it best to switch subjects. "By the way, is Jetta your real name?"

"This morning, I'm Jetta," she smiled weakly. "Next month, I'll be somebody else."

"I just want to make sure that Morton won't be able to track you down. He has resources, you know," Marshall warned.

"Everything is taken care of, Mr. Marshall" she answered. "I'm not in any national crime databank. TicToc had my records scrubbed. Right now, I don't have a rap sheet. Neither does my friend."

"Good," Marshall said. "After I drop you off, I'll let TicToc know that one component of Operation Freedom went smoothly."

Marshall chuckled. "Joe is going to be surprised to wake up and find you gone, literally without a trace."

"Well, your friend may have a slight headache when he wakes up," she said.

"You mean from the alcohol?"

"No, from something else." Jetta chuckled. "At the restaurant I slipped some Ecstasy into his drink."

Marshall chortled, delighted at the image of the egotistical prosecutor high on a party drug.

"And" Jetta added, grinning, "Tara wanted to make sure he had some staying power, so I offered him a little blue pill."

"Did you put that in his drink, too?"

"Nope," Jetta giggled. "I just straight-up offered it to him, and he gulped several down with some whiskey." Jetta shrugged her shoulders. "I had to make sure he could perform," she said impishly. "Besides, Tara wanted to enjoy herself. She needed him in the mood." Jetta paused, then added with a grin, "For a very long time."

"I can't wait to see those photos. TicToc knew what she was doing when she hired you for the job."

"Did you ever know a time when TicToc didn't know what she was doing?" Jetta asked.

Marshall hesitated for a moment. "Nope! Never have."

"Just so we're clear, Mr. Marshall. If you happen to recognize me somewhere, sometime in the future, I would appreciate it if you didn't acknowledge or approach me."

She looked at him pointedly. "It could cost me my life or," she shrugged, "or at least, my looks." She drew a manicured nail down one side of her face, then the other, across the tip of her nose, and at the corners of her mouth.

Marshall thought it wise not to ask any more questions. "Understood," he said solemnly.

Jetta yawned, and stretched languidly. She touched the lever on the side of her seat that lowered the back of her seat. Reclining fully, she turned to her side and pulled her knees up to her chest. She said, "Wake me up, please, Mr. Marshall, when we reach the airport."

Jetta closed her eyes as fatigue pressed down heavily upon her.

Her eyelids fluttered slightly as she let her body sink into the seat's contours. Images of Tara's and Morton's straining, damp bodies blurred together as they flashed across her mind. Her camera shutter clicked repeatedly, capturing lurid images of Morton's descent into carnal disgrace. Jetta did not doubt the photos would suck every ounce of fight out of him. He would have no choice but to yield to Mr. Marshall's demands.

She admired his passion and deep commitment to victims of racial injustice. But she couldn't help but wonder what lens Mr. Marshall used to navigate the world—and what it must cost him to carry that weight every day.

17

Oldest Game in Town

Morton cradled his throbbing head. Tormented by overwhelming dread. He couldn't shake an uncomfortable feeling that something awful was going to happen—but he wasn't sure what. Blackmail was an obvious possibility. How could he deny what he'd done last night? While planning to run for an elective office, he had allowed two irresistible women to photograph him engaging in sexual acts that bordered between kinky and deviant.

Hell! If the scandal came to light, he could claim to be an innocent victim of a calculated scheme designed to sabotage his chances of becoming the county's highest-ranking prosecutor.

Morton knew from past political experience that a big lie, repeated frequently and consistently, could convince the public of almost anything— especially in this era rife with conspiracy theories.

He needed to sober up fast. If he could just remember what he did! Gaps and fragments plagued him. Had he experienced some sort of alcoholic blackout? He only knew one thing for sure: it had been the wildest night of his life. Ever since reading Hemingway's *Garden of Eden*, the fantasy of having sex with two women had always teased his erotic imagination.

A knock at his door jolted him upright in his chair. He groaned again, pressing both palms to his forehead.

"Yo, Morton! You in there, Boss?" came the gruff Texas drawl. Another knock followed, making his head spin even more.

"C'mon in, Paxton, and stop pounding on that damn door."

"Geez," Paxton said as he entered the room. Had Morton looked up, he would have seen the large vein by Paxton's temple pulsing. "It was just a knock, for Christ's sake. You ask me to drop everything for a goddamn rush job, and then you try to take my head off for knockin' on your door. You know how much heat I've got on me to finish this investigative report on that double homicide?" Paxton fumed.

"Close the door," Morton snapped impatiently. "Softly, please," he added. Morton kept his eyes closed, using his elbow on the desk to prop up his throbbing head. With the other, he gestured Paxton to sit down.

Paxton studied him carefully while closing the door. He had worked on cases with Morton for years—tough, high-profile cases that could make or break a career—cases that would make most seasoned DAs short-tempered and testy—but he had never seen Morton this shaken. Paxton was more alarmed than surprised.

After listening to his panicked message before daybreak, Paxton knew immediately that Morton had really stepped in it this time. Morton's voice stirred a familiar image: the hollow-eyed panic of a defendant who knows the walls have caved in. The desperation in his voice worried him.

"Paxton! Find this girl! My future's at stake!" the voice message said. "Her name is Jetta Erzulie. This is her apartment address and her place of employment." Although his words slurred, Paxton knew the restaurant—Jake's Steakhouse and the apartment complex.

"And, Paxton," he stressed, "Go whole hog!"

There had been office gossip about Morton's romantic trysts with some very hot women, but it was only gossip. Morton had always been faithful to his wife. Paxton found it difficult to believe that he had gotten involved with some woman that sounded like she was straight out of Africa.

Eyeing Morton, Paxton couldn't resist saying what he saw. "Damn, Morton, you look like you been rode hard and put away wet. What the fuck happened to you?"

Morton removed his hands from his face and sat back in his chair. "Paxton," Morton said, his voice weak, "I think I really fucked up this time." He was trying to keep his voice from breaking.

"You mean with this .... Jetta Erzulie?" Paxton asked.

Morton sighed heavily. "A night of debauchery might have killed my chances for top DA, cost me my job, ended my career, destroyed my reputation, and will probably end my marriage."

"C'mon, Morton. Can't be that bad," Paxton said, not entirely convinced of his own words.

Morton leaned forward, resting his elbows on his desk. "I've just got a real bad feeling about this one, and I can't shake it." He sighed again and shook his head. "I woke up butt naked on a bare mattress. I could still smell the damp scent of their bodies on me."

Looking intently at Paxton, he mumbled, evidently embarrassed, "The women were gone when I woke up. They were just *gone!*" Morton sounded like he wanted to wail.

Paxton's eyebrows shot up. "*Women*!" he repeated. Paxton couldn't help but let out a disturbingly loud guffaw, despite his friend's predicament.

"Well I be damned! You only told me one name! What I wouldn't give to wake up butt-naked after a night like that!" Paxton's belly shook with laughter.

Morton snapped, "Ain't nothing funny about my situation, Paxton!" After a pause, Morton mumbled gruffly, "You miserable asshole!"

Morton's insults failed to elicit an apologetic response from the veteran investigator, but Paxton did try to suppress his laughter by slapping his hand over his mouth, which only led to violent coughing.

"Hope those cigarettes kill your dumb ass," Morton said. "You might not want a night like that if you were running for office and those women were taking photos!"

Hearing the word "photos," Paxton slapped both knees hard.

"Holy fuck, Morton! You know better than to do something dumb like that! You always told me it's not what you know; it's not what you believe; it's what you can prove! And, with photos… man…" his voice trailed off.

Paxton was now keenly aware of the urgency of Morton's request to drop everything and find this woman. Both men were now quiet.

Paxton's mind was swimming, trying to figure out what he could say to comfort his friend.

Morton broke the silence. "I think I might have been drugged. I've never felt so randy and so sexually powerful in my entire life." A slight smile appeared quickly on Morton's face, momentarily lifting his gloom. "I woke up in the bedroom around six a.m. I was in a fog. My head was pounding, and my mouth was dry. I couldn't believe it! I still had a goddamn erection! It took me a moment before I could will myself out of bed to get a drink. I was standing over the sink, cupping water, when it hit me. They weren't in the bed. They weren't in the apartment. They were just gone!"

"You hadn't called out to them? You were in the bathroom. How could you know that?"

"The furniture in the bedroom was gone," Morton said. "I rushed out to the living room area. Couch, table, chairs, music system..." He waved his arms around. "*Everything* was gone!" He paused. "Except for the stove and refrigerator. I ran around the apartment searching for mail, bills—anything that would help me get a lead on them—something that they might have overlooked. I couldn't find a thing!"

Breathing hard, Morton said, "I returned to the bedroom. The bedsheets were gone, too. No clothes were in the closet. Even *my* clothes were missing, but they left me some hospital-looking uniform and slippers to put on. I put the damn thing on, went down to my car, and got a change of clothes and travel kit from my overnight bag. I returned to the apartment and took a shower." Morton scoffed. "There was a large bath towel on the sink. I'm pretty sure that Jetta left it for me."

He continued, "I didn't trust myself to drive. I still felt groggy, so I took an Uber here." Morton paused, trying to untangle the knot that he feared would choke him. "Did you get my car from the apartment complex, Paxton?"

"Yep! Parked it in your usual spot in the underground garage."

Morton nodded his thanks.

“Honestly, Morton, it looked like a team of movers and a cleaning crew had swept through that apartment,” Paxton said. “The place was spic and span. It looked like tenants who wanted their apartment crazy clean to make sure that they got all their security deposit back.”

Morton rolled his eyes.

Feeling it was time to let his old friend know he hadn’t been loafing on the job, Paxton said, “Okay. Let me tell you what I've done. I dusted your car for prints, but I don't think anything will be found because someone wiped it down and appeared to have vacuumed it. The interior almost looked like it had been detailed. I dusted what I could inside the apartment. You know—the stove, refrigerator, and countertop. Didn’t get a thing.” Paxton shrugged. “Nothing in the bedroom, except the stripped mattress you were on.” He chuckled. “It’s a wonder that they didn’t take that, too.

“Got a friend in forensics to examine it for hair, saliva, blood, semen … you know—fluids. But, remember… ” He paused. “They took the sheets. Only prints I got were from the bathroom sink. Probably yours.”

Paxton sighed. “Honestly, Morton! Don’t think we’ll find anything helpful in the apartment or car. It’s a long shot … but maybe there's some DNA from the mattress?” His voice was uncertain.

"If they moved everything in the bedroom and apartment, I should’ve woken up," protested Morton. “I didn’t hear a thing!”

“I know you were always in the violent crime division, but you must’ve heard of roofies, liquid ecstasy, or blue nitro.” Paxton said slowly, sarcasm lacing his voice. “Those drugs will do the trick! Turn you into a fuckin’ corpse.”

Paxton searched Morton’s eyes to see if he was following. “What if someone gave you a sedative… a shot in your arm... after you passed out, to make sure you didn’t wake up while they emptied the place?” Paxton shook his head. “Yep! We need to do a tox screen on you in a private lab, just to see what's in your system.”

Morton raised his eyebrows. "A private lab?"

“C'mon, Morton! You know that everybody in the DA's office is not your bosom buddy. After your first run to become the head DA, you made some enemies inside and outside this office. What if somebody in our crime lab has a friend on the police force who has been dying to bring you down because you embarrassed him in court or dumped one of his pet cases because he withheld material evidence. Someone might just decide to leak your drug results to the press. Just think about the headlines: *Hopeful Candidate for Top DA Job Drops Blue Nitro.* Who knows what kind of drugs are in your system?”

"Okay," Morton moaned. "I get the picture."

"Besides, if your worst fear is true," Paxton continued, "we need to be able to not only prove that you were drugged—we need to control the timing of when the information is released. A private lab is essential!”

Running a beefy hand through his dyed black hair, Paxton, feeling frustrated about his lack of progress, repeated, "I went through that apartment from top to bottom. I couldn't find a thing that would help identify them. I spoke to the apartment manager. He had no problem remembering that Erzulie gal. He said that she was the hottest woman, Black or white, that he'd ever seen. At least you still got good taste," Paxton teased. “Didn't know that it ran into the exotic, though. I mean, her being Black and all.” Ignoring Morton's frown, Paxton continued," I had the manager pull her application. I've got a few people following up on personal references, addresses, phone numbers, past employment, and driver's licenses, but I bet they are all fake.”

Morton said, hopefully, “Lease application?”

“Only got one set of prints. Probably the manager. Waiting to hear back from the lab for everything that was dusted. Shrugging, Paxton repeated, “Like I said … pros.”

"What about a social security number?" Morton asked.

"Oh, yeah! Her social security number.” Paxton looked Morton squarely in the eyes. “Your girl, Erzulie. She died about fifty years ago—in Haiti.”

Morton's lips were moving, but no sound came out. Finally, he asked, "Did you contact the maître d'?

"That fool never even asked for an application," Paxton snorted. "My guess is that he was so impressed with her drop-dead looks that he skipped that requirement. However, I did persuade him to take me to her locker to see if I could find anything—particularly prints."

"Let me guess. You came up empty," Morton said dryly.

Paxton arched an eyebrow as he unsnapped the button to the pocket of his Western-style shirt. He pulled out a small piece of paper, unfolded it, and handed it to Morton.

Morton hesitated taking it until Paxton explained, "Already dusted. I don't make rookie mistakes."

It took a moment for Morton to focus. It was a short note. It read, *Tell Joe I hope he had fun.*

"That Black bitch!" Morton spat, spittle forming on his lips. "How did she know that I'd decide to sleep with her? he exclaimed in exasperation.

Paxton shrugged again. "Professional instinct, I guess," Paxton observed. "Besides, from what you told me about her, only a dead man would be safe."

Morton groaned. "Shit! I showered." He slapped the top of his desk with his hand. "I fuckin' showered! Maybe one of the girls left some hair on me. I washed away evidence. Fuck!" he exclaimed.

Paxton asked calmly, "If everything was taken, how did you dry yourself off? Did you have a towel in your bag?"

Morton looked at Paxton, confused. "I told you. I found a towel on the sink."

Paxton sighed then said, "Guess what, homeboy. They left the towel on purpose. They knew you'd shower once you saw the towel. They knew you'd be too out of it to be thinking clearly."

"Fucking, scheming cunts!" Morton hissed.

Paxton shook his head. "No need to beat yourself up about that. I bet one of those girls or somebody working with them also combed your pubic region and checked your body parts before they left you bare-assed. If you felt hands down there, you probably thought they were jerking you off." Paxton rubbed his jaw. "You were set up big time, Morton. The question is…why?"

"That's what I can't figure out, yet. Blackmail is obvious, but what's the endgame?"

"Well, where do you go from here with your dead-end investigation?" Morton said with an edge of sarcasm.

Paxton frowned. "Like I said … I got people following up on what information we do have, which ain't much. They'll be contacting the Department of Motor Vehicles, the Department of Revenue, and the State Attorney General's office, doing a records check statewide, and nationally and even checking INTERPOL. The only other thing left to do would be to get a composite sketch of the women and put a BOLO out for them. But, given the slick way they played you, I'm sure those girls could change their appearances in a heartbeat." Paxton hesitated. "My guess is they're long gone. Don't expect to find them casually having coffee at the local Starbucks."

Morton looked forlorn and desperate, then, he suddenly beamed. He almost came out of his chair. Before he could speak, Paxton raised his hand abruptly to stop him.

He said flatly, "Oh! Forgot to tell you. Someone erased the tapes on the surveillance cameras in the rental office, parking lot, and her place of employment. I'll check the security cameras on the streets, but that's probably a dead end, too. That gal, Erzulie, was probably slick enough to give you directions to her apartment that bypassed CCTV cameras."

Morton thrust himself so violently back into his chair that he hit the wall with a resounding bang that sounded like a gunshot.

Paxton said softly, "I don't know if it has sunk in yet, boss, but these gals weren't just plain old ordinary working girls. They were part of a well-thought-out, highly organized shakedown plan, but I just can't figure out why they went after you."

"Just do what you can, Paxton," Morton said weakly. "I'd really appreciate it." Color had yet to return to his face.

Paxton grunted as he pushed his bulky body up from the chair. "This one is gonna cost you a trip to Cabo San Lucas, hombre."

Morton didn't balk. "If you find Jetta, I'll give you a trip around the world."

Paxton became oddly quiet. Morton knew that pensive look from working with him in the past and asked, "What the fuck else, Paxton?" Weariness and strain didn't permit him to be polite.

"Well… just a random, out-of the-box thought, my man, but I do believe that little filly Erzulie gave you a veiled warning, of sorts."

"Veiled warning? What the fuck do you mean, Paxton?"

"Well," he paused. "Might not mean anything, but it might mean a lot," Paxton said. "I was curious about that name, Erzulie. It's unusual. So I looked it up. Thought it might give me some kind of lead. It turns out that Erzulie is a love goddess that the slaves prayed to when slave owners sold their family members off—you know—separating wives, husbands, and children."

"Jetta mentioned that. But what the fuck does that have to do with anything?" Morton asked.

Paxton tapped his temple for emphasis. "Think about it, boss. You're a white prosecutor. The majority of defendants you prosecute are Black or brown. You take away their freedom. You send them to prison. You separate them from their families. Children lose a parent. Households shift to survival mode. A breadwinner disappears. Communities change. Take enough people away and whole neighborhoods become impoverished." Paxton paused. "Because of what you do." "My gut tells me Erzulie is here to protect someone you're about to prosecute," he said, narrowing his eyes.

The last bit of color drained from Morton's face. Dumbstruck, he whispered, almost disbelieving, "Like that kid Marshall is representing?"

Paxton shrugged. "I don't know this guy Marshall, but maybe. Could be the reason for the setup." Shaking his head, he said, "Blackmail. Oldest fucking game in town."

Morton sat numb as Paxton made his way to the door. Silently berating himself, he thought, *You dumb, arrogant asshole. She told you what her name meant. She told you who she was. You just didn't listen.*

Morton's face felt suddenly hot as he recalled the dinner meeting at Jake's Steakhouse. *That Black bastard Marshall must be laughing his ass off now. And Marshall acted like he'd never laid eyes on her before.*

After opening the door, Paxton turned around and said softly, "Get something to eat, Morton. It might help."

As Paxton closed the door, Morton spun his chair around to face the window. The harsh glare of the noonday sun forced him to close his eyes. His head throbbed. He felt nauseated.

He could still smell her. Despite his shower, her fragrance lingered—a delicious, intoxicating, tantalizing essence. And the taste of her … my God! Unconsciously, he licked his lips.

"Erzulie," he said in a hoarse whisper. "That Black bitch and Marshall set me up!" Morton moaned. He swung his chair back toward his desk and buried his head in his hands.

18

The Brotherhood

Doug Joiner, known as the Professor by his students, waited on his steps with his Rottweiler, Hannibal, for them to arrive for his evening class. They were his "boys," African-American teens from the International Baccalaureate program from his wife's school, whom she'd chosen for him to mentor.

When Li'l Bits' suggested a courthouse field trip, Doug and Tawanna readily agreed, seeing it as a meaningful way to connect current juvenile court proceedings with the historical roles of the judiciary and legislature in sustaining slavery.

Doug explained to Li'l Bits, "Look! I know you're excited to see your friend, but this isn't just about observing a court in action. It's about understanding how the law works now—and how it used to work. Judges and lawmakers once declared slavery as legal and later designed penal systems after Reconstruction to supply businesses with Black prison laborers. If you pay close attention, you'll see how echoes of that same system still shape—and continue to influence—the way kids of color are treated today. This excursion isn't just a field trip. It's a window into history—and how that history continues to repeat itself."

The boys' parents were more than comfortable with a visit to the courthouse. However, the planned presentation—as a follow-up discussion—proved challenging for some. Although all the parents fully supported the goal of educating their sons about what it means to be Black growing up in a color-coded society, several felt that some of Doug's material might be too raw for their sons' sensibilities.

Tawanna learned that two of the seven students, who'd been approved to attend Tyrene's first appearance in juvenile court, might not be attending her husband's evening class.

Doug and his wife had discussed the topics he planned to cover in a debriefing session; and Tawanna, a former teacher and now a social worker, understood the need to obtain parental consent.

Due to Tawanna's insistence, Doug made material available to the parents, prepared a lesson plan, and stood ready to respond to their questions. However, the community meeting with some of the parents was disheartening.

One parent observed, "I realize that my son has been exposed to inappropriate content in the media, movies, and internet. Some of the things he's seen, I hadn't been exposed to until I was much older. But discussing lynchings, taking Black body parts as souvenirs, breeding slave women, raping children, or performing painful medical experiments on enslaved women without anesthesia," the parent paused, "Well, it might be too much. It would be too much for me," he confessed.

Nervously rubbing his hands together, the man continued, "Besides, stories like that make America seem barbaric and evil."

Trying to remain as calm as possible, Doug replied, "This isn't fiction. Everything I've written has been researched, investigated, recorded, and documented. Just read the slave narratives, testimonies from slave owners, plantation records, lynching postcards, congressional records, newspaper clipping, journalist accounts..." He stopped suddenly. His voice cracked with emotion.

"It's ugly, but it's true! It's part of American history that some educators and politicians are desperate to hide. It is the story of this country's oppression of our people."

As he spoke, he struggled to keep his emotions in check. "If we bury, distort, or hide the uglier parts of America's past—if we sanitize and romanticize its history—how can we truly understand what's happening today? Throughout its history, America has passed laws to oppress and stigmatize us, using terror and intimidation to keep us trapped as second-class citizens. This hasn't stopped. If we don't confront and understand this history, how can we fight against it? How can we create change? Pretending history is irrelevant or a thing of the past will only keep us ignorant and powerless. It's almost criminal to think otherwise."

"This is ancient history. We're past worrying about our survival," another parent said. "We need to teach our children how to stay safe when stopped by a cop, keep them out of gangs, and educate them about drugs."

"Education is the key," a woman joined in. "Get our children to college and keep them out of prison."

What started as a quiet, information-sharing session quickly erupted into a heated, acrimonious debate. Tawanna intervened as the mediator and attempted to restore order. Finally, after nearly two hours, a vote was taken. Five parents approved a modified lesson plan, while two parents opted out.

In the days leading up to the session, Doug didn't sleep well. The only thing that he could do was to prepare, prepare, and prepare some more. Tawanna gave him a few rudimentary rules about the art, science, and practice of teaching. He thought being a cop was a lot easier.

The day before the session with the boys, Doug came to a realization. He'd been so focused on educating and challenging them that he overlooked a basic rule of communication—just have a conversation. Be open. Don't try to control it. Let the boys steer the conversation wherever they want to go.

"No matter what, better light than darkness, eh, Hannibal?" he said, scratching the dog's ears. Hannibal barked his approval.

Doug picked up his cane and rose slowly off the porch steps. He winced slightly as his old bullet wound registered its nagging presence. Ignoring the pain, a smile quickly spread across his face as he began to detect the unmistakable sound of carefree, youthful energy. In a moment, they would be visible as the boys turned the corner onto his block. He took a deep breath and shouted back toward the house, "Tawanna! They're here!"

A few minutes later, the boys entered the room noisily, as usual, with the carefree abandon and boundless energy typical of bright, curious, and enthusiastic youth. It was a marvelous blend of cacophony and rhythm. Spending time with them always gave Doug a stirring sense of pride and so much hope for the future of Black Americans. Mentoring these young men made him feel that he was not only contributing to their intellectual growth and development, but also following in the revered footsteps of W.E.B Du Bois, who espoused identifying the "talented tenth"—that ten percent of exceptional Black men and women from the total Black population who would become leaders, educators, and an inspiration to uplift the Black race as a whole.

Doug chuckled. He didn't even have ten mentees, but at least it was a start. He studied them as they randomly circled the living room, deciding where to sit. He had instructed them to find a different seat at each meeting. It was his small way of inching the boys outside their comfort zones.

Positioning six folding chairs in a semi-circle at a comfortable distance from each other, he placed his chair at the top of the circle.

Although the room was less crowded, it didn't feel more comfortable. Everyone missed the other boys. The five boys attending this evening's class seemed to share Doug's disappointment as they felt the emptiness of the vacant spaces.

After they sat down, Doug scanned their faces, to carefully gauge their mental space. Their academic demands at school, athletic practices, part-time jobs, and household chores sometimes interfered with their ability to stay fully focused in the evening.

Doug admired their commitment to the Brotherhood and their desire to learn more about Black history. The boys knew what they learned and discussed in his home wasn't even touched upon in their school classes. Issues of race were often taboo subject areas. Some sanitized discussion about slavery, the Civil War, and the civil rights movement would generally occur—but devoid of any meaningful conversations about the brutal violence of those periods, the sad loss of life, or how the legacy of that era had literally bled into the present.

He cleared his throat and finally announced, "Okay, boys! Time to begin."

Doug asked, "Where is your country?"

The boys responded in unison, "The world."

"Who is your brother?" Doug thundered.

The boys again responded, "All mankind!"

The boys were smiling and, as always, Doug felt a sense of pride. He inhaled before asking the last question of the Brotherhood's adopted credo. "What is your religion?"

"To do good!" they shouted.

Doug nodded appreciatively. *How different the world would be if everyone embraced these values,* he thought.

"Li'l Bits," Doug began, "since it was your idea to visit juvenile court, why don't you update us about your friend?" Pausing, Doug asked, "What's the young man's name—Tyrene, isn't it? When you pointed him out in the jury box, I thought he could almost be your twin, except for the hair."

"Well, the bandages were a dead giveaway," Kahil interjected. "Somebody oughta teach your boy how to throw hands." Kahil—a streetwise kid, who prided himself on being able to fight—did not tolerate being dissed by anyone. Before his mom had gotten a job transfer from the inner city to the 'burbs', as Kahil called it, he'd had to fight somebody on the school grounds pretty much every day, particularly if he didn't want to get a reputation as a "bitch."

Isaiah, a dark-skinned kid with bright, intelligent eyes, asked Li'l Bits, "Is your friend Tyrene a pacifist?"

Doug interrupted, chuckling. "Hold on, boys. Let the man talk."

Li'l Bits smiled, grateful they were concerned about Tyrene. Leaning forward, he said, "His mom told me the school bully jumped him. And no, Isaiah, he is not a pacifist." Looking pointedly at Kahil, he said, "And yes, Kahil, he knows how to fight. I know because I taught him."

They had all seen Li'l Bits compete in karate tournaments. If he didn't win first place, he always left with a trophy.

"Knowing Tyrene, for whatever reason, I think he decided to just take the beating." Several of the boys shook their heads in disbelief. "That bully must've finally said something really stupid to get Tyrene to fight back," Li'l Bits ventured.

Doug shrugged. "You got to admit—words can wound deeply." He paused. "Even more so than a punch or a kick."

Isaiah said, "That boy might have made the mistake of using the "N" word. That's the one word—said to the wrong person at the wrong time in the wrong place—that can get a white boy killed."

Samuel, a slight effeminate boy, nodded in agreement, "Yeah! From what I heard Tyrene went primeval on that kid."

"Any change in the charges, Li'l Bits?" Doug asked. "The prosecutor seemed like he was out for his pound of flesh."

Li'l Bits shook his head. "I don't know much more than what we heard that day in court. But a few days later, his mom texted me to let me know that Tyrene's case had been moved to adult court. She said Tyrene was sitting with a bunch of adults, and she was waiting for his lawyer to appear. She said something about the prosecutor investigating a sexual assault charge of some sort."

Hearing the charge of sexual assault caused Doug to catch his breath. All the boys turned to look at him, curious about his reaction. "The stakes just got way, way higher for your friend, Li'l Bits. A sexual assault charge is scary not just because of the nature of the charge, but because it usually carries a mandatory sentence."

Seeing eyebrows raised, Doug explained, "A conviction for that crime means prison. It's not at all unusual for the prosecution to add as many charges as he can to pressure an accused to take a deal, but how is this sexual assault charge connected to the fight? Something doesn't add up!"

He looked at Li'l Bits. "If the prosecutor is serious about the sexual assault charge, this case has got to go to trial."

"What do you mean, Professor?" Li'l Bits asked.

"The prosecutor always offers a plea bargain—a deal," he explained. "Plead guilty to something, and other charges will be reduced or dismissed. But a sexual assault is seldom dropped and becomes the heart of the plea bargain. The stigma of it can ruin Tyrene's life if he accepts a deal like that. A plea to a sex offense is not the end of the world, but life in prison and afterwards will be very hard."

Devon, the Brotherhood's aspiring documentary filmmaker, said, "I read that only three percent of those charged risk going to trial."

Doug nodded. "That stat's pretty accurate, but what's troubling here is that someone is looking to drop this kid into a deep well." Doug looked at each boy before speaking. "Think about it. Why not keep a juvenile case in juvenile court? Why transfer it to adult court? Tack on a sexual assault charge when Tyrene was the one bullied in a school fight? Try to add an attempted murder charge?"

Doug turned to Li'l Bits. "Your friend's record is clean, right? No prior convictions, arrests, or anything else that might show up in a background check?"

"I think I would've heard something if he had gotten into trouble. I'm pretty sure his record is clean," Li'l Bits answered.

Devon said, "I've seen some documentaries about the justice system that would scare the hell out of any Black person."

"Which ones did you see?" asked Doug.

"The Central Park Five! That's the case where authorities sent four Blacks and one Latino teenager to prison for supposedly raping a white female jogger. The cops tricked them into confessing to a crime they didn't commit. DNA evidence later proved that a serial rapist had committed the crime. Still...after the convictions were overturned and they were exonerated, the prosecution continued to insist that the boys were guilty."

Jerome, a tall, lanky kid who had shaved his head to protest a friend's school expulsion, spoke up. "Yeah! I saw that one. The crime happened in 1989. One kid spent six years in prison. I think another spent almost thirteen for a crime he didn't commit."

"But the documentary that really got me was the one about Kalief Browder," Devon said. "At 16, he was sent to Rikers Island. He spent seven hundred days in solitary confinement and almost three years in county jail. Yusuf Salaam, one of the Central Park Five, spent time in solitary. I think he said that solitary can make you go crazy."

"I was shocked by Kalief's story, too," Doug said. "While incarcerated, guards and inmates repeatedly beat Kalief. He was offered a deal after thirty-three months for allegedly stealing a backpack but refused it. Said he'd done nothing wrong."

When Jerome whispered "Kalief Browder," all eyes turned to him Jerome was visibly upset. Sighing heavily, he said, "I hope Tyrene gets a better break than the Central Park Five and Kalief."

"He got out, right? Kalief got released from jail?" Li'l Bits asked hopefully.

Before Jerome could answer, Devon said quietly, a touch of sadness in his voice, "Yeah. Kalief got out. Went to community college, tutored kids in his neighborhood." Devon's voice trailed off.

"Then what?" Li'l Bits asked anxiously.

Devon couldn't speak the words. Jerome looked down at the floor. The other boys, unfamiliar with Kalief's story, looked at Devon, then at Jerome. Devon and Jerome remembered that Li'l Bits had shared with the group that he needed therapy after Tyrene's brother Duke had taken his life.

Wanting to be careful with his words, Doug finally said, "Kalief took his life, Li'l Bits. He hanged himself at his home. His mom found him." Shaking his head at the waste of a young life, Doug said, "I believe that the brutal experience at Rikers ultimately broke him, Li'l Bits. It would've broken a grown man, but he was just a kid. He was 22 when he died."

Li'l Bits rocked back in his chair. Doug reached over to put his hand on his shoulder. "You okay?"

Without answering, Li'l Bits rose unsteadily from his chair and started toward the door, his breathing ragged.

"Where are you going, Li'l' Bits?" Devon asked "Are you okay?"

Jerome's face was tight with worry as he asked, "Want some company, Li'l Bits?"

Doug raised his hand to gently quiet them, then pushed himself up from the chair with his cane and followed Li'l Bits to the door. Hannibal stirred from his nap and trotted dutifully after him, tail wagging.

"Hold on, buddy," Doug said, following him. "You going home? Do you feel sick? I can ask Tawanna to give you a ride, but let's talk first, okay?"

Li'l Bits shook his head. "Just need some air," he mumbled.

"Of course. We can all use a break. The other boys are probably feeling the same way." Doug and Li'l Bits walked down the hallway, stopping at the front door.

Li'l Bits fought back tears. "It's not right! It's not right at all! America is supposed to be a nation of laws!" He demanded, "How could something like that happen?"

Doug's words were heavy with sadness. "It's an all-too-familiar story, Li'l Bits." A pained look came over his face. "Kalief was Black, poor, and young. He was labeled a criminal, stereotyped as a thief, trapped in an unfair system that favors white people with money. His family couldn't afford $3,000 to bond him out, and he had no lawyer. He was an innocent kid imprisoned in a system designed to dehumanize."

"You didn't mention racism, Professor," he added bitterly.

Doug sighed, "Ah, yes! Racism. That, too. America's homemade poison."

After a moment, Li'l Bits said, "I overheard my mom and dad talking about Tyrene's case."

Doug's eyebrow arched. "And..."

"I didn't want to tell the group because I thought it was too personal." Li'l Bits said. "The judge in adult court locked Tyrene's mom up. Held her in contempt and locked her up! And he wouldn't set a bond for Tyrene!" he growled. "I heard that the sexual assault charge involved the bully's girlfriend."

"His girlfriend?" Doug said sharply, shifting his weight on his cane. "This case has taken a very strange turn."

"Ms. Horn sent me a text asking that we pray for them," Li'l Bits said quietly.

Doug nodded firmly. "The Brotherhood will pray for the family. We'll pray together."

"My parents have set up a meeting with our church elders to see what our members can do," Li'l Bits said. "I've got to do something to help my friend."

Doug shook his head. "There's nothing you can do, Li'l Bits. Let his mom and their lawyer handle this. Maybe the church members can take up a collection to help with a bond if one gets set. Maybe they can put pressure on the prosecutor to be more reasonable when it comes to a plea bargain."

"I can't just do nothing, Professor."

"My experience in law enforcement tells me that something rotten is going on here with these charges, particularly this alleged sexual assault charge coming out of nowhere." Doug placed his hand on Li'l Bits' shoulder. "But trying to do something, could put you at risk. Tyrene doesn't want you to wind up where he is." Doug gripped his shoulder harder. "Be smart," he said firmly.

"Be smart or be safe, Professor? You've taught us about the courage and struggle of our people throughout America's long and oppressive history—those who were assassinated for our cause: Reverend Elbert Williams, Vernon Dahmer, Medgar Evers, Fred Hampton, Malcolm X, and Reverend Martin Luther King Jr.—and the warriors who risked death because they challenged systemic racism and white supremacy Frederick Douglass, Sojourner Truth, Harriet Tubman, Ida B. Wells, W.E.B Du Bois, the Little Rock Nine, Fannie Lou Hamer, Rosa Parks, John Lewis, Bryan Stevenson, Thurgood Marshall and—"

Doug interrupted softly, "Okay! Okay! Yes! I get your point, Li'l Bits. You're right. Those individuals risked—and some lost—their lives for the freedoms we enjoy today, but *this* is not the same thing."

Li'l Bits' expression was noncommittal. "Thanks, Professor," he said quietly. "I'm just gonna step outside for a moment. Okay?"

Doug reluctantly released his shoulder. Taking a deep breath, he said, "Sure! Go clear your head. Rejoin us when you're ready, son. But come back to us, okay? We'll pray for the family when you return to the group."

Before Li'l Bits had walked down on the front steps, he'd already made up his mind. He would take action. He didn't yet know what form it would take, but he was determined to let Kalief's life inspire him.

Li'l Bits marveled at Kalief's heart and courage. He hadn't bowed to the system. Despite beatings from prison guards, attacks by inmates, months in solitary confinement, and the slow madness of incarceration, this teenage Black boy had stood firm. He didn't break. He didn't take a plea. Something mattered to him more than freedom.

Looking up at the sky—swollen with ash-colored clouds drifting past a crescent moon—Li'l Bits embraced his faith.

On several evenings, while praying before bedtime, he heard his name called. It was a soft whisper, gentle and familiar. The voice washed over him like the ripple of warm waves, and he felt a loving presence. The joy of it nearly brought him to tears.

His mind began to race. He wondered, *What possible advantage might he have over trained investigators?*

Hope eluded him until he remembered hearing about a teenager who had solved a crime the police had given up on.

Pulling out his cell phone, he began a search. Up popped Jessica Maple—a 12-year-old Black girl who had tracked down her great-grandmother's stolen furniture at a local pawn shop. The police had assumed someone with a key was responsible, since there were no signs of forced entry and large furniture had been taken. But Jessica knew only her parents had keys. Refusing to accept the police theory, she launched her own investigation and discovered that the thief had entered through an attached garage the police had failed to inspect. They had completely dropped the ball.

Li'l Bits started brainstorming, wondering what investigative leads might have been neglected or ignored. Maybe something was hiding in plain sight?

Then, a possibility hit him. It was so simple. It was a long shot—an implausible chance, of course, but he wouldn't know unless he tried. He knew who to contact if only she would help him.

"What's my religion?" Li'l Bits asked himself. The familiar, encouraging answer came. "*To do good.*"

19

The Art of Killing

TicToc couldn't have prepared Patricia for the experience she'd have with Melissa, the psychic medium. Although she had listened intently to TicToc's account of connecting with her deceased sister, Maya, hearing about it was one thing—experiencing it was another. TicToc said it was like being drawn into a shimmering light that pulsed with presence, where time unraveled, and a voice could be heard—not spoken aloud, but felt deep within the soul. After the session, Patricia had collapsed on the floor repeating over and over. "How did I not know?"

She'd been in shock during the elevator ride back down to the first floor—every second stretched thin by grief. She stared vacantly at the glass panels of revolving doors—dazed, oblivious to the foot traffic flowing around her. Her energy was spent, leaving her drained and empty. Her grasp on reality had slipped away. The soul-numbing experience left her emotionally adrift in a sea of unimaginable pain and sorrow.

In the car, TicToc was on the phone with Carl. "Can you see her yet, Carl? I got a text saying she left Melissa's office about 15 minutes ago." The strain in TicToc's voice was unmistakable.

Carl knew Ms. Horn was important to TicToc far beyond the bond of a deep, personal friendship. She had become family.

Parked on the street facing the building Patricia had entered nearly two hours ago, Carl glanced at his watch, wondering what happened to cause such a delay. Worry began to creep in—not for Patricia's physical safety, but for her emotional well-being. He'd hoped her experience with the medium would be as profound as TicToc's, but he also knew these sessions didn't always go as planned.

He wasn't naive. No two encounters could be the same. When navigating the mystery of the unknown—the spiritual realm and those who have passed over—he understood, instinctively, that there was no roadmap for a mystical, otherworldly experience.

"Carl!" TicToc's voice rang out again. "Can you hear me, Carl?"

"Yes, Boss Lady. I can hear you. I'm directly across from the building, and..." he paused, his words hanging in the air. "It looks like..." Excitement mounted in his voice. "She just stepped out of the building!"

Carl gave two quick taps on the horn, bringing Patricia to an abrupt stop. A flicker of recognition crossed her face as she turned toward the sound. She seemed lost. Her movements unsteady and hesitant. Carl tensed as she stepped into the street against the light. He blared the horn to warn her of oncoming traffic.

Tires screeched. The acrid stench of burnt rubber clawed at the air as a delivery truck swerved, missing her by inches. Furious drivers leaned hard on their horns. She barely acknowledged them, her vacant eyes fixed on some distant point beyond the cacophony of noise.

"Damn!" Carl yelled. "She just walked into oncoming traffic!"

"Get her, Carl!" TicToc shouted.

He hurried out of the car and dashed into traffic, scowling as if daring anyone to hit him. His sheer size alone was enough to make drivers slow down and take notice of the Titan striding purposefully toward a disoriented woman wandering in the street.

Carl could have easily swept her up in his arms, but the sudden movement might frighten her. Instead, he placed one arm firmly around her shoulders to guide her back to the car, while extending the other arm to keep oncoming traffic at bay. Fortunately, the light changed quickly, allowing him time to move her slowly and gently across the street. Carl flung the door open and helped Patricia into her seat. She looked shell-shocked.

He handed her his cell phone and jumped into the driver's seat. "Hang in there, Ms. Horn!" He eased the car into traffic and headed toward the highway. After a moment, Patricia slowly put the phone to her ear.

"Horn, are you okay? Sounds like you nearly caused an accident. How'd it go? Were you able to contact your son? Did you speak to him?"

Hearing TicToc's voice helped her recover her senses. Patricia began to cry softly. She tried to speak—but couldn't.

"I'm so sorry, honey," TicToc said. "It doesn't work for everyone the first time. Sometimes, it doesn't happen at all. I should've prepared you better, but I was sure it would work. Melissa helped me to speak to my sister. I thought," she paused, "I hoped it would happen for you, too."

Patricia took a deep breath, trying to ward off the swimming feeling in her head and quiet the pounding of her heart. When she was finally able to speak she said, "I saw him! I saw my baby." More tears slipped down her cheeks. "He was so…" her voice broke, "so beautiful." She took another deep breath to steady herself.

"There was a light… It was so incredibly soothing. It seemed to shift back and forth from a brilliant yellow to light gold like it was breathing—flowing over and around him like the wind. I wanted to touch him, but I was afraid that he might disappear if I tried."

TicToc felt a tear gathering at the corner of her eye. "Oh, I'm so glad, Horn. I'm so glad."

"He seemed so at peace," she whispered, wonder softening her voice. "I almost forgot to ask him why he left us."

TicToc hesitated before asking, "Did he tell you, Horn? Did he tell you why?"

"It wasn't like he spoke, TicToc. I mean… I just heard the medium's voice."

"What did she say?"

"She said, 'It's so peaceful here. I'm safe now, and I don't hurt anymore.'" Patricia started to cry again.

TicToc noted that the timbre of her friend's crying had changed—like light fading into darkness. Then in a voice that TicToc had seldom heard from her friend, heavy with the anguished emotion of loss and pain that TicToc knew all too well, Patricia said, "I want someone killed."

Although accustomed to death, a chill rippled through TicToc, as well as a deep sadness. TicToc instinctively knew she had learned something from her son—something that had caused her heart to break.

Patricia heard Carl over the intercom. “You’ll find some scotch shooters in that wooden container to your right, Ms. Horn.”

Patricia took a moment to compose herself, then she removed the lid from the box and examined the array of tiny bottles before settling on Chivas Regal. She twisted the top off and downed the gold liquid in one large gulp. With the heat of scotch in her throat and stomach, Patricia returned to the call.

"You're my friend, TicToc. I know that. You don't want me to take a step I’ll regret, but this decision ain't one of them." Wiping hot tears from her face, she asked, "You ever regret killing anyone?”

TicToc let out a sharp, involuntary laugh, “Not a damn one! Not even the very first one, I’m embarrassed to say. I figured each target did the kind of shit that deserved a death sentence. Keep in mind we’re talking about some very bad people who destroyed a lot of lives and caused a lot of pain to mostly innocent folk."

"And what did you say to God after you killed them? How did you try to make it right with Him?"

Honestly,” TicToc reflected, “it depends on *how* I kill them. If I kill from a distance, I say a prayer for their soul right after I squeeze the trigger and ask God to forgive me. If I kill up close, with a knife, and there’s time, I place my hand on their shoulder and tell them to go with God.

"Now, Horn, you need to be clear about something. I don’t necessarily hate these people. They mean nothing to me. I’m just fulfilling a contract.”

"And the men who killed your sister, what did you say to them?" Patricia held her breath, fearing that she was asking too much, that she had gone too far. But she needed to know.

TicToc answered, her voice calm and deliberate, "I cursed them. I said, 'A ring of eternal fire has been prepared for you in hell'. And if God doesn't forgive me and I end up in hell with you, I'll spend eternity killing you over and over again.'"

She paused then said, "Horn, you need to be as sure as you can that you can live with blood on your hands without regret, without remorse, and without second thoughts. More importantly, when you think about the person's death, you should feel that killing them once wasn't enough—and that if given the chance, you'd do it again without a moment's hesitation."

Patricia didn't respond—chewing her lip, turning over TicToc's words, and weighing her decision. It was a life-or-death decision, and she knew one thing for certain: if she asked TicToc to kill someone for her, TicToc wouldn't say no. Any hesitation or caution on TicToc's part didn't come from any moral qualms. TicToc wanted to make sure that she could live with her decision to end someone's life.

"I want you to kill my ex." Patricia's voice was ragged with emotion.

"Any particular way?" TicToc asked casually.

Surprised by her nonchalance, Patricia stammered, "Don't... don't you want to know why?"

"Don't care, Horn. Your reason is your own. If your reason is good enough for you, it's good enough for me."

"But I want you to know why." Patricia paused. "Because when you kill that bastard, I want you to tell him why you're ending his miserable life."

"Does this have anything to do with Duke's suicide?" TicToc asked.

TicToc was all too familiar with the sound of grief. She'd encountered it in every corner of the world. She had nearly steeled herself to its awful sound—but not completely. She heard her friend's wrenching cries and squeezed her eyes shut. Horn's sudden wail whipped the air with rage, pain, and fury.

Startled and alarmed, Carl had to refrain from pulling the car off the road.

TicToc covered her ears, tears welling in her eyes. She shouted, "Carl! Pull over—and hold her until she stops crying!"

Carl found a safe place to pull over and activated his hazard lights. He got out of the car, and opened the rear passenger door. Patricia was on her side curled up in a tight ball. Between deep breathless gasps, she moaned, "My God! My God! It hurts—it hurts so bad!"

Carl slid inside and carefully lifted her up, letting her head rest on his shoulder. She nearly disappeared in his embrace as he wrapped his arms gently around her. Carl said fiercely, "I got you. I got you, Ms. Horn." A moment later Patricia became limp and relaxed in his arms.

TicToc wiped the tears from her eyes and waited patiently on the phone. Five minutes later, Carl said, "Boss, she's asleep."

"Just sit with her for a bit, Carl." TicToc's voice was tight with worry.

"Will do," he replied. "Can't sit here much longer, though. Highway Patrol might be along soon. I don't want to have to explain why we pulled off the road. At the very least, the cop would probably think he's stumbled across a domestic violence situation."

"Okay. A few more minutes. Then take off. Let me know when she's awake?" she said anxiously.

When Patricia's breathing had become even and slow, Carl eased his phone out of her hand and disconnected the call. Then he laid her gently on the back seat and exited the car. A few minutes later he called TicToc. "Back on the road, Boss. Will check in with you later."

After 20 minutes or so, Patricia woke up. She was groggy and disoriented. Her eyes met Carl's in the rearview mirror. He saw sadness and resilience. She saw kindness and strength.

"Thank you, Carl, for helping me. It felt like you held me together."

"I appreciate that, Ms. Horn, but you did the work. Have you heard that expression, 'Things fall apart, the center cannot hold?' Well, your center refused to allow you to fall apart."

"I came unglued, Carl," she protested.

"You're still here. You didn't fall apart. Whatever was thrown at you, after all that you've had to endure, no matter how much you suffered, you held on."

After they'd driven for a few minutes Carl asked, "You ready to talk to Boss Lady again, Ms. Horn?"

"Carl, under the circumstances, I think you can call me, Patricia."

"Thank you, but no, I can't, Ms. Horn."

Patricia was quiet for a moment, then she said, "Carl, you ever kill someone?"

He furrowed his brow. "Why do you ask, Ms. Horn?"

"I asked TicToc to kill someone for me. I guess I just needed to hear myself talk about it out loud with someone."

"Let me answer your question this way, Ms. Horn," he said somberly. "The normal, average, everyday civilian forgets that there are truly evil people who commit incredibly horrific acts. The scum who kills or ravages others feels fully justified in destroying lives without pity or remorse. So, my short answer is that some people deserve killing, and that's all there is to it."

He shrugged, a hint of reverence in his voice. "Besides, there's a real art to killing. Few are as skilled as TicToc." He glanced at her in the rearview mirror. "She's made murder into a true art form." Noting her puzzled expression, he elaborated.

"Sometimes, TicToc personally interviews VIP clients to understand their feelings about the target. She usually asks, 'Do you just want the person dead, or do you want the person to be killed in a way that mirrors your feelings?'"

In a voice as casual as requesting a coffee refill, Carl asked, "How do you feel about this person you want killed? What did the medium say about why your son took his life?"

Patricia barely managed to contain the emotions about to rip her chest apart. She did not want to speak the words she heard her son say. She understood to speak them would make them more real in a way that she couldn't deny.

Would she lose her sanity? Would she go mad? Would her rage vaporize her like a blast from a nuclear explosion?

"I need a moment, Carl," she said hoarsely. Carl fell silent. The pained tone of her voice made him wonder if a part of her died in that room with her son and the medium.

"I'll tell you the worst of what Duke said, and I know you'll understand the rest." Carl thought it best not to look at her, so he kept his eyes on the road.

Inhaling deeply, Patricia said in a low, empty voice, "Duke told me his father had been sexually abusing him for years."

Carl shot a quick look at her through the rearview mirror.

Patricia began to tremble. "The worst time for Duke happened when his father took him to a place where he was sodomized by several men so that his father could have sex with another boy. Young, innocent boys. Sick, perverted men." Her voice was starting to crack. "Duke couldn't bear it any longer. The shame consumed him. He couldn't bring himself to tell me. He thought it was his fault—that it was normal for a father to do those things to his son. He thought it made his father happy. It was their secret. Duke never understood why he needed to keep it a secret. When his father let other men use him, he finally understood how wrong it was." Patricia took a long shuddering breath. "I should've known, Carl. I should've protected him."

Patricia started to sob. Quietly at first, then deep wracking sobs.

Carl didn't know what to say. He wanted to honor her pain but he didn't have the words.

Both were silent now, each lost in their own thoughts. Patricia said, "Duke wanted me to know that he's alright—that he doesn't feel the pain of those moments anymore. He even apologized for sending me the buffalo coins, but he felt that he had to. He told me his father has been living with a young, single woman with a boy about preschool age. He doesn't want that boy to experience what he did."

She withdrew into silence again. Carl listened to her breathing, shallow and rapid.

"So, Carl, how would TicToc kill somebody like that?"

Carl was silent for a moment, then shook his head. "I can't tell you. Ms Horn. All I know is that she won't have a problem doing it. She'll make him sorry that he was ever born. But first, we've got to find him."

"We need to find him quickly, Carl. When I think of what that young boy might be going through... like my son..." Patricia's voice trailed off.

"Not a problem, Ms. Horn. With any luck, it shouldn't take long."

Surprised, Patricia asked, "He's been gone for years. Why do you think you can find him so quickly?"

He paused, wondering whether to tell her. "Remember when you were in jail and the DA announced that he couldn't prosecute your case due to the victim's whereabouts being unknown?" he asked glancing at her in the rearview mirror.

Patricia nodded.

"The DA said his investigator had conducted an exhaustive search for several days with little hope of finding him. He then asked the court to dismiss your case, right?"

"Yes. How could I forget that?" Patricia replied, curiosity growing in her voice.

"Your husband didn't show up for your trial because TicToc paid him to disappear."

Patricia felt like someone just slapped her hard in the face.

Carl continued, "$50,000, I believe."

"What the hell, Carl? TicToc never told me."

"No need to tell you, Ms. Horn," Carl said calmly. "TicToc wanted him gone to secure your release from jail. She considered killing him, but didn't think it would be right unless you agreed. She finally decided to pay him off. She got him a new identity: a driver's license and a social security card, as well as a plane ticket to leave town, and an agreement never to contact you, Duke, or Tyrene again."

"I'll be damned," Patricia muttered. "That's why that low-life bastard never showed up for court. Now I know for certain he wasn't trying to do me any favors." She paused for a moment, deep in thought. "It now makes sense why TicToc told me in county not to worry about the case—that God had my back," she said.

"We'll find him, Ms. Horn. No question about that." Then, with a dry chuckle, he added, "So, TicToc might get the chance to kill him after all."

Catching Patricia's eyes in the rearview mirror, he smiled. "This time... with your permission."

20
Nothing Ventured

Li'l Bits stared at the door of his friend Sasha's house. *Maybe I should just leave*, he thought. *Just walk away and pray it will all work out for Tyrene.* His mom did say Tyrene had an excellent lawyer—a Black one, at that! Li'l Bits smiled. After seeing a white judge, a white prosecutor, white security guards, and a white clerk in court, he was so very proud that Black lawyers could fight for the rights of Black clients. Maybe Tyrene's lawyer might be able to obtain justice for him. And maybe—just maybe—he could use some help from someone outside the legal system.

Li'l Bits fidgeted with the door knocker. Anxiety and fear caused him to hesitate. *Could the Professor be right? Should he leave it alone and let the attorney do his job? But what kind of friend would he be if he did nothing? What if, by some incredible stroke of luck or uncommon favor, he could uncover some information that could upend the prosecutor's case?*

A Bible verse came to mind. *There is nothing concealed that will not be discovered, or hidden that will not be made known.*

He let the heavy door knocker drop with a loud bang and waited. He picked it up to rap again quickly two more times. No response. He frowned. He was about to knock again when he heard movement behind the door.

A young female voice called out, "It's open. C'mon in." When he opened the door and stepped inside, Sasha beckoned him to follow her downstairs. Beneath the stairwell was a door she had left ajar. He walked down the hall and stood at the top of the stairs that descended to a room below.

"C'mon down, big boy. I've got something to show you." Her voice was deliberately teasing low, sultry, and suggestive.

Li'l Bits yelled, embarrassed, "I hope your parents aren't home. Do you want to get me killed?"

She laugh. "Naw! You're safe! They're out shopping with my sister. Won't be back for hours."

Breathing a sigh of relief, Li'l Bits headed down the stairs, past a large sign emblazoned with the words *Girl Cave*, and plopped into a billowing bean bag chair beside her.

Sasha was all smiles and giggles. His eyes were drawn to her cupid bow-shaped lips which made her so alluring.

She laid her head gently on his shoulder. He acknowledged the gesture with a smile and looked around the room.

"I've never been down here before," he said.

Posters of Beyoncé and Michael B. Jordan decorated the walls. Paper butterflies of all colors and sizes hung from the ceiling. Against the wall, on a bright red futon, was an array of fluffy pillows that barely concealed the heads of what appeared to be elves and fairies with large, expressive eyes. Enormous potted plants dotted the room. The vegetation seemed otherworldly, like something out of *Alice in Wonderland.*

She took his hand. Looking deeply into his dark brown eyes, she asked demurely, "Tell me how it feels to be here with me."

Li'l Bits lowered his eyes as if he could hide his feelings. He didn't have to think about the way he felt when he was with her. It was not just her rebellious, fiery spirit that attracted him. It was how he felt in her presence. He felt alive.

Quickly looking up at the clock above her desk to avoid her question, he said, "Hey! It's getting late. I don't want to be downstairs alone with you when your dad returns. I overheard him telling your mom at your birthday party that he didn't like the way I looked at you."

Sasha suddenly stood up with her arms akimbo and yelled, "I will protect you, kind sir, if my father dares to lay a hand on your not-so-fair head."

Li'l Bits rolled his eyes and groaned. Without warning, Sasha plopped onto his lap. The beanbag chair made a loud whooshing sound that mimicked his surprised gasp. As he inhaled sharply, Sasha kissed him lightly on the lips before deftly rolling off the bag. She strolled to her chair in front of her computer desk and sat down to savor his reaction.

He managed to stammer, "You... you... smell like jasmine and roses." Flustered, Li'l Bits added awkwardly, "You taste good, too."

Sasha rolled her eyes. *Just like a guy,* she thought, *comparing me to a meal. Nothing about how he liked our first kiss.* She smiled. *Doesn't matter. I liked it!*

"My... my mom loves jasmine tea," he stammered again. "And my dad brings her roses on the third day of each month to celebrate the anniversary of their first date."

Sasha nodded approvingly. "Your dad's a romantic. You've been trained well."

"Sasha! Did you forget why I asked to come over to your place?"

She smiled. "Breathe easy, young man. No, I didn't forget. I knew something funny was going on when you asked me to find out some information about Allison Ruddick." She added quickly, "I wasn't jealous. Besides, from what I can tell from her social media, she's been head over heels for Wally Kensington for years." She swiveled her chair to face him. "Time to come clean, Matthew Michael Carver."

Li'l Bits sighed. "I didn't want you to know what I was doing because I didn't want you to get involved," he said.

"If I'm cyberstalking this girl, I *will* definitely be involved."

"Yes, but you wouldn't know why," he said quickly.

Crossing her arms across her chest, Sasha narrowed her eyes.

"Just how wrong is your plan to use this information, assuming you can find something interesting on her social media platforms." Her voice had a sharp edge to it.

"Okay, let me explain," he said quickly. He scrambled out of the beanbag and pulled up a chair to sit next to her.

"Just tell me what you hope to find!" Sasha snapped impatiently.

"Right! Okay. Here it is. Allison has accused my friend, Tyrene, of sexually assaulting her." Li'l Bits swallowed hard when he heard Sasha inhale sharply.

"But he didn't do it," he rushed to say. "I know he didn't do it. He's not that kind of guy. He's not interested in girls. After his brother died, he stopped talking. Literally! As far as I know, he hasn't said a word since Duke's death. Maybe two years. Not even to his mom."

"You haven't talked to your friend in two years?" she asked dumbfounded.

'No. I haven't." Li'l Bits shifted, clearly embarrassed. "After his brother died, he and his mom moved out of the neighborhood. He switched schools. I managed to find their phone number, but his mom told me it would be best if I didn't try to see him."

Sasha said, "I don't understand."

"Tyrene, his brother Duke, and I hung out a lot. I mean, *a lot.* You know. Basketball, overnights, dinners, video games, and stuff. The only time Duke wasn't with us was when he went somewhere with his dad. Tyrene's mom was afraid that it might be too painful for him to be around me—that I'd bring back memories of his brother.

Li'l Bits sighed. "But I did see him in court recently. He looked awful. All beaten up and wearing those awful chains."

"I'm so sorry, Li'l Bits. It had to be hard to see your friend like that."

"Yeah... it was." There was a tremor in his voice. "My mentor, Doug—we call him the Professor—is a retired cop." He thought it odd that authorities initially arrested my friend for a school fight and now plan to charge him with sexual assault. The Professor gave me the impression that he thought it was a trumped-up charge."

"Wow, Li'l Bits. Sounds whack!" Sasha began to tug on her lower lip. Li'l Bits knew that meant she was deep in thought.

"What do you think I could find out about Allison?" Sasha asked. "If she's lying about the sexual assault, I seriously doubt that she's going to post it on Instagram or Snapchat. A confession like that would be an open invitation to arrest her. Besides, if nothing else, she wouldn't risk trashing her rep and getting dissed online. For some girls, being a social outcast is a far worse punishment than going to jail."

"Yeah. I hear you, but she doesn't have to confess or admit lying about the crime. She could just express some vague regret or guilt about something she said or did. It might be a clue. I think the police call it a lead."

He saw the skepticism in Sasha's eyes. "I know. It's not much," he admitted. "But it might give us some direction."

"Why do you think she'd lie about something like that?" Sasha asked. "It makes no damn sense."

"Are you kidding me? People lie all the time about the most innocent things, but *this* lie..." Li'l Bits looked at Sasha. "It could destroy Tyrene's life and kill his chances to go to college." He shook his head in frustration.-"White girls falsely accusing Black boys of sexual assault ain't a new thing, Sasha!"

"Well," Sasha said dryly, "I've seen enough CSI to know that there might be some DNA-type evidence on Allison or her clothing to back up her story. You'll remember that Clinton didn't fare too well with his ridiculous denial. Mimicking Clinton, she said solemnly, "I did not have sexual relations with that woman."

"Maybe I'll find something. Maybe not!" Li'l Bits responded. "But I need to have faith that I *will* find something. Faith can be as small as a mustard seed, but it's not a magic jumping bean. I have to do *something*."

"Trying to find something incriminating on any of her socials is a long shot, Li'l Bits. Girls confess to all sorts of things on social media, but this would be a mad, crazy stretch. This is like fishing with no bait *and* no pole. We barely even have a piece of string to put into the water."

Glancing at the clock, Sasha said, "Let's see what we can find. I don't want Daddy to come home when you're alone with me, either. Mom usually calls to let me know when they're heading back."

She swiveled her chair back to her desk, turned on her computer and announced. "Let the Mad Hatter adventure begin!"

Sasha opened Allison's page and quickly started scrolling down the screen, looking at posts, shares, and comments about photos, events, and memories. "Hmmm! She posted that's she's in a committed relationship. Duh to that!" she said sarcastically.

"Wow! She has tons of photos of her and Wally." Sasha continued searching. "Nothing jumps out at me. Do you see anything? Let's check out the comments to see what her friends are saying."

Li'l Bits inched toward the screen. He was hoping to find one small clue—a single thread that, when tugged, might unravel a greater mystery that would lead to a eureka moment.

Sasha systematically viewed and examined the feeds, unsure when she might stumble upon a veiled reference to an alleged sexual assault. "Hmmm. Typical teenage bubble gum drama," she muttered. "Wow! Looks like her dad took off and left her and her mom! Sad stuff, here." She murmured absently. "Let's look at a few random months to see if anything is there."

Li'l Bits nodded his agreement, wondering if this was all just a waste of time. But his father always said: "You have got to risk failure to succeed." He reminded himself to have faith.

As Sasha scrolled down Allison's posts, she saw that Allison had created a video. Clicking on it, they heard her excited, bubbly voice chatting about her newly decorated room. She had painted it in overlapping shades of blue with white swirling streaks that looked like waves breaking. Above her bed hung a large framed photo of Wally holding her as they sat beneath a tree blooming with apple blossoms. Both smiled at each other as if nothing else in the world mattered but that moment.

The camera gradually scanned Allison's night table, decorated carefully with books and magazines. Over the lilt of Allison's enthusiastic commentary, the camera drifted slowly to her desk—meticulously organized, with pens and pencils neatly arranged in a holder, a self-decorated stapler, and an ornately colored book adorned with a large heart, made of miniature ruby-red jeweled glass, glued across the cover. A pen, matching the book's vibrant colors, rested diagonally across it.

Sasha stopped the video, leaned forward, and rested her chin in her hand. She murmured, "Hmmm."

Puzzled, Li'l Bits peered closely at the screen. Seeing nothing of note, he looked at her questioningly.

"What are you looking at, Sasha?" he asked.

"I see a possibility. An improbable possibility. A highly unlikely opportunity." She sighed heavily. "I also see a high-risk situation."

Li'l Bits furrowed his brow in confusion.

She pointed to the screen. "You see that book with the gaudy little red hearts on it?"

Li'l Bits squinted. "Yeah. I see it."

"Well, that ain't no ordinary kind of book, my friend," she said, a hint of self-satisfaction in her voice. "That's a diary!" She looked at him, wondering if he truly understood its significance. "Girls generally divulge their hearts and souls on those pages. You can sometimes see where ink is smudged because of tears—tears of joy, pain, anger, hurt, or disappointment."

As Sasha's words slowly sank in, Li'l Bits' eyes widened as the significance of a diary finally hit him. Their eyes met. It felt like an electric spark ignited between them.

"Yeah, baby!" Sasha yelled.

"Dat's right!" Li'l Bits responded, a big smile on his face.

They sat back laughing, marveling at their discovery.

After their laughter subsided, Sasha became subdued. Her expression suddenly fell.

Li'l Bits said, "I understand what you mean about the risky situation."

She turned to him. "You'd have to get it to find out what's in it. That means breaking into her house and hoping you don't get busted on the way in or the way out. You also have to hope she's written something self-incriminating in it."

Li'l Bits looked away from Sasha, unnerved by the worried expression on her face. His mouth felt dry. "Yeah, I know," he responded, shrugging.

“Li’l' Bits, this is harebrained." Sasha took his hand in hers and, with the other, turned his chin to face her. "What if she carries that diary around in her backpack to journal throughout the day? Breaking into her house would have been for nothing! Even if you have freakishly good luck finding it in her room, she might not have written anything in her diary about Tyrene at all.”

Her eyes implored him. "Don't do this. Let Tyrene’s lawyer handle it."

“That's exactly what the Professor said. 'Let the lawyer handle it.'" He became pensive. "If you kept a diary, where would you hide it?"

Sasha shook her head in exasperation.

Li’l Bits pressed, “Sasha! Please! This is important to me! Tyrene is my friend!”

“Alright, alright!” she sputtered angrily. “If you’re determined to make a damn fool of yourself!”

Shrugging, she said, “I journal a lot, so I have my old diaries in a cardboard box in my bedroom closet. I keep my current diary in a hollowed-out encyclopedia on my bookshelf. The typical places that a girl might hide a diary are not all that mysterious. They’re pretty obvious, in fact, like under their undies in a drawer or between their mattress and the box spring. Hell, some girls leave their diaries out in the open, particularly if they don't have any snooping kid brothers or sisters.”

Sasha noted, “She doesn’t have any brothers or sisters. Still, I wouldn’t leave an incriminating diary around for Mom to find.”

“Just imagine, Sasha! If I did find that diary," he said excitedly, "I might find proof that could completely change the outcome of the case.”

Sasha was neither hopeful nor enthusiastic—just skeptical, her doubt laden with worry.

"There's another possibility, Li’l Bits," she said soberly. "What if she journals about how awful she felt about the sexual things that Tyrene did to her? What would you do then?”

“I’m not worried, Sasha. I told you. I know Tyrene. He’s not like that. After this court mess gets resolved, I’ll introduce him to you. And, this time, I'll make sure that he and I hang out more often. We'll be just as tight as we were before his brother died."

"Well," Sasha said, resigned, "First things first, Li'l Bits. If you're determined to be stupid about this, let's see if we can locate the floor plan of Allison's house online to figure out how you can break in. By the way, when are you going to try to pull this little caper off?"

"Let's call it my mission. Caper sounds a bit suss." He smiled. "I think I'll scout out her neighborhood tomorrow morning, to get a real sense of the her house. Zillow or Realtor.com might have an archived listing. God willing, I might find something to help him."

Sasha scoffed. "God willing? You think that *She* cares what happens to your friend? There's too much killing and dying in the world for me to believe that She's concerned about one kid. Besides, you ain't no cat burglar, and you don't even have a plan."

"I know *you* will find this hard to believe, Sasha, but God's got a plan and purpose for everything." He paused. "And I mean *everything*. God is always working in our lives. All I need to do is find that diary."

"What if her mom is home?"

"If she's a single mom with a teenage daughter, she has to go to work unless she happened to buy a winning Lotto ticket."

Sasha returned to Allison's page to locate her street address. After a few moments, she said, "Not listed." Sasha saw the alarm in Li'l Bits' eyes.

"Look," she said. "I know the crowd she runs with. I'll make a few calls. If I get an address, I'll contact you tonight."

"Thanks, Sasha! Really appreciate your help," he said, touching her arm.

"Just be careful," Sasha said. "You ever hear Shakespeare's quote, 'Wisely and slow; they stumble that run fast'?"

Li'l Bits shook his head. "Uh uh. Never heard that one. Didn't take Advanced Lit." He shrugged, then said firmly, "The risk is worth it, Sasha. Nothing ventured…"

"Nothing gained?" She snorted. "Is that what you think? You do know that neurotic white people won't hesitate to shoot an unarmed

Black boy just for standing outside their front door! And if you do live, you might still be facing criminal charges of some sort! What would your parents say?"

The weight of his plan was not lost on him. Sasha was genuinely frightened for his safety.

He lowered his gaze to avoid the fearful look in her eyes. He sat back in his chair, contemplating what he should do—weighing the risks and dangers, thinking about what the Professor had said, and what his parents would think.

He had no desire to flirt with danger. He didn't see himself as any kind of hero—but the image of his childhood friend, beaten and chained, flashed in his mind. The thought of the remarkable courage of Kalief Browder— who fought to survive in a hellish environment—steeled his resolve.

He studied his dear friend Sasha—her thin arms tightly crossed over her slim frame, left hand gripping her right shoulder, right hand gripping her left. Gently, he reached over and slipped his arm around her, feeling her body tremble.

She leaned into him and laid her head on his chest. He heard her mumble weakly, "Don't do it."

With the bravest voice he could muster, he said, "Sasha, I'm sorry. I gotta try!"

21

Secrets of the Heart

A smattering of small sedans, older model cars, and work trucks lined the narrow residential streets. Garbage containers sat neatly on the curb in front of several houses.

A teenage girl, about Li'l Bits' age, walked hand in hand with an enthusiastic tot who skipped down the sidewalk beside her. A kid about 19 or 20 years old, who looked like he was part Black, rushed past Li'l Bits with a pleasant, "Whas up?"

Li'l Bits was relieved to see someone Black. His presence would appear less suspicious now. At least, he'd look like someone who might live in the neighborhood. Ambling down the opposite side of the street toward Allison's home, his walk was purposely casual, as if he had no place to go and no rush to get there.

Because it was a school day, he wore the typical backpack kids his age used to tote their books and supplies. He also wore a letter jacket he'd borrowed from a friend who attended a different school, hoping it would mislead anyone attempting to identify him. He avoided wearing clothing that might be considered 'suspicious', such as a hoodie, a cap turned backward on his head, sagging pants, or red or blue colors that could be associated with gangs. He planned to ease any fears and dispel the stereotype of a Black delinquent up to no good.

As he continued down the street, he saw Allison's house about 35 feet away. When he was directly across from the house, he glanced at the number to confirm it was the correct address. He looked again to be sure. His stomach flipped. Allison lives there!

Li'l Bits accepted what he'd planned to do was wrong, and Sasha's concern about what his parents would think troubled him. But the memory of his friend Tyrene, incarcerated in an adult jail, told him that there was more at stake than his fear of being caught or punished by his parents. He silently prayed to God to help him help his friend.

He heard a loud cry as he started to cross the street to Allison's house. It was an elderly woman. Her voice was gravelly and gruff. "Come here! Come here! Get back here, you stupid dog."

Li'l Bits couldn't see the woman at first because several cars blocked his view, but he could see a cute, tiny pup with a tail nearly longer than its body, bouncing around, running back and forth between the cars. The puppy thought the old woman was playing a game of catch-me-if-you-can. From all appearances, the pup was winning. Worried that a passing car might clip the animal, Li'l Bits dashed across the street toward them.

"It's a good thing I can't catch you, you little rat dog, because I'd kill you," she vowed. He quickly realized she was also straining to control another dog on a leash.

Li'l Bits could now see over the top of a dusty car roof to observe a tiny, withered, white-haired woman dressed in an oversized checkered flannel coat. Her right arm was fixed tightly against her body to anchor a dog's leash, while she pressed her other hand firmly against her temple to keep large turquoise, horn-rimmed glasses from falling off her face. Looking up, she was startled to see a young boy watching her.

A look of relief lit up her face. "Young man!" she said anxiously. "Can you help me? Can you catch that dog before it gets run over? I'm too old to chase after that thing."

"Of course, ma'am. I heard you yell. I was on my way to help."

Seeing that the elusive animal was nowhere in sight, Li'l Bits bent down to look under the car. Just as he had fully crouched on elbows and knees, to peer beneath the car's body, the dog suddenly shot forward to lick his face. He snatched it up with both hands, rolled over on his back, and thrust it into the air. It dove repeatedly at his face, rapidly licking him.

"Gotcha!" Li'l Bits shouted. He stood up and walked quickly around the car to show the old woman his catch. She had picked up the other dog and held him securely in her arms. The dog's leash trailed to the sidewalk, in folds, by her feet.

"Where do you want me to put him?"

She shook her head, exasperated. "Put him? I'd like you to take that nuisance of a dog to the pound, to tell you the truth. The little beast has dug a hole under my fence and comes into my yard every time my Mr. Pebbles is doing his business. I could understand if Mr. Pebbles was a girl dog, but he's not. I think that dog is definitely gay."

Li'l Bits stifled a laugh. Smiling, he said, "Naw, I think it's just a pup that likes to play. Where does he live?"

The old woman jerked her head to the house on the right. A jolt shot through Li'l Bits when he realized where he was standing. "Is this your house behind you?"

She buried her face affectionately in her little fur ball and nodded. "Yes."

"And this dog lives next door to you?" he asked.

"Yep! It's the mother's dog. But her daughter, Allison, takes care of it. I think she hates that dog as much as I do."

Li'l Bits couldn't believe his luck. "Why do you think Allison hates the dog? I think he's kinda cute."

Scoffing at his comment, the woman said, "Well, for one thing, she calls the dog 'Dumb Ass.' One day, when Allison came over to get that dog from my backyard, she told me how it had chewed up some of her homework. She was real mad."

"I would've been upset, too," Li'l Bits said, looking at Allison's house. He felt his stomach move as if a swarm of butterflies were starting to flutter inside him.

"Well, I gotta pee, so I'm going inside," the neighbor announced unabashedly. "Just walk the dog inside the gate and put it in the house. I need to leave my dog out for a while, and I don't want him pestered by Dumb Ass."

"*Inside* the house?" Li'l Bits asked. His heart was starting to pound, and he felt out of breath.

Cocking her head slightly, the old lady looked carefully at him. She said, "I don't see so well, but you don't look so good. Are you alright, young man?"

"Well, um, I don't know if I should..." he stammered. "I... I mean, put the dog inside the house!"

"Oh, don't worry about going into the house. The mother always leaves the back door open. Allison forgets her house key more often than I can count."

She looked at him closely again. "You're one of the Franklin boys who lives on the corner, aren't you?" she asked.

Li'l Bits smiled and said reassuringly, "Don't worry, ma'am. I'll make sure that Dumb Ass gets back into the house safe and sound."

She laughed, delighted that he'd adopted the name. "That's a good name for him—Dumb Ass."

"Well, I better get going so I'm not too late for school," he said brightly. He started walking toward Allison's fence while the old woman, clutching her furry treasure, hobbled toward her door.

The dog, tucked under Li'l Bits' arms, still squirmed violently, trying to get near his face. He frowned at the animal, muttering, "You *are* a psycho dog!"

Walking tentatively toward the gate, he stopped and looked back at the woman, who had not traveled far. He feared she might've changed her mind about a stranger putting the dog into her neighbor's house. But she simply shuffled away, oblivious to him and seemingly lost in thought.

Li'l Bits stood silently in front of Allison's wooden fence and spoke a silent prayer. He prayed for his decision to align with God's will and that he'd be able to locate Allison's diary.

The corroded latch almost pulled away from the screws in the wood, as he opened the gate. He stepped inside the backyard quickly and closed it behind him. He reminded himself to be calm and not rush because a neighbor might be looking out a window. Seeing someone returning a dog to its home would not be cause for a 911 call, he hoped.

He walked to the back door, praying that it was unlocked, just as the old woman advised. Bounding up the steps, he reached for the knob but stopped abruptly. Straightening up, he chastised himself.

What are you thinking? I need to make sure nobody's home.

He knocked three times and waited. Nothing. He looked through the rectangular glass pane to see if anyone was coming. Still… no one. He feared yelling might draw a neighbor's attention, so he knocked a bit harder this time pausing several seconds between each knock.

Stay calm, he thought. *Breathe! You're just returning a pet safely to its home.*

Inhaling deeply, he reached for the knob and twisted it. The door opened. He gasped, looked around, then quickly stepped inside. He yelled, "Hello! Anybody home?"

When there was no answer, he stood in the kitchen taking stock of his surroundings, while gripping the dog that had started squirming again. The kitchen smelled of fried bacon and the sickly sweet smell of syrup. With the dog secure under his arm, he walked a few feet through the tiny kitchen into the living room. The stairs were immediately to his left. The blinds to the windows on the right were drawn. Eyes wide, heart in his throat, he looked up the stairs.

I need to get moving and fast! I just hope nobody is upstairs sleeping.

Just to be sure certain, he called out, "Hello?" several times. Silence. He raised his voice a bit louder this time and said, "I got your dog! I caught it outside. Your neighbor next door told me it was okay to bring him inside the house."

Silence. Now, he could hear the ticking of a wall clock. It was quiet compared to the pounding of his heart.

He lowered the dog to the floor, and it quickly scampered off, disappearing around the corner.

It's now or never, he thought. Holding his breath, listening for any sound, he crept up the stairs like he was walking on egg shells. He stopped on the landing. Exhaling softly, he told himself to relax again.

He couldn't believe it. *He was inside Allison's house!*

Just past the bathroom, on his right, he saw the colors of Allison's bedroom. Everything was in place, as he'd seen online. The room appeared smaller, and the colors seemed bolder than in her video.

He rushed over to her desk, rifling through papers and folders. He yanked open dresser drawers, searching beneath her clothes. Methodically, he checked the books on her shelf—those large enough to conceal a diary. He peered under the bed, then rummaged through the shoeboxes stacked on her closet floor. Panic was setting in.

He removed his backpack and dropped it on the floor.

Looking down next to her bed, he saw the colorful pen that matched her diary on the floor. He picked it up. Impulsively, he snatched the sheets off Allison's bed and shook them. From somewhere between the ruffled covers flew a book with tiny crystal hearts that formed a larger heart.

Li'l Bits' heart felt a thousand times larger than the heart on the diary. Looking up, he closed his eyes and sighed, "Thank you, sweet Jesus."

He snatched the diary from the floor, stood up, and quickly skimmed through the pages—just stuff about girlfriends, jealousies, and lots of romantic comments about Wally. Words, words, and more words, but not the words he needed to help Tyrene.

Eyes wide and heart pounding, Li'l Bits kept flipping through pages, desperately hoping to see something incriminating. Close to the last few entries, something caught his eye. The pages appeared to be water stained.

Tears? he wondered. He could see where the ink had run, bleeding into the other lines.

As he read, Li'l Bits suddenly realized he'd stopped breathing. The book shook in his hands. He pulled out his cell phone. "Sasha! I got it!"

Her response was immediate. "Get out now!"

Before he could move, he heard the sound of an engine outside the house. *My God! Was it in the driveway? He bent down to shove the diary in his backpack, but froze when he heard a car door slam. Sweet, Jesus,* his mind screamed. *Someone is here!* He heard the front door open. He froze.

He heard a girl's voice yell petulantly, "Mom! I know exactly where my assignment is. It's somewhere in my room. Probably on my desk." She mumbled, "Or maybe under the bed. Don't get your panties in a bunch! I'll be out in five minutes. Put your earbuds in and listen to your audiobook. I told you there's a late school start for me this morning."

Before Allison could reach the stairs, a furry ball of energy sprang, yelping from under the couch, nearly tripping her. Surprised, she swooped the dog up, cursing and carried it to the back door.

"I thought Mom let you out this morning, Dumb Ass. You better not have crapped on the rug," she said as she tossed the dog outside.

Li'l Bits felt rooted to the floor. He'd get caught if he tried running out of the house now. Her mother would see him if he jumped out Allison's window. Besides, he might twist an ankle. He might try dashing across the hallway to hide in the other bedroom, but Allison would see him run across the hall. He could already hear Allison at the bottom of the stairs.

Hide in her closet? Slip under her bed? His mind raced, *Why didn't you leave with the diary when you had the chance instead of reading it?* A small voice answered back. *Because you didn't want to steal the girl's diary if there was nothing in it to help you.* Li'l Bits moaned.

Then he thought, *I don't have to run. She's falsely accused my friend of a crime. She has agreed to help the police by lying. I may be in trouble, but she's in a lot more trouble than me.*

When Allison entered the room, she saw a short Black boy standing about six feet away. Her mouth popped open to scream when Li'l Bits held her diary just over his head. He yelled, "You lied!"

Her diary in his hand immediately silenced her cry. Her mouth remained open, frozen in a knowing silence. Emboldened by her stunned, surprised look, Li'l Bits continued his damning accusation.

"You and those two crooked cops framed my friend on a fake sexual assault charge."

The color drained from her face. She staggered backward as if she'd lost her balance. "Give me my diary!" Allison demanded sharply. "Give it to me right now, or..."

"Or you'll do what? Call the police?" He scoffed. "Go ahead. They might be interested in your tear-stained confession."

She took a step forward. "Do you really think that diary will ever see the light of day once the police arrive? Do you know who my boyfriend's father is? Give me my diary! Leave now, and I won't report you. I promise! Now, give it to me," she demanded, "or you'll wind up in jail like your friend!" Fear and anger flashed in her eyes.

"You're asking me to believe the promise of a liar?" His face flashed with indignation. "Solomon says that one of the seven things God hates is a false witness who utters a lie. What you and those cops are doing is evil."

Allison's eyes were wild. "Are you... are you ... crazy?" she sputtered. "Are you some kind of kooky Bible thumper? You break into my house, go through my private things, take my diary, and then accuse me of offending God! You fucking hypocrite!"

"The difference between you and me is that *you* are mocking justice." Li'l Bits replied. "You intend to destroy an innocent life. I intend to save one. I may be breaking man's law, but you are breaking God's."

Screaming, she lunged at him, arms flailing, but he sidestepped her easily and guided her gently to the bed.

Gripping the diary, Li'l Bits snatched his backpack off the floor, dashed out of her bedroom, leaped down the stairs, and ran out the back door, nearly tripping over Dumb Ass in the yard.

A car parked in the driveway began blaring its horn as he ran out the back gate. He heard the car door open and someone yelling behind him as he ran.

It is about eight blocks to the bus stop, he thought. He had to get there before the police caught him. Allison was right. If the cops got their hands on this diary—or if it fell into the hands of any of the dad's cop friends—it might be destroyed...along with Tyrene's life.

Li'l Bits didn't even stop to put his backpack on. He sprinted as fast as he could, clutching it in one hand and the diary in the other. He prayed that a bus—any bus—would make a stop in time for him to escape.

Allison collapsed on her bed, crying uncontrollably. She heard her mother enter the house, calling frantically from downstairs. Trying to control her voice, she said, "I'm alright, Mom. He didn't hurt me. Call 911. I'll be down in a moment. I just need to wash my face."

Allison pulled her cell phone from her jacket and hit the automatic dial. She heard the familiar voice that sounded so much like Wally.

"Allison?" Kensington asked. "Is that you?" Allison couldn't bring herself to speak.

Kensington said louder, "Allison! Is there anything wrong? What's going on?" Kensington held the phone to his ear, waiting.

"He stole it." She was crying so hard that Kensington didn't quite understand what she was saying.

Allison repeated. "He stole it. He stole my diary."

Kensington's mind instantly blanked, and a chill shot through him. He had to restrain himself from cursing. As calmly as he could, he asked, "What about your diary, Allison?" He was gripping his cell phone so hard that his hand ached.

"He knows, Mr. Kensington! He knows. This Black kid broke into my house. I think he's a friend of that kid who hurt Wally. He stole my diary!"

Kensington was speechless.

"Mr. Kensington? Are you there? Please, say something. I'm so sorry." Allison's tears began to flow again. Not hearing any response, she said, "I don't know how he found me. I don't know how he knew about my diary."

"Is what we talked about doing for Wally in the diary, Allison? Is that what you wrote about?"

"Yes!" She cried, sobbing.

"Did you use names, Allison?" Kensington asked. He closed his eyes against the answer that he knew would come, but he hoped she would not be that stupid.

"Yes," she said quietly, but added quickly, "I didn't use your name, Mr. Kensington. I just referred to you as 'Wally's dad.'"

Kensington couldn't suppress a groan. He felt sick.

"Describe this kid, Allison. Describe him as best you can."

"Well, he's Black, light-skinned. He might be about 15 or 16. He was short—about five foot four or so."

"What was he wearing?"

"I think he had a backpack. And he was wearing a high school jacket. It had a big gold eagle on the back. I saw it when he ran out of the room."

"Okay. I've got enough to start looking for this kid. Do you know which way he ran when he left your house?"

"I don't know. My mom probably saw which way he ran. She was parked in the driveway."

"Okay, Allison. Let me see what we can do to get this situation under control."

"I'm so sorry, Mr. Kensington. Please don't tell Wally."

"Don't worry, Allison. I won't tell him, but I need you to do me a favor. Don't call the police. Tell your mom you called me, and I'll handle it."

Kensington heard a long sigh. "I bet my mom has already called the police, Mr. Kensington," she said timidly. "I heard the horn honking outside. She must've seen him run out the backyard pass her car."

Kensington groaned loudly. "Jesus, Allison! We don't want the police involved. You know what could happen if that diary gets in the wrong hands?" he shouted.

Allison's words stumbled out, haltingly guilt-ridden. "But... but... you said... that we could lie about the sexual assault... You had friends... who could help us, like that female officer who convinced my mom not to talk to me about the attack. Maybe the police would understand that the false charge is…." She hesitated, struggling to remember the phrase. Then, it hit her. "Just desserts."

Kensington groaned again, more loudly this time.

Suddenly, a new fear stabbed at Kensington. Was Allison's mother eavesdropping—listening to her confession?

"Young lady," Kensington said firmly, "I don't know what lies you are talking about, but we can talk later. I've got to run this kid down to get your property back."

Kensington quickly ended the call, wishing he had just listened without responding to her panic and giving in to his own.

Allison pulled the cell phone from her ear and stared at it, dumbfounded. She could not believe what she had just heard. *Is Wally's dad going to betray me?*

She felt hot tears streaming down her face. When she finally managed to stop crying, she sensed someone in the room. Startled, she turned around. Her mother was leaning against the doorframe, slowly shaking her head in pained disbelief—her eyes brimming with unshed tears.

"Allison," she said, her voice thick with despair. "How could you?"

22

No Way Out

Kensington went to the favorites feature on his cell phone and hit the automatic dial for Quisling. After several anxious rings, he heard a voice that sounded preoccupied.

"Hold on, Kensington, Quisling said. "Just finishing some paperwork on a shoplift."

"Where are you?" Kensington barked. "What's your location?" Quisling caught the alarm in Kensington's voice.

Immediately on alert, Quisling replied, "I'm at 12th and Elm. You know... the Texaco station. What's up?"

"We got a big fuckin' problem. I'm too far away to get there quickly. You're about fifteen minutes from Allison's house. I need you to track down a Black kid. Five-foot-four or so. Light-skinned. Carrying a backpack. School jacket with a gold eagle on it. He's probably running. He broke into Allison's house and stole her diary."

Quisling tossed the clipboard aside, started his car, flipped on his emergency lights, and roared off. "Let me guess," he spat as he maneuvered into traffic. "She journaled about *your* plan to help Wally! Goddamnit! That stupid bitch just paved our way to the joint." He screamed, "Sonofabitch!"

"We've got to find him!" Kensington yelled.

"Actually, Kensington," Quisling said, seething while he maneuvered in and out of traffic. "Finding him with the diary would be great, but it'd be way easier just to kill Allison."

Kensington was stunned. "Are you...are you fuckin' crazy?" he stammered in amazement. "That's Wally's girl! She's just a kid, for God's sake! Don't talk stupid!"

"Kid or not, she fucked up. She just exposed us! I'm not going down for her stupid goddamn mistake. If she's dead, we can write off that diary as a sick teen's bizarre fantasy if it surfaces."

Quisling gripped the wheel of his patrol car as he flew in and out of traffic. He wondered why his steering wheel felt damp. Then, he realized— his hands had become hot and slick with sweat.

"Think about it, Quisling. If she dies, who do you think would be the prime suspects? Our names are in her diary!" Kensington was trying his best to keep cool. He took a deep breath and said firmly, "Remember, we agreed to go to her to ask for her help."

"Yeah! *Your* dumb fuckin' idea!" Quisling sneered. "I should've known better. I was trying to help you and your son. My going to prison was not part of the deal!" Quisling felt like screaming. "Get rid of Allison, and you get rid of the main witness," he hissed. "Make her disappear, and the diary doesn't matter. That diary, even if found, ain't admissible in court without her testimony. And she can't testify if she's dead."

"What the fuck are you talking about? Are you out of your goddamn mind?" Kensington thundered. "You wanted to frame that kid, too! Remember?" Kensington imagined reaching through the phone to strangle him. "Did you forget all that white power shit about getting back at a nigger who nearly castrated Wally? Pull yourself together, Quisling! You sound like a damn rookie!

There was uncomfortable silence for several tense seconds. Quisling spoke first. "Let me see if I can track this nigger down. I'll call you *partner,*" he said, emphasizing the word derisively. Furious, Quisling ended the call.

Quisling thought he had almost no chance of catching the kid if he had access to a car. But how likely was it that a Black kid would even own one? What if he'd borrowed someone's car? What if the kid is hiding in somebody's house who lives in Allison's neighborhood? Too many possibilities! He slapped the wheel so hard he winced. His best bet was to watch for a Black kid moving wrong — too fast or too careful. Both meant the same thing to him.

Maybe he's running to catch a bus! *Damn!* he thought. *If that kid makes it on a bus before I get there, I won't have any chance of finding him. If he does get on a bus, which direction would he be traveling? North or South?*

Quisling blipped his emergency siren a few short blasts to get through a traffic light. He was so mad he saw red.

Kensington slumped in his car and closed his eyes to focus. He felt like his head would explode. He pressed his fingers to his forehead, trying to stop the sudden pain behind his eyes.

What had he done? What was he thinking? Quisling was talking crazy. Murder Allison? Was he out of his fucking mind? Kensington felt himself spiraling. He needed to snap out of it. This wasn't a time for *him* to panic, too. Every second counted. He had to move—*now*!

He started his car, flipped on the emergency lights, and headed toward Allison's house—just in case he could help Quisling find the kid. But what worried him more, what really rattled him, was the idea of cops responding to a 911 call at her house.

My God, he thought. *Would Allison cave and just confess to everything?*

And then he also had Quisling to worry about. "Quisling," he muttered under his breath. "I never realized you were such a loose cannon."

Kensington was suddenly pricked by a grim thought he should never forget. *Force a desperate man into a corner with no way out, and you find out who he truly is. You always knew he was a killer.*

A feeling of dread and foreboding gripped Kensington like the outstretched fingers of a dying man. Bitter regret was starting to gnaw at him. Kensington squeezed the steering wheel to refocus. "First things first," he whispered hoarsely. He had to help Quisling locate that kid, find and destroy that diary, get to Allison's house before the cops responded to her 911 call, calm her down, and hope that Lady Luck was on their side.

He activated his siren, hoping he didn't collide with another vehicle. He damn sure didn't need to be delayed by a traffic accident now. Time was of the essence.

Li'l Bits ran like a madman for about three blocks nonstop before deciding to slow down. He hoped he hadn't drawn too much attention to himself. Someone in the neighborhood would surely become suspicious seeing a Black kid hauling ass down the street. The way he was running was a dead giveaway. He slowed down as he turned the corner and almost ran into an elderly white man walking his dog.

"Whoa, young fella! Slow down. You 'bout to kill somebody, running like that." The old man pulled his dog up short and began to eye Li'l Bits.

"Oh, I'm so sorry, sir. I didn't mean to scare you," Li'l Bits said breathlessly. He did his best to look as relaxed as possible to dispel any suspicion. "I was just trying to catch a bus." His heart was pounding, and he could feel that his forehead was damp.

"Well, if you ask me, you were running like you just stole something," the old man said.

Surprised by the comment, he flinched for a moment—then caught the old man's smile and let out an awkward laugh.

"Just in a rush to catch the bus, sir," Li'l Bits repeated.

"Well, you might get there quicker if you put your backpack on," the old man observed.

Li'l Bits nodded, chuckling as he carefully put the diary inside a side pocket, then slid on the backpack.

"Wow! Must have been mad crazy when I thought I might miss the bus!" he explained.

The old man blinked his understanding and started to shuffle away. He yelled over his shoulder, "Well, you've got a few minutes. The bus tends to run 'round here 'bout every thirty minutes."

"Okay! Thank you, sir! I'll be on my way. You have a good day."

The old man didn't turn around but threw up a wrinkled hand and waved as he plodded along.

Li'l Bits took a few hurried steps, but looked back to see if Allison or her mom might be following him. Seeing no one, he breathed a sigh of relief and began a slow jog in the direction he thought would lead him out of the subdivision and onto the main street. After jogging several blocks, the rumbling sound of traffic became audible. Quickening his pace, he continued until he reached the corner.

Several cars drove by—early morning traffic. People trying to get to work. Li'l Bits looked up and down the street for a bus stop. Seeing none, he began to jog again. He couldn't help smiling as each foot hit the sidewalk. *Miracle of miracles!* He had found the evidence he needed to free Tyrene. Now, he just needed to get home with the diary and turn it over to his mom. She'd know what to do with it.

About a quarter block away, Li'l Bits saw a bench. It looked like there was a bus sign near it. Looking behind him, he saw a southbound bus about a half mile away, pulling over to unload passengers. He checked his watch. The old man was right. Looks like it comes every half hour. After reaching the bench, Li'l Bits took his backpack off, pulled out the diary, and sat down. He felt exhausted but couldn't resist rereading Allison's guilt-ridden words.

He began to read. *I know it was wrong to lie. I didn't want to, but Wally's dad made it sound so easy. He said it was just a story that could make up for what that boy did to Wally. I love Wally so much. I would do anything for him. Officer Quisling told me to tell the police that I had been raped, but I couldn't bring myself to say that. Sexual touching was okay—but not rape. What would my mom think? What would my friends say? They told me that maybe I wouldn't have to testify because the boy might accept a plea bargain. They are both cops so they should know. God forgive me.*

Li'l Bits stared at the words, *God forgive me.* Surprisingly, he felt sorry for her. He thought, *We of the flesh are so very weak.*

How does that Bible verse go? *"I do not understand what I do. For what I want to do, I do not do. But what I hate to do, I do."*

With a heavy sigh, he closed Allison's diary. He looked down the street to see the bus fast approaching. Off to his right, he saw something that caused his stomach to flip—a police car on the opposite side of the street!

With its lights flashing, it had been traveling north at a slow cruising speed, almost as if the officer were searching for someone. As the black and white pulled almost directly parallel to him, it had slowed to a crawl and made a sudden stop—a reckless move in morning rush hour traffic.

Several cars swerved around the patrol car to avoid hitting it. One car was bold enough to blare its horn.

Li'l Bits glanced down at the book in his hands, then looked up—wide-eyed—to find a police officer staring intently at him from across six lanes of traffic. The police car's siren suddenly blared as it lurched forward, then quickly slowed again in the crush of traffic. With short, urgent bursts of the siren, it began weaving through the congestion as drivers scrambled to clear a path.

He jumped to his feet, his mind racing as panic seized him. *Don't panic!* he told himself. *God didn't bring you this far to leave you now.*

He hovered anxiously at the bus stop, eyes darting down the street. "C'mon! C'mon!" he muttered, slapping his thigh. All he could do was pray the bus would arrive before the police car cleared the intersection and did a U-turn.

Li'l Bits wavered. Should he bolt back through the subdivision and hide in someone's yard or wait for the bus? Even if he had time to run a few blocks, a Black teen fleeing the sound of a siren would instantly raise suspicions. And even if he found a place to hide, other officers could be called in to join the search.

A cold realization hit him—Allison was right. Her diary would never see the light of day. No cop was going to take the word of a Black teen accusing a white cop of corruption. The bus was his best hope. At the very least, it might buy him some time. He'd be safer in a crowded bus rather than sprinting through the streets like a fugitive. He could try calling his mom, his dad, maybe even the Professor—but could he reach anyone in time?

The cop was already cutting through the jammed intersection. There wasn't much time left.

Blocked by a few determined southbound drivers who ignored its flashing lights, the patrol car was forced to slow down at the intersection just as the bus pulled up. The bus door opened, and Li'l Bits froze.

"Are you coming or not? I haven't got all day," the female bus driver said.

His heart skipped as he watched the police car whip a U-turn to clear oncoming traffic. Panicked and uncertain, he leapt onto the bus.

"You okay?" The driver studied him. "You look like you just saw a ghost."

"I'm alright, ma'am." He said as he fumbled for his bus pass. "I've just got to pray on something until I can figure out what I'm doing."

"Pray on something?" The bus driver sounded surprised. She looked at him uncertainly, like she was trying to fit his face with a place. "Do I know you? You look familiar."

"I don't think so, ma'am," he said anxiously. After showing his pass, he rushed toward the rear of the bus to see what the police car was doing. Surprisingly, the siren and lights had stopped, and the patrol car had slowed down. It appeared to be tailing the bus.

He pulled out his cell phone and hit "favorites." The phone rang repeatedly. "Pick up, Mom!" he said in frustration. He heard the automatic response, *The party you are trying to reach is not available. Please try later.* He groaned and stared at his phone.

His mind racing, he looked vacantly out the window as the bus rumbled on. Seeing a landmark he recognized, it dawned on him that he was within a few miles of the Professor's house.

A ding echoed through the bus as it jolted to a stop. Li'l Bits tightened his grip on the diary and glanced back, half-expecting the cop to blast his siren again when the passengers got off. But the officer appeared to be holding something to his ear.

Is he calling Wally's dad? Li'l Bits wondered.

He hit the automatic dial for the Professor. "Please be home," he prayed. After several rings, the Professor picked up. "Professor!" Li'l Bits nearly yelled into the phone. "Thank God! I'm heading your way. I've discovered some important evidence to help Tyrene."

"Slow down, Li'l Bits. Slow down! What are you talking about?"

Catching his breath, he said quietly, "I've got the diary of that girl, Allison, who accused Tyrene of trying to rape her."

"You've got *what*?" When the Professor said, "What!" it sounded like an explosion.

"Remember when you said that it was a bit fishy that the girlfriend of the victim is now coming forward with a story about a sexual assault? Well, I thought that I might be able to find something out—and I did!"

He was so excited he could barely breathe. "I found her diary in her house, and you were right!" he said excitedly. "She lied! And the police are involved. She wrote it all down in her diary, and I have the diary."

An elderly man seated in front of him turned around to stare. Li'l Bits whispered, "I've got proof, Professor."

The Professor was speechless. "I'll be damned," he muttered under his breath.

"Tawanna has the car. I can't come get you, but she should be here soon," Doug said, looking at his watch.

"I'm on a bus maybe three miles from your house, but I don't want you to come. A police officer is driving behind the bus. I think he might be one of the guys Allison talked about in her diary."

"Why do you think that?" the Professor asked, trying to conceal the growing fear in his voice.

"I noticed a police car on the other side of the street from where I was sitting on a bench. I was reading Allison's diary when he spotted me. It seemed like he slowed way down at first. Then, all of a sudden, he turned his siren on, changed direction, and made a U-turn. Then he turned off his lights and siren and has been following the bus ever since. I wonder why he hasn't pulled the bus over."

"He knows he's found you. He's probably calling his partner to figure out how they should play this. Maybe he wants to wait on his partner as backup." The Professor continued solemnly, "Li'l Bits, you're in danger!"

Li'l Bits thought for a moment. "Well, I'm safe for now. If he pulls the bus over, I can run."

"Maybe… if you get a chance. If the cop waits to pull the bus over at a bus stop, you can try to get away. But he'll see the bus slowing down. Then you've got to wait until the bus stops completely before the doors open." Doug shook his head. "Even if you had wings on your feet, you can't outrun a bullet."

"Would he shoot me, Professor, in broad daylight… in front of witnesses?" Li'l Bits asked incredulously.

Doug sighed, his voice suddenly heavy. "Li'l Bits... daylight and witnesses didn't save George Floyd."

"You're right, Professor," he said solemnly. "He even begged for his life… but that didn't save him."

Doug's mind ticked through safe places on that route. "You'll see restaurants and businesses along the street. If you do manage to get off, choose a store or business to run to, but don't head there directly if the cop is watching. Detour to throw him off. Call me as soon as you can. Tawanna and I will pick you up."

Li'l Bits nodded at the phone. "I understand, Professor. I'll be careful, sir."

Doug thought for a moment. "Li'l Bits, can you take pictures of the girl's diary and send it to my phone?"

"I already tried sending her confession to my mom, but I got a 'Not Delivered' message. Think the internet connection is bad."

Doug swore under his breath. "Well, take photos of any incriminating statements and save those."

"Good idea, Professor! I'll hide my cell phone on the bus if I have to run."

"No, Li'l Bits. You need to hang onto your phone until the last minute. I need to be able to reach you. If you are about to get caught, run to the nearest home or business and call me. Conceal the phone someplace safe. Okay? Hide the diary, too."

"Will do, Professor," Li'l Bits paused. "I'm sorry I had to get you involved," he added, regret in his voice.

"Look, son. No need to apologize. I'm more than happy to help. We're trying to get justice to work, right? It's a bit lazy when it comes time to work for Black people."

Li'l Bits smiled. "That's right. We need to help it work."

"That cop still on your tail?" the Professor asked.

Li'l Bits turned to look out the window behind him. "Big as day," he answered. "Can't quite see his face clearly, though."

"No matter! Just get ready to pull the cord! Then hit the ground and run like the wind."

"My legs are short, Professor, but I'm fast."

Doug laughed. "I know. I've seen you smoke a few people on the track."

Doug pressed his free hand to his forehead. "Now, photograph what you can from the diary and call me immediately, if he stops that bus. I'm calling Tawanna to see where she is. After that, my phone will be open."

Li'l Bits said proudly. "I did it, Professor! I did it. I found the smoking gun!"

"Yes, you did, sir! Ain't nothing *little* about you. You certainly made a believer out of me. Now, take those pictures! We can't let that diary fall into the hands of the police."

Li'l Bits said, "Professor, believe me. I know."

He hung up, relieved that he'd reached the Professor and grateful that he was near his house. He looked nervously out the window at the patrol car slowly stalking the bus.

He pulled out Allison's diary again, found the tear-stained pages, and began taking photos.

23

Running for His Life

Kensington heard his cell ping. It was Quisling!

"Thank God, Quisling!" he exclaimed, failing to control the mounting desperation in his voice, "You anywhere near Allison's?"

Quisling chuckled. "Better than that, Kensington, my man. I'm near Allison's diary."

"Near her diary? What the fuck does that mean?"

Quisling chuckled again, congratulating himself for locating the thief so quickly. "Saw the little nigger across the street as I was driving toward Allison's neighborhood. Looked like he was reading, just waiting on the bus. But the damn bus got there before I could pick him up. I'm riding behind the bus now."

"You're *following* the fuckin' bus?" He bellowed, "Why in God's name haven't you pulled the goddamn bus over?"

Startled and offended by Kensington's tone, Quisling's jaw tightened. "I know what I'm doing, Kensington," he snapped, his tone defiant. "I figure the kid might not be in this little caper alone. He might've arranged to meet someone on the bus to transfer the diary. We need to find out who else is involved."

Kensington bit the back of his hand to keep himself from cursing. Taking a deep breath, he began slowly, his words measured. "Quisling! What's our objective here?"

"Don't treat me like I'm a dumbass, Kensington. I found the kid. You didn't!" Quisling's face flushed crimson with anger.

Rolling his eyes, Kensington said evenly, "If that kid has a cell phone, he could be taking photos of Allison's diary right now and sending them to a dozen people. In fact, his friends could be sending those photos of Allison's diary everywhere and posting them on Facebook. Someone might even be preparing a goddamn YouTube video with our names for a thousand people to see, for Christ's sake!" Kensington's voice rose to a pitch. "So, do you understand that waiting to pull the bus over might not be the best idea, Quisling?"

Quisling went slack-jawed, then swallowed hard. He said meekly, "I'm pulling the bus over now."

"Hold up! Contact Dispatch first," Kensington barked. Tell them to notify the bus driver not to allow anyone off that bus. Tell them that a fleeing felon is a passenger, and you have to board the bus to make an arrest. But turn your siren on now!"

Quisling made several short whoops with his siren to get the driver's attention. His mouth was as dry as a sunbaked field. He paged Dispatch. The giddiness of self-satisfaction had been replaced with a cold, foreboding dread and pangs of punishing self-recrimination.

"Hello, this is Dispatch," the voice said blandly.

"This is unit 714. I'm at the approximate location of Randall and 17th, behind Bus 2256. Notify the driver that a burglary suspect is on board, and I'm about to pull it over. Let the driver know that he's not, under any circumstances, to let anybody off that bus. Do you understand?"

"Copy! Give me a description of the suspect."

"You don't need a goddamn description! Just tell the bus driver to keep everybody on the bus!" he yelled.

"Give me a description, officer," the female voice said firmly. "Do you know if he's armed and dangerous?"

Quisling snapped, "He's Black! They're *all* armed and dangerous!"

Ignoring the comment, she continued, "Well, that's a start. Black male. Height? Weight? Clothing? What else you got, officer?"

Quisling sighed heavily. "Short, light-skinned, about 21 years old. Wearing a high school jacket with a gold eagle on the back. Dark jeans. Maybe dark blue or black. Carrying a backpack."

"Weapons?" asked Dispatch.

"Don't know for sure," Quisling replied impatiently and frowned.

"Okay! I'll notify the bus driver and send backup."

"No! I don't need backup," Quisling said quickly. "It's just one kid. I can handle this."

Dispatch was silent for a moment. "You sure? That's not standard protocol."

"Just contact the bus driver so I can take this goddamn kid into custody, please," Quisling said, almost whining. "My partner is on the way."

"Okay! I'll make the call as soon as I locate a number," Dispatch said.

The driver of bus 2256 heard her phone ring and knew it was trouble. She'd noticed a police car had been behind her for over a mile. Now she realized that it hadn't just happened to be behind her—it was following her. She wondered if she had some kind of equipment violation. It had to be something minor because she was obeying all the traffic laws.

"Good morning! This is Cherry Hills Dispatch. An officer is going to pull you over."

"What's going on? I can't take another ticket."

"Not to worry! Your driving is not an issue," Dispatch said. "We suspect that a passenger on your bus may have committed a burglary.'"

The driver asked, "Let me guess. Is he a nervous-looking African-American kid with a backpack?"

"That sounds like the one. The description given by the officer is pretty general. His order is that you *do not l*et anybody off the bus—particularly that kid."

"I am happy to cooperate with the law, ma'am. Don't you worry none. I'm about to make that officer's day." She smiled broadly into the phone and hung up quickly.

A few passengers in the rear leaned toward the window, curious if the driver was about to be ticketed. But Li'l Bits didn't have to look—he already knew what was about to happen.

Looking over her shoulder, the bus driver yelled, "Young man! You with the gold eagle on your jacket."

Surprised, Li'l Bits looked toward the front of the bus and pointed to his chest to make sure that he was the person the driver was addressing. Passengers' eyes turned toward the driver's object of interest.

She yelled, "That's right! I'm talking to you. Move it! Get up here quick!"

Li'l Bits reached the middle of the bus when he heard several more quick blasts of the police siren that made him jump.

The driver yelled at him again, but more sharply this time. "You need to move it, son, and I don't mean tomorrow. Get up here now!" she commanded.

He darted down the aisle of the bus, passing the apprehensive eyes of aging seniors clutching bags of groceries and the questioning stares of high school students. The siren made several long whoops and a few short blips, but the driver kept driving as if she'd heard nothing. Li'l Bits took the seat behind the bus driver.

"I know you," she said. Then, she quickly corrected herself. "Rather, I know *of* you." She looked at him through her rearview mirror.

Confused, Li'l Bits leaned around the plastic shield behind her so he could see her face more clearly. About sixty years old, with red high-lights and streaks in dyed black hair, her wrinkled, dark brown face now beamed as she looked at him.

Looking out through the dusty windshield of the bus, Li'l Bits saw that they were approaching a bus stop where a passenger was waiting. To his surprise, the bus accelerated, ignoring the man who stood motionless on the sidewalk. Li'l Bits saw a perplexed look on the man's face as the bus sped by. He then shot his arm straight into the air to give the driver the finger.

This time, the siren let out a long, wailing scream. The bus driv-er chuckled to herself, but didn't slow down. All the passengers were alarmed, staring out their windows at the police car with its flashing lights and siren.

One of the passengers yelled nervously, "Hey, lady! That cop wants you to pull over! "

With a laugh, she said, “It’s okay, folks! I’ve always wanted to give a cop a run for his money!”

She looked through her rearview mirror at the small Black boy. He was anxious and afraid.

She said, "Don't worry, son. He won’t get you—not if I can help it."

Startled and completely bewildered, Li’l Bits asked, "You know he's after me?" The police car pulled alongside the bus, and Li’l Bits could see the cop’s arm motioning them to pull over.

"Where do you need to get off?" she asked calmly, ignoring the agitated hand gestures from the police car.

"Just a little ways up ahead, ma'am, near the next stop. I need to get off there." His heart was pounding wildly.

"Hold on!" she said. "I'm going to get you there as close as I can. I've got to be careful. This fool may try to cut me off. If he does, you go to the rear exit. Sit directly across from the door. He’ll board the bus. I'll open the front. When he gets on, let him approach you. When he’s close, but not too close, step to the door. He’ll yell for you to stop. Wait for the green light before you touch the door. The door will open in 0.2 seconds if you don’t trip the sensors too quickly. When those doors open, he will come at you hard. I’ll close and lock the doors before he can exit. That should give you a head start." She added, “By the way, stuff that jacket in your backpack. It’s a dead giveaway.”

She could only drive another one hundred feet before the police car suddenly accelerated. She gripped the wheel, anticipating a collision.

"Here we go," she said. "I think I just got on Po-Po’s last nerve." As the patrol car swung sharply in front of the bus, Li’l Bits asked, "Why are you helping me?"

She gave him a magnificent smile, then said, “I go to your church occasionally. I've seen you when the Spirit has moved you. It's the most amazing thing I’ve ever seen.” She shook her head, "Someone has probably got a lie out on you—sayin’ you committed some kinda burglary—so the Lord put it on my heart to help you."

The patrol car careened wildly in front of the bus, stopping about fifteen feet away. Li'l Bits was about to explain, but the bus driver barked, "Go!"

Li'l Bits ran back near the rear exit and sat down. He removed the high school jacket and stuffed it in his backpack. He made sure that Allison's diary and his cell phone were secure before zipping it back up.

The bus driver announced over the intercom, "Ladies and gentlemen, we've got company. Don't be alarmed. Just stay put." She paused and then added, "Whatever you do, please don't make any sudden movements. Better still. Don't move at all. He's not here for you. Put both hands on the seat in front of you and don't leave your seat. I don't want anyone shot on my bus."

Quisling exited his car in a rage. He turned the siren off but left his emergency lights flashing. He ran to the front of the bus and pounded on the door.

The bus driver assumed an air of complete bewilderment. She opened the door and gave the impression of being slow-witted.

Quisling stood in the street glaring at her. His hand gripped the butt of his gun. He felt swollen with rage. If not for the fact that she was in a public place, with a host of witnesses present, he would have snatched her Black ass off the bus, senior citizen or not, and thrown her to the ground. Quisling resisted the impulse to shoot her in the face.

Nodding timidly at the officer, who swore under his breath, she hunched away to avoid angering him more. Quisling stomped up the stairs, pausing to growl at her as she stared down at her feet. "Are you fuckin' deaf, you stupid bitch?"

At the top of the aisle, he slowly scanned the bus packed with morning commuters. Quisling eyed the passengers looking for the light-skinned Black kid in a white jacket.

Fuck, he thought. *No white jacket but several light-skinned colored kids. Damn, Mongrels! They all look alike.*

"Who was the last person to get on this bus?" he barked.

Several heads quickly turned to glance in Li'l Bits' general direction. Quisling noticed and started cautiously down the aisle. Quisling thought, *He might be packin' heat.* He had only advanced a few feet when he spotted Li'l Bits by the rear exit. The boy's terrified expression gave him away. Quisling exclaimed, "Gotcha!"

He took slow, deliberate steps toward his anxious suspect. Quisling unsnapped his restraining strap to free his gun. The bus driver watched the officer's movements through her rearview mirror.

Li'l Bits' attempt to appear nonchalant failed as he stared out the window. He watched the officer approach out of the corner of his eye. As Quisling lumbered forward, Li'l Bits swung his legs into the aisle, acting as if he were looking for something he'd dropped on the floor. The sound of footsteps came ominously closer. Still looking down, he perched himself on the edge of his seat and leaned imperceptibly toward the exit.

"Don't you move another inch, boy!" Quisling shouted.

When Quisling was within fifteen feet of Li'l Bits, the bus driver shouted, "Hey, cop! Behind you—gun!" and slammed her palm against the horn. Quisling dropped low, drew his weapon, and swung around.

The passengers began yelling and screaming. A few yelled, "Gun! Gun! Get down!"

Panicked, Quisling stayed in a low crouch trying to locate the threat while pandemonium raged in the bus.

Li'l Bits shot out of his seat and the driver flipped the switch, opening the exit door. In one seamless motion, he bounded over the steps and took off running.

Furious, Quisling glared at the driver and bolted toward the exit. Just as he neared the stairs, the driver immediately slammed the door shut.

Quisling howled like a wounded animal after colliding forcefully into the door. He then began to pull and bang on it violently.

Passengers began to yell and scream again. Several slid down into their seats. A few toward the rear distanced themselves as far as physically possible from the raging officer. Those closest to the front got up and dashed out the front entrance behind the fleeing driver.

Realizing that the door would not yield to brute strength, Quisling gave up, gasping. Fearing he would lose sight of his prey, he thundered down the aisle and looked out the window, scanning the street. Within seconds, he saw a small Black boy with a backpack running toward a green belt area within a subdivision.

Quisling bounded down the aisle to the front door, spouting a stream of racist epithets, even though the driver was already gone. At the very least, he wanted to backhand her.

Quisling had little time to apprehend the boy. Once he got deep into the residential area, he might disappear into anybody's house. The kid would be gone, so would Allison's diary, and so would his career. Initiating a house-to-house search was risky because that would mean enlisting the assistance of other officers, and Kensington did not want anybody else involved. He had to get this kid on his own, if possible.

Stumbling down the steps at the front entrance, he prevented his fall by grabbing onto the bus railing. Checking his fall caused a sharp, wrenching pain in his left shoulder. He cursed out loud. "Sonofabitch!"

Gun still in hand, Quisling sprinted to his patrol car parked at an awkward angle, partially blocking a passing lane. Traffic slowed to navigate around it, but he didn't care. Hopping onto the hood, he strained to spot the boy. The aluminum hood groaned and buckled under his weight leaving a sizable dent behind.

About thirty yards ahead, the boy darted down a winding sidewalk between rows of houses. Damn, that kid can run! Quisling noted the pedestrian corridor was large enough for his patrol car.

Jumping off the hood, Quisling fell and stumbled to the ground "Fuuuck!" he yelled as pain shot through his sore shoulder. Jumping up, he scrambled to his car and tossed his gun onto the passenger seat.

With the siren blaring and lights flashing, he shot across two lanes of southbound traffic into northbound lanes, while cars blared and braked hard. He barreled on, unfazed. He had his target. Tires screeching, he tore into the subdivision, blowing through a stop sign without so much as a glance.

Up ahead, the kid raced downhill, his speed relentless. *Where's he going? Does he have a plan—or is he just running for his life?*

Quisling pressed on, observing the terrain. The path dipped and plateaued in intervals, with a sharp drop further ahead before leveling out for several hundred feet. The undulating ground demanded caution—one wrong move at this speed and his car could flip.

Li'l Bits had run down nearly three hundred feet of slightly curving and dipping hillside. He ran on the grass instead of the winding sidewalk—it was a more direct route to the Professor's house. When he passed the corner ranch-style house on his left, he would be able to see the Professor's home. Then, thirty yards to safety.

The rumble and bounce of the patrol car sounded threateningly close. Glancing over his shoulder, Li'l Bits gasped realizing he might not make it in time.

As he reached the house on the top of the cul-de-sac, he decided to hop the four-foot wooden fence. While in mid-air, the patrol car flew past, barely missing him. It shattered fence posts and railings, sending wood fragments and debris everywhere. The lights and siren of the patrol car blared wildly as it bounced down the hill.

Seeing the kid turn left into the cul-de-sac, Quisling locked onto his path and the house he was running toward. He couldn't make a sharp turn unless he wanted to risk rolling his car or winding up in someone's house or backyard. He had to slow down carefully and back up.

If he rolled his car, the kid would get away for sure. He carefully pumped his brakes. The tires of the car ripped the turf violently as it started to vibrate and shudder, sliding and grinding to a halt.

As the car was correcting itself, Li'l Bits flew across the bulb of the cul-de-sac, feeling as if his body were moving in slow motion.

When he glanced up, the Professor was already at the open doorway, waving frantically and shouting for him to hurry. He looked like one of those sports dads at a track meet, cheering his son near the finish line." However, Li'l Bits didn't hear excitement and exhilaration in his voice—he heard fear.

As his feet hit the edge of the yard, he saw the Professor's car parked in the driveway. The Professor looked back into his house and shouted, "Tawanna! Code 9! Code 9!"

The Professor turned back to the street and saw the patrol car. It was about to drive across the grassy area into the cul-de-sac when his neighbor, whose fence had been smashed by the police car, backed out of his driveway, deliberately blocking the patrol car.

A moment later, Li'l Bits vaulted over the two porch steps. The Professor barely had time to step aside before Li'l Bits hurled himself through the doorway with Hannibal at his heels barking wildly.

Relieved, the Professor smiled at Li'l Bits as he leaned forward, hands resting just above his knees, still panting hard to catch his breath.

"I told you I could run," he gasped.

"Yeah, it's a damn good thing you're fast because you sure are out of shape!" The Professor smiled, shut the front door, and turned to face the visibly shaken and exhausted boy who was frantically searching through the backpack he'd dropped on the floor.

Tawanna walked out of the kitchen with a cell phone in her hand and a shoe box in the other. Hannibal bounded across the floor to sniff the contents of Li'l Bits' backpack.

"I made the call," she said, her eyes wide with apprehension. The Professor gave a slight nod of his head. Tawanna walked up to her husband, trembling, and quickly handed him the box. He stared at it for a moment, lost in thought, remembering—then met his wife's eyes, brimming with tears.

He gently caressed her hand. "Everything is gonna be okay." He took the box and turned to Li'l Bits.

Before the Professor could speak, Li'l Bits thrust a thin book—decorated with beads, sequins, and hearts—into his hand. As his fingers closed around it, he caught the low rumble of a car pulling up outside. The Professor realized that the siren had stopped, and the car was driving across his lawn.

"That sonofabitch is crazy!" he muttered under his breath. "This the book, son?" The Professor asked as he heard a car door creak open.

"Yes, Professor. It's Allison's diary," he said excitedly.

"Tawanna," The Professor said, "Take the book and Li'l Bits next door to Mr. James. Safeguard that book, and don't let Li'l Bits out of your sight. I'll take care of the cop."

All three jumped as they heard a car door slam. Hannibal started barking again.

"Go!" The Professor ordered.

Tawanna grabbed Li'l Bits' hand and ran toward the back sliding door that led onto the deck.

Li'l Bits asked breathlessly, "What's Code 9? I heard the Professor tell you to call Code 9."

Sliding open the door, she said, "Code 9 alerts our community to the presence of a rogue cop. Many of our neighbors, or their families and friends, have had some very unpleasant experiences with overly aggressive cops—boys with toys who don't know how or when to use force."

"That's awful," Li'l Bits murmured as they ran across the wooden deck. Tawanna held up a hand to slow him down. She peered carefully around the corner of the house before jumping to the ground. She motioned for him to follow, and together they slipped into the neighbor's backyard.

In the living room, Doug opened the shoebox and pulled his Glock 17 from its leather holster. The cool metal felt light in his hand. He inhaled the sharp scent of gun oil. He studied his weapon, admiring its cold, deadly simplicity. A flood of memories assailed him—none of them good.

He tossed the box aside, ejected the magazine, and checked for all seventeen rounds. Pulling the slide back, he chambered a round, placed the muzzle against his lips, and kissed it. Lowering the gun to his side, Doug stepped to the front door. Hannibal swung his head toward him when his master spoke. Taking a long, deep breath, the Professor said, "Well, boy…let's go say hello to one of our city's finest."

24

The Standoff

Doug didn't know if the air had turned unusually cool or if it was just his nerves. He hadn't fired a gun in years, but he hoped his training and muscle memory would kick in. At least, his focus remained sharp; he noticed the alarm in the officer's eyes as they locked onto the weapon resting against his thigh.

Hannibal bolted outside, brushing his leg. At the snap of Doug's fingers, Hannibal halted, positioning himself ten feet away, directly before the visibly shaken officer. Hannibal lowered his massive head, tensed his powerful shoulders, and waited—poised and ready.

A low guttural growl caused Quisling to flinch, his eyes widening in fear. He'd seen what K9 dogs could do to a man. Quisling observed that the dog was on high alert—waiting for his master's next command.

Quisling regretted holstering his weapon before exiting his car. He was at a significant tactical disadvantage. As he hand inched toward his holster, Doug shouted, "Freeze, mister! Unless you've got a nervous twitch in that arm, you best keep your hand away from that gun—if you want to live."

Eyeing the gun in the man's hand, held low by his side, Quisling thought he might be able to take him, if it weren't for the dog. He noticed that the man appeared to stand slightly off-balance, which gave him a slight advantage.

However, something made Quisling hesitate—the look in his eyes. There was no fear—just a cold, hard, unflinching stare that said he had faced down death before and would kill Quisling without hesitation if he made the slightest move for his gun.

Quisling hoped Kensington would arrive soon to provide cover. He had radioed him the address after he parked on the lawn, but he hadn't anticipated being challenged by a homeowner who believed in the Second Amendment.

Quisling said derisively, "Help is on the way, boy! You need to put your gun down, call off Cujo, and get out of my way. You are aiding and abetting a felon! I saw him run into your house. Give him up!"

Doug smiled. "Where do you think you are, Opie—in the Mississippi Delta? This ain't the middle of the night, and you ain't coming in some old, defenseless uncle's house to snatch up a young Black boy. You blink wrong, and you'll die on my lawn."

Quisling's face flushed hot with anger. *What's up with these stupid niggers calling me 'Opie'?* He was about to reconsider his decision to draw his weapon when he heard several chirps from a police siren. He looked up the street to see flashing red and blue lights.

Under his breath, Quisling muttered, "Here comes the cavalry, nigger."

Emboldened, Quisling yelled at the man. "Get that damn dog inside if you want it to live. And if you want to avoid any more trouble, you need to put that gun down now! I'm not telling you again!"

Kensington roared down the street and parked. He exited his car slowly, wisely choosing not to escalate the situation by drawing his weapon. He had contacted the Criminal Intelligence Unit to conduct a background check on the homeowner, which revealed that he was an ex-cop with an outstanding record and a disability discharge from the force. CIU reported he'd received numerous commendations for heroism and public service awards.

Not a man to be taken lightly.

Kensington noted two surveillance cameras angled in different directions high above the door's entrance. Another camera was affixed above the garage door. Kensington knew that negotiation, rather than aggressive action, was the best strategy, but stood slightly behind his car door in case negotiations failed or Quisling did something reckless.

Doug yelled, "Ready!" Hannibal instantly erupted, barking ferociously and snarling, his lips curled back to bare sharp teeth, saliva foaming at the corners of his mouth.

Quisling inhaled sharply, stumbled back, and gripped his gun but resisted the impulse to pull it from the holster. Instinct told him that he might be the first casualty in this situation.

Kensington raised both hands in appeasement and said, "Please call off your dog, Mr. Joiner! We're not looking for any trouble." He started to step from behind his door—but not so far that he couldn't use it as a shield if bullets started to fly.

He had only taken one step but stopped immediately when Doug raised his left hand, just slightly above his head, to signal him to halt. Then he pointed a finger to a second-floor window in a home across the street. He snapped his fingers once, and Hannibal immediately returned to an alert stance.

Kensington cautiously turned his head to see where Joiner was pointing. He noticed a window slowly opening and felt a chill run through his body. He thought he saw a curtain move but could only see darkness within the large rectangular frame. He strained his eyes, trying to see if someone had him in their sights.

He called out to Quisling, "We got company—possible threat behind us, one o'clock. second-story window." Quisling's eyes widened in fear. He turned his head very slowly to avoid triggering an attack from the dog. He was now aware of the dark window that could spell his death.

Was someone up there with a weapon? Could there be more than one person? The window was large enough. He turned back to face Joiner, who was smiling broadly. Frustration and anger caused Quisling to sweat.

What kind of neighborhood had they wandered into? Kensington wondered. Ordinary Joe Blow citizens didn't act this way. Kensington spoke carefully, hoping to appeal to reason.

"We're not looking for a shootout here, sir. We're just trying to do our jobs. You were a cop once. You wore the badge same as I did. You know the drill. You 're obstructing a police officer in the lawful performance of his duty. You can be arrested. We can arrest anybody who helps you."

"Yeah!" he said dryly. "Used to be a cop until I was shot stopping a convenience store robbery by another cop who knew me." Doug paused and then asked, "Any of you boys ever been shot?" Quisling and Kensington looked blankly at him. Quisling twisted his mouth.

"Well, if you've never been shot, have you ever been shot at?" he asked, smirking.

The men still didn't respond. Both shifted nervously and looked at each other, wondering if he might start shooting.

Nodding toward the window across the street and slapping his Glock against his thigh, Doug said, "If you're lucky enough to live, it hurts... a lot."

Quisling's mouth had gone dry when he heard that the Black man facing him used to be one of their own. He might have been in far more danger than he realized if he'd tried to draw on him before Kensington arrived.

With all the authority he could muster, Quisling said firmly, "We just want the boy."

Doug spat on the ground. "Do you want the boy, or do you want what the boy has?"

Kensington looked down at the ground and sighed. He forced a poker face before replying. "Mr. Joiner, he broke into somebody's residence and stole her property. That could mean a prison sentence for him and a prison sentence for you for aiding him."

Kensington studied Joiner's eyes when he noticed that he was no longer paying close attention to Quisling or him. Instead, he appeared more relaxed, looking casually behind them—first to Quisling's left and then to Kensington's right.

Kensington sensed a physical presence behind him. Across the street, a small crowd of people stood with cell phones, recording the unfolding drama in their neighborhood.

Kensington fumed, *Damn! Bad enough to be caught on security cameras—but live witnesses, too?*

Behind him, he heard cars approaching fast. A Ford Raptor stopped in the middle of the street, directly across from the house. A pot-bellied white man with shoulder-length silver hair jumped out, grinning—dressed in a tie-dye shirt and military fatigue pants.

Two more vehicles pulled up across from Joiners' home, parking partially on the street and partly on the sidewalk, with about fifteen feet of space between them. The drivers stayed in their seats.

Kensington yelled to the hippie, "Get back in your truck, mister."

Holding both arms high in the air, the man said, grinning, "I'm not armed, officer." Nodding toward the men seated in their cars, he said, "I'm not, but..." jerking his head toward the other drivers, he shrugged. "But they might be."

One driver, wearing an NRA cap, nodded and smiled. The other chewed hard on a wad of tobacco, then spat into the street.

Still grinning, the man yelled, "Hey, Professor! Community Cop Watch reporting at your service. Looks like you got two of our true and blue here. What's going on?"

"They want to come into my house, Charlie, but they don't have a warrant," he said.

Quisling yelled, "We don't need no goddamn warrant. We got a fleeing felon who might destroy important evidence. We got the law on our side."

Charlie said, "Not if you don't have a warrant, sir. You remember the 4th amendment, right? Man's home is his castle. You boys should know that."

"What evidence might the boy be destroying, officer?" Joiner taunted the officers. "I thought that he'd stolen something. Was it drugs he stole from the victim's house? You can flush drugs down a toilet. If he'd stolen drugs, a judge might say you had exigent circumstances to enter my house. Anything else, like a TV or a computer, might be pretty hard to destroy." He paused and said. "Unless it's something you can burn."

Kensington groaned. Quisling grimaced. They exchanged a glance—tight and uneasy—each seeing their worst fear mirrored in the other's eyes. Their shared look said it all: *He knows.* Joiner smiled.

Kensington cleared his throat. "Whatever he stole, mister, it's still evidence, and we want the boy and that property he stole. We don't need a warrant for a fleeing felon."

Kensington was starting to feel uneasy with so many people around. He knew that if things got out of hand, he and Quisling had no chance of controlling the situation. Calling for backup could trigger a shootout— something he was determined to avoid. Worse, some by-the-book cop might seize the diary and hand it over to the DA, and that was a risk he wasn't willing to take. Kensington's mind raced, trying to figure out the best move.

Meanwhile, Quisling looked around in amazement at the crowd. *Where the hell did all of these people come from?* He couldn't believe that some white people were also here—helping this nigger! He turned around to see a few people on the sidewalk inching closer.

Quisling thought, *It looks like the fucking United Nations. I've never seen so many mud people appear so damn quick in a middle-class suburb.*

"Don't take another step, folks!" he yelled.

"These are my neighbors, officer," Joiner said. "They're good people. They live in this neighborhood. They all respect the law. All of them are here as law-abiding citizens. They just want to make sure our interaction remains friendly."

Acknowledging their presence with a warm smile and a broad flourish, Joiner turned to the two perplexed officers. He said, "So… go get your warrant, and I'll be happy to let you enter my home."

Out of the corner of his eye, Kensington saw movement behind a house next door to Joiner's home. He did a double take—he couldn't believe what he just saw. Dumbfounded, he beckoned Quisling to approach him.

Kensington stepped away from the car door that partially shielded him and raised both hands to his shoulders. He announced, "Just need to talk to my partner for a moment, folks, and we'll be out of your hair."

Quisling stared at him, befuddled.

Forcing a smile, Kensington beckoned Quisling over. When he didn't respond, Kensington began walking toward him. Quisling shrugged, shook his head and scowled. He strode slowly toward Kensington, attempting to display as much bravado as possible as he walked.

When they were within a foot of each other, Kensington leaned over and muttered, under his breath, "You took your damn time. Let's get out of here!"

Quisling was stunned. "Leave now? We'd look like … like … a bunch of pussies." He started to protest violently, and Kensington unwisely raised his hand to calm him. Quisling slapped it away. His face felt hot, and his eye twitched in anger.

"Why leave now?" he hissed under his breath. "That little nigger is in there—and my future's in there with him. I'm not leaving without that goddamn book."

Kensington leaned in. "Trust me, Quisling! Let's just leave now, unless you plan on trying to kill everyone here. Didn't you see the surveillance cameras on Joiner's house? Everyone here is recording us! We're wasting time." There was restrained panic in Kensington's voice. "We need to go *now*. Trust me on this, Quisling!"

Crestfallen, Quisling shrugged again and stomped back to his patrol car. He looked like he was going to have a heart attack.

Just before Quisling got to his car, Joiner delivered a parting jab. "Hey! Law and Order! You'll be getting a bill for tearing up my lawn." He added, "You need to pay for my neighbor's fence, too."

Quisling gritted his teeth and slid into his seat.

Slamming the door, he leaned out his window as far as he could, and spat on the lawn.

Kensington looked up at the second-story window and saw it fully opened. He decided it was a good time to leave. Some gun nut might be inclined to make a name for himself.

He cautiously returned to his car, got in, started the ignition, and tapped his horn twice. Charlie, the community watch guy, drove his truck forward to make room for their exit.

As the officers drove off, the crowd followed them down the street recording their departure with their cell phones.

Kensington had no doubt that some, if not all, of the neighbors were armed. The woman with the large tote bag might have had a few surprises for them, too. He wondered if anyone would have opened fire if they had tried to enter the house. He was certain that Joiner would have defended his home with his life.

Kensington radioed Quisling. "Follow me. The rabbit just left his hole. We may still be in luck."

"What the hell are you talking about? What fuckin' rabbit?" Quisling asked, still seething.

Kensington explained that the kid had taken off as they stood in front of Joiner's house.

"That ain't necessarily good news, Kensington, if he left the diary with those people! Maybe he's just creating a diversion by running."

"I hear you, but my gut tells me he still has Allison's diary. Besides, I think he took off on his own. I can't imagine his friends letting him run off so we could catch him again. Did it seem to you that any of those people trusted cops?"

"Yep!" Quisling said, sighing. "We're riding the knife's edge on this one—but at least we are going to get that Black son-of-a-bitch!"

As Kensington made a right-hand turn down a street that would wind past a high school, he considered several possible escape routes the boy might have taken. But, an uneasy thought started to gnaw at him. The boy seemed to have waited at the rear of the next-door neighbor's house until he was certain that Kensington had seen him. Only then, after being seen, did he take off running.

Perplexed, Kensington rubbed his brow slowly. "What kind of cat n' mouse game is this kid playing?"

He knew they were in a precarious situation. Only a miracle could save them now. Shaken by this bizarre turn of events, he was once again overwhelmed by a profound sense of regret.

Is this who I am? he wondered. *If the worst happens, will they just remember me as a dirty cop?*

Kensington's fear hung cold and heavy, like the chill of iron against his skin.

25

Lost and Found

A few minutes later, Kensington radioed Quisling. "I called the school resource officer to be on the lookout for a short, light-skinned African-American kid running toward or past the school, wearing a white jacket with a gold eagle. I'm gonna swing by to canvass the area. You cover the park area east of the school in case he made it that far."

Quisling balked at the plan. "The nigger is fast, but he ain't no Usain Bolt. He couldn't have made it that far!"

"*You* couldn't have made it that far—not with that gut on you," Kensington snapped. "But that kid is running for his life. Just do what I say!"

Within minutes, Dispatch interrupted his thoughts. The voice said flatly, "The RO has got your runner. Report to the principal's office."

Kensington was dumbfounded. Whistling through his teeth, he exclaimed, "That kid must have run straight to the RO!" He thought, *What game is he playing?*

Kensington pulled into one of the parking spaces reserved for police and leisurely opened his car door. He didn't have to rush, anymore—not now. He had time. His thief had been caught. But unlike his incarcerated friend, this boy wasn't mute. He could talk—and he had a lot to say about two cops pressuring a young girl to lie about a crime that never happened.

Kensington had to create a convincing narrative about Allison's diary—one that could explain why she would accuse him of pressuring her to lie about a crime.

This won't be easy, he thought. *What would be her motive to malign the father of the boy she loves?* His mind whirled for explanations, but none satisfied him. Even if he could convince Allison to admit she had fabricated everything—that none of it was true—why would she write something so outrageous in her diary in the first place? What would be her motivation?

If push came to shove, he could only deny, deny, deny, just like the lying politicians do when they are caught red-handed breaking the law. Plausible deniability was his best strategy.

Take slow, deep breaths, Kensington told himself. *Go to the principal's office like it's a routine investigation. Remember! You are the law!*

He walked up the steps and stood before six metal-framed doors that channeled student traffic in and out of the school. Despite his mental mantra to remain calm, his heart was starting to race again.

A scenario flashed in his mind: the principal may have already notified the DA about the diary. Detectives could be on route to the school right now to question him, gather statements, and lock in a damning narrative *before* he could control it.

And he'd bet that cops were already responding to Ms. Ruddick's 911 call. God help him if Allison leaks what's in her diary when questioned.

Any damning admission would make for a difficult situation, but not an impossible one. Allison has no independent proof. No one to corroborate her story. Her accusations couldn't be verified. One thing for certain, Wally would not help her send his dad to prison.

Then Kensington paused. He wondered, *But what if her mother heard any of her panicked phone call?* Shaking his head, he muttered, "Can't worry about that now. Gotta focus on the next few minutes."

If a call to the DA has already been made, he would play dumb and act incredulous in the face of outrageous accusations, protesting that he had no idea what Allison was talking about. It was his word against Allison's. It was Quisling's word against hers. It was Wally's word against hers.

Kensington sighed. He hoped he didn't have to discredit Allison. But, like Quisling had said, "It's her or us." But choosing "us" didn't mean she had to die. Quisling was wrong! Allison had created a serious problem for them, but he still believed that there were less lethal ways to handle it.

If he convince Allison to tell one last lie—to back his claim that her story was fabricated—that would get everyone off the hook. Everyone except her, that is. If the DA was pissed enough, she could be charged with false reporting. Even then, Kensington was confident he could swing a diversion deal and keep her out of the system.

Kensington sighed, poor, sweet, naive Allison. She would've done anything to please Wally. How could he have let himself become so guilt-ridden that he allowed his son, basically a child, to influence him into committing a crime?

Elsa, his beautiful wife, would have told him, "You are not the man I married. I don't know you anymore."

Why was he feeling so disgusted with himself? Was it because he'd done something despicable, or was it because he'd been caught?

Kensington pulled out his cell phone and called Quisling. After several rings, Quisling responded. "Where are you? I'm still circling the park. Not a damn thing, yet." His words came at Kensington in a rush.

"You can stop your search," Kensington said dryly. "The rabbit has been snared."

"Hot damn! Hot damn! Hot fuckin' damn!" Quisling yelled. He slapped the steering wheel of his car. "You at the school? I'll meet you over there!"

"Yes, I'm at the school. But, no! Do *not* meet me here! I'll handle this." Kensington held his breath, anticipating Quisling's outraged response. He yanked the phone from his ear as soon as the stream of profanity erupted, holding it at arm's length as if Quisling's words might scorch his skin.

Quisling was panicking—on the edge of losing control. He didn't want to risk him causing a scene in the principal's office. After a few moments, Kensington put the phone back to his ear.

"Kensington! Kensington! Are you there? Answer me, you sonofabitch!"

"Don't you fuckin' blow me off, goddammit!" Quisling yelled. "You put my ass in this sling, and I am not gonna let you hang me with it. I have as much right to be there as you do!"

"I know you do, Quisling," Kensington said calmly. "I'm not trying to cut you out of anything. Hey, you found him first. I didn't, but I got him now. We're working on this as a team, right? We don't need to arouse suspicions unnecessarily." After a few moments he asked, "We good?"

"I'm coming to the school," Quisling replied.

Kensington smacked his head and blurted, "What?"

"I'm still coming to the school, but I'll wait for you in the parking lot."

Kensington sighed. "Okay! The parking lot works."

"I want this Sambo bastard, Kensington," Quisling snarled. He sounded almost bestial. "He don't get to scare me, taunt me, get his friends to confront me, sic a dog on me, and have a gun pointed at my face. *I'm* the law!" Pausing, he yelled, "I am a white man. My ancestors would roll over in their graves if I let this nigger go unpunished."

Suddenly, Kensington felt drained—sick of hearing Quisling's tired reminiscing about his glorious white ancestors.

"I don't know how long this meeting will take. The boy is in the principal's office. I've got to play this one by ear. A strong possibility exists that the principal may have already made several calls—one to the police, another to the DA's office, and a third to the Attorney General. Whatever you do, please stay in your car. If you see a squad car pull up, call me!"

Quisling snorted. "If I see a squad car, don't expect me to hang around, Kensington. You're on your own. I'm outta here." Quisling's phone went silent.

Entering the building, Kensington motioned to a student walking by. The boy removed his earbuds and looked inquiringly at Kensington. "Yes, sir?"

"Principal's office … which way?"

"You'll never find it from here." The boy smiled. "Follow me," he said amicably.

They walked down the hallway and around a series of corridors. Turning another corner, the kid pointed to a large, enclosed glass room occupied by several desks. Kensington turned to thank him, but he was already walking away.

Kensington stepped through the open doorway and stopped, anxiously waiting to catch someone's attention. A few curious heads turned his way but returned quickly to work. A door opened to the right of a woman, who was loudly raging at the copier.

A tall, athletic-looking woman in a smart blue pants suit walked out. She gently squeezed the shoulder of the frustrated woman at the copier. She said, "I know. Been buggin' ADMIN for a year, trying to get a new one."

She looked up, startled to find Kensington watching her. She made a quick mental note of him. Tall. Solidly built. A slight paunch. Keen, dark eyes. Graying hair. He was making a conscious effort to appear relaxed. Throwing him a quick, knowing smile, she walked up to him with an outstretched hand.

"I'm Principal March," she said. Her dark brown eyes studied his face carefully, wondering why he looked so pale and drawn. Kensington felt his stomach knot under her scrutiny.

He forced a smile. "I appreciate your help, Principal March. I've been on quite a chase today, running down this boy." His voice was flat but all business.

She cocked her head and eyed him. "Matthew Carver."

"Excuse me, ma'am?"

"His name is Matthew Michael Carver. We call him Li'l Bits. If you've seen him, you'd know why." She smiled politely again.

"Well, I only got a glance at him because he took off kind of quick, but I'm looking forward to meeting him."

Kensington wondered how much she knew about Allison's diary. Whatever she knew, she was holding her cards close to her chest. He paused. "Sounds like you know him. This looks like a fair-sized high school—close to a thousand kids or more? I bet you get to know all the troublemakers."

Her eyes showed surprise. "Some kids you get to know because they get into trouble. Some kids you get to know because they are exceptional. You can't help but notice them. Pretty much everybody around here knows and likes Li'l Bits, including me. He's no troublemaker."

Kensington scoffed. "Even good kids screw up occasionally."

She nodded in agreement. "But if Li'l Bits 'screwed up' as you say, I'm sure that he has a good reason. That's just who he is."

Who in the hell is she talking about? Is she actually talking about this little Black boy? Sounds like this principal is one of those white progressive administrators who believe that the legacy of slavery causes dysfunctional behavior in Black kids. The possibility that March thought this Carver kid was faultless almost made Kensington roll his eyes.

"Did he tell you what he did?" he asked casually.

"Yes. But not in detail. He told me he went into a stranger's home, uninvited, but wouldn't tell me why." She paused, searching Kensington's face again, then added, "He said you'd know why." The knot in Kensington's stomach tightened.

"I told him that I need to call his parents, but he said he wanted to speak to you alone first before I called them."

"So you haven't called the police?" Kensington asked.

She looked puzzled. "Why call the police, Officer Kensington? I knew you were coming."

Kensington suddenly felt an inexplicable surge of hope. He shrugged slightly. "Right! Of course!"

"Follow me, please."

She opened her office door and waved Kensington to a seat in front of a small, light-skinned boy who sat at a conference table. He sat ramrod straight, his hands folded in front of him. His face appeared damp with perspiration.

Principal March paused at the door, silently observing both of them.. Turning her attention to Li'l Bits, she asked, "You okay?" Then she eyed Kensington. Li'l Bits smiled slightly and nodded.

When Kensington heard the door shut and her footsteps trail away, he walked up to the table, bumping it hard, and assumed a menacing stance. If he had this kid at the police station, he could find out what he needed to know in a heartbeat.

Kensington barked, "Give me your cell phone."

Hesitantly, Li'l Bits pulled the cell phone out of his pants pocket and placed it on the table. Kensington looked at it to see if it was recording.

"What's your password!"

Li'l Bits said, "1225."

Kensington turned on the cell phone and searched for the photos icon. He accessed it and searched for the most recent. His knees nearly buckled. He dragged a chair back from the table and sat down.

Slowly, he read Allison's confession. Kensington sighed, and shoved the phone across the table. Li'l Bits caught it before it flew on the floor. He wondered where the diary was.

"Read my name in her diary?" he asked.

"You weren't named, sir. I just guessed who you were. Tyrene's mom told me that Wally's dad was a police officer. Allison told me, too. Not too hard to put two and two together."

"How did you know I'd be the one to come to the school?"

"You love Wally, right? You want to protect him. I figured it would be Wally's dad who'd walk through that door."

Li'l Bits bent over and searched through his backpack. After finding what he needed, he straightened and placed Allison's diary on the table.

Kensington let out a slow whistle. "So this is it, huh?" he said, not expecting a reply. "Allison's precious diary," he added sarcastically. Kensington flipped through the diary until he located the words that condemned him. His face drained of color.

Closing the book, he fell back heavily into his chair. Part of him wanted to rage, to lash out at this kid. Another part wanted to thank him for putting an end to this criminal charade. Then, a realization struck Kensington—he felt a flicker of admiration for a boy willing to risk his life to help a friend.

His life? Why would his life be at risk for a diary? Then Quisling's mind-numbing statement about killing Allison came to mind.

A wave of panic screamed at him to seize the phone and diary and bolt from the office. But what good would that do? It was too late! Anyone with half a brain brain could figure out what he had done. And Li'l Bits—and maybe others—had copies of the pages.

The standoff at Joiner's house would be seen for what it was: two desperate cops involved in a criminal conspiracy, trying to seize and destroy incriminating evidence. A handwriting expert could easily identify Allison as the author. And with enough pressure and coaxing, the DA could make her talk.

Kensington folded his hands, leaning across the table. He asked, "Did you make a video of Allison's diary, too?"

Almost apologetically, Li'l Bits explained, "It wasn't my idea, Officer Kensington. But Mr. James, the neighbor's house that Ms. Joiner and I ran to, suggested we make a video, just in case. He had all the equipment because he makes YouTube videos about gardening. He asked me to narrate what I had found, and then he filmed the most telling diary entries. Didn't take long," he added.

The certainty Kensington once felt about avenging Wally had leached away like lead into soil — slow, poisonous, irreversible. His ill-conceived plan to frame the kid who'd hurt his son in a school fight seemed colossally stupid now.

He remembered berating Wally after his wife died, convinced she could've been saved if she had cried out—that Wally would've heard her if he hadn't been lost in his music with those damn earbuds jammed in his ears. But, maybe she'd never cried out at all. Maybe she just died—suddenly and alone.

Tears threatened the corners of Kensington's eyes as he thought of her. He pushed himself away from the table, stood and walked to the window facing a large expanse of ground. Looking out, Kensington saw nothing—his mind consumed with a storm of self-condemning thoughts. Elsa would have been so disappointed in him.

What happened to me? How could I have taken this path?

Gradually, through the mosaic of his conflicted mind, the distorted picture became clear. He'd lost his moral compass.

Then came Quisling, desperate for help. At a time of profound loss, Kensington felt needed. The one place where he felt most needed was his job. Carelessly, he let down his guard and let Quisling in. Quisling's comment about "a knife coming in handy" should have tipped him off. Quisling entertained him and Wally with stories from the "good old days"— a time when society openly oppressed Black people through laws, customs, and the full force of the state to maintain a rigid caste system. Strangely, Kensington felt a perverse sense of power hearing those stories. When a Black boy hurt Wally, it made sense to Wally that he was entitled to his revenge. So Kensington helped him do just that—with a lie—spun together with a racist and Wally's girlfriend, to brand an innocent Black boy for life. Kensington suddenly felt soul-sick.

Racial hatred is so seductive, he thought—alluring, enticing, and insidiously destructive. Constant exposure to messages of racial intolerance—subtle or blatant, from evangelicals to politicians, from social media to family dinners, from art to culture, from podcasts to communities— seeps into daily life making the urge to hate feel as natural as breathing.

Kensington stared off into space as he mentally recoiled from the words of unmitigated hate he had heard from his son—*I want that nigger to pay.*

What did Elsa say was one of God's greatest commandments? *Thou shalt love thy neighbor as thyself.*

Confused by the unexpected change in Kensington's demeanor, Li'l Bits remained perfectly still, quietly studying the slightly bowed head and broad sloping shoulders. Kensington was looking out the window, but Li'l Bits wondered if he was actually looking inside himself.

"Excuse me, sir."

Kensington glanced almost absent-mindedly over his shoulder. He felt tired and drained. He turned and walked listlessly to the table. Lowering himself into the chair, he asked distractedly, "What is it, Li'l Bits?"

"I didn't understand, at first, why you did what you did. I mean, that story you made up about Tyrene. I was angry when I read it in Allison's diary." His eyes expressed his pain. "The only thing I can figure is you had to have been deeply hurt to create that lie. You must've wanted revenge."

Kensington winced hearing the boy's truth. His throat felt unusually tight and dry.

"My hope was to find something—some evidence—to prove that my friend didn't sexually assault Allison. I know God helped me find her diary." He paused. "During the entire bus ride—with that other officer tailing us—I kept turning it over in my mind: who should I give the diary to? At first, I thought about giving it to my mom. Tyrene's lawyer seemed like the best option—but I knew I had to talk it over with my family first. Taking the diary to the police was out of the question."

Kensington smiled wryly at his concern—knowing that another cop who valued brotherhood over his sworn oath—would have destroyed the diary.

The kid's eyes suddenly brightened. "The bus was going right past the Professor's house. He's an ex-cop. He'd know what to do."

"That guy with the gun? You call him Professor?"

Startled, Li'l Bits asked, alarmed, "The Professor had a gun?"

Kensington scowled. "Yeah! He had a gun and was ready to use it, too."

The color drained from his face. "I had no idea. I didn't want anyone to get hurt."

"Is that why you ran ... so we'd follow you?"

"Yes. I didn't want my friends to be in trouble. I knew that if I ran, you'd come after me." Li'l Bits opened his phone to write a text.

"What are you doing?" Kensington asked.

"Please! Just a minute." He rapidly tapped a message and hit send. "I sent a text to the Professor before you arrived at school, asking him to hold onto the photos and video until you and I could talk. I just wanted to make sure he didn't forget."

Almost immediately, his phone pinged. Chuckling, Li'l Bits said, "The Professor just texted me to remind me of the story about the scorpion and the frog."

"What about a scorpion and a frog?" Kensington asked.

"It's a fable. A cautionary tale," he explained. "The frog helped a scorpion cross the river on his back. The scorpion stung the frog before he reached the other side. When the frog asked the scorpion why it had stung him, the scorpion said that he couldn't help it. It was his nature. They both drowned. The moral is never forget the true nature of the thing you are dealing with. If it's deadly, like the scorpion, it will kill you."

"So I guess I'm the scorpion?" Kensington mused. He picked up the diary again, stared hard at it, then set it back down. "Why would you even want to talk to me? With that diary, with that book as evidence..." his voice trailed off.

"You made a mistake, sir." Li'l Bits shrugged, "A really bad one, but I'm not the one to judge you or any of your friends. If the diary ended up in the hands of a policeman—someone who took their oath seriously—it could destroy your lives: Allison's, that other cop, maybe even Wally's, and yours. So, I came to a decision that I think is fair for everyone. I decided that I didn't want my friend Tyrene to have to defend himself in court against a lie."

Leaning forward, Li'l Bits said, "If you can get that sexual assault charge dropped, Officer Kensington, then there's no need to give copies of Allison's diary or the video to anyone. I just want my friend to have his day in court, about the fight at school."

Kensington sank back against the chair. He could hardly believe what he was hearing. This was the miracle he needed—he only had to convince the DA to drop the sexual assault charge.

Emotion prevented Kensington from speaking. He felt his eyes beginning to burn and blinked rapidly to stop the tears. Li'l Bits could see that Kensington was struggling to say something but raised his hand.

"No need to say anything, sir. Life can get pretty hard sometimes—brutal even. People get confused and make poor decisions. Any decent person can lose sight of what's right. I think that deep down you want to be a good man. What you did is now between you and God."

He continued, "So we're clear, sir, once the sexual offense charge is dropped and the trial is concluded, win or lose, all the evidence will be destroyed. I'll make sure of that."

Kensington's head was reeling as he felt a swirl of emotions lift him. He looked deeply into Li'l Bits' compassionate eyes and knew he could trust him. Now, he no longer cared that a tear streamed down his cheek.

Overwhelmed with gratitude, he reached for Li'l Bits' hand and silently held it. Li'l Bits nodded his understanding and grasped Kensington's hand with his, causing him to jump, as if an electric circuit had been closed.

As he looked at Li'l Bits, a soft radiance began to emanate from him. The air shimmered faintly as a golden aura gathered and enfolded him—gentle and diffuse, like the first light of dawn drifting through the mist. Then suddenly, a burst of brilliant light broke through — nearly blinding him — cascading into a halo of whirling light.

Kensington was awestruck, uncertain whether he was dreaming or hallucinating—the sight was utterly breathtaking. Gradually, the light ebbed gently, like waves returning to the sea. An uncanny calm settled over Kensington as he gave himself over to the wonder of the moment. A feeling unlike anything he'd ever known stirred within him.

His breath caught in his throat, a surge of emotion, a sob rising behind it. *Is this what grace feels like? Amid his bewilderment, a single thought emerged, threaded with quiet awe—Who is this boy?*

A sharp knock at the door abruptly brought the surge of emotion to a halt. Then a long pause, as if the person outside the door was waiting for an invitation to enter. Kensington quickly wiped his cheek, reluctantly released Li'l Bits' hand, and sat up straight in his chair. The luminescent aura surrounding him faded like a wisp of smoke carried off by a gentle breeze.

Another polite knock. The door slowly opened, and the principal stuck her head inside the room. "Sorry, gentleman. I need my office. Meetings, you know."

Sensing something palpable in the room, Principal March looked at Kensington, who sat eerily still.

Slowly, he turned his face toward her, and her breath caught in her throat. She had seen that look only once before—in church, with her grandma. Years later, when she was much older, she came across the words of a Christian mystic that explained what had astounded her that Sunday morning. The mystic wrote, "*It is the true light that shines in everyone. It is the light of Christ.*"

Standing up, Kensington realized he was somewhat unsteady on his feet. He felt light-headed, but his voice remained clear. "Everything has been resolved, Principal March. You can let his parents know that no charges will be filed." He added with a smile, "I'll leave it up to you and his parents to discuss his consequences."

Principal March entered her office and exclaimed, "That's wonderful news, Officer Kensington! His family will be so appreciative. A little communication can go a long way," she added. She shot Li'l Bits a disapproving look, who glanced down at the table, looking sheepish.

"Li'l Bits, you've got some explaining to do to your parents," she said. "I'm glad the trespass has been cleared up with the police, but you still have your parents to deal with—and they won't be happy."

Kensington walked slowly to the door, distracted, appearing to reflect deeply about something heavy on his heart. The principal studied his face, noting the dramatic change from his no-nonsense, take-command attitude when they'd first met. She asked, "You alright?"

Kensington looked back at Li'l Bits, whose eyes were bright and warm. Turning to the principal, he said quietly, "I'm better than I've been in years."

Looking at Li'l Bits, he said, "I'll call you later, young man, about your request. Hope I can get an answer soon."

Li'l Bits responded with a relieved sigh.

Principal March's curiosity piqued when she heard mention of a request but said nothing. *Best not to get involved unless asked,* she thought.

Kensington was nearly out the door when Li'l Bits called out to him.

"Officer Kensington, don't forget this." He held up Allison's diary.

"Right!" Kensington said absentmindedly as if the book no longer mattered. "I *do* need to get this back to Allison." The principal walked over to retrieve the book from Li'l Bits.

Before handing it to Kensington, she examined the cover and turned it over carefully. "Is this evidence of the crime?" she asked.

Kensington took the book from her. "You might say that," he said with an ironic smile.

"So this misadventure involved more than a just a trespass." Principal March narrowed her eyes at Li'l Bits, who thought it best to say nothing. When she looked at Kensington for confirmation, he gave a faint smile and shrugged.

Kensington considered the book for a moment, thinking how it had led to a road he wished he had never taken. But then, he thought, *I never would have met Li'l Bits.*

He touched two fingers to his forehead in a polite salute and nodded his head. "Thank you both for your help. I'll return this little treasure to its owner immediately. You know how troubled a teenage girl can get when she thinks her private thoughts might be exposed."

Still reeling from his unexpected good fortune—and humbled by Li'l Bits' unimaginable grace—Kensington walked out of Principal March's office with a light heart, but not quite a clear conscience.

26

Untermensch

The awful sense of foreboding had drifted away like a storm passing out to sea. Kensington heard Li'l Bits speaking excitedly to the principal as he closed the door. He walked past the receptionist's desk and entered the hallway. He did not worry that Li'l Bits would reveal what he'd done. The book in his hand was a pledge of faith that had sealed their promise.

Kensington strode briskly down the corridor, reflecting about Li'l Bits, remembering his wife, and recalling a lyric she used to sing. He mouthed the words, "I am born again. I've been made free."

As pleasant thoughts drifted through his mind, a deep, resonant voice called out to him, snapping him out of his reverie.

"Officer Kensington! Got a moment?"

He turned to see a uniformed policeman jogging toward him. He was very tall and thin, with freckles and sandy red hair that was too long for standard dress. Kensington wondered how such a commanding voice could come from a man who looked like a good wind would blow him away. Kensington looked up at the officer, who was clearly out of breath.

"I had to run from the other side of the building to catch you. The principal told me you just left her office," he said, tucking in his shirt. "She forgot to tell you that I wanted to speak to you before you left."

"How can I help you?" He searched for the officer's name tag. "Officer Pete?"

"*I* took Li'l Bits to the principal's office," Pete said.

Kensington nodded. "Got you. You're the resource officer."

"Right. I've worked at the school for about six months, and—"

"And you know Li'l Bits." Kensington interrupted him before he could finish.

"Yes! I mean, no. Well, I don't know him, but I know *of* him."

"So, what is it you know, Officer? Li'l Bits seems to be well known around here."

"Well, when you radioed to look out for a runner, I was surprised to discover that it was Li'l Bits because he's kind of a..."

Kensington smiled again and finished Officer Pete's sentence— "a special kid."

"Yes," Pete said excitedly. "Do you know he got an award for saving a police officer's life?"

Kensington shook his head slowly. "Hadn't heard that. I just met him."

"Yeah! He did! He was on a ride-along with an officer who had made a traffic stop. The officer was in the street, speaking to the driver. Li'l Bits saw a kid in the side mirror coming up the sidewalk. He thought the kid was acting odd, so he slouched down in his seat, keeping a close eye on him through the mirror. When the kid stopped just in front of his door, Li'l Bits saw a red bandanna hanging from his rear pocket.

"The moment he saw the kid reach inside his jacket, he kicked the car door open, slamming it into his back. Turns out he had a gun and was going through a gang initiation to shoot a cop, but he was knocked off balance. The shot missed the officer. Li'l Bits got a Citizenship Award for saving the officer's life."

Kensington made a whistling sound. "Wow! That's impressive! I'm starting to appreciate just how special he is."

"Well, sir! I couldn't imagine that Li'l Bits was in trouble with the law. I just needed to find out what was going on."

"It was all a big misunderstanding, Officer Pete. Everything has been straightened out. Don't worry, he isn't in trouble."

Officer Pete appeared relieved. "Well, I'm glad." Touching the radio attached to his shirt with his right hand, Pete grew quiet, listening. Then he excused himself. "Gotta go. Disturbance in the cafeteria. Catch you later."

Pete dashed off down the corridor in a half sprint as kids scampered out of his way.

Kensington walked out of the school and stood at the top of the steps. His tranquil mood immediately vanished upon seeing a heavy, squat figure in a police uniform perched on his car.

With clenched fists and arms tightly crossed against the front of his body, Quisling rocked back and forth rapidly on the hood after seeing Kensington exit the school alone. As he hopped off the car, Kensington sensed an incredible amount of anger and hostility emanating from him.

As he approached Quisling, Kensington reassured himself, *Doesn't matter what Quisling says or thinks. He and Allison needn't worry about any blowback. I'll take care of everything, and I don't need his vote.*

Face contorted and mouth twisting each time a profanity was spat out, Quisling bellowed like a wounded bull. He slammed his fist several times on the hood of Kensington's patrol car.

Quisling was causing a scene, and a crowd of kids began to gather and gawk. Kensington calmly pointed toward the group forming around the parking lot—several had already pulled out their phones to record the raging officer. It took Quisling a few seconds to register Kensington's silent message.

Quisling looked around and bellowed, "Now we got fuckin' *teenage* gawkers." He stopped venting just as abruptly as he'd started. His round face was red and damp with sweat.

Kensington hissed under his breath, "This is exactly why I didn't want you showing up—you're a loose cannon!"

"Where's the little nigger?" Quisling asked. "Why ain't he standing next to you in cuffs with snot running down his nose?"

"I want you to listen carefully." Kensington said through clenched teeth. "If you interrupt me, I'm leaving your fat ass here. Nod if you understand."

Quisling managed to give a perceptible nod.

"The kid gave me the diary. Do you understand? I got the goddamn diary! The only thing he wants us to do is to make the sexual assault charge go away. Once that charge is dismissed, all evidence of Allison's diary will be destroyed. There will be no mention of us lying, pressuring Allison, false charges, our involvement, or police corruption. He is letting us off the hook!"

Kensington felt winded. Drawing in a breath, he huffed, "A meeting with the DA's lead investigator is absolutely crucial—my highest priority. Getting Allison to agree to drop the charge—that'll be easy. Once that charge is dropped.... It's over. We're in the clear."

Quisling opened his mouth, but Kensington cut him off with a sharp wave of his hand. "I'll make this right. Do you understand? I'll handle it. The only thing you need to do is forget it ever happened."

Quisling wiped his damp face with his hand. His lips were trembling. "That boy made me look like a fool. He had his nigger friend pull a gun on me, and we did nothing. Not a goddamn thing! We're white, we're the law, and there's a damn price that needs to be paid when Black scum messes with the law. These streets belong to us."

Kensington sighed and shook his head. Quisling's words left him exhausted, wrung out like a wet rag. "Get away from my car, Quisling. I've got a diary to deliver," he said dismissively. He opened his car door and sat down wearily in the seat.

Quisling moved to the driver's side window as if he was going to say something.

Kensington shut him down. "Zip it, Quisling. We can talk later. Think about what I just told you and do me a favor, please. Don't call me until I call you."

He added, "And don't visit Wally at the hospital. Things have gotten twisted, particularly with Allison. I don't want you aggravating him. I just need time to smooth out the wrinkles with her."

Quisling's mouth dropped open, but he closed it quickly. He straightened up as Kensington began to pull out of the parking space.

Kensington stopped the car and leaned out the window. "Quisling, I'm truly sorry for getting you involved." He paused. "Trust me. I'll make this right."

Quisling watched Kensington pull his car out onto the street. His mind was numb, but his gut began to churn with anger again. He dragged himself over to his patrol car and got in. Then he grabbed the steering wheel, squeezing and releasing it, while staring mindlessly at the instruments on his dashboard.

"The kid brokered a deal with Kensington? That Black bastard wants the sex charge dropped?" Shaking his head, he mumbled, "That diary, if used by a competent lawyer, could probably get the whole case dismissed."

He pressed his hands to the sides of his face, squeezing it with increasing pressure until he winced in pain.

He wondered, *Is this a trap?*

Looking up, confused and upset, he traced the school's steps and saw the double doors fly open. A torrent of kids streamed out, rushing loudly down the steps to their cars. After the first wave of kids drove off, a small figure emerged slowly from a crowd of stragglers. He meandered at the top of the steps, wearing a familiar white jacket. Quisling's heart jumped.

"It's him!" he exclaimed bitterly. "The monkey is walking around with his flunkies like he's king of the jungle. He's probably telling all his homies all about how he punked two dumb white cops."

He was starting to rage again. All the other kids became a blur. The target of his hatred almost disappeared in a glowing red haze.

His mind assaulted him with his great-granddaddy's words—uppity niggers who had forgotten their place, educated coons who mimicked the King's language, and dumb-ass monkeys who dared to challenge the law.

He was feeling something that he hadn't felt in a long time. He felt as though he were being sucked into a dark, empty void—a chasm of aching emptiness that consumed his soul. His mind screamed at him, but he felt paralyzed. How could this overwhelming despair reclaim his life again? Years ago, he discovered something that saved him. What was it? He shut his eyes, trying to focus.

Then it struck him—the exhilarating sense of purpose and belonging he'd felt when he first joined the Fraternity of the Southern Cross. His self-loathing had vanished. With each meeting, uncertainty, confusion, and hopelessness fell away. For the first time, he believed he was somebody. He was told that he and his brothers were destined for greatness—that they would protect and preserve the purity of the white race. He hungered to learn weaponry, field tactics, and hand-to-hand combat—the skills he knew would be vital when the race war began. The movement had given him a powerful new identity— but over time, he had strayed from the path. His passion dulled. Though he crossed paths with a few Aryan Brothers in the corps, it wasn't the same as standing shoulder to shoulder with true believers, men who had pledged to live and die for the Cause. The hatred that once fueled him, that had given his life meaning, began to fade.

He stopped attending meetings at the Sacred Hall. He drifted away from the fellowship of true believers. He stopped reading the Word."

Yet, he told himself he was still committed—still loyal to the cause. He kept reading *The Turner Diaries*, *Mein Kampf*, Tom Metzger's *Third Position*, and subscribed to *American Renaissance*. But now he saw the truth: he'd been deceiving himself. This wasn't an ideology to hold at arm's length—to slip on and shrug off like a secondhand jacket. It way a way of life. It was a calling. It demanded total devotion. Casual belief was not enough. He had lost his way—and he knew it.

Deep from within, from the very fiber of his being, a small voice whispered, *Yes, Quisling! This much is true. With those angry, violent men, you did feel that you belonged, and your life had purpose.* The voice paused. *But did you ever feel a sense of peace?*

Quisling seethed at the mere suggestion that questioned his convictions. His anger crackled—he felt he could ignite the air around him. Sitting transfixed in his car, he stared at the Black boy casually ambling away. A storm of muddled thoughts about vindication and righteous retaliation whipped through his mind, yet no clear plan emerged. How could he satisfy his thirst for revenge with impunity—like in the 'good ole days' when killing a nigger was met with the same indifference as killing a snake.

Quisling pulled out of his parking space while watching the boy, who had crossed the street with two white students. He could see the trio of kids walking away casually. They were talking, gesticulating wildly, and laughing.

Quisling exited the school parking lot, turned left, and slowly approached the three-way stop. He lingered at the intersection longer than necessary, quietly watching the group to see if they would change direction. Then he pulled his patrol car over and let it idle.

When the sidewalk curved, he briefly lost sight of them but quickly caught up, keeping a safe distance. After about twenty feet, they reached a footpath. The white boy and girl hugged the Black boy, waved goodbye, and turned onto the walkway.

Seeing the girl touch the Black boy's skin made him sick. He wanted to smack her and her companion. Quisling thought, *Got something for you, colored boy. Just you wait. Gotcha for sure, this time.*

"Your ass ain't on no bus now, boy!" he chuckled. "No house to run to!"

After driving another twenty feet or so, Quisling glanced down the footpath to confirm the white boy and girl had disappeared. Continuing a bit farther, he gave a light tap on the horn. The kid glanced over his shoulder and slowed, locking eyes with Quisling. Quisling waved and offered a forced smile. The boy stopped on the sidewalk as Quisling pulled up beside him.

Quisling leaned toward the passenger side of his car and said, in the most exuberant voice he could muster, "Hey! I'm glad that I could catch up with you!"

Li'l Bits looked puzzled. "Do I know you, Officer?"

"No, no, no!" Quisling said, smiling and shaking his head. "Officer Kensington wanted me to bring you to the police station to talk to you again. He said he had some good news, but he wanted to tell you in person. You made quite an impression on him."

Hoping that Officer Kensington had already made some headway with his promise to get the charge dismissed, Li'l Bits smiled. "Wow! That was quick! Praise God!"

Caught off guard by the reference to God, Quisling stumbled over his words. "Yes! Right! Praise Him! That's for sure!" he said, but the sound of his voice was hollow.

Li'l Bits was used to people appearing confused or uncertain when he expressed his gratitude to God, so he smiled politely at Quisling's awkwardness.

Scanning the officer's face carefully, he hesitated and took a step back. He saw a large depression in the hood of the car.

"What happened to your car?"

Surprised, Quisling forced a laugh. "Oh, that! Some homeless drunk got upset and jumped up and down on it when I told him he couldn't pan handle in front of a store."

Li'l Bits lowered his body slightly to get a good look at Quisling. "Are you the officer who chased me through the Greenbelt?"

Quisling screwed up his face as if he had no idea what the boy was talking about. "Nooooo! That wasn't me. That officer was called back on patrol a while ago. Kensington called Dispatch to locate the closest cop to the school. I just happened to catch the call."

Li'l Bits leaned his head to one side. "This isn't your usual district, is it? I don't remember seeing you around. I do ride-alongs now and then." He moved closer to the passenger side window.

"I'm assigned to a different district, but we received a call to respond to a possible disturbance. Some domestic dispute. Everything is fine now."

Quisling leaned back in his seat, trying to appear casual. The kid's face was just inches from the passenger door frame.

"Well, I'm glad you weren't the guy chasing me." Li'l Bits took a deep breath before continuing. "There was something scary about the way that he was trying to run me down with his car."

"He tried to run you over with his patrol car?" Quisling asked, eyebrows raised.

"No, not really. He was just trying to catch me. But he almost hit me." He paused, thinking. "It felt like he would've run me over if he'd had the chance. I mean, he was driving like a maniac through a greenbelt—where people walk their dogs and ride their bikes." He shook his head, dismayed. "He could've killed someone just to get to me."

With feigned ignorance, Quisling joked, "What did you do? Shoot somebody?"

Li'l Bits laughed. "If I'd shot somebody, I wouldn't be here talking to you. Officer Kensington would have taken me downtown and locked me up in a cell. Let me just say that I took something from someone to help a friend. I gave it to Officer Kensington. It was just a book."

In the most sincere voice that he could manage, Quisling said, "Well, young man, I'm glad that you got away from that maniac cop. Officer Kensington clearly would've been upset if you had gotten hurt."

Li'l Bits nodded his understanding. "The other officer was just trying to do his job, I'm sure! I know how things can get crazy and out-of-control when there's a police chase."

Li'l Bits stepped off the sidewalk and leaned comfortably into the passenger side of Quisling's car, resting his elbows on the window frame.

"How did you even find me?" he asked quizzically.

Quisling hesitated, pretending to adjust something on his instrument panel. Then he said, "If you've ever done a ride-along with a cop, you know the kind of databases we can access. Kensington found a photo of you somewhere and sent it to me. He figured you might still be at school, so he told me to get over here fast and look for you." He chuckled. "I got lucky—I spotted you walking through the parking lot."

His smile was ingratiating. "Get in! I have to get back on patrol soon. I'll take you to Officer Kensington."

Li'l Bits started to reach for the door handle but stopped.

Quisling almost panicked. "What's wrong?" he asked.

Li'l Bits looked off in the distance. "I told my friend, the Professor, that I would be coming to his house during my afternoon break."

"Hey! You can text him on the way to the station. I'm sure the Professor would want you to speak to Kensington first, so he can help you fix whatever needs to be fixed," Quisling said reassuringly. "By the way, what is your friend's name?"

"His name is Tyrene!" Li'l Bits said enthusiastically.

He opened the door and was about to climb in the front seat when Quisling said, "I hope you don't mind, but could you ride in the back seat, please? Departmental policy. This ain't a ride-along," he said cheerfully.

"Sure!" Li'l Bits opened the back door and slid across the seat. Quisling checked his rearview mirror and casually turned his head to ensure no one was watching. A car with kids passed them, but they never looked his way. A few cars were in driveways, but the neighborhood appeared quiet.

"Say, Officer! You're looking around like *you* just broke the law." Li'l Bits said, with a laugh. Leaning forward, he extended his hand over the seat. "My name is Matthew Carver, but everyone calls me Li'l Bits. What's your name?"

The seat groaned as Quisling turned around. He took Li'l Bits' hand and gripped it hard. Quisling smiled as he saw Li'l Bits wince from the pain. "Nice to meet you. My name is Officer Quisling."

Li'l Bits' mouth dropped open. Alarmed, he exclaimed, "*You ARE the other officer that Allison wrote about in her diary*!"

Li'l Bits jerked his hand back—but Quisling lunged forward and tased him in the neck.

Quisling leered at the sharp, crackling zapping that made Li'l Bits jerk violently, his body twitching in spasms. "How do you like that, li'l nigger?" he sneered, jamming the Taser harder into his neck.

The acrid stench of burning flesh made him smile—*You do smell like burnt pork, he thought.*

"Mess with me, will you? I've got something for your Black ass."

As Li'l Bits convulsed, Quisling yanked his flashlight from his utility belt and brought it down hard, slamming it onto the boy's forehead. He smiled at the dull, hollow crunch of the impact. A low whistle escaped his lips as he saw the skin split open, blood oozing slowly from the wound. Li'l Bits slumped over, unconscious, in the back seat.

"Sorry about that. Didn't mean to draw blood. I must have been more upset than I thought." Quisling chuckled.

Looking up, he scanned his surroundings. He breathed a sigh of relief. No one was around. He exited the car and opened the passenger door. He leaned into the car, jerked Li'l Bits' hands behind his back, cuffed him, and taped his mouth. He then backed out of the car, went to his trunk and opened it. He pulled out a blanket, slammed the trunk closed, re-entered the rear passenger side of the car and threw the blanket over the boy's body. After scanning the street for witnesses and finding none, he returned to the driver's seat.

For a moment, he toyed with the thought of contacting Kensington just to piss him off. He quickly dismissed it as a bad idea. Glancing over his shoulder at the blanket embroidered with the Southern Cross, he hissed, "Yeah, baby! I'm going to have some fun with this boy."

Quisling started his car and quietly accelerated down the street. His mind raced faster than the car engine, teasing through the kinds of punishment he would inflict. Right now, he needed only to drive away slowly. Just another officer on the road who has pledged to serve and protect.

He checked his watch. A few hours left on his shift. He needed to call in. He could use the time off to plan. He knew an idea fitting the occasion would eventually come to him, and then he would know exactly what to do. He chuckled, "The boy had no idea who he was messin' with."

Quisling was grinning now. He hoped for a full moon tonight—someone had once told him at the Sacred Hall that blood looked almost black in the cold light of the moon.

He wondered, *Could anything be more beautiful than blood bathed in moonlight?*

Now that we've got the diary, he thought, *any copies of Allison's confession don't mean shit. All we need to do is make her admit she made it up—like it was some sick, twisted fantasy she thought was funny.*

He scoffed. *Who's going to take the word of a family of niggers over a white person, anyway? Haven't they figured that out yet? White is always right!*

Cruising past the street where the chase had first begun, Quisling muttered, "You said you wanted this nigger to pay, Wally. Well, this boy's gonna wish he was never born."

A dark voice whispered to him, *But whatever you do, it must be spectacular. Make an example of the untermensch. Make your great granddaddy proud.*

Quisling's lip curled as he caught his reflection in the rearview mirror. He nodded slowly, then murmured, "It's gonna be magnificent."

27

Missing

Doug ambled out of his house past the scarred earth where the patrol car tires had ripped through his lawn. The air reeked of torn earth and crushed grass—a bitter, green sharpness mingled with the damp, loamy scent of exposed soil. His next door neighbor had already cleaned up the debris from his broken fence that had exploded into the street.

"Those bastards were really out to get Li'l Bits," he growled. "Thank God he'd been home when he called."

He paused at the top of the cul-de-sac, leaning heavily on his cane. This morning's encounter with the police left a dull ache in his legs and back. Standing on the porch during the face-off had stressed his body more than he'd realized.

The greenbelt path winding past his house toward the high school was quiet, dotted only with a mother pushing a stroller and an older man walking his dog. Doug turned to look back toward the street that fed into the cul-de-sac, wondering which route Li'l Bits had taken to return to his house. Frowning, he walked gingerly down the middle of the street hoping he would appear. Scanning the sidewalks, he saw a group of students heading west toward the bus stop. But still no Li'l Bits.

A tingling in his ears—an old cop's instinct— always warned him when something was off. It had served him well when he was an undercover cop. Checking the time, he felt the familiar sensation.

"Li'l Bits said he'd be at the house during his break period," he muttered. "He should be here by now."

He stopped short, tapping his cane, unsure whether to drive to the school or wait. Limping forward, he pulled out his phone to dial Li'l Bits. No response. He dialed his wife. "Tawanna! Any word?"

Tawanna detected a note of uneasiness in his voice. "Honey! he hasn't called. You know he'd call you before he called me. Did you try any of his friends?"

Doug rubbed the back of his neck. "No… no," he said hesitantly. "But I got another idea, babe. What's the name of the school resource officer? He had a last name that sounded like a first."

"Hold on! He's in my contacts." A few moments passed before Tawanna responded. "His name is Officer Pete. Sending it now."

"Okay, thanks! You call his friends while I try to get in touch with Pete. If he can't locate him, I'm going to the school. Li'l Bits said everything was fine when Officer Kensington left. They'd worked out a deal, and he felt confident he wouldn't be charged with breaking and entering. He asked us not to do anything with the copies of the diary or the video until he talked to us. He was really clear about that. He didn't even tell Principal March what was in Allison's diary."

Doug continued, "He sure sounded excited about this deal he struck with Kensington, but I'm still worried."

"About what, honey?" Tawanna asked.

"Those men are desperate, Tawanna. A lot is at stake for them. Do you trust those cops to leave their future in the hands of a Black kid?" He paused, his voice sharpening. "Especially that fat one who chased him down the greenbelt and drove his car up on our lawn. Something is really off with that guy. He shouldn't be on anybody's police force."

"I hear you, Doug, but think about it. Li'l Bits felt he was safe to meet with Kensington in the principal's office. Kensington didn't arrest him—he left him at school. And when Li'l Bits called after their meeting, he said he felt like angels were in the room."

She smiled. "Remember what he said about how you need to walk in the world?"

Doug shook his head. "Nope! Probably another Bible verse, though."

"Be shrewd as snakes and innocent as doves!"

"Well, I think I know what that means, but we shouldn't forget that he's still a kid dealing with two dirty cops. Kensington didn't move up on my hit parade list because he struck a deal. It was the smartest thing for him to do."

"Look! There's no need to worry yet, honey. So relax! Call Pete. I'll contact the Brotherhood. And please, get back to the house soon. Can't you hear Hannibal barking for you?"

Doug smiled faintly. "Right. On my way." He limped gingerly back toward the house, nearly holding his breath as he dialed Pete.

The phone rang once, twice—than continued four more times. Doug's jaw tightened with each ring. Finally Pete answered.

"Officer Pete here," he said pleasantly.

"Officer Pete," Doug exclaimed. "Glad I could reach you. This is Doug Joiner—the boys call me 'Professor.'"

"Yes, sir! I remember you. What can I do for you?"

"I'm looking for one of the kids I mentor. His name is Matthew Carver, but everybody knows him as Li'l Bits."

"Li'l Bits. Of course, I know him. Don't think that a whole lot of people *don't* know him."

"Well, I live a ways up the street from the school," Doug explained. "Li'l Bits told me he'd be coming my way after his break. But it's been a while— he hasn't shown up and hasn't called. I know he had a meeting with an officer by the name of Kensington at the principal's office this morning."

"I saw Officer Kensington just after he met with Li'l Bits. He was heading to his car, but Li'l Bits wasn't with him." He paused a moment before adding. "Kensington was in a real thoughtful mood. Quiet, but friendly."

"You mind telling me what you talked about with him if it wasn't anything official?" Doug asked.

"Nothing official at all. I was checking on Li'l Bits' situation. Everything seemed fine. I got the distinct impression that Officer Kensington liked him."

"Really?" Doug said skeptically. "Is Kensington on the tall or heavy side?"

"Nope! Not heavyset! Not as tall as me, but tall," Pete replied.

Thinking about the confrontation on his lawn, Doug said, "Yeah. Had to be the tall guy. He had a cooler head and was more of a negotiator."

"Don't know about the negotiation stuff, but he seemed like an okay guy."

Doug's voice tightened, "I need you to do me a favor, sir. I'm worried about the boy. Could you please try to find him for me as quickly as possible?"

"Why are you worried?" Pete sounded confused.

"I can't explain now, but I need you to find him!"

A disquieting silence hung on the line. Pete hesitated but decided against pressing for an explanation. "I'm on it," he said. "Keep your phone on. I'll call you back—soon." Before hanging up, he added, his tone sharp. "By the way, Professor—you need to tell me what's going on. Principal March told me it was 'personal.' Officer Kensington called it a 'misunderstanding.' Cops don't swing by my school for the hell of it. And now you're worried because you don't know where Li'l Bits is?"

Doug sighed. "That's fair. I can give you some info, but not right now. I'll tell you more after I know that he's safe."

As soon as Doug hung up, his phone rang.

Tawanna's voice sounded rushed. "I called Principal March, but she was tied up in a meeting. I also contacted three of his buddies, but none of them have been in touch with him. I told them to spread the word that we need to find him immediately. I also sent a message to our Community Watch Group, asking them to contact us if they see him. I attached his picture to the text."

"Nice work, sweetheart. Did Li'l Bits' parents sound worried that you were looking for him?"

"No… well… I tried, but I couldn't reach them. I left voice messages."

"Okay," Doug said. "We'll keep trying. Officer Pete's checking on Li'l Bits' whereabouts at school. Could you grab copies of Allison's diary for me? I need to take another look just in case I overlooked something."

With the diary copies in hand, Tawana stepped outside, scanning the area for a police presence. She waved to her husband as he approached—clearly unsettled about Li'l Bits. Hannibal bounded out of the house and barreled into him, nearly knocking him over.

Tawanna sat on the step, watching as Doug walked slowly toward the house. His limp appeared to be worsening with age.

"Sit here by me, honey, and rest those ailing bones. Feast your eyes on Li'l Bits' miracle," she said, smiling. Doug groaned as he dropped down beside her. He rested his cane on the steps and commanded Hannibal to sit.

He shuffled the pages back and forth, a perplexed look on his face.

Tawanna said, "A page of the diary got stuck in the printer. Mr. James brought it over when you went out looking for Li'l Bits."

Doug frowned. "Did you read this part where the girl says there was something creepy about this guy Quisling? That he has this 'I hate Blacks' thing going—how it was an abomination for a Black man to touch a white woman's skin, even accidentally. Allison seemed to believe he was weird—a bit off—because he was beginning to act like the lie about the sexual assault was true."

Doug's voice deepened. "Quisling is actually thinking that the sexual assault really happened! He said things to her like he was going to avenge her honor. That crazy bastard is unhinged."

Tawanna's eyes widened as the weight of his words sank in. She thought, *Another cop might be targeting a young Black male. And, this time, it wasn't Tyrene. It was Li'l Bits.*

Doug read the page recovered from the printer. He grew quiet, his thoughts weighing heavy on him. After a moment, he looked up, his gaze lingering on the damage to the lawn.

"Li'l Bits became a prime candidate for murder when he stole that diary. Now that Kensington has the diary, does that really change anything?"

Tawanna shook her head, refusing to accept the idea of murder. "Too many people know about the diary now," she protested. "What are they going to do? Kill everybody?"

"Right now, there's you, me, Mr. James next door, and Li'l Bits." He shrugged, "That's not too many witnesses to kill. Ain't a village, Tawanna. A gas line explosion or strategically placed bombs could take out both houses."

He rubbed Hannibal's massive head as he thought. "I just don't think you understand, hon. For some cops, shedding blood ain't no big deal, especially if a lot is on the line." He met her eyes and added somberly, "And there's a lot on the line."

"But, Doug," Tawanna protested, "What about the deal Li'l Bits was so excited about? He said everything had been worked out with Kensington!" Her voice broke, "He thought everything was fine."

Doug shifted his weight, stretching his leg. "I damn sure hope so, but this diary might still be worth killing for."

Tawanna's voice sounded like a plea. "They must realize that they've lost control over this situation now, Doug." She reached over and slid her hand over his. "There's no need to hurt Li'l Bits now."

He gently squeezed her hand. "Diary or not, Quisling may be the kind of psycho cop who'd take pleasure in killing a Black person just for kicks."

Doug tapped the pages. "Even with the diary in their possession, Li'l Bits could still represent a problem for them. He's a material witness." His brow furrowed deeply. "What if they lied to him—told him what he wanted to hear to catch him off guard and trick him? They could set him up, get him alone, and then kidnap him." He looked hard into her eyes and said, "Desperate men are known to do desperate things."

Tawanna eyes widened in fear as she stifled a cry.

Clutching the diary pages in his hand, Doug grabbed his cane and stood abruptly. Deep in thought, Tawanna jumped, startled by his sudden movement. He kissed her gently on the top of her head. Hannibal started barking again as Doug hobbled to the car. He flung the car door open, then paused before getting in. Throwing an anguished look back at his wife, he said, "There ain't nothing more dangerous than a desperate cop. And if you add corruption to the mix…" His voice trailed off.

Tawana stood up and asked, "Do you want a physical copy of the video or just email the file to you?"

He shook his head. "I have everything I need for now." After a moment, Doug added, puzzled, "I still don't understand why Li'l Bits gave Kensington that diary. He could've handed it over to Tyrene's lawyer who might have been able to get the whole case dismissed."

"You should know by now that Li'l Bits doesn't think or act like most people."

Doug nodded his agreement. "Well, you got that right! I asked why he had returned that diary like it was a lost library book, after he left Principal's March's office. I thought it was sheer madness to give it to that cop."

Doug scoffed. "I could hear Li'l Bit smiling through the phone when he said, 'It's going to be alright, Professor. I prayed on it.'"

Tawanna lifted her chin, a soft smile played on her lips. "That's our Li'l Bits! God bless him. If it is, indeed, madness, Doug, it flows from a power greater than we understand."

Doug fell silent—her words striking something deep within him. Pressing his lips together, he thought, *Time to go. Time may not be on our side.*

He turned and gently patted Hannibal on the head. "Stay," he said softly. Then he eased himself into the car and closed the door.

Tawanna watched the front bumper strike the bottom of the driveway violently as he backed up and sped off down the street. Moments later, the tires squealed as he rounded the corner.

In her mind's eye, she saw Li'l Bits' engaging smile and heard his vibrant laugh. Then, suddenly, her thoughts clouded with fear—she could no longer see his face. A chill swept through her, and she trembled. She wrapped her arms around her shoulders to stem the hollow feeling rising in her stomach. It was the same feeling she'd felt the day her obstetrician delivered the words that broke her heart—her baby was dead inside her.

"Li'l Bits. Where are you?" Her heart pounded against her ribs, each beat echoing louder than the last. A tightness gripped her chest, making each breath a struggle. She sat back down on the steps, her elbows digging into her knees. Clasping her hands together she prayed, "Please, dear God! Let Li'l Bits be okay!"

28

Amber Alert

Officer Pete peered through the glass pane on the door to the principal's office before knocking. He could only see the back of the man sitting in front of the principal's desk, his posture rigid with tension. *Must be the Professor,* he thought.

Looking over the man's shoulders, he saw the pained, angry expression of the principal as she slowly seemed to digest the last page of a document. At that moment, he knocked.

"Officer Pete, please come in," she said, looking up. Her voice sounded distant, her mind clearly preoccupied.

Using the edge of the principal's desk for support, Doug stood and offered his hand as Officer Pete entered the office.

"Nice to see you again, Professor," Pete said as he shook his hand. Doug offered a faint smile before quickly settling back into his seat.

Almost in unison, the principal and Doug asked, "Did you find Li'l Bits?"

Pete shook his head. "No luck. I checked everywhere—the cafeteria, gym, library, and the activity centers. Nothing!" Exasperation flickered on their faces. "I asked the maintenance people to keep a sharp eye out for him, but there's been no sign of him ~~yet~~."

"He hasn't shown up for his period six class." The principal said. "Ms. Bishop, his teacher, said she hasn't seen or heard from him. So I had my secretary page Li'l Bits over the intercom system, but there's been no response. We called his house, but I couldn't reach his parents. I tried to reach his dad at his office. Still waiting."

"Officer Pete, did you speak to any of his friends?" Doug asked.

"Sure, I did. Every kid I passed who I thought might know him. No one has seen him! I still need to review the surveillance cameras outside and around the building. The recordings should show who he was with when he left school."

Taking a deep breath, Pete demanded, "Now, would somebody tell me what the hell's going on? Should I be sending out a BOLO alert or what?"

The principal looked plaintively at Doug. "Tell him, Professor!" Her voice nearly broke when she spoke.

Doug looked into Pete's eyes, where worry lines were etched at the corners. Pointing to a stack of papers, Doug explained. "On the principal's desk are photocopies of a girl's diary, in which she confesses that Kensington—the officer you spoke to this morning—and another cop pressured her to file false sexual assault charges against Li'l Bits' friend."

As Doug recounted how the situation had unfolded, a riot of emotions raced across the officer's face. Shaking his head, Pete said, "This is bad!"

"Li'l Bits gave Officer Kensington the diary," Principal March added. "No mention was made of a video, though—just the diary. Do you have the video?"

"Not with me," Doug said. "My wife has a thumb drive at home. Mr. James, my next door neighbor, made copies."

March leaned across her desk. "I wonder if Li'l Bits told Officer Kensington about the video."

"Knowing Li'l Bits," Doug sighed, "I'm pretty sure he did."

Raising an eyebrow, Pete asked, "Was Officer Kensington definitely one of the cops?"

"Yep! His name isn't specifically mentioned in the diary, but he *is* referenced as Wally's dad. Kensington responded to my home as backup for the other cop when they were trying to arrest Li'l Bits."

Pete's mouth twisted. "Are you talking about Wally Kensington from Thomas Jefferson? I heard that boy is a bully!" He shook his head. "Where's the diary now?"

Doug shrugged. "Right now? Anybody's guess. I don't know. As Principal March said, Li'l Bits gave the diary to Kensington just before he left her office. Kensington said he was going to return it to the girl, Allison. It seems like Li'l Bits and Kensington struck a deal about Tyrene's case, but I'm in the dark about the details."

"Damn! When I contacted Li'l Bits, he probably had the diary in his backpack," Pete said.

"I suspect Kensington may have deliberately misled Li'l Bits into thinking he had secured a deal for a favorable outcome in his friend's case to get that diary."

Doug glanced at the principal and then back at Pete. "He was supposed to come to my house during a break to explain the details of their agreement. He made me promise not to do anything with the copies and video until we talked. He sounded excited and relieved."

"So you think he may have been set up?" Pete suggested. "Make him think everything is fine, then..." Pete's voice trailed off.

Doug shrugged. "Snatch him. Snatch him to quiet him. Snatch him to quiet me. Snatch him to ransom copies of the diary and the video."

Agitated, Doug stood up and began pacing stiffly. "I can only guess what their plan might be, but I did read one thing that scared the hell out of me."

Doug furrowed his brow. "This cop Quisling, according to the girl, seems slightly off. She thinks that he's creepy and an inveterate racist."

Pete inhaled deeply. "The cop I met seemed pretty decent. I didn't get the sense that he was a slimeball."

Pete narrowed his eyes, replaying the interaction between himself and Kensington in his mind. "I think it's probably that other guy that we need to worry about. What does he look like?"

"He's a big man. Stocky. Bit on the hefty side. About 5'9", two hundred fifty pounds."

Pete shook his head, "Definitely not the guy I talked to in the hall."

March exclaimed excitedly, "Wait a minute! Wait a minute! What if Kensington was going to follow through on whatever he and Li'l Bits had agreed to, but that other cop, Quisling, came up with his own plan?"

"Hmmm," murmured Doug thoughtfully. "Maybe you're right, Principal March," he said, frowning. "Li'l Bits would never have blown me off—not with something as important as this. Someone had to stop him from coming to my house. If he was good with Kensington, then it must've been Quisling."

Pete walked over to the principal's desk and held out his hand. She seemed confused until she realized he wanted to see the photocopies of the diary.

Pete groaned as he flipped through the pages. He said, "Assuming this stuff is true, those cops have got a serious problem! I'm surprised the man I talked to would get mixed up with someone like Quisling."

All three became silent, trying to fit together the jumbled pieces. Doug broke the tense silence. "I know someone who might be able to help. He's an assistant DA in a neighboring county. I haven't talked to him in years, but he worked on a couple of my cases. I can take the evidence to him. He can help me get it to the DA assigned to the case. A DA can light a fire under the police department to help locate Li'l Bits. After all, he's now a material witness to a criminal conspiracy and official misconduct."

March quickly added, "And God forbid, maybe a kidnapped victim." She shook her head. "My staff will create and circulate flyers."

"Sounds like we need to do an Amber Alert," Pete said. "Li'l Bits is still seventeen.... right?"

Doug replied, "For a few more months."

Pete cautioned, "He's only been missing for about an hour or so. If you two are wrong about this, and he's sitting in a coffee shop with a buddy somewhere, there'll be hell to pay."

"What would you rather deal with? A dead kid or department ridicule?" Doug asked.

Pete blanched. Embarrassed, he said, "Right. Okay. Let's get on it. We each know what we need to do. Let's find him!"

Doug made his way slowly out the door. Pete rushed past him, speaking to dispatch on his two-way radio. "Amber Alert. I'll send you a picture of the abducted child in five minutes."

Doug could barely feel his legs as he limped down the hall. He reached his car as quickly as he could and sat down, breathless.

He called his wife. "Li'l Bits isn't here," he huffed. He heard Tawanna groan. "We're sending out an Amber Alert. The school will print flyers. Do me a favor. Look in my office for my old phone directory. It has Larry Kincaid's personal number. He's a prosecutor's for Garfield County. Tell him I'm coming. He'll remember me."

"The case isn't assigned in that county, is it? Why not contact the county where the case is being prosecuted?" Tawanna asked.

"This is the most effective way to get the assigned prosecuting attorney's attention. One district attorney speaking to another carries far more weight than the word of a retired Black police officer."

Doug heard muffled crying. "Tawanna," he said softly, "We need to keep a clear head about this. Please try to reach Li'l Bits' parents. They still don't know."

"You can count on me, Doug. I just need a moment. I'll have it together before I call them. See you soon."

"Meet me in the driveway with the thumb drive, okay?" he said.

She whispered, "Love you," but Doug had already hung up.

Speeding down the highway to Kincaid's office, Doug recalled his advice to Li'l Bits during their break at the Brotherhood meeting. "Stay out of it. This could be dangerous. Let Tyrene's attorney handle things."

Doug knew a competent attorney could make the difference between getting a case dismissed, securing an acquittal, or negotiating a decent plea bargain. Moreover, Tyrene's attorney is Black. Fully aware of the racial biases embedded in the criminal justice system, his attorney would dig deep. No stone would remain unturned. Tyrene wouldn't be a case.

He would be a cause. The fight for Tyrene's freedom had to be relentless. And, under these circumstances, ruthless

Doug recalled the determined look on Li'l Bits' face the night the Brotherhood met. He thought of a quote—attributed to Hannibal the Great—that he had once shared with the boys during a lesson on great Black military leaders. He wondered if those words had influenced Li'l Bits' decision to help Tyrene.

The brilliant military strategist, who dared to cross the Alps with elephants to invade Italy, once declared: *I will either find a way or make one.*

29

A Promise and a Prayer

Kensington was running late—but, hopefully, not too late. He'd underestimated the time needed to deliver Allison's diary. He'd had to smooth things over with Ms. Ruddick and the officers responding to her 911 call.

Kensington glanced at a few older attorneys exiting the courthouse, briefcases in hand. Some were with clients. Others were alone. A few carted several boxes of large files. Maybe a medical malpractice case, where someone had died during a botched operation. A well-dressed young man sat forlornly on the steps, mumbling incoherently with his head in his hands. Maybe a father who recently learned that his child support payments had increased. If so, when his lease expires, he would probably have to move out of his two-bedroom apartment.

Kensington hadn't been to the courthouse in a while. Thinking back, he'd been in a conference room with a DA and an investigator as late as midnight. Maybe Ron Michaels, a diehard street cop turned investigator, was still in charge. That man never smiled. He would probably be upstairs still working. He'd know which DA was prosecuting the Horn case as well as the assigned investigator.

A burly security guard shouted, "Kensington! You lost? The bad guys aren't on this side of town." Looking up, Kensington recognized a rookie he had trained in the academy.

"Just need to chat with someone in the DA's office," he replied amicably. "They still on the same floor?"

"Same place. Take the elevator. Third floor. Make a right off the elevator. Immediate right at the next corner."

"Good seeing you, Andrews. Thanks!" Kensington said over his shoulder as he strolled across the marble floors toward the bank of elevator doors. Kensington entered the elevator, mulling over his day, which seemed to span a lifetime.

His mind retraced each event, each one a potential disaster: Allison's panicked call about her stolen diary; Quisling's irrational reaction to kill her; the confrontation at the ex-cop's house with his bizarre Community Watchdog neighbors; trying to control Quisling's outrage at the school; returning the diary to Allison's house; dealing with her emotional anguish and her mother's restrained fury; and finally, the highly suspicious cop who responded to the 911 call about the stolen diary.

Kensington found it strange that, instead of reflecting on the extraordinary moment he'd experienced with Li'l Bits in Principal March's office, his mind was swarming with fears—sharp, persistent fears like Gremlins biting and scratching, refusing to leave him alone.

His wife of deep faith would have told him that he had received a blessing from Li'l Bits. *Did his lack of spiritual depth keep him from fully embracing a moment that would profoundly transform most people's lives?*

But Kensington was in survival mode now. More fight than flight. After he secured a commitment from the DA's office to drop Allison from the case, he thought he might finally have time to process what he had experienced in Principal March's office.

The doors sprang open. Kensington adjusted his patrol cap on his head and stepped out. He thought the cap added more authority to his appearance. Strolling down the corridor to the DA's office, he felt an odd mixture of dread and excitement. Just one final hurdle to clear—and with Allison's cooperation, everyone could finally breathe easier.

He cringed at the memory of how Allison and Ms. Ruddick had reacted to the news that her diary had been recovered. As upset as they both were when Kensington arrived, they'd said nothing to the officers about his plan to frame the Horn kid. According to the officers, the family had only reported a break-in, described the intruder, and told the police that the only missing property they could identify was a personal journal.

Allison told the officer that she had called Kensington because he was her boyfriend's dad. She explained that her mom had called 911.

While at Allison's house, Kensington was certain that the officer taking the report was highly suspicious. The cop couldn't understand why Allison was so upset about a book. It wasn't as though someone had stolen a prized family heirloom.

Kensington also learned that the officer's partner took a statement from the older woman next door. She reported seeing a young, light-complexioned teenager who helped her stop Allison's dog from running in the street. The only clothing she remembered was a high school letter jacket. The old woman said the jacket was white, with a large blue letter J stitched over the heart and a football and lacrosse patch on a sleeve. The officers appreciated the old lady's help because Allison, surprised and frightened by the intruder, couldn't recall any details about his clothes. She only remembered that he was wearing a white high school jacket.

Kensington had learned all of it from the lead officer after arriving at Allison's house. He'd arrived just as the officers were preparing to leave. Kensington walked through the open front door into the living room and declared, "Found something you might want."

When Allison spotted her diary in Kensington's hand, she let out a shriek. However, all eyes turned instantly to Ms. Ruddick.

Allison's mother pushed her thin, bony figure from the chair, and abruptly walked toward the kitchen. Allison looked horrified. Ms. Ruddick paused at the doorway just long enough to shoot Kensington a disgusted look. The officers looked at Kensington, puzzled, wondering what role he had played in this strange affair.

"Allison! Get in here and bring that damn diary!" Ms. Ruddick snapped.

Allison looked like she would break into a thousand pieces. "Yes, ma'am," she said, and rushed into the kitchen.

Kensington smiled sheepishly, apologizing to the officers. "Ms. Ruddick doesn't like my son. I think Allison told her about some very private things she wrote in her diary. It could've been very embarrassing if that book had gotten around. If you've got teenage girls, you'd know exactly what I mean."

One officer nodded. The other just looked at Kensington quizzically. Then he asked, "Did you catch the kid?"

Kensington extended his hand to introduce himself. "I'm Kensington, would-be hero, finder of lost property," he said with a wry smile.

"I'm Crandall," the tall, gray-haired man said shaking Kensington's hand. "Did you catch him?"

Kensington feigned frustration. "No. He got away. He tossed the book as he was running. I lost him in an apartment complex near 8th and Elm."

"What was in the diary?" Crandall asked. "Her mother seemed pretty pissed off, but she seemed scared, too. Kids write about all kinds of things in their diaries. Sometimes criminal things, like drug dealing or sex trafficking."

Kensington shook his head. "You don't know Allison. She's an angel. Nothing remotely like that."

Crandall asked again, "But you didn't read the diary after you found it? You didn't even look inside? You weren't even curious why she would be so panicked about a stolen diary?"

"Yeah, I was curious—but not enough to violate her privacy. Besides, it wasn't my business. Allison's my son's girlfriend. They're planning to get married. So… like I said, Allison's mom just doesn't like him."

"Yeah," Crandall said begrudgingly. "Maybe you got a point." Crandall tucked his pad and pen away, signaling to his partner that it was time to go.

Glancing toward the kitchen, Crandall said, "No need for me to bother them again. Looks like you have this under control."

Kensington said, "Appreciate your help, Crandall."

Relieved they were gone, Kensington stood in silence, staring blankly at the closed door. He heard the police car start, but it didn't pull away. Holding his breath, he wondered if they would come back. Had they bought his flimsy excuse about why Ms. Ruddick was so furious? If they returned with more questions the family might crack.

He heard a car door close and inhaled sharply. Footsteps grew louder as someone approached the front door—then suddenly stopped. A pause. Muffled voices. The footsteps retreated. A car door opened, then closed, and the vehicle finally began to pull away. Moments later, Kensington heard the wail of a siren. He exhaled in relief and muttered, "Thank goodness. They got an emergency call."

He started toward the kitchen, but Allison appeared before he could enter. She looked lost. Her eyes were red, swollen, and brimming with tears. The diary was no longer in her hand.

He stepped forward to console her, but she shook her head stepping away from him. When he tried to speak, she held up her hand to silence him. She looked desperate and helpless.

It took everything he had to remain silent.

What I did to this young girl—who loves my son with all her heart—is unforgivable, he thought bitterly.

It took a few moments before Allison spoke. When she did, her voice was small and weak.

"Everything will be alright, Mr. Kensington," she whispered. "My mom knows. She knows everything, but it'll be okay."

Kensington became aware of a faint but distinct smell. It was smoke—something was burning, coming from the kitchen.

Allison avoided his gaze as he looked at her. "My mom is burning my diary. Could you leave now?" He started to speak, but she met his eyes and said firmly, "Leave now! Please! We'll be fine. I need to work this out with mom."

Dumbfounded, Kensington nodded. "Tell your mom that all the kid wants is to get the sexual assault charge dropped. He won't say anything about what you wrote in your diary. I'll tell the investigator and the assigned DA that you changed your mind about testifying. I'll explain that your mom doesn't want you to be re-traumatized."

Allison stared at him, but said nothing. Kensington continued, "Rape victims recant all the time for a lot of reasons. The sexual assault team in the prosecutor's office is accustomed to victims recanting their statements."

Allison rolled her eyes and took a deep breath that shook her slender frame. When she looked at him again, Kensington saw burning anger in her eyes. She said coolly, "Another lie to cover a lie, Mr. Kensington?"

Pressing his lips together to keep from saying more, he forced a weak smile, gave another nod, and slowly walked to the door.

Before Kensington walked out, Allison said, "Please tell Wally not to call me for a while. Okay?" She'd barely finished speaking when a flood of emotion overwhelmed her. Sobbing, she dashed up the stairs, her footsteps echoing behind her.

Torn by the pitiful sound of it, Kensington knew what he had to do next. He had to honor his promise to Li'l Bits. He needed to get to the DA's office and deliver the news of Allison's decision not to testify.

Of course, he'd say her mother fully supported the choice. Her boyfriend, Wally, didn't want her subjected to the embarrassment of a trial or the humiliation of testifying.

Kensington would paint Allison as a fragile, vulnerable teenage girl who would be unnecessarily re-traumatized by publicly reliving a vile, ugly experience. Besides, there was no need to pursue the sexual assault charge when a conviction on felony assault was practically guaranteed.

He'd stood by his car outside Allison's house, his head throbbing and every muscle taut with stress. The house behind him seemed to radiate a silent reproach. His shoulders slumped, and his head dropped to his chest as he let out a long, weary sigh.

As he lowered himself into the car seat, Kensington focused on the one task that remained: honoring his promise to Li'l Bits to get the charge dropped. He was confident he could make it happen. No—he was determined to make it happen. He just needed to get to the courthouse and wrap this package up with a big, bright bow.

As he mentally checked off the laundry list of points to persuade the DA to drop the sexual assault charge, a faint smile crossed Kensington's face. Given the circumstances, the DA would surely see that dropping the charge was the only humane thing to do.

Now, standing in the secured visitor area at the DA's office, Kensington asked the receptionist to buzz him through. She shook her head and informed him that policies had changed—too many threats had been made against public officials. He'd need an escort.

Even behind her thick glasses, her eyes appeared tired. She asked who he wanted to see. "Chief investigator Ron Michaels, if he's still here."

Chuckling dryly, she said, "He's always here. Please take a seat. Who shall I…?"

He said, "Just tell him Kensington. If he hasn't gone senile, he'll remember me."

Grateful to be off his feet, he removed his cap and laid it on his lap. He rubbed his throbbing temples, then closed his eyes. Tilting his head back, he exhaled deeply.

His thoughts drifted back to the miraculous moment in Principal March's office. He was determined to keep his promise to Li'l Bits.

Silently, he did what he had seen Elsa do countless times over the years. He prayed for a second miracle.

30

Professional Courtesy

Ron Michaels, the head DA investigator, had a penchant for offending people who were incompetent or unreliable. He was known to openly castigate a subordinate in meetings when evidence had been overlooked or mishandled at a crime scene. Under Michaels' watch, an investigator either improved and advanced in the ranks or got verbally shredded so many times that they simply disappeared, often quitting without notice.

Although Kensington towered over him physically, Michaels remained an imposing figure due to his intense, uncompromising presence.

Without exception, Michaels would never tolerate a last-minute request from anyone, badge or not, to speak to one of his best and busiest investigators. However, he believed Kensington's request merited a pass: a veteran police officer's son had been viciously assaulted and maimed, and the other victim was his son's high school sweetheart.

Even though the workday was nearly over, Michaels agreed to connect Kensington with the investigator assigned to the Horn case.

Kensington sat watching the sweeping second hand of the clock tick away his precious time. It was getting late. He couldn't count on Allison's mother to remain silent. She might have a change of heart—especially if she dwelled on how he'd coerced her daughter to commit a crime.

Dropping the sexual assault charge—that was his best insurance. She might stomach what he'd done, but only if that charge disappeared.

The acrid stench of the burning diary still lingered in his nose. Allison's pale, haunted face continued to unsettle him. Then his thoughts turned to Quisling. How was he handling the collapse of his criminal scheme—a plan undone in an instant, after the improbable discovery of a girl's diary.

A soft smile crept across his face as he recalled his golden moment of grace in Principal March's office.

Relax, he told himself. *Take a few deep, calming breaths, like the trauma counselor taught you years ago.*

"Mildred," a voice boomed. "Just buzz him through."

"Straight down the hall and to your left," the secretary said.

Kensington glanced at the clock. He'd been waiting nearly an hour. Still, he was relieved he'd have the opportunity to make his pitch to get that sexual assault count dumped. He didn't want to waste any more time when so much was at stake. Too many people were counting on him.

Welcoming a momentary breather from the stack of files on his desk, Hastings, the lead investigator on the Horn case, offered Kensington some instant coffee, which he'd politely declined.

"Nothing like a little caffeine to get you through a long day," Hastings said, blowing on his coffee as he settled into his chair. Hastings leaned back, scrutinizing Kensington, and took a quick sip. Then he sat up abruptly."How can I help you, officer?"

Kensington removed his cap and ran his fingers through thick, graying hair. After a long, calculated sigh, he spoke. "My son, Wally, is the assault victim in the Horn case. Allison, his girlfriend, is the sexual assault victim. She's having second thoughts about testifying."

"What's the defendant's name?" Hastings asked.

"Tyrene Horn," Kensington said. "The case started in juvie and then got transferred to adult court."

Hastings was suddenly animated. "Hey! I heard something about the kid's mother being jailed for contempt of court." He started laughing. "If I remember correctly, Ms. Horn told Judge Davidson that he should be wearing a white sheet instead of a black robe."

Kensington, made a whistling sound through his teeth. *This is one hell of a family Li'l Bits is trying to help.*

Hastings grinned broadly. "Yeah, I thought that was a real hard-ass move on her part. That woman takes that truth-to-power shit seriously." He leaned forward slightly. "Got an agency number, Kensington?"

Kensington shook his head. "No."

"No? Well, I guess we'll have to do this the old-fashioned way." Swiveling his chair toward a filing cabinet, he pulled out a drawer. Hastings hummed under his breath as his fingers flitted across files in the cabinet. He had a disdain for the digital age and always asked his secretary to make hard copies for him. He prided himself on being a Luddite.

"Found it!" Hastings turned his chair back to his desk and started reading the file.

A few more minutes passed as he thumbed through the file.

"Not much going on yet. The DA's made a few investigative requests. Hmmm," he murmured. "Looks like the precipitating event was a school fight between your son and Horn." He read more of the file then stopped abruptly. "Damn."-Looking up, he asked, "I hope your son—Wally—is okay. He sustained a nasty injury."

Without waiting for a response, Hastings returned to reading the file. "There are a lot of witnesses to be interviewed." He grunted. "Great! Looks like some surveillance footage is available. Not much here on Allison." Going to a folder inserted in the file, Hastings pulled out a two-page handwritten statement and a supplementary offense report.

"Here we go. Got her story and an attached note from the prosecutor about adding charges." Hastings sat up and pushed himself away from his desk. "Now help me out, here! What makes you think that she doesn't want to testify?"

Kensington took a long breath before speaking. "Well," he paused, "According to her mom, she has nightmares, crying fits, and is unable to eat or focus. She doesn't even want to go to school."

Hastings frowned. "The question for me is whether she's reacting to what the Horn kid did to her, her fear of testifying in court, or both." He picked up a pen and began tapping it slowly on his desk. "You know, Kensington, with time and support from the Victim's Advocate Office, some of these victims find the courage to see the case through, but a major factor is support from their parents."

"Parent," Kensington corrected him. "Just the mom. Dad has been out of the picture for a while."

"Close mother-daughter relationship?" Hastings probed.

"Yep. Very tight. But this decision not to go to court comes from Allison, not her mom." Kensington quickly added, "Ms. Ruddick supports whatever Allison wants. She doesn't want her daughter to have to deal with the ugliness of her peers and the brutal harassment that can start on social media once the charges are made public. The shaming in high school can destroy an innocent girl's life. Worst possible time for a teenage girl. I mean...for something like this to happen."

Hastings shifted his position in his chair and took another sip from his cup. "There ain't no good time to be sexually molested, Kensington. You know that." Hastings leaned forward. He asked, concerned, "You're not the cop on the case, right? That would be a major conflict of interest."

"Definitely not, but Allison is very special to me. She's my son's high school sweetheart. They've talked about getting married. They both agree they don't want this thing hanging over them." Kensington could see a perceptible change in Hasting's expression.

Telling lies is so much easier when you can salt them with enough truth to make them palatable, Kensington thought.

"Sorry about Allison, Kensington. Not the kind of experience kids want to start a future with." Hastings looked down at the file, deep in thought. Looking up, he asked, "What do you need from me?"

Shrugging, Kensington said, "I don't know the policy about dropping these kinds of charges now. Back in the day, the prosecuting attorney could make the call. Now it seems the decision to dismiss needs to be run up the flagpole."

"Well, you got the flagpole right, but it's even more complicated now, with a new law on the books."

"What new law?" Kensington asked.

"A prosecuting attorney has been given legal authority to issue a warrant for any material witness in a domestic violence or sexual assault case who refuses to testify."

"You mean a DA can arrest and jail a rape victim if she doesn't want to testify?"

Hastings nodded. "Yep! That's the dubious wisdom of one of our 'get tough on crime' legislators who shepherded a bill through the state legislature."

Kensington thought, *How can you sleep at night knowing you locked up some poor woman who'd already been traumatized?*

Recriminating thoughts about his own criminal conduct quickly reined in his self-righteous indignation.

Kensington pushed himself to stay focused. He explained to Hastings Allison's inner struggle—her battle between wanting justice, but fearing the social fallout that could result from pursuing it.

The investigator listened intently, signaling his agreement as Kensington spoke, punctuating key points by tapping his pen.

After eight demanding years in the sexual assault unit, Hastings had heard countless stories of regret, guilt, fear, and confusion—yet he remained deeply sympathetic to survivors.

His experience had also taught him that women who were initially willing to testify sometimes came to regret their decision. That regret typically surfaced after an enraged husband retaliated by harming their children—or when a rape victim is murdered days before the trial was set to begin.

"Most men can't begin to grasp what it takes for a woman to follow through on a sexual assault report. It takes a kind of courage that a man can't comprehend..." Hastings paused, then added quietly, "unless he's been raped. If it were my daughter, I wouldn't want her to go through that kind of public embarrassment and humiliation. But then, I have to say, whoever was stupid enough to touch my daughter would experience a fatal accident of sorts, if you know what I mean."

"I'm glad you understand Allison's situation," Kensington said. A note of genuine relief in his voice. "I'd really appreciate it if you could speak to the assigned prosecutor on our behalf."

"Joe Morton is the DA," the investigator volunteered. "He's a slick, sonofabitch. He can be hard as nails, but he owes me a favor or two. He won't like this, but as long as the dismissal can be spun to make him look good, he'll probably go for it. Besides," he paused to take a sip of his coffee, then gave a contented sigh, "it's just one count. It won't sink the entire case."

Hastings added, "You know, he's tough on crime, but back in the day, before he became political, Morton used to say that sometimes showing compassion for a victim means more than getting a conviction. With that philosophy, dismissals tended to be easier."

Hastings paused, looked down at the file and then back at Kensington. "It would help if Allison is willing to submit a victim impact statement as an aggravating factor at Horn's sentencing—assuming he's found guilty. Getting a victim impact statement from her should help convince Morton to dump the count."

The investigator chuckled. "Morton spares the girl and her family unnecessary heartache and can still argue for an aggravated sentencing range before the judge. Can't beat that politically, and Morton is all about politics."

Kensington feigned uncertainty for a moment, then he said, "Let Morton know she'll write the statement—as long as she doesn't have to appear in court."

"Alright. I'll touch base with Morton tomorrow. He might want me to meet with Allison in person. You know. Just to confirm what you said."

Kensington smiled. He was confident that Allison would agree to a short interview with a sympathetic investigator, particularly if that meant her involvement in the case would end. All she had to do was tap into the emotions she'd been experiencing with her mother to convince Hastings of the trauma this case had caused her.

Allison can play-act this interview with Hastings in her sleep, Kensington thought. *And as for the impact statement to the court—hell, he could type it and have her sign it.*

Kensington jumped as he looked at his watch. "I didn't realize how late it was. Wally's still in the hospital. I've gotta go see him." Kensington stood and extended his hand.

The investigator pumped it hard and said, smiling, "I'm good with this. I have a backlog of cases to catch up on, but I'll let Morton know there's no point wasting my time—or taxpayer dollars—on a charge that can't be proven beyond a reasonable doubt, especially if a frightened teen might recant or refuse to show up in court."

Winking, Hastings added, "Now, get out of here. Go see your kid. I'll be in touch." As Kensington walked away, he heard Hastings yell, "Call me tomorrow!"

As the elevator descended to the ground floor of the near-empty building, Kensington breathed a deep sigh of relief. This morning, he felt like a tornado had ripped through his world. Tonight, he felt as if he'd stumbled out of the wreckage—bruised and battered, but still alive.

As he walked down the steps of the courthouse, a feeling of longing made him pause. On impulse, he decided to take a brief detour before heading to see Wally. His visits had been rare—too painful to make.

Forty minutes later, he found himself standing quietly in a church cemetery at Elsa's grave. The cool night air brushed his skin, carrying the faint scent of damp earth and pine. He stood in silence, eyes lifted to the sky, where stars blinked behind a thin veil of cloud.

He could almost hear the soft whisper of grass beneath their feet as they walked in silence through the park beneath a moonlit sky. He could feel her hand — smooth and warm — in his. Without looking at her, he knew she was smiling. The air, sweet with the scent of evening primrose, and the memory of her soft image, caused his heart to swell.

Now he strained to hear her voice, but the silence held.

He whispered, "I promise to do better, sweetheart."

31

A Moment of Grace

Kensington had just entered Wally's hospital room when a book hit him on the shoulder. He winced. Another book came flying, but he managed to block it with his elbow.

"Whoa, Wally!" he yelled. "Get yourself under control!"

Standing in the corner of the hospital room, Wally's eyes, wild and teary, darted from the bedside table to the nightstand, looking for something else to throw.

Kensington slowly walked toward him, his hands raised in surrender. But Wally hobbled awkwardly to the bathroom and slammed the door behind him.

Kensington walked to the doorway, checking the hall to see if the commotion was loud enough to draw attention. The last thing he needed was an audience. After Quisling, Allison's mom, and the cops. He was drained.

Sighing heavily, he strolled over to the bed and plopped down, facing the bathroom door. He felt like he'd collapsed across the finish line in a marathon race—dead last. Under the bed sheets, Kensington felt something hard. Sliding his hand under the sheet he pulled out his son's cell phone. Entering Wally's code, his mother's birthday, he unlocked the phone and went straight to messages.

Of course! Allison had already texted him. Not really a surprise. Kensington knew she would reach out to him—just not this quickly.

Kensington cringed at the memory of Allison's hollow, vacant expression as she walked away from him.

The text was short, but Kensington felt the pain beneath her words:

My mom told me to break up with you, Wally. She said you and your dad used me like a dumb two-bit whore. Don't call or text me.

No wonder Wally was so angry at him. He swore under his breath, cursing himself for ignoring the obvious—the devastating pain that a failed plan would cause them. It had always been a possibility, but one he'd dismissed as too remote to matter, especially given his determination to keep his promise to his son.

Staring at the bathroom door, he said, "Allison caused the problem, Wally. She didn't mean to. Guess it was dumb luck someone discovered her diary. I didn't have time to do anything except damage control. You understand that, right?" When there was no response he said, "C'mon out, Wally. We need to talk."

"Your genius plan cost me my girl, Dad." Wally said from behind the door.

Kensington heard a loud sound as if Wally had punched the door, or maybe he had rammed his head against it.

Kensington barked, "Knock it off, Wally." Then, in a voice heavy with frustration, he added, "Please."

Kensington dragged himself off the bed, walked to the door, and rested his forehead against it. He listened for movement inside the bathroom but could only hear ragged breathing. If he entered the bathroom now, things could only get nasty. Maybe physical. Best to wait until Wally came out on his own.

Wally," he whispered, "I'm sorry. This is nobody's fault but my own. I was supposed to be the adult—the one who made the right decision. When you asked me to go after that kid, I wanted to get him too—for what he'd done to you. And maybe, deep down, I was trying to make up for the sorry way I treated you after mom died." His voice softened. "Things were finally going well between us, don't you think? We were laughing again, talking, doing stuff together. When you asked for my help, I didn't want to let you down. I should've said no. God, I wish I'd said no."

His eyes burned with unshed tears as he spoke. "I love you, son. Please… you're all I've got. I need you."

Kensington heard something muffled behind the door, but the words were inaudible and broken. "Wally?" He asked. "Did you say something?"

Emotion stole Wally's words. His voice trembled. "I… I guess you're all I got now, too, Dad." A sob caught in his throat. "Allison told me not to call or text. She wants me to leave her alone. Her mom wants her to break up with me." His voice cracked.

Kensington pressed his forehead hard against the door. He took a deep breath before speaking. "It's not over between you two. She adores you. We need to give her time. That's all. Her mom is just trying to protect her. I'd tell you the same thing if I thought your relationship with Allison caused you problems. Let's give her some time. You know... you'll still see her at school, but you should keep your distance unless she approaches you."

Wally was silent. Kensington held his breath and waited. When he heard the door click, he stepped back. It swung open slowly. Wally stood quietly in the doorway, his face damp with tears.

Kensington snatched Wally up in his arms and held him tight. Slowly, he could feel Wally's arms wrap around him. Silently, they held on to each other.

Wally dropped his head against his dad's chest, sighing, "We did wrong, Dad."

Kensington whispered, his voice tight with emotion, "I know, Wally—but it was worse than wrong. It was criminal."

"I didn't realize how awful it was—what we asked her to do—until I heard Allison crying. She felt so ashamed, so embarrassed, so hurt."

"You talked to Allison?" Kensington asked, surprised.

"Just for a moment. She had to get off the phone before her mom caught her. She was crying something awful. She told me that the kid who stole her diary was just trying to help his friend."

"His name is Li'l Bits," Kensington said.

Wally looked at his dad disbelievingly. "You met him? You met the kid who took Allison's diary?" he asked with a stunned expression.

"Yeah! He's quite something," Kensington mused. "Let's sit down, and I'll fill you in."

With his arm securely around his son's waist, Kensington carefully guided him to the bed and helped him sit. He then reached down, gently lifting his son's ankles to swing them onto the bed. After adjusting a few pillows behind him, Kensington sat down beside him. Wally reached over and took his father's hand.

Wally said quietly, "You look tired, Dad. Don't think I've ever seen you this tired."

Kensington squeezed Wally's hand. The doleful expression on Wally's face was gradually lifting.

"Been hell today, son! It all blew up when Allison's diary was taken. Did she tell you what she'd written?"

Wally frowned. "Not really. We only spoke for a quick minute before she hung up. She won't answer any more of my calls." Wally scrunched up his face. "Did she really write about our plan in her diary?"

Kensington nodded.

Shaking his head, Wally said, "Not too smart to confess to a crime in writing—even in a private journal." A perplexed look crossed Wally's face. "But how weird is it that this kid found out she had a diary and then breaks into her house to find it! That's just insane!" he exclaimed.

Kensington agreed. "What are the odds? Just incredible! Must have meant to be, as Mom would say. You know... God's will."

Wally shifted his body against his pillows. "But you returned the diary to Allison?" he asked.

"Yeah! I did, but that's not the most amazing part, Wally."

Kensington sounded as if he had snatched victory from the jaws of defeat. "I may be able to do a total reset if Morton, the DA, can be convinced to drop Allison from the case." He quickly added, "Of course, Allison and her mom must agree. But given the trouble that this lie has caused them, I have no doubt they will be more than eager to get that count dumped."

Wally looked puzzled. "Wait! I don't understand, Dad. Get what count dumped?"

Kensington couldn't help but smile. "Li'l Bits—the kid who took Allison's diary—made a deal with me. He said he'd destroy all the evidence, if the DA dropped the sexual assault charge. It was a fair ask. He just didn't want his friend prosecuted on a false charge."

Wally blinked rapidly, stunned. He shook his head. "Wait—you're saying he caught us red-handed, with proof we lied… and all he wanted was for you to agree to drop the charge?"

Shrugging, Kensington said, "I didn't believe it either—but he didn't want anything else. He just wants his friend to have his day in court... without the phony charge. Li'l Bits didn't threaten to go to the police. He didn't threaten to go to the press. He said he didn't want our mistake to ruin our lives."

Kensington was drawn back to the mystical moment, his mind grasping for words to express a feeling that defied description.

"The truly amazing thing about this kid," he said slowly, "was that he didn't even seem angry. He was so forgiving—so compassionate—like he genuinely understood why we'd do something so awful."

Kensington's thoughts flashed back to the image of Li'l Bits, surrounded by a soft, luminescent glow—a brilliant aura that seemed almost otherworldly. He glanced at Wally, debating whether he should try to explain that moment… that moment of—

Then he heard Elsa's voice, inside his head—gentle, certain, and filled with love, clear as if she were standing beside him: "Grace."

Wally shook his head, his face a mask of confusion. "I just don't get it. I don't understand. Why didn't he want some kind of revenge? We were trying to destroy his friend's life."

Kensington nodded, his face solemn, but illuminated by a deep understanding. "He's not about revenge, Wally. All you had to do was look into his eyes to understand that… he's about forgiveness."

"Why didn't you just destroy Allison's diary, Dad? You could've saved yourself a lot of trouble!"

Kensington grew thoughtful. “Never occurred to me,” he said. “I didn’t even think about it. Besides, it wouldn’t have fixed our problems. Copies of her confession had already been made. And I promised Li’l Bits that I’d return it to Allison. Like I said, it was the start of a reset—getting her property back to her.”

Kensington heard anxious concern in Wally’s voice. “Where is the diary now, Dad?”

Surprised, Kensington looked at Wally. “So Allison didn’t tell you?”

“No, I told you. We didn’t have much time.”

“The diary’s gone, Wally.” Kensington corrected himself. “Well—at least, the incriminating pages. Her mom was burning it in the kitchen while I was talking to Allison in the living room.”

“Wow,” Wally said, relaxing further into the bed. “It’s gone! What a relief!”

Kensington shook his head. “We’re not out of the woods yet, Wally. I told the investigator on the case that Allison doesn’t want to testify—that she wants to avoid the shame and embarrassment of a public trial. The investigator may still need to speak with her about her decision, but that’s all.”

Kensington added, “I called Allison’s mom several times just before I came to the hospital, but she didn’t pick up. So I called Allison. It was important for her to convince her mom to talk to me. Understandably, Allison refused. Why should she trust me? I explained the agreement that I made with Li’l Bits and my discussion with the investigator. I had to plead with her. It took awhile. Convincing her wasn’t easy. Finally, she consented. She said she’d ask her mom to call.” Kensington chuckled. “Her mother took her sweet time, probably just to make me sweat.

“When she finally called me back, I explained what I’d done—and what she and Allison needed to say if the investigator called.” Kensington paused, remembering the hurt and anger in her voice.

“Ms. Ruddick is deeply upset. Not just with me—she’s struggling with all of it. She’s worried about Allison, feeling so disappointed and shocked by her daughter's behavior—fearful of the scrutiny, all the attention that a trial would bring.

"And that's exactly what the investigator needs to hear, I told her—her fear and worry for Allison. If she speaks from that place—protectiveness, concern, distress—it might be enough to get the charge dropped."

Kensington smiled ruefully and said, "Damn, Allison's mom gave me an earful. I don't think God ever intended a mouth to be used that way! She said she'd have me arrested in a heartbeat—if she could do it without dragging Allison down with me."

Kensington continued, "Hopefully, Morton, the DA trying the case, won't feel a personal need to follow up with a one-on-one interview with Allison to salvage the count. Sexual assault for a prosecutor is a lot juicier than a school fight."

Wally paused, taking it all in. He exclaimed, "So Allison's mom burned the diary pages to protect her."

Kensington sighed. "Yeah. Now she's implicated, too."

"Implicated? What do you mean, Dad?"

"She destroyed evidence of a criminal conspiracy that could be filed against us. The DA can charge her with destruction of evidence, accessory after the fact, or obstructing government operations."

"A case against us," Wally echoed. "And a case against Allison's mom, too!" he moaned.

It suddenly hit him—Wally hadn't even considered the potential blowback if the scheme fell apart.

Kensington had considered the risk, but only briefly—then arrogantly dismissed it, certain he could manipulate the system, even if it meant committing a serious offense by defrauding the court with a false charge, fabricated evidence, and perjured statements.

He winced at the thought: *I weaponized the entire judicial system to pursue a personal grievance. How petty! How despicable!*

"What a profoundly stupid thing I did, Wally," Kensington admitted. "Looking back, I don't even recognize myself." He paused, his gaze distant. "I thought about that when I spoke to Li'l Bits in the principal's office."

Kensington fell silent. When he spoke again, his voice was husky with emotion. "I feel so ashamed. I took an oath to serve and protect."

"You know what Mom would say, don't you?" Wally asked softly.

Kensington shook his head. "No. Not exactly. I can think of a few things, though. All bad." Kensington made a feeble attempt to smile.

"She'd say, 'Now, it's between you and God.'"

"Yeah. You're right. She *would* say that." Kensington paused. "Li'l Bits told me the same thing. '*Now it's between you and God.*' That's what he said in the principal's office."

Wally's eyes grew large. Worry creased his face. "I hope you were alone with him when you made that deal."

"C'mon, son!" Kensington said. "I know I screwed up, but give your dad a little credit. Of course, we were alone. If we weren't, I might be in cuffs right now, courtesy of Principal March."

Wally apologized. "Sorry, Dad. I just want this thing to go away."

"Me too, Wally. It's been a nightmare, but I think I've covered all the bases now."

"Does Quisling know? What does he say about all this?" Wally asked.

"Don't worry about him. If I can clean this up without dragging him into it, he'll be perfectly fine with everything."

Suddenly, Kensington felt too exhausted to hold his head up. "Wally, I'm gonna just close my eyes here for a moment. Grab some shut-eye on your couch."

Wally offered a supportive nod, "You had a long, hard day, Dad. You rest."

Kensington lumbered over to the small couch. As he sank down into the cushions his mind kept racing, replaying every calculated step he'd taken to clean up the mess. Though he believed he'd done everything possible to salvage the situation, a vague, unsettling feeling gnawed at him. No matter how often he reassured himself he'd carefully navigated a dangerous minefield, he couldn't shake the growing dread that something might still go wrong—something beyond his control.

Quisling! I just need to keep him in line, Kensington thought. *That's all I need to do.*

Clinging to that final, rose-colored thought, he allowed himself to drift off to sleep.

32
Urban Fruit

Dead tired and disoriented, Kensington couldn't remember where he was for a moment. Suddenly, the chaotic memory of yesterday jolted him awake like a bucket of freezing water. It wasn't a dream—it happened! Damning, irrefutable evidence of the criminal conspiracy had been uncovered.

Kensington glanced at his watch. He'd overslept. He'd have to haul ass to make it to his 6 a.m. roll call at Headquarters. Careful not to wake Wally, he tip-toed out of the room.

His body felt stiff from sleeping on the makeshift bed, and he needed a shower and a fresh change of clothes. His back ached, too.

As he trudged toward the exit, he caught sight of a security guard idling by the reception desk who looked vaguely familiar. Then, he remembered.

Several years ago, the man had been fired from the police force for killing a civilian, and his certification to be employed as a police officer had been revoked.

The man was a rookie—just six months out of the police academy. He had shot and killed a Black woman sitting in the front passenger seat during a traffic stop—two blocks from her house. Kensington learned later-that she had refused to cooperate with the officer after the driver took off running.

According to the officer's Use of Force Report, the woman refused to identify the fleeing suspect or show her ID. She supposedly got loud and announced that the rookie cop was nothing more than a Badge Bunny and a second-rate security guard. Each time he ordered her out of the car, she challenged him, "Read me my rights if you're arresting me."

After the cop's repeated orders to exit the car, she finally said, "Alright, then," and she reached down inside the car.

He emptied his gun into her point-blank, claiming he felt threatened. In his Use of Force Report, he wrote, "She looked at him with the face of a demon."

It turned out that the elderly woman—about eighty-five years old and weighing no more than 115 pounds—had bad knees and was just reaching for her collapsible cane to get out of the car.

He claimed that he yelled at her repeatedly not to move, to keep her hands visible. However, no one was there to confirm or contradict his statement. The dash cam did not capture the rookie standing by the door. The patrol car had no external microphone, so there was no audio recording of their confrontation. Body cams weren't in use at the time.

The district attorney ultimately decided not to pursue criminal prosecution based on the officer's repeated warnings, her failure to comply with verbal commands, the furtive movement inside the car, and the officer's stated fear for his life. The district attorney considered the nine rounds fired into her body as circumstantial evidence of the officer's fear.

Every poor Black neighborhood in America knows the sound of gunfire. Her neighborhood responded quickly. Angry neighbors, friends, and relatives surrounded the cop within minutes. The on-duty supervisor had issued an OIS, an officer-involved shooting, coupled with a code 3 emergency response, to indicate an urgent incident.

Kensington arrived on the scene with a hundred others in riot gear. After the rookie's police car had been flipped on its side, the protesters marched to the police station and tried to burn it down.

Communities no longer tolerate police violence, Kensington thought. *Passive acceptance of police brutality is a thing of the past, especially with the emergence of the Black Lives Matter movement.*

Kensington hoped he wouldn't get an OIS call today. The intense drama of the past twenty-four hours had completely drained his energy, leaving him with no reserves to draw from.

If not for Li'l Bits, he could have shared a similar fate as the disgraced rookie. He offered the man a sympathetic nod, but the man only glanced at him before quickly turning away.

Since his first shift didn't start until 7 a.m., Kensington decided to keep his mobile data terminal off and listen to a jazz radio station as he began to ready himself for today's urban mayhem.

As he drove toward HQ, he reminded himself to call Hastings at the investigator's office when he had a break. Hopefully, Hastings would be able to corral DA Morton before the morning docket began in district court. Otherwise, Kensington might have to wait until the end of the day before he could hear news about the DA's decision to dump the attempted rape count.

He was cautiously optimistic. Hastings had given him the clear impression that he knew how to work Morton.

Kensington smiled. Li'l Bits would be the first person he'd call. He anticipated a "praise God" response from the young man. Then, he would call Allison's mom, who would probably be hostile and implacable. Later, he would touch base with Wally. He knew he could count on an enthusiastic, over-the-top yelp. And after Wally, maybe Quisling?

The thought of dealing with Quisling almost gave him a headache. Acting stupid didn't seem to bother that man at all, even in front of a crowd of high school students. If he did call Quisling, he would probably curse him out before hanging up on him.

Sighing, Kensington decided that it didn't matter how anyone responded. He would be grateful. He could start a fresh, new relationship with Wally. And, in time, Wally could mend his relationship with Allison.

As for Quisling, he knew the relationship had become toxic. He could no longer stomach the stories of the "good ole days" that reeked of bigotry and hate. It was time to end the relationship.

Heading toward work, he looked up at a brooding sky, which seemed unusually dark this time of morning. Rather than getting lighter, the sky appeared to darken. *Strange,* he thought. He wondered if the weather was being affected by the approach of errant thunderstorms. He heard the sky rumble and saw flashes of lightning in the distance.

Near the entrance to HQ, he saw three or four camera crews and vehicles from several local news stations setting up. There was also a cable news truck from CNN. Something was up. Something big. The last time he had seen this kind of news frenzy was over allegations of police brutality. A police officer shot an unarmed Black man at his home after the man made a 911 call seeking help for his mentally ill son.

Kensington wondered, *How will the Chief handle the media this time?* His PR man always had a stock response ready:

We appreciate your interest and will provide a comprehensive update as soon as possible. Until then, we ask for your patience as we prepare to address your questions. Thank you for understanding.

The Chief no longer expected to be quoted accurately or in context by news reporters. Experience had taught him that some news reporters selectively quoted his statements in ways that heightened tensions within the community. After being misquoted countless times, he embraced an observation attributed to Mark Twain: "If you want to be misinformed, read the news."

Driving past the designated public parking area to HQ, Kensington spotted a dark blue Ford Crown Victoria with tinted windows. Approaching the car slowly, he noticed it had a small, mounted antenna on the right front fender. He took a quick look at the plate. "US Government" was printed over the plate's flag.

"Feds," he muttered. It was unusual for the feds to come to HQ—rarer still for them to come this early in the morning. Even in cases involving a police shooting, they never took part in a media blitz.

Kensington considered logging into his computer to find out what was going on but quickly changed his mind. *No more drama,* he told himself. Whatever this story was could wait until he had a hot cup of coffee. Besides, someone would damn sure tell him. Cops always hear when another cop screws up.

If a civilian had been killed, whoever killed that poor bastard was probably doing some creative report-writing.

Standard phrases routinely used to justify a killing came to Kensington's mind: "officer safety," "appropriate adherence to standard police procedures," "reasonable exercise of deadly force," "officer feared for his life," "perceived imminent threat," "the suspect failed to comply"—or some combination of boilerplate police language.

Kensington suddenly felt that these hollow, legalistic phrases—crafted to absolve a police officer of murder—infuriated grieving parents, reducing their profound loss to a scripted defense.

Kensington paused. He felt different. Something within him had changed. Had he developed a moral uneasiness about this suspect jargon used to justify the deaths of unarmed men. Somehow the pat phrasing seemed to obscure the humanity of the deceased. He wondered, *Had Li'l Bits affected him in more ways than one?*

Using his electronic key, he opened the chain-link fence to the authorized personnel area. Pulling in quickly, Kensington parked in the first available space. He noted that the parking lot was almost full. Entering the side entrance, he jogged down a hall leading past the break room to the locker room.

As he passed the break room, he was surprised that hardly a table was vacant. Several officers occasionally glanced at the mounted TV set while drinking their morning coffee. A few others sat together at their tables, mindlessly eating breakfast, periodically stealing glances at the TV. Other officers sat with arms folded or elbows resting on the table. They all seemed to be waiting for something to happen.

Kensington slowed his pace, drew himself up, and stopped. Something was off. He hadn't seen this many people in the break room since the OJ Simpson's verdict. Something didn't seem right. His gut told him that it concerned the camera crew and TV reporters on the lawn.

As he headed down the hall to the locker room, it hit him—the silence! Typically, officers were bantering, teasing, and joking, but it was eerily quiet, everyone seemed—almost grim.

Kensington groaned. Maybe the news teams were out there for something far worse than he imagined. A mass shooting at a mall? Maybe several cops had died in an ambush. Now, that would make the news! It might even explain the presence of the FBI, particularly if a terrorist cell was involved.

Kensington was in the process of opening his locker when Smitty came out of the shower. Smitty was a barrel-chested veteran who had served several tours in Afghanistan and had worked undercover with him on the streets years back. Old scars from several bullet wounds on his upper shoulder always seemed more pink when he got out of the shower.

"Where the fuck you been, Kensington? The watch commander has been calling everywhere trying to reach you." Smitty eyed Kensington carefully. "You okay? You look like you just crawled out from under a rock. Did you turn your radio off? Have you checked your patrol computer? Have you been listening to the news?"

Before Kensington could speak, a cadet in police fatigues appeared at the door. He seemed agitated.

Breathlessly, he said, "Smitty! It's started."

Smitty snatched his robe from his locker and put it on as he rushed into the hallway. Without looking around, he yelled over his shoulder, "You might want to see this!"

What the hell is going on? Something about Smitty's tone unnerved him. The visible agitation of the cadet added to the mystery. Kensington dreaded to admit it, but something more gut-wrenching may have occurred. *God! Please don't let it be another school shooting.* Kensington's body suddenly felt heavy. He shook his head and followed them out of the locker room.

Before Kensington could get within ten feet of the room, he heard the shuffling of bodies and the scraping of chairs. The energy in the air was wild and palpable. When Kensington entered, it was standing room only. Every eye was fixed on the TV.

A newscaster stood on a hill north of the interstate. His coat danced about him as the wind whipped it around. Given the morning hour, the sky was extraordinarily dark—almost black. Gray clouds, like snarled, twisted fingers, slowly drifted across a brooding, dismal sky. It seemed like a thunderstorm might be brewing. Quick flashes of light licked the sky. Thunder rumbled.

Kensington saw crowds of people standing behind portable security fencing that had been erected across the highway. A group of people pressed against the barricades, trying to breech them. Police officers in reflective vests were redirecting both foot and vehicle traffic. Flashing lights from strategically placed police cars signaled that the area was closed off. Some people carried signs and waved placards, while others carried flowers. A group appeared to be kneeling in prayer as someone conducted a service. Some individuals wandered aimlessly, while others crisscrossed the highway.

Several officers positioned along the barrier waved back those trying to take photos, while others maintained the integrity of the perimeter. Some officers, wearing riot gear, appeared to be barking orders through a bullhorn.

The newscaster was speaking, but Kensington couldn't hear. Someone yelled, "Turn it up!" Kensington recognized the newsman. Usually, he appeared on the evening news. They must have pulled him from his usual beat to cover this early morning assignment.

"If children are in the room, I strongly urge you to remove them," he advised. "What I am about to report is not appropriate for the young or even adults who are sensitive to or offended by images of violence. If so, I caution you to change the channel."

He hesitated for a moment before he began. Collecting himself, he said, "I'm standing on Interstate 40. About a hundred yards behind me is the bridge that traverses the highway.

"At approximately 3 a.m. this morning, reports of a body hanging from the bridge began flooding our newsroom. Initially, our reporters dismissed it as a hoax or a sick joke. However, individuals traveling the highway took photos and sent them to us.

"At first, we thought it was an effigy or a dummy that pranksters had hung from the overpass. What appeared to be blood on the body could have been nothing more than dye or red paint. Our newsroom immediately contacted law enforcement, but they had already been notified and dismissed the reports as a prank." He continued, "Our news team arrived before they did."

He paused. He seemed to be holding back tears. "By the time I arrived, there was a horrendous traffic jam. Several cars were involved in accidents that required assistance from emergency vehicles. Because of the size of the crowd, the cars, and police barricades, I could only get within three hundred feet of the body."

He stopped again. A shudder visibly shook him. "I looked up, but I couldn't believe what I saw. I had to look into a high-power camera lens to be sure. It was not a dummy. It was not an effigy. It was a shoeless teenage boy with a noose around his neck. He was wearing a high school jacket. A sign pinned to his jacket read, 'urban fruit.' Unconfirmed reports indicate that the sign may have been written with the boy's blood."

The shaken reporter continued. "We did not understand what the sign meant, so we asked our research team to check our databases. They concluded it was a taunting reference to an anti-lynching song, 'Strange Fruit', sung by Billie Holiday in 1939. The first stanza reads:

Southern trees bear a strange fruit
Blood on the leaves and blood on the root
Black bodies swingin' in the Southern breeze
Strange fruit hangin' from the poplar trees."

He then read the last stanza:

"Here is a fruit for the crows to pluck,
For the rain to gather, for the wind to suck,
For the sun to rot, for the tree to drop,
Here is a strange and bitter crop."

Kensington's knees buckled. He staggered back, but firm hands behind caught him and held him up.

"Gotcha!" a voice said. "You okay?"

Kensington didn't respond. He took a faltering step forward to regain his balance. The newscaster's voice still reached his ears, but it seemed distant. He could no longer make out the words. His head was spinning.

The scene cut to a close-up of the body. In the background, Kensington heard a helicopter thumping overhead and the confused, frightened voices of spectators on the pedestrian overpass.

Yellow tape draped over, down, and around the bridge. The camera moved steadily and slowly, inching toward the body hanging motionless in the air. The figure wore a high school jacket with white sleeves adorned with football and lacrosse patches. Dark stains partially obscured the letter J stitched over the heart.

His mind screamed, *No! No! No! It can't be!* He clutched his chest, the pain so excruciating that it momentarily paralyzed him. It wasn't a heart attack he felt—it was his heart breaking.

His mind screamed, *Quisling! You crazy, stupid, fuckin' sick racist bastard! What have you done?*

Overwhelmed by the full, horrific reality of Quisling's sadistic act, Kensington's body felt white-hot, infused with indescribable pain, sadness, horror, grief, and something else—something murderous.

Behind him, two large hands tried to grab his arm to steady him, but Kensington tore himself away and rushed blindly into the bathroom across the hall, slamming the door open so hard it boomed like a cannon shot.

Watch Commander Wheeler came down the hall just in time to see Kensington bolt into the bathroom.

Wheeler walked up to the door and heard the sound of violent retching. Standing outside quietly, he radioed the Division Chief. "Found him! Be up in a couple minutes! Seems like he's sick."

Wheeler fell silent, listening intently to the response. "No," he growled. "I will *not* go into the bathroom. My days of watching grown men puke are over." Then he added, "Trust me! He ain't going nowhere."

Several minutes passed, and Kensington was still in the bathroom. Wheeler could hear him dry heaving. Wheeler banged on the door and shouted, "Kensington, sick or not, I'm waiting on you. The Chief wants to see you *now*! The FBI is with him."

Kensington managed to mumble, "Hold on! Hold on! Just need a minute." Several more minutes passed. Wheeler heard a faucet running.

Kensington slowly emerged from the bathroom, his eyes looked vacant, confused, and uncertain. Water dripped from his face.

"Drank a bit too much last night, Kensington? Kinda dumb when you got an early morning shift."

"No! No, Commander! It's nothing like that at all. Think I got a virus. Stomach bug or something. Maybe food poisoning. Just hit me hard and sudden. I don't feel well…" His voice drifted off.

Wheeler looked him over again and frowned at the vomit on Kensington's shirt and pants. He radioed the Chief again. "Chief! He's a fuckin' mess. We need about fifteen minutes for him to shower and dress." Wheeler's face contorted as he listened to the Chief's reply. Wheeler yelled, "If you want your office to smell like puke, I can bring him up right now! Those fuckin' 'suits' can wait!"

Nodding, Wheeler muttered, "Right! Right! I got you! I'll stay with him."

He barked at Kensington again. "Get your ass in the shower and make it snappy! Chief wants to see you 'cause you got visitors. Visitors you love to hate!"

Wheeler trailed behind Kensington on the way to his locker. Kensington felt his body quaking, almost vibrating.

Was he having a seizure? Why was it so hard to breathe? He felt weak, disoriented. He told himself that he couldn't pass out. He had to remain conscious.

A hot tear burned slowly down his cheek while his guts felt like they had been ripped open with a dull knife and stirred with a red-hot poker. Bile rose up and burned the back of his throat.

The dismissal of the sexual assault charge no longer mattered. His plan had collapsed. Everything had changed—the universe had shifted.

He hadn't escaped the tornado. He'd heard it now—the low, thunderous roar of a freight train charging through the darkness. The wreckage of his world lay scattered around him. No welcoming light pierced the gloom. Only the terrifying sounds remained: the howling wind, the crack of thunder, and a deep, unrelenting roar that seemed to mourn with him, amplifying his grief.

And worst of all.... *Li'l Bits has been murdered.*

33

Person of Interest

Kensington showered and dressed robotically for the meeting with the Chief, knowing he needed only two items—his badge and gun. Afterwards, the Chief would tell him to place them on his desk. The rest of his duty gear would be locked away in storage until the investigation ran its course. The FBI's presence made it clear just how precarious his situation was.

As Kensington fumbled with the last buttons of his uniform, he fought the impulse to walk out, drive to Quisling's place, and put a bullet in his head. But he couldn't just disappear—people were waiting for him. People who were angry with him—his Chief and the damn FBI.

He shut his locker and pressed his forehead against the cool, smooth metal. Images of Li'l Bits' kind eyes and compassionate smile floated before him. An indescribable quality about him profoundly touched Kensington in a way he couldn't fully comprehend.

Why? Why? Why? He wanted to scream. *It was so senseless!*

He punched his locker, leaving a deep dent in the metal door. The explosive bang resonated in his ears. He turned from his locker and walked slowly down the narrow aisle. He moved through a thick emotional fog, willing himself toward the door where Wheeler waited.

Li'l Bits' death had shaken him to the core. He'd lost Elsa, and that grief had nearly undone him, but this was something new. Quisling's stories of lynching, once just grim history, now landed with a force that sickened him. For the first time, he began to grasp what Black families had been forced to endure for generations. It was a nameless horror that had no end.

He inhaled deeply and shoved the door open. He barely managed two steps into the hallway when he heard his name.

"Kensington! Don't move! I'll be right there."

Commander Wheeler was an old war horse by-the-book, die-hard dinosaur. But he was as solid as they come.

Wheeler had one pet peeve, though. He couldn't stand feds. He had been embarrassed one too many times after cooperating with their joint investigations.

Kensington followed Wheeler to the elevator. If the FBI wanted to see him, he was clearly under suspicion—but suspicion of what, he didn't know. Never in his wildest dreams had he imagined that the phrase "person of interest" would ever apply to him.

The elevator chimed, and the two men silently stepped inside. Wheeler pressed the top button.

"You look dehydrated, Kensington. You need to get some water in you. Passing out won't go over big with the Chief." Wheeler cocked his head to look at Kensington's face. "Your eyes are red, too, but I guess you already know that."

Kensington shrugged and cleared his throat. "Allergies," he muttered.

"Food poisoning *and* food allergies! A perfect storm of ailments really fucked you up today, huh, Kensington?" Wheeler scoffed. "Well, you better get your shit together, before you see the Chief and those feds. They're out for blood. You want to make sure it ain't yours."

Kensington managed to nod. It was an effort to get the words out. "Thanks, commander," he said. But his voice was hollow.

Both remained silent as the elevator ascended. The elevator doors would open soon, and Kensington readied himself to step into the corridor with his designated police escort. He began to close his hands tightly into fists and slowly released them.

Gradually, his breathing became synchronized with the rhythmic squeezing and releasing of his hands. Kensington could feel himself regaining control.-The doors opened after an excruciatingly slow ride. Wheeler stepped out first.

Kensington had been summoned to the Chief's office after Elsa died and the reports of excessive force rolled in. Only a few rooms were on this floor: a conference room, an interviewing room, a waiting room, and a small cadre of secretaries who shared a room divided by tight cubicles south of his office. Kensington took some comfort in sensing where Wheeler was leading him. He was heading to the Chief's office, not the interview room. If Wheeler had dropped him off there, his chances of leaving the building would have been less than fifty-fifty.

Did they get photocopies of the diary? Did they speak to Allison and her mom? Do they have Quisling in custody in another room? Has Quisling made a statement? How much do they know?

There was no way to know how much they had uncovered. That was always their hold card. Law enforcement used highly effective interrogative techniques to elicit incriminating statements, admissions, and even false confessions from a person of interest. Ask a suspect critical questions that the interrogators already know the answers to; ask the same questions in multiple ways; put words in the suspect's mouth; set up a person to make factual errors; confront the suspect with statements of other witnesses; challenge the suspect with conflicting facts; make him backtrack on their story; scare them with lies about evidence they don't have, and then drop the net. And, if all else fails, use psychological pressure, emotional manipulation, and physical coercion.

Cool and careful. Cool and careful. That's the way to play this, he reminded himself. Be responsive without being defensive. Appear to cooperate without cooperating. Use righteous indignation at strategic moments. The stakes had changed. He could be up for a murder rap, along with that bastard Quisling. This might be a capital offense crime. His jaw suddenly clenched so hard it hurt.

Quisling killed Li'l Bits for what? Kicks? Southern hillbilly stupidity! The sick cause of white supremacy? Or just because he thought that he could get away with it?

Kensington's head began to spin again, but it stopped cold as Li'l Bits' face flashed before him. The crushing sorrow gave way to a heavy, burning sensation in his gut—his grief solidifying into seething rage.

Just keep it together a bit longer, he reminded himself. *You don't want to forfeit your chance to get to Quisling.*

Wheeler led Kensington to within a few feet of the Chief's door—just close enough to eavesdrop. Angry voices spilled through the doorway and filtered down from the ceiling vent. He recognized the Chief's deep rumble, along with two unfamiliar male voices.

One of them snapped, "Kensington is as crooked as they come."

Wheeler pulled Kensington to a safe distance, ensuring no one could overhear their conversation.

Wheeler hissed, "Did you have anything to do with getting that boy killed?" His pale blue eyes had morphed into a deep glacier gray.

Stunned and surprised, Kensington's mouth dropped open in shock. He realized that Wheeler had tricked him, drawing him in with feigned concern only to set him up for a question that the Chief and feds would soon demand an answer.

Wheeler's eyes had now assumed an incredibly menacing quality.

Kensington's voice was husky and barely audible. "No... In the short time I spent with Li'l Bits at his school, I got to like him. I got to like him *a lot.* If you ever met him, you'd know how special he is. He's one in a million." Kensington's voice cracked.

Wheeler held Kensington in a relentless stare, his eyes scanning every strained feature, searching for the slightest flicker of deceit. But what caught him off guard—what he hadn't expected—was the sudden flash of anguish that broke across Kensington's face. Wheeler's gaze softened, then he stepped back.

"No, Kensington," Wheeler said ruefully. "Not how special he *is. Y*ou mean, how special he *was.*"

The voices from within the Chief's office were louder now. Wheeler jerked his head toward the room. "Sounds like they're pretty hot in there. If you get a bit closer, you might be able to make out what they're saying."

Wheeler threw a glance at the Chief's door. Kensington understood. He nodded.

"I need to use the restroom, but I'll be back in a few minutes. I'll radio the Chief that we're on the way."

Wheeler started to move away as Kensington slid closer to the room filled with angry voices. Suddenly, he turned and gripped Kensington's forearm, squeezing it so hard that Kensington winced.

"If I find out that you were in any way involved in that kid's death, Kensington—and I do mean any way," Wheeler paused, raking him over with his eyes, "I'll put you down myself."

Kensington murmured meekly, "I understand, but you have nothing to worry about because I have nothing to worry about." Wheeler released his arm and started walking away. Without looking back, he muttered, "I damn sure hope so."

Kensington inched toward the ceiling vent and assumed a nonchalant posture in case an administrative secretary walked by. He wasn't concerned that other officers might see him because no cop came anywhere near the Chief's office unless summoned.

"He's dirty, and you know it," one of the men said. "You're gearing up to do that brotherhood-in-blue bullshit, and it's gonna get you and your whole damn department embroiled in a federal investigation."

Division Chief Jackson's baritone voice shot back, "You ain't on an Indian reservation now, son. Save those threats for people who don't know better. I'm letting you sit in on this interview as a goddamn courtesy—and I mean, *sit in*. No questions! You step out of line, and I'll have both of your asses escorted out of the building."

A second voice chimed in, "We got him, and you know we've got him! His son's girlfriend, Allison Ruddick, claims Kensington pressured her to lie about a sex crime and commit perjury on the witness stand. Then, the kid who steals her diary turns up dead less than twenty-four hours later. That's no coincidence, Jackson."

"It's *Chief* Jackson to you, *Mister*. Don't forget whose office you're standing in."

The agent continued, his agitation and frustration rising. "We have enough evidence to take him into custody right now under our federal hate crimes statute. Why didn't you call IAD after the DA faxed pages of Ruddick's diary to you."

"Don't tell me how to do my job," the Chief fumed. "There's always time to get Internal Affairs involved. And your highly questionable belief about probable cause is pure speculation. Until I hear from someone further up the chain, our state criminal jurisdiction applies. This is a state murder investigation under *our* hate crimes statutes, not yours. As for probable cause—no one has interviewed Ruddick. She's the key to clearing up this mess. She's missing now. Both she and her mom are gone. The house is being staked out in case she returns."

"Ms. Ruddick and her daughter ain't stupid," the first agent said. "How long would you hang around with your daughter when the kid who stole her diary winds up dead?"

Before the Chief could respond, the phone in his office rang. The room became quiet.

Kensington leaned back against the wall for support. *They know a lot more than I thought—but no Quisling and no Allison. They can't drop the net. Not yet.* Struggling to keep his breath steady, he wiped the fine beads of sweat from his forehead with slightly trembling hands.

Looking up, he saw Wheeler standing a few feet away. He was eyeing him closely. His craggy visage had visibly softened. Wheeler walked up to him and handed him several damp paper towels and a cup of water. Kensington downed it in a single gulp. Meeting his gaze, Kensington pointed to the Chief's door with his chin and whispered, "It's gonna get real hot in there."

Wheeler took the cup from Kensington and said, softly, "If you got nothing to hide, like you said, you'll get through it."

Kensington folded the towels in half and wiped his neck and face. Wheeler casually looked up and down the hall and then headed toward the Chief's door. After tossing the towels in the trash, Kensington followed, fighting back a sudden surge of panic.

Kensington overheard the Chief on the phone. "Gotta go. Will get back to you in about an hour. Try to track down Ms. Ruddick at work and her daughter at school. Talk to her neighbors. See if you can locate any relatives or friends. Get a warrant to pull the mother's bank records to see if you can get a hit on her credit card. Put a BOLO out on her car. Get a physical description of them to everyone in the field."

There was momentary silence then, a loud bang resounded against the wall, like someone had kicked a trash can into it.

"Goddammit! We need to get a better handle on this mess!" the Chief yelled.

Wheeler leaned toward Kensington and whispered, "You ready?"

Kensington's eyes flashed with resolve. He said, "Let's go."

They walked up to the Chief's door, and Wheeler rapped twice in quick succession. "Come in!" the Chief barked.

Wheeler opened the door and brusquely motioned Kensington to enter. Kensington straightened up, squared his shoulders, taking a deep breath before stepping into the room.

Kensington saw two men in dark suits standing near the Chief's desk. One was tall and angular, in his late thirties, with a pronounced widow's peak, and a flat face with cold, watchful eyes. The other man was about fifty, sporting a silver-cropped crew cut. His stiff posture indicated that he was ex-military. He wore a mean scowl and stood with thick arms folded across a massive chest. The Chief jabbed at a chair for Kensington to sit down.

Before Kensington could seat himself, the Chief bellowed, "Where the fuck you been? You look like shit!"

"You going to introduce me to your new friends, Chief?" Kensington asked casually.

Without looking at Kensington, the Chief said dismissively, "Agent Cavalessi and Agent Barnes. Cavalessi is the tall one." He turned back to Kensington. "I repeat, where the fuck have you been?"

Kensington strolled to a chair and sat down.

Tilting his head slightly to the side, he asked quietly, "When?"

The Chief looked like he was going to explode. Catapulting himself from his chair, he towered over the desk, fuming. Kensington had forgotten how tall he was.

"Don't get fuckin' cute with me, Kensington. Any more smart ass responses, and I'll let these suits have you."

Kensington placed his hands in his lap. "I'm not trying to get smart with you, Chief. You got to help me out here. You need to give me some kind of time frame." Kensington continued, "Are you talking about this morning, yesterday, or last week?"

The Chief appeared to relax a little—but only a little. The sudden flash of anger subsided, and he sat back in his chair. Kensington noted that his temper hadn't improved over the years.

"I'm under a lot of pressure here, Kensington. Let's talk about yesterday morning when you were at a civilian's house." He flipped open a file. "Doug Joiner, ex-cop. His home!" The Chief's voice became stern and flippant. "Quisling was there, too. You remember Quisling, don't you? He's the lead cop on the Horn case. Does that ring a goddamn bell?" he sneered.

"Of course I remember, Chief! Yep, I was there! I was trying to collar a kid who'd broken into my son's girlfriend's home and stolen her property."

The Chief looked pointedly at Kensington before he spoke again. Almost on cue, the two federal agents moved closer to Kensington to gauge his reaction. The Chief said, "Well, Matthew Carver, the kid you chased yesterday morning ended up hanging from a noose over the interstate highway. People have already started to riot throughout the city."

Kensington steeled himself before speaking. He said solemnly, "I caught the news before Commander Wheeler told me you wanted to see me." The note of genuine sorrow in Kensington's voice caught the Chief off guard. The FBI agents' expressions remained impassive.

The Chief continued, "This is the same kid that you had a private meeting in Principal March's office with. I know because I spoke to her this morning."

"It wasn't a private meeting, Chief. It was a consensual interview about the crime that he'd just committed."

"Did you take a written statement?"

"No."

"Did you give him a court summons?"

"No."

"Did you take the case to the filing DA?" snapped the Chief.

"No," Kensington said slowly, feigning exasperation.

The Chief continued, "I can't find any report or record indicating that you checked in with Dispatch when you contacted the neighbor's house, spoke with the school resource officer, or talked to Principal March and the victim." His eyes were ablaze. *"Why the fuck not?"*

"It was a rushed situation, Chief—fast, fluid, and chaotic. Allison Ruddick, my son's girlfriend, called me about the theft of her property, and I got a call from Quisling that the Carver kid was hiding at a neighbor's house. Everything was happening so fast that I skipped procedure until I could chase him down at the school."

Kensington continued, his voice steady, as Chief Jackson glared at him. "Allison told me she just wanted her property returned. She didn't want anyone to get into trouble." He shrugged. "She's soft-hearted that way. I had a heart-to-heart with Carver in Principal March's office, gave him a stern warning, and retrieved her property."

Chief Jackson shook his head in disbelief.

"I caught the kid! He confessed to the crime. I recovered the property. I gave him a break and let him go with a warning. Principal March was going to follow up with a call to his parents. I delivered the property to Allison." Kensington yelled, "I did my job! What's the goddamn problem?"

"*Property*? *Property*, Kensington? You mean the girl's diary? The one with her confession about you and Quisling pressuring her to accuse a kid of sexual assault?"

The two agents moved closer. Kensington felt someone's hand resting on the back of his chair but resisted the urge to look.

Now it was Kensington's turn to act outraged. He jumped out of his chair, voice rising as he shouted, "What the fuck are you talking about?" The feds flanked him, braced to take him down if necessary.

The Chief screamed back, "Are you telling me that you don't know what's in that diary?"

"No! I have no idea what's in Allison's diary!"

"Bullshit!" One of the agents yelled.

Ignoring him, Kensington protested, "I never read it. Yeah! That's what I'm telling you. The only thing that I know is that my son, Wally, told me that he had broken up with her because Allison had been making stuff up. Crazy stuff, according to Wally."

"Stuff! What kind of stuff?" the Chief asked.

Kensington shook his head and shrugged, "I don't know. Wally didn't say. I didn't ask, and I didn't push him. As far as I was concerned, the breakup was between Wally and Allison."

"Maybe he'll tell us," the Chief challenged.

"Maybe. You can try. I think he may be released from the hospital soon, but he's my son. He's a minor, and he won't say a word to you unless I'm with him. All I know is that if it was something really important that he wanted me to know, Wally would have told me." Kensington sat down again. Eyes wide and innocent, he asked, "Have you got the diary? What does it say?"

Without looking at Kensington, he said quietly, "During your so-called consensual interview with Carver, did you ever get his story as to why he stole Ruddick's diary?"

"I've been a cop for twenty years. That's not including my five years as a detective. Part of my job as a detective was to uncover a motive, finding out 'the why.' Of course, I asked him! He said he did it on a dare to impress some girl who disliked Allison because she stole Wally from her. It was just dumb teen shit."

Kensington paused to catch his breath. "Are you gonna let me see the diary, Chief?"

"Fuck no! But we do have a thumb drive of a very interesting video narrated by the murdered boy and photos of the diary from Doug Joiner that was given to the DA's office." The Chief snapped. "All you need to know now is the video and photos incriminate you and Quisling in a plot to set up Tyrene Horn by falsifying criminal charges. Seems like the Carver kid was childhood friends with him. Isn't that the kid who maimed your son in a fight? It sure seems like you two concocted a scheme to get payback for your son."

The Chief huffed. "That story about a teen dare and a jealous ex-girlfriend smell to high heaven, Kensington." The Chief added, his tone grim, "That diary is a motive for murder."

"That's a fucking lie!" Kensington boomed.

"You and your buddy Quisling were too busy to notify Dispatch about a burglary and theft or to file a report about multiple field contacts? I find that kind of suspicious. You aren't trying to hide anything, *are you,* Kensington?" The Chief's tone mocked him.

"I'm not lying. You got your information wrong. Sounds like you're looking for an easy scapegoat for Carver's death."

The Chief's face flushed. "Watch your mouth, Kensington, or I'll snatch your ass up right now and throw you in jail."

Kensington looked at the three men and sneered. "You and the men in black, here, are out of your minds. Whatever you think you got don't amount to shit. It's all circumstantial, and you know it. And whatever else you're thinking, well... it's pure speculation."

The Chief bellowed, "I got enough probable cause to arrest you right now. And once I get that girl and her diary, I will have enough evidence to lock your sorry ass up and get the DA to file charges. If nothing else, Kensington, you're facing a grand jury indictment."

"Probable cause? Are you dreaming, Chief? You better make it good because I will sue your ass and take your house, your car, your bank account, and your pension."

The Chief spat, "You got motive. Carver knew about your scheme to get Allison to lie, and you killed him to keep him quiet."

Kensington laughed out loud. "Right! Return the diary—the only solid evidence that might link me to your murder scheme—to the girl who wrote it? Two cops were already at her house when I brought it back. Allison could have handed the diary over to them, but you already know that, don't you? You pulled the police contacts for Allison's address, didn't you?"

Kensington rolled his eyes. "I returned the diary to her! What sense does that make if I was guilty of something?" he shouted. "Hell, if I had read the diary and it says what you think it says, I could've destroyed it myself!" Breathing hard, Kensington added, "If nothing else, I would've confronted Allison about what she wrote. I guess that's the 'crazy stuff' that Wally told me about."

"Yeah, Kensington!" the Chief snorted. "Your plan might have worked, but you didn't count on Carver. You didn't count on your plan being discovered. Everything went to shit when he found Allison's diary."

The Chief hunched forward, narrowing his eyes. "Your partner told you, didn't he? He told you that Carver had to go."

"I know the name of this game," Kensington said ruefully. "Rush to judgment!" Close a high profile case as quickly as possible just to quiet the city and keep the politicians off your back."

"We got you in a box, Kensington," the Chief intoned, "and you know it. When we find the Ruddick girl and the diary, I'll slam it shut."

"Right now, Chief, you got a lot of holes in that box, and it's full of hot air." Kensington looked around to meet the feds' hostile looks and the Chief's accusing stare. "I'm innocent. I did nothing wrong! I had nothing to do with Carver's murder. I am a victim of circumstance." Kensington's voice nearly cracked when he said "murder."

He took a deep breath. He had to convince them that the case they thought they had was as flimsy as a dime-store paper lantern. He needed his freedom, just for a short while. He had to be able to get to Quisling. Hopefully, Allison and her mother could evade apprehension for another twenty-four hours.

"Okay, guys! Let's play with the timeline. I leave the school a little past 2 p.m. I take the diary directly to Allison and talk with her, her mother, and the two cops responding to the 911 call. I leave their house around 3:30 or 4:00. I get back on the road until my shift ends at 5. All you have to do is to check my car's GPS to track my whereabouts. I didn't return to the school. I didn't go back to Joiner's house. I don't even know where the Carver kid lives. Then, I went to see my son at the hospital, and I stayed the night."

"In your fluid and chaotic situation, Kensington, didn't you forget something? Did you omit something from your timeline?"

The Chief paused briefly as Kensington furrowed his brow and acted confused. "Courthouse, maybe? Why did you go to the courthouse, Kensington? Your GPS shows you were there a few minutes after five until nearly 8 pm. What were you doing?"

"Oh, that! Yep! Forgot about that. Wasn't important. Just checking on an old case I had worked on as a detective years ago. Heard there was an appeal. So I wanted to review the file."

"It's only a matter of time before we find out who you met with…" The Chief paused, locking eyes with Kensington. "And why." He glanced at his watch. "The courthouse opens in about five minutes. Smitty is on his way there now. As for the hospital—we know you were there. The nursing station confirmed it. You were seen sleeping around the time Carver was lynched."

"I told you I didn't do it."

The lines in the Chief's wrinkled forehead deepened as he studied Kensington. The Chief had seen his share of brutal murders. He'd been at countless crime scenes and examined dead bodies, but the sadistic, mutilated killing of this young Black boy had affected him deeply.

Maybe, it was because a cop was the most likely killer. Maybe, it was because the act was so bestial and primitive. Maybe, it was because this violent desecration of life revealed the thin line between a civilized and primitive society.

The Chief thought, *Carver was not a casualty of war, where unspeakable atrocities are expected. He was a good kid, with hard working parents, from a decent Christian family, who had once saved a cop's life.*

"Maybe you didn't put the rope around that poor kid's neck before dropping him over the rail. Maybe you weren't the one to drive the nails through his hands and feet. Maybe you weren't the one to cut his ear off or beat his face to a pulp, but you could've definitely given the kill order."

Kensington's voice wavered, "No one… no one should ever die like that." Rage and grief flashed across his face. Something within him shifted, like tectonic plates colliding beneath his emotional core, searching for a place to settle. An eerie calmness overcame him. His face was suddenly devoid of emotion. The change was unmistakable.

Barnes and Calvalessi exchanged glances. Barnes was familiar with that look. It was not an easy one to forget. It's that moment when a soldier accepts that a decision he has made might cost him his life. Kensington's expression carried that same resolve—a willingness to die for something, but Barnes didn't know what.

Kensington's voice was flat and even. "I didn't kill him. I couldn't do that. He was the most decent human being I ever met. I had nothing to do with his death." Challenging each man with a defiant stare, Kensington added, "And I don't give a fuck whether you believe me or not."

The ex-military suit shot back, "Where can we find Quisling?"

"I don't know. Check the duty roster," Kensington said.

The Chief snapped, "He was a no-show today, smartass. How do we find him? He disconnected the GPS on his cruiser. A BOLO is out for him and his vehicles."

Kensington snapped back, "Are you kidding me? How would I know how to find him? Check his personnel file. This ain't rocket science, boys."

"We did, Kensington! All we got was a damn PO Box number," the Chief growled. "Quisling made sure that he couldn't be found easily. His banking and credit cards list to his PO Box address. Same with utilities. He used the department's address to register his truck. His last two addresses on file are dead ends. No forwarding addresses. The records division is checking GPS logs to see if he drove his patrol car to an address that might be his home. He must be a renter 'cause we can't find any real estate records."

The Chief narrowed his eyes as he leaned forward. "Don't play fucking games, Kensington. You must have some idea where he lives! You ever been to his house?"

"No!" Kensington lied.

"Where did you guys hang out?" Agent Barnes asked.

"The cop bar down the street. The pizza parlor around the corner from the bar. Denny's. Hamburger joints. Places like that," Kensington responded. "Try tracking him down using his cell phone or his pager."

"We tried that, genius," snapped Barnes. "He's not answering his pager and has apparently disconnected his mobile data terminal from all power sources. He appears to have gone dark late yesterday. Can't contact him if the devices are shut off. Can't triangulate his cell phone location if he disabled his cell."

Kensington shrugged impatiently, "I don't know what to tell you, Agent Barnes."

"The truth would help, Kensington." The Chief said sarcastically. "Even if you didn't have anything to do with Carver's murder, but you know where Quisling lives, you're impeding the apprehension of a wanted suspect. You're complicit in the boy's death. You'd be an accessory after the fact."

"Is that supposed to scare me, Chief?"

The Chief snorted, "Have you met any of Quisling's relatives?"

"No! I think he's from the South. Maybe the Deep South. He's told me stories about some of his relatives, but no names or places."

The Chief sat back in his chair. "Well, Kensington, you've been no fuckin' help. You need to give me your badge and gun," he said dismissively.

Kensington wasn't surprised. This wasn't the first time he'd surrendered his badge and gun to the Chief, but he knew the stakes were much higher now. This time, he didn't give a damn about keeping his job. But if they wanted him for a murder, he would give them one.

Kensington stood up stiffly, removed his badge and waistband clip holster with his Glock, and placed them on the Chief's table. "You're making a big mistake, Chief, but it won't be the first time."

"Get out of my office! Don't leave town! We're not done—not by a long shot! You are to check in with my office each hour on the hour until I tell you to stop calling. You miss one goddamn check-in, and I'm arresting your ass. You clear?"

Kensington was silent. He met the Chief's stare with a grim smile. He had a score to settle. He owed it to Li'l Bits. No need to get into an ego contest with the Chief. Ignoring the contemptuous stare of the agents, he strolled to the door.

Before Kensington could open it, the Chief said, "By the way, I know that you met Quisling at the school less than thirty minutes before you met with Principal March and the Carver boy. He was still there after you left her office. There's a surveillance tape of him pounding your car." The Chief asked mockingly, "Was he upset about something, Kensington?"

Kensington stopped, sighed, and looked over his shoulder at the Chief.

"Quisling remained at the school after you left, didn't he, Kensington. Waiting to see if the kid appeared? Waiting for his victim?"

The Chief pursed his lips, his grin sharpening into something cruel. "How did you describe the kid? 'The most decent human being you ever met'? The Chief's lip curled into an ugly sneer. "You knew exactly what Quisling was like. Rumor has it you befriended Quisling after he killed a Black man. Yesterday, he terrified a busload of morning commuters. He smashed through a neighbor's fence trying to hit Carver. Tore up Joiner's lawn with his car. Did you forget how unhinged he was, pounding on the hood of your cruiser like a madman? That wasn't a cop out there—that was a thug. And you left that boy's fate to someone like him."

His voice was cold and condemning.

Kensington felt the Chief's cheap shot land like a kidney punch. It took every fiber of his being to manage an indifferent shrug before walking out. He tried his best not to slam the door. He was not successful. After the door banged shut, he heard an explosion of angry voices behind him, barking like a pack of frenzied hounds that had treed a fox.

Wheeler was right. The feds want his ass, and the three of them want blood—his blood.

34

Shots Fired

After leaving the Chief's office Kensington headed down to the lobby. His gait was unsteady, and his hand shook. A profound sadness began to grip him. But soon, it would be swallowed by a black hole of rage. Consumed by emotion, he didn't hear the administrative secretary ask if he was okay as she passed him in the hallway.

The horror of what he'd heard in the Chief's office left him with a silent scream in his throat. Fortunately, his police experience conditioned him well as he listened impassively to the horrific details of Li'l Bits' torture and murder. Away from the accusing eyes and accusations of his interrogators, he could barely control himself. He felt like he would be sick again, but now was not the time. He had something to do. He had a debt to pay. Then, he would allow himself to grieve Li'l Bits' death.

He placed his card against the electronic detector and entered the lobby. His only thought was to get to his car to check if his gun and ammo were still in the trunk. As he approached his patrol car, his steps quickened and became more deliberate.

Before opening the car door, he hesitated. Should he go see Wally before the cops did? Suddenly, his mind calmed. He knew what he needed to do—what he wanted to do. There was no need to try to see Wally now. The cat had crawled out of the bag, and Kensington didn't think Lady Luck would put it back. Besides, if he delayed longer, Quisling might be arrested before he could get to him. Maybe, he was already on the run. Pulling out his cell phone, he called Wally.

"Dad. Hey. You at work?" Wally asked groggily.

"Hey, Wally. How's my boy?" Kensington tried to sound as upbeat as possible, but Wally picked up a hint of sadness in his father's voice.

"You okay, Dad? Is everything all right?"

"Have you watched the news today, Wally?" Kensington asked nervously.

"No, Dad. Your call woke me up. Didn't sleep too good last night. I was having some bad dreams."

"Wally, I need to make this quick 'cuz I've got to get on the road. I want you to do everything I ask. Understand?"

Puzzled, Wally asked, "Is this about the diary, Dad?"

Kensington sighed heavily. "If anyone asks about the diary, don't say anything. I need some time. Tomorrow morning, you can tell them the truth. Let them know it was my idea to frame that kid."

"What! I can't do that! I won't do that! You'll get in trouble for sure, Dad!" Wally's voice quaked with fear.

"Wally, don't lie. They already know. It's just a matter of time before they have proof. Just tell them the truth. Tell them it was my idea, please," he pleaded.

Wally was quiet. It sounded like he was starting to cry.

"One more thing, son. Don't watch the news. You'll hear some awful things. I just want you to know I had nothing to do with it."

The phone was silent. It seemed like an eternity before Wally spoke. He asked, "Is this about Quisling?"

"I think so. I don't know for sure, but I'm… I'm gonna find out."

"Be careful, Dad."

Kensington tried to keep his voice as even as he could. "I love you, Wally. Never forget that! I'll call you as soon as I can."

Wally said quietly, "I'll be waiting."

Kensington reluctantly ended the call, then quickly walked to his car and opened the driver's side door. He popped the trunk and moved to the rear of the vehicle. Inside, amid various police gear and equipment, he found the wooden gun case containing his .357 Magnum. Removing his uniform shirt, he donned a covert bulletproof vest and adjusted it for comfort. He then put his shirt back on, leaving it unbuttoned, and untucked. After retrieving the silver-chromed firearm from its velvet-lined case, he closed the trunk firmly.

He slipped into the driver's seat, placed his weapon on top of the case, and began buttoning his shirt. The slight whiff of gun oil brought back fond memories of Wally and him cleaning their handguns after target practice.

He did a perfunctory check of his rear view and side mirrors. Then he reached over to caress the contours of his gun. Kensington chewed softly on his lower lip. His breath was starting to quicken. He looked up to catch his eyes in the rearview mirror.

If eyes were indeed the windows of the soul, Kensington thought, *then something inside him had died.*

Kensington picked up his weapon and whispered, "Hope you've got yourself right with God, Quisling."

Sixty minutes later, Kensington's patrol car bounced through ruts in the dirt road, jostling him from side to side. A strong wind stirred up plumes of dust, partially obscuring his vision. When he stopped the car, the dust gradually settled, momentarily casting Quisling's house in a brown, cloudy veil.

He looked around, but neither Quisling, the truck, nor his patrol car were in sight. *Maybe he's already on the run,* Kensington thought. He grabbed his firearm, checked it again, and placed it inside his belt under his shirt.

Kensington exited the car and quickly stepped away from the weather-beaten path Quisling called a road. The wind still gusted strongly, clouding the air. If Quisling suddenly appeared, he didn't want to be a vulnerable target with dust blowing in his eyes.

His memory drifted back to the moment he sat in Quisling's trailer—eager to persuade him, anxious to lay out his plan to frame Wally's attacker. He had little doubt that Quisling would refuse: convincing Quisling to join a corrupt scheme to destroy a Black youth's life was an irresistible enticement, like dangling raw meat before a rabid animal.

He recalled Quisling's so-called art display—a blatant declaration of his commitment to white supremacy. The print of the dead man hanging on his wall now felt like a weight around Kensington's soul, its horror magnified by the knowledge that Quisling had probably acted out a morbid fantasy.

He wished Quisling had talked him out of it, convinced him the risk wasn't worth it. But deep down, he knew Quisling never would—that was precisely why he'd chosen him. The scheme catered to his irrational hatred of Black people. The moment Kensington decided to fabricate a lie, his life veered onto a path from which there was no return.

The gun's weight against his lower back reminded him that each step forward marked a point of no return. With determination, Kensington willed himself toward Quisling's home, each step feeling heavier than the last.

Killing Quisling now would extinguish any hope of his future as a free man. He stood at a crossroads with no escape: face prison for corruption or face prison for murder. Either path led to imprisonment. In a cruel twist of fate, the only act that might restore a fragment of his self-respect was, paradoxically, murder.

Kensington, sighing heavily, paused to admire the tall, slender trees swaying behind Quisling's house. The clouds had parted, allowing the late morning light to shine through. The branches danced rhythmically in the wind as they whirled, spiraled, and leaped through the emerald-green canopy. Sunlight flickered off the foliage, momentarily calming Kensington's troubled spirit.

Then, out of nowhere, a tiny bright-colored body, no heavier than a coin, with inordinately large eyes, demanded Kensington's attention. It hovered just inches from his face, darting from side to side as if studying him. After a few quickened heartbeats did he recognize the creature: a hummingbird!

Kensington couldn't imagine where it had come from; no nectar-rich flowers grew in this area. Yet, here it was floating, seemingly suspended in midair. He could only marvel at its beauty. Was it beckoning him? Was it here to deliver a message? Kensington stared at it mesmerized, until it flew away.

He felt his spirit lifting. He began to smile. Kensington thought, *Seeking revenge was the same kind of dumb decision that got him here in the first place. Hadn't he learned anything!* Recalling his supernatural experience with Li'l Bits, he knew that he would not want anyone murdered in his name. Li'l Bits sought only justice for his friend. Arresting Quisling to stand trial for his murder would be enough.

A sense of relief settled over him. Unlike Quisling, cold-blooded murder was not something he desired nor wanted on his conscience. A thought sickened him. What if Quisling kept Li'l Bits' ear and put it in a jar as a souvenir? Kensington squeezed his eyes shut. He felt his stomach churn.

Kensington shook his head to dispel the image and was about to contact the Chief when he noticed a slight movement behind a window. Squinting to see more clearly, he saw a flash and heard a report. Before he could fully register what had happened, he felt a sledgehammer-like impact strike his chest. Stumbling backward, he fell hard on one knee, struggling to stay on his feet. As he reached for his weapon, another bullet grazed his throat, and a third struck his shoulder, knocking him back.

Through a haze of searing pain, Kensington heard the creak of Quisling's front door open. He made out the sound of feet stumbling, almost falling down the steps. Muffled footsteps shuffled toward him, and then he heard Quisling's voice.

"Sorry, Kensington! I meant to shoot you in the head." Quisling started to laugh. "My target placement is a bit off. I'm a little drunk."

Kensington struggled to maintain his focus. He saw a small-caliber handgun in Quisling's hand and heard the slosh of liquor in the bottle clutched in the other. Quisling loomed over him, reeking of alcohol, sneering as he watched the life slowly drain from Kensington's eyes. Kensington pressed his hand to his throat. Warm. Wet. Burning. Blood seeped between his fingers with each pulse.

Quisling's words slurred. "I figured you were comin' to get me. I thought you might be upset if I killed that nigger. So I told myself, 'Self', if he's comin' to get you, he's nothing but a race traitor anyway, and he needs to be put down, too.'"

Quisling dropped heavily to his knees by Kensington's head. Using his gun's muzzle, Quisling stroked Kensington's forehead and temple. The barrel was hot, causing Kensington to flinch.

"Ya see, Kensington, you'd be no good to us when the race war starts. You'd be worse than dead weight." Quisling giggled. "No pun intended." He continued, "You'd fight with the mud people, the queers, and the Jews, and I can't have that."

The bottle glugged as Quisling took a swig. He slurred, "I can't have you killing our very fine white people for that vermin scum. Your death was inevitable. You might as well die sooner than later."

Quisling tried to focus on the small trickle of blood oozing from a small round hole in Kensington's shirt, but his eyes were becoming increasingly blurry. "Damn! This shit is really starting to hit me, Kensington. Glad you came when you did. A little bit later, and I would've probably missed hitting you altogether."

Quisling lifted Kensington's shirt slightly to reveal his body armor. He tapped on Kensington's vest, causing Kensington to wince in pain. Quisling said vacantly, "Hmmm. That shot may have broken some ribs. I used a full metal jacket with a tungsten core just in case you wore a vest."

Quisling took another swig and shoved Kensington's head with his gun. "Stay awake, Kensington. I need to tell you something 'bout killing that boy," he shouted. "Hey! Keep your eyes open. Look at me!" Then he slapped Kensington's face—hard.

Kensington strained to open his eyes but felt incredibly tired. Kensington didn't want to die—not like this. He thought about Li'l Bits: he hadn't wanted to die either.

"You want a little drinkie for old times' sake?" Quisling saw the bubbles of blood form at the corner of Kensington's mouth. "Maybe not a good idea. Looks like maybe you got a big, ugly hole in your chest—maybe your lung?" He took a long sip from the bottle.

Quisling looked up at the sky and sighed. "I always loved living here. Felt free out here, away from all the freaks and clowns." Kensington heard the bottle hit the ground and fall over.

Quisling placed his hand gently on Kensington's arm. "There was something really strange about that kid. I mean really, really strange." Quisling hesitated, trying to explain what had unnerved him. "I was doing my best to hurt him, but he never cried. He never asked me to stop. He never begged! He never pleaded with me to spare his life. Not once."

Quisling shook his head, confused and disbelieving. "It's as if he knew he was gonna die and accepted it. Accepted it completely." Shrugging, Quisling asked, "Who the fuck ain't afraid to die?"

Kensington heard Quisling searching the ground for the bottle. He heard him take a sip. "He never cried out—even when I drove the nails into his hands and feet, he never cried out. He just took huge, gulping breaths every time I drove a nail into his flesh, and his body would just shudder and convulse."

A distant edge crept into Quisling's voice as he muddled through his drunken stupor, struggling to make sense of Li'l Bits' behavior.

"I will never forget that look in his eyes, Kensington." A sob caught in his throat. "You've never seen a look like that." Bewildered and confused, Quisling shook his head. "No hate. No fear. Something else. Something unnatural. I can't explain it. It almost felt…." His voice drifted off. "He was supposed to beg me for his life! He was supposed to *beg*!"

Quisling whimpered, "His death was supposed to be magnificent." He blurted out, "How could he look at me that way? Like he knew something that I didn't."

Quisling looked at the sky as if it held the answer to a mystery he couldn't comprehend.

Kensington grimaced as he tried to smile. He understood something Quisling never would.

"Perfect love casts out fear," Elsa would tell Kensington when he felt stressed by life. She would've understood the look in Li'l Bits' eyes. Elsa would have told Quisling that Li'l Bits was being held in the palm of God's hand.

Quisling took another swig. Suddenly, there was anger and outrage in his voice. "You think you fuckin' know me, Kensington! You don't know me! I never knew my father!" The words erupted from him like steam coming from a busted radiator.

Kensington heard him cock the hammer and felt the gun pressed firmly against his temple. Quisling's words were surprisingly clear. "Time for you to go sleepy."

Kensington inhaled sharply and felt pain radiate through him as his ribs shifted in his chest cavity. He squeezed his eyes shut and didn't try to speak, but Quisling managed to read his lips as he mouthed the word, "Elsa."

Kensington held his breath, waiting to die, when he heard the crack of a high-powered rifle and the almost instantaneous sound of bone exploding. Warm liquid and clumps of loose flesh sprayed his face.

He heard the sudden roar of an engine gunning down the road. Within seconds, it slid and skidded in the dirt. Two car doors opened, followed by the thud of feet scrambling.

Someone spoke. The voice was familiar. It was Agent Barnes, the ex-military fed from the Chief's office. Footsteps walked briskly past him. "The perp is dead," the Barnes said. "I'll get help for Kensington."

Checking Kensington's condition, his partner, Cavalessi said, "You can call, but unless there's a hospital around the corner, they won't make it in time." He shrugged. "Flight for Life will be too late but call anyway." He sighed. "The best we can do is make him comfortable." He gently wiped blood and flesh from Kensington's face.

Cavalessi then placed his hand over his neck wound. After unbuttoning Kensington's shirt, he loosened the Velcro straps and quickly pressed down on Kensington's chest to slow the bleeding. Barnes placed a makeshift pillow under Kensington's head and draped a jacket over his shoulders

Kensington wanted to smile in appreciation but couldn't. His life was ebbing away. He struggled to speak, knowing these words might be his last. Blood oozed from his mouth. Gasping, he gurgled, "Tell Wally... "

Cavalessi said gently, "We heard everything, Officer Kensington. We caught Quisling's confession with our laser mic. I placed a tracking device on your car while you showered at HQ. Wish we had arrived before he ambushed you."

Kensington felt a light touch on his shoulder. "We'll tell Wally that his dad helped us take out the bad guy."

Kensington felt a deep sense of peace. He thought about the hummingbird that came to visit him.

That was a magical moment, he thought. *How many people have ever had a visit like that? A winged blessing! A gift of beauty before I died.*

Kensington could barely understand what the agents were saying now. Then, he heard the faint sound of a third voice. He strained to recognize it but couldn't.

The voice was getting increasingly louder, as if the person understood he was slipping away and that it was necessary to lean in closer to whisper in his ear. The chilled darkness was starting to overtake him. He had no more fight left. Standing at the edge of his fading existence, he envisioned death as a shadowed crossing over black water, reserved for corrupt souls—a shrouded ferryman waiting in silence at the threshold of his life. But it wasn't a stranger who stepped across the veil. It was not a man's voice he heard—but a woman's.

The sound was indescribably lovely. It seemed like an eternity since he had heard that voice. It was more wind than sound. It was Elsa, his wife, calling to him.

Elsa whispered, "Take my hand, sweetheart. Time to come home."

35

Over a Barrel

Clayton Marshall slammed several motions on the prosecutor's table in front of Joe Morton, who sat hunched over his pad and pen. Morton knew that Marshall would come to court fully armed with a battery of motions once the news about police corruption broke.

Marshall announced, "There's a motion for a special prosecutor, a motion to dismiss for prosecutorial vindictiveness, a motion to dismiss for outrageous police conduct, a motion for change of venue, and a motion to return the case to juvenile court with accompanying memoranda for each motion." His voice bristled with raw emotion.

Morton didn't flinch. He didn't even bother to look up. He continued to make notes on his yellow legal pad, seemingly oblivious to Marshall fuming behind him. Outwardly, Morton appeared preoccupied with paperwork. Inwardly, he suppressed a visceral urge to spring from his chair and punch Marshall.

After about twenty seconds, Morton carefully laid his pen down, reached forward, and shoved the documents with such force that they flew off the table, landing several feet away. He picked up his pen again and resumed writing.

When Marshall slammed his fist on the table Morton stopped writing and leaned back, studying Marshall's furious scowl. He folded his arms across his chest and asked, "Do I need to call security, counselor, or are you just having a hissy fit?" He snorted. "Either way, I'm not impressed."

Genuinely pleased that Marshall was outraged and struggling to control himself, Morton savored his delicious moment.

"Aren't you jumping the gun a bit, with these motions, Marshall? The court has to decide first whether the case against your client stays in district court or is returned to juvie. We've got a long way to go yet, boss, before he entertains those other motions," Morton said sarcastically.

When Marshall heard the news about Li'l Bits' murder, his body went still. Then he sat on the bed and sobbed. The centuries-old trauma of racial terror crackled within him. Another Black child murdered. Now, Morton's arrogance stirred something violent in him. He wanted to hurt him — physically. The kind of hurt that couldn't be undone. Jetta was wrong — Blood can redeem blood.

No one deserves to die like that, he raged silently.

Marshall backed away to sit on the edge of the bailiff's table, his heart beating furiously. *Breathe,* he told himself. Glaring at Morton, he inhaled deeply, his chest rising as he summoned composure.

"One of your cop buddies murdered my client's friend who found evidence about that bogus sex charge," Marshall yelled, his voice filled with rage. "Your cop mutilated that young boy—strung him up and tossed him over a rail like he was a sack of meat. I wonder when dumb, sick, white bastards like that are going to lay down and die."

"Those are serious allegations about a bogus charge, counselor. You got any facts to back that up?"

Marshall walked toward Morton while reaching inside his jacket. "I've got a few things that might interest the judge." Marshall pulled out a pen. It was the pen Patricia Horn had with her in Tyrene's hospital room when Quisling visited. It was a recording device. Hitting the playback button he held the pen high. Morton recognized Patricia Horn's voice and scowled.

The male voice on the tape said, "We *will* get your son. You can count on that, even if I have to bend the law to do it."

"If that was a cop," Morton observed coolly, "he'd claim that his statement was inappropriate, made in the heat of anger, without any intention of abusing his position as a law enforcement officer." Morton chuckled dismissively.

"You won't be able to get by with glib explanations this time, Morton. The FBI recorded that same cop admitting to murdering Matthew

Carver, Tyrene's friend—right after he ambushed his partner and just before they put a bullet in his head." Marshall clenched his fist.

"Nasty story, Marshall, I give you that. But I don't see how it has anything to do with the prosecution of this case."

"Why are you trying to play dumb, Morton? Doug Joiner provided copies of Allison Ruddick's diary and a thumb drive to a district attorney, from a neighboring county, who attempted to deliver the evidence to *your* office, but you refused to meet with him."

Marshall clenched both fists now. "The girl mentioned two cops, Quisling and the vic's dad, Kensington, who pressured her into lying about Tyrene Horn sexually assaulting her."

Marshall took slow, deliberate steps and stopped in front of Morton. Leaning forward, he planted his palms flat on the table. This time, Morton stiffened and leaned back. Marshall's face was less than a foot from Morton's.

Marshall's nostrils flared. His voice, a low growl. "When your secretary stone-walled the DA, Joiner immediately contacted the Chief of Police and the FBI. He identified the two police officers who had kidnapped Carver and warned that they might kill him because he possessed incriminating evidence of a criminal conspiracy."

Marshall straightened up. "The FBI remained noncommittal until the lynching was broadcast on national TV. Now the case is being jointly investigated as a hate crime by the Civil Rights Division's Criminal Section of the US Department of Justice and your local sheriff's department." Pausing, Marshall smiled, "One of the feds assigned to the case blew Quisling's head off."

Morton shrugged. "I don't know what you're talking about. I wasn't aware that a DA from another county was trying to contact me. He damn sure didn't leave anything with my secretary."

"I never expected you to admit it, but it doesn't matter."

Morton smirked. "You think you got me backed into a corner, don't you, Marshall? You think that your theory of corrupt cops has crippled my case—will get it dismissed and get your client off—but you forgot something. You forgot which judge you are in front of. He's worst than Judge Davidson. That so-called evidence of corrupt cops will never see the light of day."

Morton shook his head. "Dead cops! One killed by the FBI! The other killed by his own partner! The judge will rule that it's irrelevant to this case and overly prejudicial to the People. The jury will never hear it." Morton's voice reached a crescendo. "That evidence will be ruled inadmissible."

Morton paused, stabbing his finger at Marshall. "Besides, I still have the assault charge, and I have plenty of Wally Kensington's friends to say that Horn started the fight." Morton smiled. "Horn is going down for that attack. And if I'm at my oratorical best, the jury will also convict him of assault with a deadly weapon—his teeth—given the unusual nature of the injury. Kensington could have bled to death if the paramedics hadn't responded so quickly." Morton's feigned attempt to appear empathetic nauseated Marshall.

"You're a despicable bastard, Morton! You've got a hard-on for my client because you still want to believe that I screwed your wife twenty years ago. You're using my client to get at me." Marshall shook his head in disgust. "If this incident had involved two white kids, you'd be sending them both to juvenile diversion with sandwiches and Starbucks Frappuccinos."

Morton shrugged. He was enjoying Marshall's outraged frustration. "Yeah! You got me. I'm a card-carrying bigot with a license to prosecute anybody I choose."

The doors to the courtroom opened. Morton and Marshall both turned and heard a soft "Ahem!" They stared blankly at the intruders. A division clerk meekly entered through the courtroom's double doors, accompanied by a wide-eyed courier. The courier had a large brown envelope in his hand and looked nervously from Morton to Marshall.

The clerk walked to the well of the courtroom, speaking as he approached them. The mail courier stayed tight on his heels, nerves visible in every step.

"Folks on the morning docket are starting to line up out there." His voice echoed concern. "You gentlemen have less than ten minutes to wrap up. Turning toward the courier, who looked anxious to leave, the clerk announced, "He has a package for DA Morton and insists on delivering it to him personally."

With raised eyebrows, the clerk asked, "Did a wind gust blow those papers on the floor?"

"Sorry! I got it," Marshall said. He quickly gathered his motions and placed them on the defense table.

Flustered and hurried, the courier gestured to Marshall, "Is he Joe Morton? It's very important to deliver this package to the right person!" The courier looked behind him like he was being watched.

Swallowing hard, the courier explained, "An incredibly *ginormous* Black guy told me" the courier's voice cracked, "He told me, 'Make sure you get this to Joe Morton and nobody else.' He refused to give me a physical description. He said someone in the courtroom could identify him. "The guy was Black, so I figured that the envelope was for, uhm, a Black man."

Morton swung around in his seat to face the gangly young courier. "I'm Morton," he said, extending his arm for the envelope.

The courier looked like he had been rescued from certain death. "Thank God! Delivery confirmed." With that pronouncement, the courier hurried out of the courtroom banging the doors open.

The clerk yelled at the fleeing man to slow down. Grumbling complaints and curses immediately filled the hallway as he threw the doors open to exit.

Shaking his head in disapproval, the clerk returned to his desk to review the docket sheet.

"Think there's some kind of toxic material inside?" Morton asked Marshall jokingly while inspecting the envelope. He tested its weight in one hand and examined it with the other.

My name is on it, but there's no address! Not even identifying labels.

Morton held the package in his hand loosely, turning it over and around several times to examine it. Something inside shifted.

His stomach flipped.

"Get him! Get that courier. Stop him now!" Morton yelled.

The clerk sighed, dropping his head. "Mr. Morton, c'mon," he groaned, stretching out the words for emphasis. "I don't have time to chase people down this morning. I can call the deputies downstairs to try to catch him before he leaves the building, but my plate is full today."

An amused expression flashed across Marshall's face as he quietly took a seat at the defendant's table.

"Try to catch him at the elevator!" Morton screamed. "Call the deputies, if you miss him!"

The clerk frowned, and reluctantly started to drag himself out of the courtroom. He suddenly stopped to answer his phone.

Morton screamed, "*GET A MOVE ON!*"

The clerk shot Morton an irritated look and quickened his steps to the doors. He opened the door wide and announced the division would not be open for another twenty minutes.

Marshall asked, "Should I lock the door, Morton, so we won't get interrupted again?"

Morton ignored him. He was preoccupied with the mysterious brown envelope. Morton's infuriating arrogance was gone—along with the cocky self-confidence and smug superiority that came with it.

Marshall watched him intently, barely able to suppress a grin. *My turn, Morton. Let's see how much you like your surprise.*

Morton stared wildly at the package. He felt paralyzed. He looked over at Marshall, sitting relaxed with his legs crossed. His expression was as placid as still water. Marshall's agitation lessened as Morton's anxiety grew.

Marshall gestured to the envelope. "Aren't you going to open it, Morton? It could be a love letter from someone you prosecuted."

Morton leveled his gaze at Marshall. His words were low. His voice trembled. "You know what this is, don't you Marshall? Don't act fuckin' clueless!"

Straining hard to maintain his composure, he inhaled deeply. He pushed his chair back from the table. Morton announced, with false bravado, "Hell! Let's see what's inside."

The sound of ripping paper felt like a part of him was being torn away, as if his innermost secrets were being exposed for all to see. He feared he'd be left naked before the world.

Morton peered cautiously into the package, clinging to a vague, distant hope. Then he gasped. His instincts about that night were right—Jetta had set him up! These salacious photos would shred his whole life piecemeal.

Taking great pains to shield them from Marshall, Morton carefully pulled several photos from the package. His mouth went dry as he tried to swallow. There was no doubt. No mistake. That body was his. Although the woman's face was not visible, he'd recognize that exquisitely shaped Black body anywhere.

Morton wondered, *Where can you run when there's nowhere to run? Where can you hide when pressing a computer key can expose your shame to the entire world? What can you do when there's absolutely nothing you can do?*

Death by a thousand cuts would have been preferred to this.

Morton looked up at Marshall. "You did this, you Black son of a bitch! You set me up!"

Morton snarled. Something ugly moved across his face. He threw his chair back — it crashed to the floor. He lunged at Marshall. Marshall's hands shot up. "Whoa, Mr. Prosecutor. Whoa." Marshall said, a lilt in his voice. "Slow the devil down." Morton froze. Eyes wild. Chest heaving. Slowly. Very slowly, he straightened up. A whimper escaped.

"There's a way out of this, Morton," Marshall said calmly. "You can salvage your life, your career, and your reputation." He paused, "Or you can roll the dice. It's up to you." Marshall met the fury in Morton's eyes with serene detachment.

"You Black bastard. I could kill you for this."

Marshall heard the hallway door to the courtroom open and looked over to see a female clerk enter. She said, "I heard yelling." Stunned at seeing Morton's furious expression, she stopped talking immediately. She looked over at the Black man sitting still at the defendant's table and asked, in a hushed voice, "Do I need to call a deputy, Mr. Morton?"

Morton didn't respond at first. He needed a moment for the blood to stop pounding in his ears. Taking several deep breaths, he finally answered, his voice quaking, "Can you let us use a room back there? Maybe a jury room so we can talk?"

"No one is allowed in the hallway now, Mr. Morton, since admin implemented those new security measures. Only authorized personnel are allowed."

Morton sighed and inhaled deeply. "Fifteen minutes, please—just fifteen minutes. That's all I need." Marshall nodded his agreement to the clerk. The clerk was suspicious of this Black stranger, but he was wearing an expensive-looking suit. She thought, *Drug dealer.*

Sensing the clerk's apprehension, Morton added, "He's not a defendant, ma'am. Believe it or not, he's an attorney."

Marshall arched an eyebrow and smiled. *I should wear an attorney placard with my bar number on it.*

The forlorn look in Morton's eyes persuaded the clerk to accede to his request. Shrugging, she said, "I shouldn't do this, but you are an officer of the court. Follow me."

Placing her badge against the sensor, the clerk pushed the door open. Morton quickly grabbed the envelope from the table.

Morton and Marshall dutifully followed the clerk out of the courtroom, into the hall, to a door with a sign that read 'jury room'. Using her key, she unlocked the door.

"Fifteen minutes," she said firmly.

Morton walked into a room that could barely accommodate twelve people. A long rectangular conference table made of hard oak occupied the middle of the floor. The chairs were evenly spaced around the table.

Although warm sunlight flooded the room, Morton felt an unexplainable chill. He walked to the far side of the table and placed the envelope down.

"Talk," Morton demanded as Marshall sat down.

"Two cops are dead. An innocent boy has been murdered. My client has been locked up far too long. He'll carry the guilt of his friend's death for the rest of his life."

Marshall stopped, letting the words sink in. He eyed Morton, trying to read his reaction. He spoke quietly. "There's been enough pain, Morton. Too much death. We're officers of the court. Prosecutors have a higher ethical duty to seek justice. Can't we try to work out a little justice in this case? No one wins here."

Morton snapped, "Why don't you just fucking say it, Marshall! You want a deal! With these photos, you want the deal of the century. I know you! If you get the deal you want, you win! You beat me!"

Marshall sat back in his chair and stared hard at Morton. "Didn't Carver's death mean anything to you, Morton? How he died and why he died? He was just an innocent kid trying to help his friend."

Marshall sighed and shook his head. "Every time a Black person is murdered because of hate, a part of me dies. The pain is so intense that I feel like I want to destroy something—mindless, apocalyptic destruction. When I think about the suffering my people have endured," his voice trailed off.

Marshall had to summon all his willpower to remain calm. Grief was about to overtake him. He said, "But then you hear about a kid like Matthew Carver, whose spirit tugs at your soul and whispers to something deep inside you—to do good, to be kind." Unconsciously, he placed his hand on his chest. "His life urges me to keep hope in my heart, to try to make a difference."

Morton scoffed, his words laced with derision. "I truly don't care about you or your people's pain. This world is full of pain. We all live with some kind of pain. Black people don't have a monopoly on suffering."

Marshall cursed himself. He knew better. Letting Morton see his pain— casting pearls before swine.

"What do you want for the photos, Marshall?" Morton asked sharply. "I assume that if I give you the deal you want, the copies and originals will be destroyed."

"To be clear, Mr. Prosecutor. I'm only asking for a fair deal under the circumstances," he said dryly.

'Which is...?" Morton asked flatly, one eyebrow arched high.

"Allow Tyrene Horn to plead no contest to fighting in public with unsupervised deferred prosecution for three months, dismissal upon good behavior, and completion of an anger management class. I think that's more than fair, Morton. If you do that, you have my word that those photos—I mean all the photos, originals, and copies—will be destroyed."

Marshall's declaration that the photos would be destroyed made Morton laugh. But what other option did he have? He couldn't think of one that would keep his life unscathed. He had no doubt that if the photos went viral and hit the press, the public would crucify him. Forget career. Forget marriage. Forget forgiveness. Reluctantly, Morton thought, *It's time to be practical. Time to be realistic. Time to be smart. I need to deal this case.*

Morton countered, "Twelve months with an unsupervised deferral, the anger management course, seventy-five hours of community services, and a letter of apology."

Marshall didn't blink, knowing Morton would play hardball. "Nope," Marshall huffed. "When hell freezes over… definitely no letter of apology." He cocked his head. "You know you've got no hand to play here, Morton. You do understand I'm just indulging you. I'd hoped you'd be arrogant enough to push the envelope so I can tell my client and his mom that we can't reach an agreement."

Morton's eyes narrowed. "You want to destroy me, don't you, Marshall?"

Marshall smiled, "Yep! I do, but I want to leave that choice in your slimy hands."

Morton's tone was matter-of-fact. "If any of these photos ever appear in social media or anywhere else, you know I'll kill you."

Marshall reassured him, "Do the deal, and you have nothing to worry about from me." Marshall shrugged. "If you want this thing to go away, Morton—and I mean, *really* go away, like disappear completely," pointing to the envelope, "The deal must guarantee a clean record. His mother won't accept anything less. 'The system will not stigmatize my son,' she said."

"So," Morton declared crisply, "if I don't go along with this proposal, those photos hit the media?"

"Twitter, TikTok, Facebook, Instagram, national and local print media, cable news, wire services, to name a few," Marshall replied casually.

Morton laughed derisively. "Why don't you tell me to dump the whole damn case, or else you'll fuck me like Jetta did! You know that you have the leverage to make me do it."

Marshall was thoughtful for a moment. "If I took advantage of you that way, Morton, then I really would become the bad guy. That's not my style. Besides, given the stories I've heard about Matthew Carver, he wouldn't want your life ruined, as sorry and worthless as it is."

Marshall paused. "I spoke to Mr. and Mrs Carver about their son. One thing that impressed me about him was his deep sense of mercy and compassion. I feel compelled to honor what he stood for." Marshall smiled grimly. "But if it were entirely up to me, all the prayers in the world wouldn't save your sorry white ass."

Marshall admitted, "I hate going outside the law to make you do what's right, but I've learned from experience that those within the system are too often compromised by personal ambition, social prejudice, political expediency, racial bias, and public pressure. You know this to be true." Marshall shrugged. "Besides....justice doesn't happen on its own. Sometimes, it needs a little help."

Morton's wounded pride caused him to delay announcing a decision he already knew he would have to make—that he must make. The media frenzy around those photos would be unimaginable. It would be a shit-storm. Reporters would torment family members, friends, and colleagues about his character. He couldn't tolerate that burning embarrassment and shame. He wouldn't want to inflict that kind of unwarranted punishment on his wife.

Marshall looked at his watch. "That clerk will be here soon to kick us out. I need an answer before I leave this room." He paused. "And I changed my mind about the deal. You took too long to accept. Forget the anger management class and the public service hours! My deal or nothing." He stood slowly, narrowing his eyes. "You gonna accept it or not?"

Morton turned his back to Marshall and stared out the window.

Marshall turned to exit the room. He placed his hand on the doorknob and looked back at Morton, who stood stiff and motionless with hunched shoulders. "You might want to let your wife know what's coming because I'm gonna light your ass up."

Morton spun around quickly to face Marshall. "Wait a minute, goddammit," he said breathlessly. "Let's set the case over for tomorrow. I can get the paperwork ready by then."

"Hell, no! Tomorrow is not an option!" Marshall barked, turning fully to face him. "My client is grieving the death of his friend. Put the paperwork together this morning, and I'll take it to the jail for Horn and his mom to approve. Let's just tell the judge that I'll waive my client's appearance and enter a plea for him. The judge will permit that procedure with a deferred prosecution misdemeanor offer. We can conclude the deal before the morning docket ends today. I'm sure that the judge has seen the news broadcast of that lynching. When he finds out that it was my client's friend who was murdered by the cop assigned to the case, I'm confident that, with your recommendation, the deal will go through."

Morton ran his fingers through his hair. "I prefer you leave out that part about the boy's death unless"—he paused—"unless the judge decides to reject it."

Marshall said, "I'm okay with that. But let's be clear, Morton! We need to do this today so that my client gets released."

"Is that release part of the deal, now, too? Do it today, or else?"

"Yep," replied Marshall indifferently. "By the way, contact the victim's advocate to obtain verbal approval of the deal from Wally Kensington. Pretty sure he won't care. And before I forget," Marshall added, "restitution for your vic's injuries is off the table. That condition is also part of the deal."

Morton was about to bluster when Marshall stopped him short. "Kensington was the initial aggressor. There was no provocation by Horn. Kensington hit and kicked him repeatedly while Horn was on the ground. Horn acted in self- defense against a bully. No jury would convict him."

"What! The court won't accept that," Morton protested.

"Yeah! The judge will, particularly if you stipulate. I've got footage from the school that shows your vic attacking my client relentlessly for nearly 9 1/2 minutes. That's about the same amount of time that Derrick Chauvin knelt on George Floyd's neck. The Court will have no reasonable doubt that my client acted legally in self-defense after he sees that tape."

Marshall smiled. "Think about it as a penalty for Kensington, like the cost for perpetuating a fraud on the court." He opened the door leading into the court's hallway. "Let's wrap this up quick, Morton."

Morton dropped his head and shrugged, fully recognizing that he could not negotiate, bargain, or argue. He groaned inwardly, *Blackmail. Oldest game in town.* He quipped, "What's the fuckin' rush, Counsel? Got a date with Jetta?"

Marshall didn't try to to conceal his contempt. He said coolly, "My client needs to get ready for a funeral."

Before closing the door, Marshall turned to lock eyes with Morton. "By the way, counselor, just so you know—the beauty of my people is defined by the power of their spirit and the brilliance of their resilience, not by their hardship and pain. Don't mistake suffering with weakness. Our suffering has only made us stronger."

Winking, he said, "Enjoy the photos."

36

A Terrible Legacy

Pine needles and night dew scented the cool, misty air. A hint of twilight appeared in the coal-black sky. A milky thread of light, almost invisible to the naked eye, softly emerged. Soon, it would rouse the world from its deep slumber and, with each stitch of muted light, a gradual awakening would occur. In a matter of minutes, the crossbeams would become fully visible. And, in an hour or so, the three towering crosses atop the distant mound of Mt. Calvary would be awash in sunrise hues of red and gold.

A large crowd of people had already arrived at the amphitheater. Many more would soon be coming. They would wait patiently in the still darkness until the morning light dispelled it, signaling the beginning of the memorial service.

The mood of those present was unquestionably somber, which couldn't be explained simply by the early morning hour. It wasn't just the occasion that dampened their spirit. The prevailing mood stemmed from an uncertain, uncomfortable feeling that something unnatural had happened with the murder of Matthew Michael Carver.

Not only had their lives been profoundly affected, but a dreadful fear had seeped into their collective consciousness, breeding a necrosis of despair. They realized that the America they thought they knew, imagined, hoped for, and strived to build was nothing more than a myth. America was far from the inclusive "Shining City on the Hill" that Ronald Reagan had envisioned. In truth, Reagan's America was as imaginary as King Arthur's legendary Camelot.

This brutal murder had stirred many from a dream-like slumber and resurrected the terrible legacy of lynching that America had sought to ignore, if not erase, from its collective national memory. The permeating chill in the sentient night air had become an all-embracing chill in their hearts.

Someone lit a candle. An audible sound of relief greeted the tiny flame from those nearby. Another candle was lit, followed by another and then another, until a sea of human shadows was transformed into small pockets of brilliant white light floating aimlessly, like luminous paper lanterns on water, paying homage to the dead.

An outdoor memorial service at sunrise was somewhat unusual for Mt. Calvary, but Li'l Bits once told his parents that he wanted to see the glory of God's presence blazing across the heavens when he died. His mother had remembered the three crosses at this cemetery that Li'l Bits said spoke to every living soul—the cross of Jesus that granted eternal salvation, the cross of a sinner who repented, and the cross of an unrepentant sinner. She knew he would be pleased with this choice for his service.

His parents never imagined that they would outlive their son or that he would be taken away from them in such an unspeakable manner. His mother cried out, "Only the devil himself could have murdered our boy in such an obscene way."

Ruth Carver was too wounded and grief-stricken to hear the words that her husband would save later to speak.

In time, he would tell his wife, "Was not the manner of Jesus's death obscene? Did Jesus's death not bring glory to God?" Then, putting his arms around her, he would say, "No matter how hard, difficult, or painful this is for us, we cannot fathom or understand God's way. We can only have faith in His divine will."

With his forehead pressed tenderly against hers, he would whisper, "God can send light into the darkest places. We must cling to our faith."

Li'l Bits, when stirred by the Spirit, had preached about Jesus's willingness to sacrifice himself to free everyone from sin. He also spoke of the deep, abiding, and perfect love that Jesus shared and lived unconditionally.

"Love thy neighbor as thyself," Li'l Bits would often say. And he did his best to embrace the fruits of the Spirit expressed in Galatians 5:22-23, which is why his entire community—church congregation, neighbors, relatives, friends, and high school students—was expected at his memorial.

A local media personality predicted several thousand mourners would attend, hoping to understand why members of American society continue to be so twisted and perverse. Some, confused and bewildered, would be present to seek a form of catharsis from a soul-wrenching experience. However, the majority would be present to bear witness to the brief life of a very special person.

As the morning dawned, a procession of funeral cars slowly passed the meandering crowds. Pedestrian traffic lanes were clearly marked with stanchions and rope, carefully monitored by a team of ushers in formal attire.

The men wore black suits, white shirts, and solid black ties. The women wore starched white dresses, stockings, small caps, and gloves. Any person attempting to gain entrance to a non-designated route would be firmly, but politely, redirected to a predetermined route.

The route guided them away from the rear of the stage, directing them toward the front and outlying areas. Here, a crowd of people stood, stretching back to the sloping grounds that led up to the three crosses—which loomed silently, overlooking the unfolding human drama.

Approximately twenty feet in front of the stage, a troop of male guards would maintain a protective buffer between The Carver family and close friends and the crowd. They, too, were dressed in formal attire. The men stood at arm's length from a wall of restless people waiting for the service to begin. Although the mourners were mainly silent and subdued, occasional deep, shuddering sighs broke the stillness.

The last limousine to arrive attracted more attention than others. On each side of the car was a phalanx of men walking in tandem as the car inched along. When the car stopped, no one approached it. As the driver's door opened, the security team stood immediately to attention.

If Carl's exit from the car was filmed in slow motion, it might seem to an onlooker that the towering man needed a full thirty seconds to stand up straight. Though in truth, he moved with the grace of a panther, rising instantly to survey his surroundings.

Feeling his phone vibrate, he pulled it from his pocket and answered, "Yes, ma'am. We're here." He continued to look around as he spoke. "You were right. She complained just like you said she would. Said we were overdoing it with all this security." He paused for a moment listening to the voice on the other end. "What did I tell her in response?" he asked. "I underscored the fact that a memorial service is an extremely vulnerable, but predictable target."

Carl continued, "She had a hard time buying the idea that someone would attempt to shoot her or Tyrene at a memorial service. I think she forgot about the nine Black worshippers murdered while praying in the South Carolina church and the ten Black victims gunned down at a Buffalo Supermarket. She finally understood that the best time for an assassination is when everyone's guard is down, and the unimaginable is not contemplated. When I explained that a white supremacist sympathizer or cop friend of Quisling might try to avenge his sorry ass, it finally clicked. She said, "So kill the kid who got him killed?"

He walked to the rear passenger door and stopped before opening it. "Tell her what?" he asked. "Really?" he replied with a surprised smile, cocking his head. "That was quick work." He paused, listening intently. "So you decided not to kill her ex," he said.

He nodded approvingly and added, "I think you're right about that. Better for Ms. Horn to have a little blood on her hands than someone's life, even though that bastard deserves to die." Listening quietly again, he responded, "That's true!" He shrugged. "She can always kill him herself later if she wants to."

Carl chuckled, "So that's what the buffalo nickel was all about. A little help from the Spirit world, huh?" He reached for the door handle and asked, "You want to talk to her?" Then he nodded knowingly. "She won't like it, but I'll tell her you'll be in touch soon."

He paused again. "Okay. Safe trip! Let me know when and where I can reach you." He nodded several more times, digesting her instructions. "Don't worry. I'll let her know." He closed softly with, "Be safe, Boss!"

Carl didn't like leaving TicToc without his personal protection, but he knew how much she cared for Ms. Horn and her son. He would die for them as easily as he would die for her.

But death will not claim a victim today, he thought. *Not if I can help it.*

Carl had meticulously planned for their safety. Limousine drivers and their passengers had been screened and cleared by Protective Support. Carl had personally scouted the area multiple times with his team, checking for explosives and identifying vulnerable surveillance points. His men would be strategically placed in and around the large crowd, using real-time 3D facial recognition scanners to identify domestic terrorists. The team had activated a surveillance drone to monitor the entire area. Any suspicious behavior would be captured via aerial camera, triggering a 'red alert.' TicToc wanted assurance that her friend and son could attend Li'l Bits' service with minimal risk.

The one threat TicToc feared most was a trained elite sniper, like herself, who could make a headshot from over a mile away. Fortunately, the terrain surrounding the amphitheater didn't permit adequate concealment or camouflage for a sniper hide, and no buildings within range provided good visibility.

Before selecting a site, Carl asked Reverend Davis to provide a list of five locations that could accommodate a large crowd. They quickly eliminated three church sites within city limits: too much activity; too much exposure; and not large enough for the anticipated crowd. After personally scouting the remaining two sites, outside the city, Carl chose an open amphitheater after consulting with TicToc and obtaining approval from the Carver family.

Besides having limited road access, it was a simple open-air amphitheater design with a stage facing a grassy area shaped like a baseball diamond. About twenty feet from the top of the diamond's semi-circular arc were one hundred stone steps built into a hill that climbed at a thirty-degree slope. The hill rose about 75 feet above the surrounding area. At the top, asphalt pavement had been laid where hikers could rest on gray stone benches. An elevated artificial dirt mound stood in front of the benches, where three crosses had been erected. The central cross, dedicated to Jesus, stood 15 feet high, while the other two measured 12 feet each.

Carl carefully opened the car door, and Patricia spryly bounded out of her seat. Although a tall woman, her head barely reached Carl's chest.

"Step back a bit, Carl. I'll break my neck if I want to look you in the face," she said in jest. Carl smiled at her attempt to be lighthearted, but he could see sadness in her eyes.

"I still find it hard to accept that you and TicToc believe that we might be in danger at a celebration of life service. People get unhinged, but not that unhinged."

Carl laughed. "You still upset about needing to change your outfit?"

"Well, yes!" she said plaintively. "I had purchased a perfectly nice boat-necked long-sleeve black dress, and then TicToc tells me that the dress won't work with a bulletproof vest."

Laughing, Carl said, "Well! You have got to admit that it would be hard to conceal a vest under that dress.

"Besides," he added placatingly, "the black suit jacket and the matching pants look great on you. You can't even tell that you are wearing one."

She shrugged. "Well, I could see by the look in my son's eyes that he wanted me to wear it, and he seemed okay with wearing one himself. “So," her voice drifted off, "I guess, like TicToc said, 'Better safe than sorry.'"

Carl leaned down to whisper into her ear. She could smell the fresh scent of soap on his skin. "Not a lot of questions right now, Ms. Horn," he said quickly, "but TicToc wanted me to let you know she has taken care of Duke's concern."

She began to stammer, repeating, “Is he...?” several times, but her voice trailed off. She couldn't bring herself to say the word.

Carl held her gaze, demanding her full attention. “He's not dead. He's alive.” Carl thought, *After what they did to her ex, he might have wished they had killed him.*

Patricia gasped—sharp and shuddering. Carl couldn't tell whether it was relief, disbelief, or something else entirely. Maybe this wasn't the best time to tell her. Carl reminded himself that she was still not entirely comfortable with the nature of their work.

"TicToc was afraid you wouldn't be able to live with yourself if you had a death on your conscience. So she made sure he'd never get the chance to hurt another kid."

Patricia frowned, uncertain of his meaning.

Carl said softly, "A frozen FedEx package will arrive a few days after you get to Canada. Make sure Tyrene doesn't open it."

Uncertainty flickered across Patricia's face—then Carl's message suddenly registered. She nodded with grim approval. "No more fathering new victims. No more molesting anyone ever again."

A Bible verse came to mind. She recited it to Carl, "If anyone causes a child to stumble, it would be better for them to have a millstone hung around their neck and be drowned in the depths of the sea."

Carl, mildly amused, remarked, "A clean slash beneath his trachea is a lot simpler than cutting off his jewels or drowning him. But TicToc figured this way, you'd have time to think about whether you really want to take that final step."

Patricia replied with a wry smile, "I'm good with this for now. I imagine he'll be limping for a while." She chuckled at the thought.

"By the way," Carl said, "The buffalo coin was more than a message to get your attention, Ms. Horn."

"What? What else did the coin mean?" Patricia asked.

Carl took her arm as they walked past the security officers standing watch on the side of the car. He could feel her eyes searching his face. Rounding the back, they reached the rear passenger door.

Before opening it, Carl leaned down to Patricia and whispered again, his voice light and slightly amused, "The buffalo coin wasn't just a way to get your attention, Ms. Horn. It was also Duke's way of telling you where to find his father." Carl's eyes twinkled as he spoke, "We found him in Buffalo, New York, working as a sanitation worker."

Patricia jerked her head back in stunned disbelief and then she gave a slight chuckle. "Thanks, Carl!" she said. She looked up toward the sky. "Thank you, Duke."

She clasped both hands together, close to her face in prayer, and closed her eyes. She murmured, "My dear, sweet boy." With eyes tightly shut, she released a long, shuddering sigh. Carl watched as she took a deep breath, relaxed her shoulders, and opened her eyes.

Carl sensed a sudden, fragile vulnerability in her. The sadness had returned to her eyes, and now it echoed in her voice. "This is going to be a hard day," she said quietly.

Carl opened the rear passenger door and stepped back politely. Tyrene sat motionless. Though the tinted windows filtered most of the morning light, she could still see his face—pale, damp, and expressionless. His eyes, glassy with tears, stared vacantly at the back of the headrest in front of him.

Patricia reached down gently to touch his arm. Emotion threatened to overtake her. She cleared her throat several times before trying to speak, but despite her best efforts, her voice still broke.

She whispered softly, "Time to say goodbye, son."

As Tyrene stepped out of the car the dawning light revealed to everyone within view that more time was needed for Tyrene to heal. His deep purple bruises had faded to yellow and orange. A tiny blood blister on his lip stubbornly lingered.

Tyrene, however, refused to feel anger about the beating. Wally was now an orphan after his father had been killed in a deadly ambush.

Thanks to TicToc and his lawyer, he'd been released from county with a clean record after the court dismissed his case.

After conferring with Paxton, his seasoned investigator, Morton decided to drop the entire case—an act of self-preservation to ensure the damning sex photos never came to light.

Paxton said, "Sure, the case has gotten a lot of press—but not because you're going after a celebrity defendant. You know that. It's because of a horrific murder committed by a racist cop. Not exactly the kind of case you want your name tied to."

Morton hesitated, but Paxton pressed. "And with those photos of your bare ass floating around, you don't have a pot to piss in or a window to throw it out of. For your own peace of mind—just dump it."

Morton informed the reassigned judge that Officer Kensington had been killed while attempting to arrest a fellow officer who had murdered the defendant's friend. Morton also informed the court that Wally, as his father's sole beneficiary, would receive fallen officer benefits from multiple governmental programs, which would provide financial support for most of his adult life.

Marshall emphasized that Quisling, the officer responsible for both murders—Wally's father and Tyrene's friend—was also the lead investigator on his client's case. However, he deliberately withheld the fact that the police chief had cautioned him about pursuing allegations of corruption within his department. With both Kensington and Quisling dead, the Chief deemed the issue of police corruption irrelevant.

"Leave it to reporters to muckrake and sell their newspapers." Chief Jackson advised Marshall. "You stay out of it! Whatever they pay you won't be worth what I will put you through. I can make your life a living hell." He paused. "Find another hill to die on."

Marshall rolled his eyes and scoffed. Had the Carver family been inclined, he was more than ready to file a §1983 action and sue everyone including the governor of the state.

No longer confined to the adult jail, Tyrene now sat safely beside his mother on the dais. Li'l Bits had been laid to rest days earlier in a private ceremony. This moment was bittersweet.

Tyrene sensed someone watching him. He turned and spotted a man with a cane at the end of a row, leaning forward to offer a smile. It was a smile steeped in pain—one that never reached his eyes. Tyrene thought he recognized him — the man who had sat beside Li'l Bits at his first court appearance. Tyrene lifted his chin in response.

Next to him sat a striking woman Tyrene assumed to be his wife. She turned slightly and gave him a faint smile. She sat perfectly rigid. Tyrene thought of Grandma Emma's crystal glass teetering on the edge of a table.

She looks like how I feel, Tyrene thought.

He offered a polite nod, then quietly turned away.

Tyrene understood all too well the hollow emptiness the Carver family was about to face. The approaching trio of holidays would only magnify the ache left by Li'l Bits' absence.

He remembered his first Halloween, Thanksgiving, and Christmas without his brother. Then came Duke's birthday—and, hardest of all, the painful effort to transform the anniversary of his death from a day of mourning into one of remembrance. Those were hard days.

His mother reminded him that Mr. and Mrs. Carver would be seated on the dais in the front. His mother would seek them out after the memorial service, just as she had after the funeral. The guilt that Tyrene felt when he hugged the Carvers was crushing. But for him, their son would still be alive. He hoped they would someday forgive him.

How had this happened? Tyrene silently lamented.

It was just a stupid school fight. He let his memory drift back to the moment right before he lunged at Wally and bit him. Why hadn't he just taken Wally's final kick? Why hadn't he just let it go? Then, he remembered Duke's voice and the comforting touch of his strong hand on his shoulder.

It's time to put an end to this bad boy's stupid act, echoed in his mind.

Had he known three people would die—if he had known his childhood friend would be murdered because of what he did to Wally that day—he would have told Duke, "It's okay, Big Brother. I can take it. Remember, I'm your Little Man Dude."

Tyrene struggled to hold back the burning tears welling in his eyes again. His mom caught his pain and gently reached over to squeeze his hand. "It's not your fault," she said firmly.

After his release from jail, his mother had told him about Li'l Bits' death. In a hoarse, ragged whisper, she'd gently repeated what Clayton Marshall had told her.

Marshall's account differed sharply from the version the prosecutor presented to the judge. In Morton's telling, Kensington was cast as a hero; in Marshall's, he was a remorseful criminal seeking redemption.

His mother knew Wally's father was no hero. To her, he was no more than a street thug hiding behind a badge. He had betrayed his solemn oath, and his reckless, unlawful scheme had led to their friend's brutal death.

Still, Tyrene said nothing after she told him about Li'l Bits. But when his anguished wail tore through the silence, it shattered her. She clung to him as tightly as she could, terrified that his sanity might bend like a fragile reed in a violent storm—until it finally broke.

Now, at his dear friend's memorial service, his mother repeated—more fiercely this time—"It's not your fault." She spoke to him in a rush, breathless and urgent, about the mystery of God's plan and His unfathomable will, as if the sheer speed of her words might somehow dull his pain.

Her voice had apparently become too loud because she heard an elderly voice rasp from across the aisle, "Excuse me, sister, but the song is about to end, and the Reverend looks like he's gettin' ready to preach."

She blinked her apology to the octogenarian.

Patricia held her son's hand tightly and turned her attention back to the rich, powerful rendition of an iconic spiritual—a song that had long carried the hope of a better day.

Swing low, sweet chariot,
Comin' for to carry me home.
Swing low, sweet chariot,
Comin' for to carry me home.

37
Give Me Strength

As the recording of Pie Jesu played, Reverend Gabriel Davis waited anxiously at the lectern. He was no stranger to death. He'd presided over many memorial services, but this was a brutally haunting moment that conjured up the lynching of Emmett Till. This time, the world was forced to witness the tortured body of a Black child hanging over an interstate highway.

The Reverend fought back tears as his eyes burned fiercely with grief and anger. His chest felt heavy. He struggled to catch his breath. Images of those two dead children, separated by over three generations, were unsettling to his mind and spirit.

Struggling to distract himself from the brutal images, he looked out at the thousands of troubled faces before him. The crowd was a veritable cross-section of race, ethnicity, and class—all united in mourning. They desperately needed words of comfort and hope, seeking some understanding of the inexplicable.

They seemed lost. He felt lost. The barbaric murder of Li'l Bits deeply traumatized the Black community, once again shattering its sense of safety and security. The murderer had been a guardian of the law—an agent of the state. Like George Floyd's killer, he was a cop.

Once the ghastly details of Li'l Bits' death were made known by the press—nails hammered into a child's hands and feet—the public and media drew dramatic parallels to the crucifixion of Christ.

The Reverend sighed heavily. Innocence and purity destroyed by mindless, insatiable hate. Could he do this? Could he speak for Li'l Bits?

He should have declined the Carver family's request to speak this morning, but they knew how much he loved their son.

Mr. Carver had told him, "I'm not looking for the Sermon on the Mount, Reverend. If it's rage you feel, show it. If it's sadness you feel, tell it. If it's love you feel, express it. No matter what you say, you can't do this wrong."

There was an implicit expectation that a dedicated servant of God would sustain mourners spiritually, give them hope, and bolster their will to endure, but the Reverend had doubts.

Can I, in my deep emotional pain, comfort them? Can I, despite my anger, give them hope? Can I, in my spiritual confusion, uplift their spirits? Please, God—help me say what needs to be said.

Lowering his head, he closed his eyes to pray. After a moment, he heard a commanding voice. "Speak the truth. Speak in love. Speak from the heart. The Holy Spirit will be with you."

Startled, his eyes snapped open as if expecting to see someone standing by his side. No one! A *welcomed spiritual message,* he thought. And, then, he smiled.

He recalled a scripture in Luke, reminding him that the Holy Spirit would provide the right words when the time came. Relief and gratitude surged through him. Under his breath, he murmured, "Thank you."

Stirred by the voice, the Reverend felt called to not only honor and bless Li'l Bits but, more importantly, to confront an enduring psychic illness: a centuries-old pathology deeply rooted in white America.

The Reverend believed this pathology could be understood if America could find the courage to answer a simple question—*Why did white America fear the Black man?*

He was with the Carver family when two uniformed officers arrived at their home late in the evening. The conversation was direct, dispassionate, and deliberate. One officer spoke evenly: "Mr. and Mrs. Carver, we have some bad news. We found your son. I'm sorry for your loss—your son is dead."

Despite his best efforts, he couldn't erase the memory of Mrs. Carver's heartrending cry. It was a mother's cry, ancient and undying, echoing through generations—overwhelming his mind, crushing his heart, and nearly driving him to his knees.

It was one word. She just said one word—a word that was at once a plea, denial, disbelief, and fury; a word charged with unimaginable anguish that electrified the air. She screamed, "No!" The terrible sound of it reverberated throughout his soul.

He felt empty.

He looked up at the sky, where a rosy pocket of light was forming beneath the awakening sun. Swaths of red, orange, and gold twisted through layered clouds like Christmas ribbons draped across the heavens — resplendent, brilliant, alive. They splashed across the three crosses on the mound.

Whenever the Reverend preached about the Passion of the Christ, Li'l Bits seemed to fall into a trance. Congregants were certain that he was filled with the Holy Spirit as he spontaneously began preaching about the redemptive blood of Jesus. During those brief, rapturous moments, the Reverend believed he saw God's glory radiating from Li'l Bits—an ineffable glow that arrested his breath and filled his soul with sacred wonder. To the Reverend, Li'l Bits was a marvel, a miracle, and a mystery.

The Reverend fervently believed that, after millennia of silence, God had chosen to grace humanity once more—in the form of a young Black boy.

Folding his hands together, he bowed his head in fervent prayer. As the hymn nearly reached its stirring finish, the ethereal sound of Pie Jesu buoyed his spirit, carrying him on each beautiful lyric to a serene place of enchantment and comfort. He waited for the Holy Spirit to touch him, drawing in a deep breath and releasing it slowly.

He prayed... *God give me strength.*

The soothing requiem reached its tranquil end. Pressing his fist against his mouth, he coughed several times, clearing his throat.

Ceremoniously, he turned to quietly acknowledge the civic leaders, family members, and close friends on the dais behind him before turning to address the entire multitude of mourners and spectators before him.

With his head lifted high, his grand baritone voice boomed across the stage.

"Brothers and sisters, welcome! On behalf of the Prince of Peace Community Church, the loving parents of Matthew Michael Carver, and our beloved son—whom we affectionately call Li'l Bits—we thank you for joining us today to mourn, honor, and bless him.

"This is a hard day!" he declared. "Another beautiful, innocent Black child has been stolen from us because of sick, mindless hate."

The timbre of his deep baritone voice fell suddenly.

"I used to imagine that Li'l Bits might be our Martin Luther King, Jr. for this century," the Reverend reflected. "He was blessed with an extraordinary spiritual gift. And like Reverend King, I believed that, in time, history would have touched and blessed him."

His mind flashed back to a joyous memory. "If you had seen him moved by the Holy Spirit in our church, you would understand what I mean."

The Reverend felt his mood lifting. "So many people came to the Lord because of him. Members of our congregation were drawn to him—they said that just being in his presence, when he was moved by the Holy Spirit, dispelled any doubt about God's existence."

The Reverend said, awe filling his voice, "This child was truly blessed——the Holy Spirit touched him, and through him, we all felt God's love more deeply." A broad smile spread across his face—a sparkle dancing in his eyes. "I baptized that little fella when he was a baby. Lord knows how he cried when I sprinkled him with holy water!" The Reverend chuckled. "At his baptism, his father shared with me the extraordinary vision he had when his wife was pregnant.

"We now understand that what Mr. Carver witnessed was the divine foretelling of an extraordinary birth, the significance of which would unfold over time."

The Reverend said, "Mr. and Mrs. Carver often invited me to dinner. Li'l Bits would offer a beautiful prayer to bless the food, and afterward, the four of us would have a Bible study."

Mr. Carver shouted, his voice breaking, "Those were truly blessed occasions, Reverend."

"Once we had closed the Bible, Li'l Bits and I would talk about school, his friends, and books he liked to read." Pausing, the Reverend said, "He never failed to mention his friend, Tyrene. It was for Tyrene that Li'l Bits risked his life. Despite his mentor's urging to leave it to the police, he refused to be dissuaded."

Doug and Tawanna looked at each other knowingly. Doug leaned over, whispering, "I know, sweetheart. He was guided by a power greater than we could understand." A tear streamed slowly down Tawanna's cheek.

The Reverend's face brightened with admiration. "What a noble expression of love and sacrifice! As Jesus said, *Greater love hath no man than this, that a man lay down his life for his friends."*

Tyrene inhaled sharply as he gripped his mother's hand. She wrapped her arm around him, trying to steady him against the heartache she knew was tearing through him.

The Reverend heard muffled sobs and weeping behind him. Pausing to respect the expression of grief, he inhaled slowly, then began again.

"It was such a joy and privilege to watch Li'l Bits grow into a fine young man of deep faith who possessed such an amazing spiritual gift. To me, he was an anointed soul—beautiful, radiant, and full of grace. The most remarkable thing about Li'l Bits was witnessing the Spirit of the Lord descend upon him."

The Reverend's face almost glowed as the mystic thread of memory transported him back in time. "When the Spirit moved him, you could see a dazzling white light rush like the wind through our church. An indescribable joy filled everyone's heart. The woes of the world seemingly disappeared. Some claimed to see Jesus, while others felt they stood in the Promise Land. The river of living waters within our church swept over us washing away our worries and fears, filling everyone with a sense of the divine. It was pure jubilation!"

His eyes swept over the crowd. "When I looked down upon my congregation during those remarkable moments, I saw members seated in prayer, radiating a golden aura." He repeated, almost in disbelief, "A golden aura! Others knelt with their hands clasped, rocking back and forth, their faces ecstatic, occasionally raising a hand and shouting, 'Praise Jesus'!"

Someone on the dais behind him exclaimed, "Yes! My God! Yes! I was there! I saw it, too! It was glorious!"

Reverend Davis smiled. "I feel Li'l Bits now. I feel his love! I feel God's love." His smile now reached his eyes. "God has a way of bringing forth goodness even out of the depths of evil."

"Yes, He does!" came an impassioned voice from behind him.

Inspired and alive with energy, he glided gracefully across the stage, his black robe billowing about him like wings, his heart overflowing.

"Though his life was painfully brief, Li'l Bits planted seeds of kindness everywhere he went—seeds that will take root, grow strong, and bear lasting fruit in our beloved community. In time, his beautiful spirit will return to grace us again, in a way only God's mystery and wonder can reveal."

With a heavy sigh, he intoned, "I am so tired for my people… so tired of the pathology of white America." He paused, then clarified, "It's a cultural pathology—embedded in white supremacy—that perpetuates Eurocentric values, false beliefs, and myths crafted to justify the systemic exploitation and dehumanization of Black people. It's a dark, perverse sickness that has inflicted centuries of pain, anguish, and death upon my people."

A female voice from the dais yelled, "Tell it!"

Acknowledging the comment, the Reverend nodded. "My people have carried relentless sorrow and trauma—from before this nation's birth and through every generation since."

With a vigorous shake of his head, he declared, "Driven by merciless avarice, nearly two million Black souls were wrenched from their homelands and condemned to the hell of the Middle Passage—where they perished in chains, suffocating in filth and darkness, their cries lost to men like John Newton, a sea captain and slave trader who later composed Amazing Grace. And," he paused, "after enduring 246 years of chattel slavery, hundreds of thousands of descendants of those stolen people were re-enslaved once more after Reconstruction ended in 1877. Plantation slavery was replaced by chain-gangs and convict leasing. Corrupt courts, greedy politicians, and mercenary police devised unlawful schemes to arrest, convict and fine Black men for petty offenses like vagrancy, changing employees without permission, or riding freight cars without a ticket. Unable to pay the fine, illiterate and jobless men were forced to work for the county until the 'debt' was paid off. Tens of thousands worked on chain gangs in mines, rock quarries, and railroads or as leased convicts to farms and lumber camps. Thousands died as a result of exhaustion and overwork, beatings and torture, starvation and disease, and even murder. It was another kind of slavery that lasted until 1945." He paused to let his words sink in.

"During this time period, we were subjected to relentless racial violence and terror by the Klan, vengeful mobs, or white citizens seeking complete domination: thousands of Black victims were lynched, lives extinguished in acts of unspeakable cruelty and barbarism, while state and federal authorities turned a blind eye. Specifically, in the bloody Red Summer of 1919, white mobs rioted—looting, robbing, and killing—in over 25 U.S. cities, burning homes, destroying businesses, and slaughtering thousands of Black men, women, and children. It was a bloody reign of racial terror."

Breathing heavily, he sighed, "Our progress—Black progress—has always sparked murderous white rage and resentment."

His eyes flashed anger and pain. "Each succeeding decade saw a campaign of hate and oppression in every sphere of life for Blacks—social, political, economical: Jim Crow segregation, exclusion from unions, denial of government benefits during the Great Depression and after WWII; red lining and predatory lending, restrictive covenants, voter suppression and disenfranchisement, and rabid violence over school desegregation."

Uttering a derisive laugh, he said, "The country was shocked when the National Advisory Commission on Civil Disorders concluded that racism—white racism—had sparked the civil disorders that erupted in over 20 urban cities in the summer of 1967. The commission identified repressive and violent policing as part of the tinder that helped ignite the flames."

Exhaling heavily, he looked up to the sky and closed his eyes again. The weight of America's racial fault lines felt ugly and crushing, hollowing him out like a gourd scraped clean for a drum, its skin stretched tight with the grief of generations.

"Tell me—have any of you here who self-identify as white ever had to give 'The Talk' to your child? The talk that might be the only thing keeping them alive when they're confronted by police?"

His eyes swept slowly, deliberately over the crowd. "Did you know that from 2015 to 2020, at least 135 unarmed Black men were killed by police in this country."

Bitter contempt laced his voice. "Unarmed. No weapon. No threat—just a deadly fiction born in the minds of those who call themselves our protectors. Think about those murdered—lives tragically stolen during routine traffic stops: while seated in a car or outside their car with hands raised; shot in the back while fleeing or because a cell phone was mistaken for a gun." His voice trailed off.

"Many white Americans, however, had long shielded themselves from Black trauma—cocooned in willful ignorance, until the brutal, public murder of George Floyd in Minnesota forced them to confront a reality they could no longer ignore."

He scanned the audience, his gaze pressing into them as he let the weight of his accusation settle. "On a raw, visceral level, white Americans were forced to confront the tortured death of a Black man on a public street in broad daylight. For the first time, they witnessed—with undeniable clarity—the brutal cruelty of police violence, a reality Black Americans have known and protested for generations. Social media and news outlets thrust the brutal murder into the faces of white America, forcing them to see what Black Americans have always known."

Raising his voice, almost to a strident pitch, he said, "The world watched in stunned, muted horror as George Floyd cried out to his deceased mother while the police officer slowly squeezed his life from him."

Waving his hand dramatically over the audience, he said, "A profound shift in white awareness of anti-Black police violence hit like a rogue wave, crashing violently into white consciousness that sparked outraged demonstrations worldwide."

Narrowing his eyes, he declared, "To truly embrace George Floyd, to accept his full humanity, America and the world had to strip away the distortions of stereotype and prejudice. The merciless way he was killed demanded that he'd be seen as a human being—not as some looming threat in the white imagination, not as a criminal shaped by police narratives, not as a thug painted by politicians and media. He was a man!"

With an arched eyebrow, he asked, "Did you ever stop to wonder how recognition of his humanity pierced though white apathy and numbness?" His eyes swept slowly across the audience, searching their faces.

"Somehow, white America found it in its heart and soul to mourn an ordinary Black man—not a global icon like Reverend Martin Luther King Jr., but a man with a criminal record, a man who had served time, a man battling addiction. A man scraping by at the margins of society. One could say that George Floyd stood as both a symbol and a representative of countless marginalized Black men trying to survive America's minefield of white grievance, resentment, and hate.

"Yet, despite his personal failings, America embraced the murdered man—perhaps in an effort to salvage its moral integrity, or even its very soul."

His voice thundered, "The man who murdered Li'l Bits masqueraded as a guardian of the law—a die-hard white supremacist cloaked in a badge. He, too, was indifferent to the humanity of my dear friend and slaughtered him like an animal." His breath caught in his throat.

"The misguided individuals attracted to this ideology of hate fantasize about the myth of white supremacy—a toxic nostalgia rooted in the outmoded desires of segregationists, racists, bigots, and hate-mongers," he said with bitter contempt.

"Let me share with you a conversation I had with an entertainer from South Africa who grew up in its apartheid regime—a system considered by some historians as more harsh than Jim Crow segregation. The man told me that the first time that he felt real hate is when he came to America. He told me there is so much hate in America because he believes there is so much anger." He placed a hand on his chest and spoke with emphasis, "Hate and anger. Anger and hate.

"Why do some white people hate us so much that they want to kill us?" the Reverend asked. "What have we done to them?"

He continued, "Historians, politicians, economists, and sociologists agree that Black people have played a foundational role in creating the economic success of this country. Black soldiers have fought in every war, even when segregated by law. We created gospel, blues, jazz, R&B, ragtime, soul, and hip-hop and rap music. The whole world celebrates the pop culture created by Black artists. Our Black scientists have contributed to notable advancements in agriculture, science, technology, and medicine. We have been the veritable foot soldiers trying to make America a more perfect union. The words of David Walker, author of *An Appeal to the Coloured Citizens of the World,* remain as powerful and true in 1829 as they do now: 'The greatest riches in all America have arisen from our blood and tears.'"

Opening his arms wide in supplication, he asked, "Should we be hated because we have created a beauty in America that would have been impossible without us? Should we be hated because we have marched, sacrificed, and died to be first-class citizens? Should we be hated because we demand that America make good on its promise of inalienable rights to life, liberty, and the pursuit of happiness?"

The Reverend scoffed. "After 400 years of unrelenting oppression by white America, the unshakable resilience of Black people lays bare the deep cracks and inherent fragility of white supremacy."

Anguish creased his face as his expression darkened. "White supremacy," he muttered, curling his lip. "It hasn't been a difficult challenge for me to forgive the racist who murdered my beloved friend."

Shrugging, he said, "Reverend King Jr. would probably have just dismissed the killer as one of his sick white brothers who was ignorant and knew no better. Remember what Jesus said while dying on the cross. *'Forgive them, Father for they know not what they do.'*" He paused to collect himself before continuing.

"It's not the killer who should be solely condemned for this atrocity! No! He is a mere puppet for white supremacy! America should be condemned for failing to teach students how the institution of slavery has profoundly impacted American society, contributing to systemic racism that continues to shape laws and policies affecting every aspect of our lives today. America should be condemned for normalizing white supremacy by honoring traitors who fought to enslave and exploit Black people. America should be condemned for enacting laws that have created the new Jim Crow of mass incarceration."

In a measured tone, he said, "I understand white weakness. White supremacy is like the sirens' call in the legend of Ulysses. Few can resist. Few can withstand it because it offers privilege, advantage, and power."

Glancing over the audience, he asked, "Do you remember Amy Cooper, the white woman who walked her unleashed dog in Central Park? All was well until a Black birdwatcher asked her to put her dog on the leash required by park rules. Well! She was miffed. She didn't want to comply with a simple request. The Black man had disturbed her worldview. He dared to challenge her whiteness. She called the police, reporting that an African-American man was threatening her and her dog."

The Reverend screwed up his face. He asked, "How did she learn about white supremacy? Do you think she took a college course? Had she read a book? Did family and friends tell her? What had society taught her? Or did she instinctively understand, based on her lived experience in America, her whiteness carried meaning—had power—that she could, on a whim, potentially unleash the lethal force of the state against an innocent Black man with a fake distress call?"

Shaking his head, he said, "She claims she is not a racist. And, really," he paused, "it's not necessary to label her as such. But think about the white people who supposedly create race-neutral policies and supposedly craft facially-neutral practices in education, healthcare, legislation, or law enforcement. They perceive themselves as fair, decent, bias-free, color-blind, well-intentioned people, but they are oblivious to their unconscious racial bias. Like Amy Cooper, they don't believe they have a racist bone in their body."

He paused, letting the silence spread across the field like a wave. Then, arching an eyebrow, his voice low and deliberate, he asked, "If white racism does not exist in these institutions — then why?" His voice lifted into the open air. "Why do respected government studies and peer-reviewed journals document the same story, over and over again — disparities in health care, in employment, in education, in housing, in criminal justice?" The words rolled out over the thousands standing beneath the open sky like thunder finding the horizon. "Not in one domain. Not in two. But in every domain where Black life intersects with American power."

He let them sit in it. Then his voice dropped to something that felt, despite the thousands present, almost private.

"Li'l Bits didn't die in a vacuum. He died in a system. He died because of a system. And that system has a name."

Folding his hands in front of him, he said solemnly, "We are creatures of culture. No one is immune to the pervasive cultural forces in America that perpetuate whiteness as the ultimate power backed by the state. The siren call of white supremacy beckons every white person. Some consciously embrace it, while others subconsciously succumb to it."

Raising his finger heavenward, he cautioned, "But there will be a reckoning when people have tired of asking, negotiating, protesting, and marching to achieve racial justice and social equality. Remember the African-American spiritual, 'God gave Noah the rainbow sign. No more water, the fire next time.'"

He slowly approached the lectern, pressed his lips together in thought, then spoke with quiet empathy: "I know that white supremacy is not your fault. I know that white supremacy was not your idea. But you must understand that, as white people, you become complicit in maintaining its power when you ban books that expose it, censor books that celebrate diversity, and tolerate hate that sustains it.

"You can't sit on the fence any longer—who has the courage of Viola Liuzzo? You can't pretend it's someone else's problem — who has the commitment of Reverend James Reeb? You must speak out — who has the conviction of Heather Heyer." Shrugging his shoulders, he said, "Otherwise, you who claim to believe in a just and equal society betray us with your silence." He slowed to catch his breath. He said, "If you see something, say something." Reverend Davis implored, "Together, we as a community, as a nation, must dismantle the dehumanizing and depraved structure of white supremacy or risk losing our God-given freedoms, our cherished values, and our democratic republic to autocratic leaders."

He stretched his arms wide, as if he could gather every spectator into them, as if he were embracing the whole crowd. Boldly, he proclaimed, "We are all part of an elaborate, vibrant, and intricate tapestry of life—brilliant and magnificent, like Joseph's biblical coat of many colors. If we can truly embrace the aspirational promise in these words—'We hold these truths to be self-evident, that all men are created equal, endowed by their Creator with certain inalienable rights, including life, liberty, and the pursuit of happiness'—then we may yet witness a new dawning in America."

Inhaling deeply, he said, "If Li'l Bits had lived, I truly believe that, in time, he could have been the architect of the bridge to connect the beauty of our diverse cultures."

A note of sadness crept back into his voice. "Nevertheless, we must treasure his memory — let it become the legacy that sustains us, that keeps us moving forward."

He surveyed the massive crowd: among them, news reporters, who would broadcast the story of Li'l Bits' brutal murder, a stark reminder of America's enduring racial shame. He looked down at them. They looked up at him.

"Let us use the wonderful memories of Matthew Michael Carver and the mystery of his relationship with Jesus to dedicate ourselves to doing good works in the world—to make a difference; to transform the character and heart of America! Let us reach out to each other in love and kindness, recognizing that we are all part of the miraculous tapestry of life—that what touches one of us touches us all; that what touches our community touches the world.

"Are we not all God's children? Are we not our brother's keeper? Did God not make us all in His wondrous image? Do we not mirror the kaleidoscopic brilliance of His boundless love for us? Like our iconic Representative John Lewis urged us to do, let us go out into the world and make good trouble. Together, let us put our knees on the neck of white supremacy until it dies." Inhaling deeply, he said, "Brothers and sisters, please, bow your heads.

"Dear Father in Heaven, we ask, in Your Son's precious name, to bless and protect the people who have come here today to honor your fallen son; to help us to forgive and be strong. Let your wondrous grace extend to everyone who values brotherhood, love, and freedom. We ask that you strengthen our faith and give us the courage to make America what it is meant to be: a just, loving, accepting, merciful, and compassionate land. Let America flower into a magnificent garden where everyone can flourish."

Raising both arms high, he concluded, "On behalf of the Carver family, we thank you for being here. In the name of Jesus, Amen."

It seemed as if mourners and spectators had collectively held their breaths during the last moments of the Reverend's prayer. The crowd finally exhaled as one.

White doves were released from cages nestled in a niche on the high ground. Cage after cage, wave after wave, they ascended into the clear morning air, their fluttering wings and whistling calls rising with them. They soared and wheeled, beautiful winged messengers against the sky.

Patricia sat with her arm tightly around Tyrene, their faces damp with tears. Looking up, she marveled softly, "Hundreds of feathered angels to guide his journey home."

She laughed then, sudden and free.

Looking at Tyrene, she said, smiling, "TicToc must have purchased every white dove in the Southwest to honor your friend."

Around them, the crowd broke into exclamations of childlike wonder, clapping as the winged creatures whispered and spiraled gracefully into the air.

"How absolutely glorious!" Patricia said aloud. "Beautiful. Just beautiful."

Stifling a sob, she cried out, "Fly to God, dear sweet boy. Fly home to Jesus."

38

Welcome Home

Patricia Horn swung her legs into the car next to Tyrene as Carl closed the rear driver's side door behind her. Having secured them in the limousine, he strolled over to check in with two of his agents assigned to guard Horn and Tyrene. He wanted to know if anything seemed out of place or if anyone looked suspicious before he left for the airport.

Carl worried that providing protection at a memorial service in an open air amphitheater with this size crowd was a high-risk situation. Restricting movement to limited spaces made the challenge far more manageable.

The bulletproof car suggested by TicToc was an extra precaution.

Experience had taught her that extremists sometimes took advantage of vulnerable moments—like a memorial service or funeral—to do a "hit."

Despite meticulous planning, they might have overlooked some small detail or made a faulty assumption, which would provide a window of opportunity for a professional assassin or an ex-military neo-Nazi.

Carl wasn't naive. He knew there were no rules in killing—only targets to be eliminated. The occasion didn't matter: a cemetery, a church, a child's birthday party, a retirement barbecue. Nothing was off limits. Death never takes a holiday. He'd made a pledge to TicToc to protect them.

Wheels turned in his head like a fine Swiss watch. Old memories of revenge killings came back to him. One misstep could unravel their careful planning. You can never be too careful. After thirty years, someone still tried to kill Salman Rushdie after the Ayatollah Khomeini issued a fatwa against him and offered a death bounty in 1989.

While Carl gave last-minute instructions to his agents about a revised exit route from the memorial venue, Patricia's heart ached as she watched Tyrene sitting quietly, slumped over, with his head bowed, arms hugging his body, and shoulders tucked about himself like a wounded bird.

He was doing his best not to cry anymore. She knew it would be difficult for him to stop if he started again. Her last few days since his release from jail had taught her that. She was relieved that he had gotten through the service so well. She speculated that Reverend Davis' scathing criticism of America may have triggered more anger than tears.

Reaching over, she gently pulled him to her. His body collapsed heavily against her as he nestled his forehead partially against the side of her face and shoulder. Almost immediately, she felt him exhale deeply. Horn sensed a swirl of emotion flowing through him. Her heart dropped as she heard him release one pitiable sob that shook his body.

She didn't know how to help him. She had tried to shield him from the details of his friend's murder, but that had proved impossible. Li'l Bits' death sparked a media frenzy, and Tyrene quickly learned what the killer had done to him.

Tyrene's heart pounded wildly against her side. Alarmed, she shushed him softly, trying to calm him, to settle him down. She pressed her head down gently on his as if her physical connection with him could take away his anguish. Would he ever again be able to breathe freely, to find a moment of peace without the awful weight of his friend's death?

The helpless feeling that torments every parent hoping to ease their child's distress plagued her now, but several thoughts consoled her: *My boy is alive. He's free. He's with me. TicToc kept her promise to keep him safe.*

But now, it was Patricia's responsibility to help him heal. She felt powerless. She knew that she had failed to help him recover from his brother's suicide. What could she do now to help him heal from his friend's murder? She sighed heavily.

"Tyrene," she whispered, "Breathe with me, baby. Follow my breathing. Take a long, deep breath, hold, and exhale slowly. Okay?" she added.

"Just focus on your breath. Don't think. Let thoughts pass by like clouds." She felt him acknowledge her with a slight nod of his head.

Carl opened the car door quietly and lowered his massive body into the leather seat without speaking. Shifting his body slightly, Carl adjusted the rearview mirror to get a better view of his high valued passengers. He sat watching them—a mother holding her son tenderly, rocking him from side to side slowly. He slid back the glass privacy partition. "You two okay?" he asked.

Patricia nodded. She sensed that something was on Carl's mind.

"Okay to talk?" he asked.

She took a moment to note that the pounding of Tyrene's heart had slowed.

"Yep! You can talk, Carl," she said.

Turning toward Patricia, he said, "I've been thinking about how hard it's been for you and Tyrene these past weeks. This experience has been a nightmare for both of you. Tyrene was locked up and denied bonds on bogus charges. You were held in contempt and jailed. And finally, after the dust settled," he hesitated, searching for the most delicate way to say it, "Tyrene's best friend is no longer with us."

Patricia wondered, *How could a school fight turn into a murderous nightmare that's devastated so many lives?*

"I just want to let you know that you two are troopers. I'd gladly have you on my team any day!"

Tyrene pulled away slowly from his mother. Sitting up, he kissed her quickly on her cheek while taking her hand in his. He squeezed it gently.

The pain in Tyrene's face was palpable. He no longer possessed the eyes of a child. The thought of his grievous loss triggered a physical sensation that made Carl's heart skip.

Looking into the rearview mirror, Tyrene met Carl's eyes, which revealed deep caring. Nodding politely, he managed to give Carl a subdued smile.

"Something else on your mind, Carl?" Patricia asked, noticing his pensive look.

Shrugging, he said, "Well… yeah… there is."

"You want to talk about Li'l Bits?" she asked.

Without waiting for Carl's response, she asked Tyrene, "You good with him talking about your friend?"

Eyes now bright and alert, Tyrene lifted his shoulders with polite indifference. "Go ahead, Carl," she prompted.

Sadness crept into his voice. "Listening to Reverend Davis describe him and the incredible impact he had on people, I just wish I'd had the chance to meet Li'l Bits. He seemed like an extraordinary young man."

Patricia turned to look out the window. Memories stretched back, lulling her into a peaceful moment from her family's past. "I know his mom. Our boys played together when they were younger—sleepovers and everything. Li'l Bits was a delight to be around. You know how special he was; he was my son's best friend." She shot Tyrene a quick, loving look, and Tyrene smiled back broadly.

"Yeah," Carl said, smiling, looking over his shoulder at Tyrene. "Two damn fine men!"

After repositioning himself in his seat, Carl said, "Time to go." He closed the partition to give them privacy. Signaling the agents he was taking off, Carl started the car. The gravel scattered wildly, pelting the undercarriage, as the limousine surged forward, veering off the shoulder onto the paved road.

While driving, he periodically checked the side and rearview mirrors. His men were tailing them at a safe distance. After a few miles, he saw another of his team's cars parked on the side of the road. She waved as he whizzed by.

Carl finally started to relax. He loosened his grip on the wheel, letting his eyes drift to the thick green clusters of trees lining the roadway. He noted that the main highway would appear in a few more miles, where another set of cars would join them en route to a private airport. TicToc had arranged for a safe house in Canada for the next few months.

Suddenly, a call came through Carl's earpiece. The agent's words were pressured, rushed, and difficult to understand. It reminded him of a civilian who had barely managed to survive a terrorist attack, but this man was no civilian. Carl floored the accelerator. The unexpected explosion of power and speed flattened Patricia and Tyrene against their seats. Patricia gasped loudly.

Carl looked back to see if his men were keeping up. He caught a glimpse of Horn's panicked eyes in the rearview mirror.

"Slow down! I can't understand you!" Carl said into his mic. "Who is this? Is this Dawson?"

"Sorry, Chief! It's Dawson, sir! I'm Sector 12. You know..." he stammered, "I was assigned the perimeter area around the mound, along with Jamison."

"Is this a Code Red? Has there been a security breach? Is there a threat in that area? Any shots fired?"

Dawson seemed confused. "Yes! I mean, no! I mean. This isn't a Code Red unless... unless this is a diversionary tactic, but I don't think—"

Carl's interruption was sharp. "What the hell is going on, Dawson? Where's Jamison? Is anybody hurt?"

Dawson sputtered, "No! No! No! It's nothing like that, Chief. Everyone is safe. No weapons were fired." Dawson sounded as if he couldn't catch his breath. "Just give me a moment, please," he said. "I can explain..." He corrected himself. "I mean ... I think I can explain."

"We have a drone, Dawson! Put Sector 12 on the screen!"

"The signal is down, Chief! I'm sorry. The connection is lost! Someone's working on the transmitter."

Carl stifled a groan. "Just report what you're seeing! Can you do that?"

Patricia glanced over at Tyrene, whose knee was bouncing rapidly. He had both hands pressed firmly against the seat, as if bracing for a collision. She double-checked their seat belts to make sure they were secure.

Watching the scenery blur past, she estimated Carl was pushing well over a hundred miles an hour. Yet despite the tremendous speed and power, Patricia had heard only the initial roar of the engine when Carl accelerated; now there was just a quiet hum. She reached over and held Tyrene's hand.

Their eyes met, and she said calmly, "Everything is going to be fine." For a fleeting moment, though, she wondered if the real threat wasn't a bullet or a bomb—but a violent crash in a custom-made SUV.

Leaning forward in her seat, Patricia strained to catch Carl's words, but the privacy partition muffled his voice. She slid it back a few inches. Although she couldn't make out the details of what Carl was being told, one thing was clear: he was angry.

Patricia slid the partition back a few more inches. "Carl!" she said softly enough to be heard but not loud enough to be intrusive. He didn't respond. She heard Carl ask someone named Dawson about a drone being operational. Patricia didn't whisper this time. She blurted out, "Carl!" which startled him.

Ms Horn!" he said firmly. "Please sit back. We'll be slowing down very soon. Just got confirmation from Jamison that this isn't a Code Red! No shots were fired! Everyone appears safe, although I'm not sure what's going on. Everything is under control. Just trust me."

"No Code Red! That's a relief," she sighed, patting Tyrene's hand as she sat back in her seat.

Patricia had to ask, "What's going on, Carl?"

"Not sure yet. But I can tell you my guy is highly agitated, which is totally unlike him. I told him I'd get back to him when I can pull over to a secure spot."

"Carl! There are speakers back here. Can you connect me to the audio so I know what's going on."

"The call caught me off guard. Everything had been going so smoothly, but operations rarely go off without a hitch. I got too complacent. Now that I know there's no immediate threat, I can let you listen in. If circumstances change, though, the partition stays shut and the rear speakers stay off. You understand, Ms. Horn? You could become a distraction."

Nodding, she said, "Makes sense, but I have another ask."

Carl sighed. He didn't try to hide his exasperation. "What else, Ms. Horn?"

"Dawson said he is trying to get a drone working, right? If it's operational, I've got a screen back here. Can I watch the video, too?"

Carl hesitated. He knew things on the mound could get unpredictable, maybe even violent. He didn't want to expose them to unnecessary trauma or re-traumatize Tyrene.

"If I think it's safe for viewing, I'll connect you to the screen. In the meantime, I can let you listen to the audio. But I want you to use the headphones in the console. Put those on! I think it's best to leave Tyrene out of this drama."

"Okay," she responded. "Now, can we please slow down?"

"Yes! Yes! Sure!" he said haltingly, watching the road as if looking for something to appear. "Almost there," he mumbled to himself.

Carl reduced his speed so he didn't overrun a predetermined site on the road that would provide decent cover. He had scouted this highway before and had made mental notes about various landmarks that offered protection. Looking alongside the road, he exclaimed, "Found it!"

He saw a sizable, weathered boulder that had probably rolled down the mountain during a rockslide years ago. It sat back from the road about forty feet like a silent sentinel. He carefully pulled around the back of it and parked. The boulder was just large enough to shield the passenger compartment of the limo, if positioned correctly. The cars trailing Carl took positions in front and back of his limo, leaving enough room for Carl to maneuver in case of an emergency.

He said to Patricia, "Headphones." She eagerly put them on. Returning to the transmission, he said, "Okay, Dawson, let's start over. From the beginning—tell me about this 'thing' you mentioned."

Dawson words tumbled out, "I've been trying to tell you, Chief! It's phenomenal—unbelievable! You've never seen anything like it. You have to see it to believe it! I wish you were here!"

Carl couldn't imagine what Dawson was talking about. He was still trying to pin down the emotion in Dawson's voice. Was it fear? Excitement? He sounded completely overwhelmed.

"Before you start, Dawson, just confirm this is not a Code Red!"

"No Code Red, sir, but you won't believe what I'm going to tell you… what I'm seeing! This can't be real."

Carl relaxed against his seat. He said dryly, "Okay, Dawson! Let's have it!"

"I've been watching the flow of crowds exiting on the amphitheater grounds below. Maybe fifteen or twenty people, instead of heading to their cars, started hiking up the steps to the elevated level where I was standing—you know, at the mound." He sounded breathless.

Carl refrained from telling him to hurry up and get to the '*thing*' he had to see to believe.

"My back was turned partly toward the mound because I was watching people resting on benches and others just strolling around. Then I saw the expression on an elderly couple's faces—their eyes looked like they were about to pop out of their heads. They were pointing at something behind me. So, I turned around… Then I saw it."

His voice shook with emotion. "I looked around to see if others were seeing what I saw. Some people seemed frozen, unable to move. Others pointed, mouths open in disbelief. A few had already pulled out their phones to take pictures." He paused as though gathering his thoughts. "It's beautiful and terrifying at the same time, Chief! But my mind refused to accept it—it had to be an optical illusion, a visual trick, some kind of clever light projection. I kept searching for a scientific explanation… but this isn't science, sir."

Dawson sounded strangely exhilarated. "It reminded me of the three children who saw the Blessed Virgin Mary at Fatima."

Carl scrunched his face. *What the hell is the Blessed Mary of Fatima?* he wondered. He had no clue what Dawson was rambling about. Carl's impatience was boiling over.

"Dawson! Tell me what you see or send a video from your phone!"

Excitedly, Dawson exclaimed, "No need now, Chief! You can see for yourself—the signal is back. The drone should be transmitting!"

Patricia yelled, a question in her voice, "Carl?"

"Be patient, Ms. Horn. I need to check this out for myself first."

The transmission kicked in. The drone first showed an aerial view of the stairs leading up to the mound, then floated higher, sweeping over to capture the crowd gathered at the mound's perimeter.

Carl instructed, "Zoom in on the people on the mound!"

The drone camera swept past the three crosses on the mound, then hovered, lingering over a cluster of people inching toward a strange halo of light, faint but unmistakable at the far edge of the screen. Suddenly, the drone swung around, zeroing in to reveal the full source of the unnatural glow.

Carl narrowed his eyes. Against his better judgement, he thought Horn needed to see this because she'd doubted the possibility of danger at a memorial service.

He yelled, "Don't let Tyrene watch the screen!" He waited for her acknowledgment, then activated the display.

The moment Patricia saw the image, she gasped. "There are *four* crosses! Carl!" she shouted, "Do you see the fourth cross? It's *burning*!"

Carl's mind screamed. *This is a breach—but definitely not one I ever expected.*

His security plan focused on guarding against bullets, bombs, and booby traps—physical threats, not psychological trauma or emotional assault. Some racist pig had managed to plant a burning cross, the Klan's infamous symbol of hate and terror, to desecrate the sacred memory of a grieving Black family.

"Maneuver that drone to the cross that's burning," he said bitterly.

The cross—nearly large enough to crucify a grown man—appeared to be made of wood and stood adjacent to the other three structures.

Flames licked and engulfed it from top to bottom and swept across the beam—but not like a raging, furious blaze. Instead, the fire seemed to flutter eerily, its flames waving and billowing in near silence.

Why aren't the people standing at a greater distance to protect themselves? Why do they appear to be drawn to it?

As the drone's camera shifted, Carl shook his head in disbelief—some people were actually reaching out and touching the flames!

"What the hell are they doing?" he muttered. His mind raced wildly.

Patricia stuttered, "No! It can't be! It's almost like—she inhaled sharply. "It's like the vision Moses saw in the wilderness at Mount Sinai."

What would TicToc make of this? she wondered.

Carl stared at the screen, straining to hear any crackling or popping from the burning wood. Nothing. No sound. To his amazement, the people touching the flames neither yelled in pain nor cried out.

As he kept watching, he puzzled over the spectators' odd behavior, especially those with their hands in the fire. They looked like they were worshipping at a sacred shrine.

Curious, skeptical, and uncertain, he leaned in, his face just inches from the screen. He saw people kneeling at the cross, heads bowed low in reverent worship. Some, with hands folded and eyes closed, appeared to be praying. A few stood with arms outstretched toward the sky, swaying gently, while others lay prostrate on the ground.

Someone exclaimed, "There's an angel in the fire! Do you see the angel?"

Carl scoffed, shaking his head and rolling his eyes. Angel? What angel? Were these people losing their minds? *It's like staring at clouds and claiming to see a white elephant.* He quickly dismissed the idea as the product of an overactive imagination and turned his thoughts back to the real mystery—the fire that didn't blister flesh.

"This is an elaborate hoax," he muttered, "but impressive. A lot of planning went into staging this illusion!"

Then he saw something that completely bewildered him. Carl blinked hard, staring at the sight. Squinting, he was drawn closer to the screen. Suddenly, a chill swept over him.

Was this the thing that Dawson was trying to explain?

He whispered to Patricia, "Are you seeing what I'm seeing?" Stunned disbelief echoed in his voice.

Patricia didn't answer. She sat entranced, staring at the screen, her mouth agape, eyes widening with each passing second.

More people now gathered around the burning cross, their hands moving slowly in and out of the flames. Each radiated a mysterious golden aura around their heads, while their bodies began to glow with an otherworldly light.

Carl looked on, befuddled. This was no hoax, he thought. "This is … this is amazing…." He didn't know what to make of it.

Patricia asked, in a hushed voice, "My God. What is happening here?"

"Zoom in on some of the faces," Carl demanded. "I need a close-up of the faces of those touching the flames!"

The camera zoomed in on several people with their hands in the flames, moving slowly from one face to the next, then another, and another. Their expressions were strikingly similar—almost identical.

Some had their eyes softly closed; others stared wide open. Their expressions were serene, almost blissful—as if standing on a remote mountaintop, experiencing perfect harmony and inner peace.

Years ago, Carl had experienced a similar moment while solo backpacking in Colorado. Standing on a mountain peak in the chilled air, he'd felt overwhelmed by the spiritual essence of the natural world, losing himself completely in the breaking dawn, as the sun's palette of rays slowly pierced the gray mist, revealing the world's breathtaking beauty.

Carl was deeply moved as he watched their faces. His breath caught in his throat as a numbness crept over him, his eyes fixed on their extraordinary, unwavering expressions. To him, they radiated an otherworldly adoration that could only be described as spiritual bliss.

Patricia mumbled, awestruck, "Their faces are so… beautiful!"

Carl felt the hair on the back of his neck slowly rise. An electric surge shot from the crown of his head down through his limbs, setting his body vibrating with an astonishing energy that heightened his senses.

He was beginning to understand the mystery, now—not with his mind, but with his heart. It was something that Reverend Davis said when the Holy Spirit touched Li'l Bits.

He sifted through fragments of memory, searching for the Reverend's words that might explain this bewildering phenomenon. Suddenly, his mind erupted in a flash of clarity. He remembered.

An image of a transcendent Li'l Bits crystallized like a revelation. In those ineffable moments when the Holy Spirit touched him, the Reverend had seen God's glory shining in his face. Reverend Davis also spoke of his congregants radiating a golden aura when the Holy Spirit descended upon Li'l Bits.

Incredulously, Carl thought, *Are these people being touched by the Holy Spirit? Are they encountering something sacred?*

The thoughts racing through his mind made no sense. He wasn't religious or spiritual, but his curiosity about the possibility of a spiritual realm had been sparked when Ms. Horn told him she was able to communicate with her son.

Carl had no answers. This was a world completely alien to him. He felt conflicted and mentally adrift, but he knew logic and reason were useless here. All he knew was what he saw and what he felt.

Then an epiphany shook him. He remembered the prophetic words of Reverend Davis. During the service, those words had sounded like the sorrowful longing of a grieving man hoping to see his friend again in another life—but now they carried a deeper meaning. The Reverend had known, without question, that Li'l Bits would return—his wondrous spirit would grace us again.

Had Li'l Bits somehow returned, like Ms. Horn's deceased son? Could his spirit be embodied in that cross? The very idea of it froze his mind.

Carl's thoughts abruptly stopped, as if someone had flipped a switch and cut the power. Like a relentless sea pounding a child's broken sandcastle, his doubts began to crumble. His mental defenses were giving way. Then a voice, deep from within, spoke—*Let go.*

His mind went blank. All physical sensation ceased. His sense of self dissolved as he felt himself irresistibly pulled into a mystical reality that defied the laws of the physical universe. He felt fear—not of physical death, but of something much more, a kind of death he couldn't name.

Carl inhaled sharply as his breath deepened. Heart thumping wildly, he felt his chest expanding. Carl sensed himself being sucked into a vortex of light.

The voice repeated, more commanding this time: *Let go!*

Carl could no longer resist—he had to surrender. Something within him fractured, and his heart finally broke open. He gasped, forcefully, as if taking his very first breath of life. A rush of air and warmth surged through his body like a celestial wave. His soul flooded with a peace he had never imagined possible. He blinked hard, fighting back tears. His chest heaved as he sucked in large gulps of air. His body felt drained of strength, overcome with a weakness that felt wrapped in wonder.

Astounded and exhilarated, he glanced over the seat at Horn, who was quietly weeping. Carl knew instinctively—they were tears of joy.

Eyes glistening, Tyrene and his mother held hands tenderly, marveling at the screen. They watched in quiet reverence, captivated by the remarkable expressions of those touching the flame. Then Patricia heard a raspy voice.

The voice sounded vaguely familiar, yet slightly different—deeper, older. In a weak, breathy tone, it said, "Li'l Bits."

Patricia clearly remembered the therapist's prediction about the moment Tyrene might speak again: "The need to speak will be so great that Tyrene won't be able to resist."

With the utterance of Li'l Bits' name, the fourth cross vanished as quickly and mysteriously as it had appeared. Then the transmission stopped. The screen went dark. Carl, Patricia, and Tyrene were stunned into silence and left dizzy with their thoughts.

Patricia's heart nearly leapt from her chest. Words caught in her throat as she pulled Tyrene into a tight embrace, holding him as close as she could. She sobbed with gratitude. The trauma of Duke's suicide, which had stolen Tyrene's voice, had been healed by the miraculous vision that had graced them.

Now, it was Patricia who couldn't speak. Her throat felt strained and raw, as if it burned with emotion so powerful that only water from heaven could soothe it. She held her son tightly. And Tyrene clung to her like he'd never let go.

He wept freely now, whispering hoarsely, "I love you, Mama."

She drew back and pressed a kiss to his damp cheek, their tears mingling. Resting her head lovingly against his, she wrapped him in a trembling, protective embrace and whispered, "Welcome home, son."

About the Author

Spike Adams is a retired Colorado judge and a proud father of three sons, having shared 35 wonderful years of marriage with his soulmate. Before ascending to the bench, Adams served as a trial attorney in both private practice and the Public Defender's Office across three counties. He handled felony cases ranging from sexual assault to aggravated robbery and murder. His courtroom experiences—and the lives forever changed within that system—helped shape the themes in his novel, *The Fourth Cross*, alongside the enduring tragedies of Emmett Till and George Floyd. In his free time, Spike Adams enjoys reading, watching movies, and savoring good food.

www.ingramcontent.com/pod-product-compliance
Lightning Source LLC
LaVergne TN
LVHW100248210926
848480LV00003B/865
* 9 7 9 8 2 1 8 7 3 3 7 1 1 *